# *DRIVEN by GROWTH*

## POLITICAL CHANGE IN THE ASIA~PACIFIC REGION

Studies of the East Asian Institute, Columbia University

# THE EAST ASIAN INSTITUTE OF COLUMBIA UNIVERSITY

The East Asian Institute is Columbia University's center for research, publication, and teaching on modern East Asia. The Studies of the East Asian Institute were inaugurated in 1962 to bring to a wider public the results of significant new research on Japan, China, and Korea.

# DRIVEN by GROWTH

## POLITICAL CHANGE IN THE ASIA-PACIFIC REGION

### CONTRIBUTORS

Thomas P. Bernstein
Chai-Anan Samudavanija
Chan Heng Chee
Tun-jen Cheng
Harold Crouch
Sung-joo Han
Shinichi Ichimura

Ikuo Kabashima
Jamie Mackie
James W. Morley
Yung Chul Park
Sukhumbhand Paribatra
Bernardo M. Villegas
Zakaria Haji Ahmad

## JAMES W. MORLEY, Editor

**An East Gate Book**

*M. E. Sharpe*

ARMONK, NEW YORK
LONDON, ENGLAND

An East Gate Book

**Library of Congress Cataloging-in-Publication Data**


Driven by growth: political change in the Asia-Pacific region /
edited by James W. Morley:
contributors, Thomas P. Bernstein . . . [et al.].
p.   cm.
Includes bibliographical references and index.
ISBN 1-56324-013-0.
ISBN 1-56324-014-9 (pbk.)
1. Asia, Southeastern—Politics and government—1945–
2. Asia, Southeastern—Economic policy.
3. East Asia—Politics and government.
4. East Asia—Economic policy.
I. Morley, James William, 1921–
II. Bernstein, Thomas P.
JQ96.A2D75   1992
950.4'2—dc20
91-28995
CIP

Printed in the United States of America

The paper used in this publication meets the minimum requirements of
American National Standard for Information Sciences—
Permanence of Paper for Printed Library Materials,
ANSI Z39.48–1984.

BM (c)   10   9   8   7   6   5   4   3   2   1
BM (p)   10   9   8   7   6   5   4   3   2   1

# Contents

# List Of Tables And Figures

**Tables**

**Figures**

# Preface

THE PACIFIC Basin Program was inaugurated in 1986 at Columbia University by the East Asian Institute and the Center on Japanese Economy and Business for the purposes of advancing knowledge of the region and providing opportunities for graduate training involving comparative and international approaches to the region as a whole.

This volume, which is one of several multinational projects sponsored by the program, is the outgrowth of concerns voiced at a workshop held in New York in December 1986, when a group of Asian and American political scientists and economists gathered to evaluate the high economic growth that had been rejuvenating so much of the region. The group included Thomas Bernstein, John Bresnan, Gerald L. Curtis, Chai-Anan Samudavanija, Chan Heng Chee, Sung-joo Han, Shinichi Ichimura, Hugh Patrick, Juwono Sudarsono, and myself. It became immediately apparent that while the fact of the growth, its causes, and the probabilities of its effects on future economic developments were receiving great attention, its political consequences were being largely ignored—except for the widespread assumption that since nearly everyone wanted growth, it must be a good thing. But was growth having a stabilizing or destabilizing effect on the governments involved, and was it driving them in more authoritarian or more democratic directions? How could one explain that high growth in China was compatible with communism; in Japan, with democracy; and in the other countries, with a bewildering variety of authoritarian, quasi-democratic, or democratizing regimes? Had growth no political bearing? Or were the dynamics of its impact too subtle to analyze? We decided to investigate.

A second workshop was held in Kyoto, Japan, in June 1987 with the cooperation of the Institute of Southeast Asian Studies of Kyoto University. Most of the original group were there, joined by Harold Crouch, Kondo Shigekatsu, Nakajima Mineo, and Yasusba Yasukichi. It was agreed that a comparative study should be launched of those political systems in the region that were politically autonomous, that had a record of sustained high economic growth, and for which at least a useful amount of data seemed to be available.

The final conference was held at Hua Hin, Thailand, in June 1988, cosponsored with the Institute of Security and International Studies of Chulalongkorn University, and was attended by all of the paper writers in this volume with the exception of Tun-jen Cheng.

Ideally, we should like to have been able to assemble a team of individuals as skilled in economics as in political science, with a broad knowledge of the entire region and a bent for theorizing from comparative data. But given the state of scholarship—the country-specific nature of much of our knowledge, the continuing isolation of the economics and political science disciplines, and the relative weakness of political science theorizing—we felt it advisable to recruit a team largely of country and subregional specialists, particularly political scientists since the output of the interaction we were interested in was politics, but drawing in economists as well where their input seemed particularly vital. We would try to make up for our deficiencies by a more than usually intensive interaction among the members of the research team, each criticizing the others' work and each revising his or her own work in response.

The research design also required special attention. It would have been extremely convenient if we could have turned to a body of well-accepted theory with which to inform our study, but there are today in the fields of political economy and political change at least a hundred flowers blooming—Marxists, modernizationists, *dependencistas*, institutionalists, and statists, to name a few, of many different persuasions. Moreover, there was a sentiment among the scholars from Asia in our group that they did not wish to go on simply trying to test and apply the ideas of Western theorists. They were familiar with these theories, but they felt that what was needed was a new approach—or perhaps a return to an older, inductive approach—of total immersion; that is, of inviting each participant to immerse himself or herself in the experience of the country at hand, probing it for evidence of the interaction of economics and politics, and in the process confirming or refuting existing theories or offering such new ones as seemed to be most explanatory. There was a danger, of course, that we might end up with our own hundred flowers. In part we have, but in the end, when we came to compare our various country studies, most of us found that it was largely by standing on the shoulders of some of the modernizationist and statist theorists that we could perceive a dynamic pattern emerging from the welter of conflicting appearances.

The pattern we propose is, of course, at best only a probability, for besides calling for testing in other regions of the world, it rests in large part on an intuitive base. The statistical data are supportive, but all too frequently inadequate. The questions that social scientists are interested in are not necessarily those that governments find most useful. In any event, some countries have stronger data-collecting and publishing traditions than others. Even for the strongest collectors, it was not until the 1960s that the United Nations brought some consistency into the statistical reporting of its members. It should also be recognized that there is an inevitable distortion in converting monetary values into U.S. dollars (which we have usually done to enable comparisons to be made) if one uses the exchange rates, since purchasing power parities may differ substantially. The values, therefore, should be understood to be more or less indicative, not exact. The result is that many of the economic, social, and political changes that we believe to be important cannot be reliably documented and compared. In these circumstances, each author has gathered and evaluated such statistical material as he or she could, but in the end, each has also faced the necessity of making judgments in many cases on the basis of scanty evidence.

Chapter 1 sets out the nature of the problem. It contrasts the common experience of high economic growth in the region with the diversity of political systems that obtain there and asks what, if any, is the impact of economic growth on political change. Nine chapters follow, in each of which this question is explored in one particular country. These chapters can in fact be read alone since they stand as historical analyses of the political economies of these countries during the period of high growth to 1990. Their essential prupose, however, is to form the data base for the final chapter, where we attempt to set forth the explanatory framework that we believe emerges from the country studies.

A few cautionary notes: The use of "economies" to refer to our subjects when we are referring primarily to their economic behavior, and "polities," "regimes," or "political systems" when referring primarily to their political behavior, is not meant to reflect on their "countryhood" or international diplomatic status. Nor are our uses of "Korea" or "South Korea" to refer to the Republic of Korea, and of "Taiwan" to refer to the Republic of China, meant to reflect anything but everyday conversational usage. Similarly, we hope that individuals who are referred to by one of their names when they would prefer to be known by the other will forgive us. Readers unfamiliar with the diversity in this region should know that custom in these matters differs not only from country to country, but from ethnic group to ethnic group within certain countries.

Finally, I should like to express the thanks of the group for the advice given at various stages in the project by those mentioned above who were not participants in this final volume, as well as Philip Oldenburg and Hadi Soesastro, and for the hospitality shown by the Institute of Southeast Asian Studies of Kyoto University and the Institute of Security and International Studies of Chulalongkorn University. We should also like to express our deep gratitude to the supporters of the Pacific Basin Program, which made this effort possible, including Dengen Kaihatsu Corporation, the Henry Luce Foundation, Kansai Electric Power Company, Nissho Iwai, Nissho Iwai of America Corporation, the Rockefeller Brothers Fund, Tokyo Electric Power Company, and Tokyo Gas Company.

James W. Morley

# Contributors

THOMAS P. BERNSTEIN is professor of political science and member of the East Asian Institute, Columbia University, New York.

CHAI-ANAN SAMUDAVANIJA is professor of political science, Chulalongkorn University, Bangkok.

CHAN HENG CHEE is director of the Institute of Policy Studies, Singapore.

TUN-JEN CHENG is assistant professor of political science, Graduate School of International Relations and Pacific Studies, University of California, San Diego, in La Jolla.

HAROLD CROUCH is senior fellow in political and social change, Research School of Pacific Studies, Australian National University, Canberra, and associate professor in political science, Universiti Kebangsaan Malaysia, Selangor.

SUNG-JOO HAN is professor of political science and member of the Asiatic Research Center, Korea University, Seoul.

SHINICHI ICHIMURA is director of the Institute of International Relations, Osaka International University, Osaka, and vice-chancellor of the university.

IKUO KABASHIMA is associate professor of political science, Institute of Socio-Economic Planning, Tsukuba University, Tsukuba.

JAMIE MACKIE is professor of political and social change, Research School of Pacific Studies, Australian National University, Canberra.

JAMES W. MORLEY is Ruggles Professor of Political Science emeritus and research associate of the East Asian Institute, Columbia University, New York.

YUNG CHUL PARK is professor of economics and member of the Research Institute for Human Settlements, Korea University, Seoul.

M. R. SUKHUMBHAND PARIBATRA is director of the Institute of Security and International Studies, Chulalongkorn University, Bangkok.

BERNARDO M. VILLEGAS is senior vice-president of the Center for Research and Communication, Metro Manila.

ZAKARIA HAJI AHMAD is associate professor of political science and head of the Strategic and Security Studies Unit, Universiti Kebangsaan Malaysia, Selangor.

# DRIVEN by GROWTH

## POLITICAL CHANGE IN THE ASIA-PACIFIC REGION

# 1

# Introduction: The Varieties of Asia-Pacific Experience

## Shinichi Ichimura and James W. Morley

THE RISE of new states in Asia and the Pacific presents an opportunity to restudy an old and perplexing relationship, that between economic growth and political change. Few regions of the world offer so many varieties of recent experience.

Economically, the resource endowments of such countries as Malaysia and Singapore are totally different. The growth strategies pursued by countries like China and South Korea have moved down different paths. The levels of development achieved by countries like Japan and Indonesia are worlds apart. Nevertheless, except for Myanmar (Burma) and the smaller Communist countries, the economic trend for all has been up, and for some, steeply so. Among those that have relied most heavily on the market, South Korea, Taiwan, Singapore, and the Crown Colony of Hong Kong have set the pace for newly industrializing countries; and Japan, emerging from the devastation of war, has become the economic standard bearer for the world.

Politically, however, the currents of change do not appear to have flowed all in the same direction. South Korea, a country with a very impressive newly industrializing economy, has moved through a succession of military coups to emerge as a struggling democracy, while Singapore, at an even higher economic level, has been tightening the system. Among the developing countries of ASEAN, the coup-ridden but relatively stable political system of Thailand seems gradually to be liberalizing, while its neighbor, Malaysia, has been tilting uncertainly in the opposite direction.

Why is economic growth apparently having such a variable impact on the political systems of these Asia-Pacific countries? What is there, if anything, in each country's specific growth experience that helps explain why it is more attracted to a Leninist system or to democratic forms or—as in most cases—to an authoritarian pattern of its own making? And what is there in that experience that may help explain why one state is more stable than another in the political choices it makes?

3

These are the questions we intend to take up here by analyzing the experiences of nine states in the Asia-Pacific region. We have felt forced to exclude the smaller Communist states, which have not achieved sustained growth or for which the data are insufficient for our purposes. We have excluded also Myanmar, where comparable data also are not easily available; Brunei and the Pacific island states, where independence has been achieved only recently; and Hong Kong, for reasons of its colonial relationship.

Of the remaining states, six achieved national independence or established new political systems in the post–World War II period: China, South Korea, the Philippines, Indonesia, Malaysia, and Singapore. We shall, therefore, be analyzing the experience of each of these states or systems since founding. The other three—Japan, Taiwan, and Thailand—have longer continuous state histories. On the other hand, two of these underwent regime changes—that is, changes in the structure of power and the forms through which it is exercised—also roughly in this period. The Nationalist Chinese regime suffered a vast change in circumstance by having to retreat to Taiwan in 1949, and Japan reemerged from occupation with a democratic system in 1952. As for Thailand, a slightly longer span of time seems appropriate to consider since its contemporary political evolution dates back to the overthrow of the absolute monarchy in 1932.

Our sample, then, consists of the experiences of nine states for varying lengths of time, but roughly in the years since the end of World War II, with particular emphasis on the last two decades or so when economic growth became such a common experience (table 1.1).

To introduce our search for the dynamics of the relationship between economic growth and political change in these countries, we begin with an overview of their economies, recounting the commonalities of their achievement: the effectiveness of their strategies in meeting what appear to be universal growth requirements and the impressive rates of growth they have achieved. We also point out, however, the significant differences among these strategies, and the variations in levels of income that have resulted. Next we present an overview of the various political regimes that have evolved during this period, and we conclude by introducing briefly the key concepts and the general approach that animate the inquiry in the country studies that follow.

## Economic Growth

The economic performance of these countries over the last several decades has surprised everyone in the world. Asia was once known as the place of Oriental despotism and widespread, irreducible poverty. Even as late as 1968 the "Asian drama" was conceived as a tragedy of stagnation by the best-known authority, Dr. Gunnar Myrdal (1968). This pessimism gradually yielded to optimism, however, as most Asian underdeveloped countries began to follow suit to the fast growth of the Japanese economy, which quadrupled its GNP in that decade.

Table 1.1

**The Sample: Country and Period**

| Country | Date | Explanation of beginning date |
| --- | --- | --- |
| China | 1949– | Founding of the People's Republic of China |
| Indonesia | 1945– | Founding of the Republic of Indonesia |
| Japan | 1952– | Independence from occupation |
| Malaysia | 1957– | Founding of the Federation of Malaya[1] |
| Philippines | 1946– | Founding of the Republic of the Philippines |
| Singapore | 1965– | Independence from Malaysia |
| South Korea | 1948– | Founding of the Republic of Korea |
| Taiwan | 1949– | Restriction of the GRC to Taiwan |
| Thailand | 1932– | Overthrow of the absolute monarchy |

[1]With the addition of Sabah, Sarawak, and Singapore to the peninsular Malay and Straits Settlements in 1963, the Federation of Malaya became the Federation of Malaysia.

Even so, the most authoritative study, known as the Hla Myint Report, undertaken by an Asian Development Bank study group just before 1970 predicted only a modest 5.5 percent growth rate for East and Southeast Asian countries in the 1970s (Asian Development Bank 1971). The actual performance turned out to be 7.4 percent, the countries in this region achieving faster growth than those in any other region of the world, whether industrialized or underdeveloped and including the oil-rich Middle Eastern countries. These rates slowed in the 1980s, but, with the exception for a time of the Philippines, they have remained highly respectable and have kept well ahead of population increases (table 1.2).

The result in most cases has been an impressive rise in the per capita level of income. (See table 1.3. For data in constant 1980 U.S. dollars and in international dollars, which show roughly similar orders of magnitude and the same rank-order of countries—with the exception of China when calculated in international dollars, a phenomenon that will be commented on later—see table 1.4.)

As table 1.3 indicates, while all these countries have grown rapidly, they have not developed at the same rate nor to the same degree. On the basis of their growth performances, they fall into four different groups. Japan is alone as an industrial economy; it is highest in GNP per capita as well as the largest in output. Singapore, Taiwan, and South Korea form next a cluster of newly industrializing economies (together with Hong Kong often referred to as the Asian NIEs), this terminology having been proposed by the OECD in 1979 to designate

Table 1.2

**Average Annual Growth Rates of GDP and Population in the Asia-Pacific Region, 1965–87 (percent)**

|  | 1965–80 | | 1980–87 | |
| --- | --- | --- | --- | --- |
|  | GDP | Population | GDP | Population |
| Industrial |  |  |  |  |
| Japan | 6.3 | 1.2 | 3.8 | 0.6 |
| NIEs |  |  |  |  |
| Singapore | 10.1 | 1.6 | 5.4 | 1.1 |
| Taiwan | 9.8 | 2.3 | 7.6 | 1.4 |
| South Korea | 9.5 | 2.0 | 8.6 | 1.4 |
| Developing |  |  |  |  |
| Malaysia | 7.4 | 2.5 | 4.5 | 2.7 |
| Thailand | 7.2 | 2.9 | 5.6 | 2.0 |
| Philippines | 5.9 | 2.9 | -0.5 | 2.5 |
| Indonesia | 8.0 | 2.4 | 3.6 | 2.1 |
| Giant |  |  |  |  |
| China | 7.4 | 2.1 | 10.4 | 1.3 |

*Sources:* Except for Taiwan and China, all data are from World Bank, *World Development Report* 1989: 166–67, 214–15. Taiwan data are calculated from those for 1965–79 and 1980–87 in the Republic of China ERCUSA 1989: 4, 23–25. China GDP data are those for "net material product," calculated from data for 1970–79 and 1980–84 in United Nations 1983–84: 95; China population data are calculated from data for 1965–79 and 1980–87 in People's Republic of China 1988: 75.

certain middle-income developing economies whose per capita GNP in 1978 had reached U.S. $1,600 or more and whose industrial structure and trading activities had begun seriously to impact the global economic system. Then come Malaysia, which in some ways resembles the NIEs but is not customarily included with them, Thailand, the Philippines, and Indonesia. These countries make up the ASEAN countries of Southeast Asia minus Singapore and Brunei and are often identified as the ASEAN 4; we shall refer to them simply as developing economies. China is a developing country as well, but its size generates such unusual problems and opportunities that it is often useful to distinguish it as a giant economy.

There has been an inclination in recent years to seek the explanation for the similarly rapid growth rates of these economies in some peculiarly "Asian strategy" of development. But there has been no such single strategy. In fact, three different strategies were initially pursued, depending on resource endowments.

Table 1.3

**GNP per Capita in Current U.S. Dollars in the Asia-Pacific Region, 1967-87**

|  | 1967 | 1970 | 1975 | 1980 | 1985 | 1987 |
|---|---|---|---|---|---|---|
| **Industrial** | | | | | | |
| Japan | 1,190 | 1,930 | 4,490 | 9,870 | 11,270 | 15,760 |
| **NIEs** | | | | | | |
| Singapore | 660 | 950 | 2,540 | 4,550 | 7,620 | 7,940 |
| Taiwan | 249 | 360 | 890 | 2,155 | 2,892 | 4,630 |
| S. Korea | 140 | 260 | 580 | 1,620 | 2,160 | 2,690 |
| **Developing** | | | | | | |
| Malaysia | 350 | 390 | 820 | 1,680 | 1,970 | 1,810 |
| Thailand | 170 | 210 | 360 | 670 | 810 | 840 |
| Philippines | 210 | 230 | 360 | 680 | 570 | 590 |
| Indonesia | 50 | 90 | 210 | 480 | 520 | 450 |
| **Giant** | | | | | | |
| China | 100 | 120 | 180 | 290 | 320 | 290 |

*Sources:* Except for Taiwan, all data are from World Bank, *World Tables, 1988–89 Edition*: 14–17. Taiwan data are from Republic of China DGB 1989: 93.

The resource-poor economies (Japan and the NIEs) pursued a strategy that was designed to overcome their weakness in natural resources and take advantage of their human capital. The first step was to develop labor-intensive, light industries like textiles and footwear and then to increase productivity and export the products. The next step was to use the foreign exchange earned in this way to import capital equipment to invest in infrastructure and in these and additional export industries. Exports were further expanded and higher levels of industrialization attained. Government support in various forms of subsidies usually played a crucial role in the early stage of industrialization.

The resource-rich economies (the ASEAN 4, which we have designated the developing economies) pursued a different strategy, centering on the exploitation of the natural resources that they have in abundance. The first step was to explore for oil and other mineral resources or to develop the primary (agricultural, fishery, and forestry) industries. These natural resources, primary products, and processed raw materials were then exported, the foreign exchange earnings being used to pay for imported capital goods, which were invested in infrastructure and resource exploration, agro-industry, and resource-related industries, or, if the government desired, in light industries. The economies following this

Table 1.4

## Per Capita Income in the Asia-Pacific Region, 1967–87

| | GNP per capita in constant 1980 U.S. dollars | | | | | | GDP per capita in current international dollars |
| | 1967 | 1970 | 1975 | 1980 | 1985 | 1987 | 1987 |
|---|---|---|---|---|---|---|---|
| Industrial | | | | | | | |
| Japan | 5,100 | 6,910 | 7,750 | 9,070 | 10,670 | 11,720 | 13,135 |
| NIEs | | | | | | | |
| Singapore | — | — | — | — | — | — | 12,790 |
| Taiwan | — | — | — | — | — | — | 5,907 |
| South Korea | 700 | 890 | 1,210 | 1,580 | 2,120 | 2,750 | 4,832 |
| Developing | | | | | | | |
| Malaysia | 880 | 930 | 1,090 | 1,720 | 1,770 | 1,670 | 3,849 |
| Thailand | 430 | 490 | 550 | 680 | 760 | 830 | 2,576 |
| Philippines | 480 | 530 | 610 | 710 | 580 | 630 | 1,878 |
| Indonesia | 190 | 240 | 340 | 510 | 570 | 580 | 1,660 |
| Giant | | | | | | | |
| China | 160 | 200 | 240 | 290 | 450 | 510 | 2,124 |

*Sources:* GNP per capita in constant 1980 U.S. dollars, except for Singapore and Taiwan, is from World Bank, *World Tables, 1988–89 Edition:* 18–21; Singapore data are calculated by applying the relevant U.S. deflator to data in current U.S. dollars, ibid.: 14–17; Taiwan data are calculated by applying the relevant U.S. deflator to data in current U.S. dollars in Republic of China 1989: 93. GDP per capita in current international dollars is from U.S. Agency for International Development 1989: 132–33, where GDP in current U.S. dollars has been converted into "international dollars" using purchasing power parities (PPPs), following the procedures described in Summers and Heston 1988.

model usually required a significant amount of investment in human capital, because they were seriously short of skilled workers, engineers, bureaucrats, and businessmen. Only after a preparatory stage of development did a gradual shift to a higher degree of industrialization become possible.

The Chinese situation was different. As a giant economy, rich in both human and natural resources, it did not feel forced to follow exclusively either of these strategies. Instead, it found it possible to undertake development on several different fronts at the same time. The first step was natural-resource exploration and agricultural development. Industrialization was pursued simultaneously for a considerable period by utilizing out-of-date technology and without relying much on external trade or foreign investment. Capital was largely squeezed from domestic savings and invested in infrastructure and certain strictly protected, labor-intensive industries. Exports were limited to selected natural resources, primary products, and light industrial products. Imports were restricted to a minimum essential for industrialization. Eventually, of course, this simultaneous effort to develop autonomously a capital goods industry tended to retard techno-logical progress, so that as the pace of development fell behind that of surround-ing industrializing countries of smaller scale, demands were generated for "opening up" the economy.

An important explanation for the economic success of these Asia-Pacific economies, therefore, is not that all pursued the same "Asian strategy" of devel-opment, but that each devised a relatively appropriate combination of economic policies for matching its domestic comparative advantage to the requirements of development. These requirements are that a virtuous circle of export-led growth be instituted—that domestic efforts increase exports, and that the foreign ex-change earnings from exports support the import of new capital goods and tech-nology, which in turn are fed into the development of new domestic industrial capacity. While open economy policies were not adopted by all countries from the beginning, China being a notable example of a late opener, eventually all have sought to promote international trade, foreign direct investment, and inter-national loans.

A second explanation for the success of their strategies has been the support-ive nature of the international environment. A virtuous circle can hardly be constructed or sustained unless importing countries' markets are open for devel-oping countries' exports; unless industrial countries are willing to supply the necessary capital equipment, financial loans, technology, and management know-how; and unless international regimes provide fair competition for trade and a peaceful political environment.

Fortunately for the Asia-Pacific economies, the international environment was indeed generally favorable. The United States played a particularly important role in Japan's development throughout; and both the United States and Japan have been indispensable partners of the others (table 1.5). The United States, for example, took 11–34 percent of the exports of these countries in 1975 and 14–38 percent in 1984,

Table 1.5

**United States and Japanese Share in Asia-Pacific Trade, 1975–84 (percent)**

| | Exports to | | | | Imports from | | | |
| | US | | Japan | | US | | Japan | |
| | 1975 | 1984 | 1975 | 1984 | 1975 | 1984 | 1975 | 1984 |
| --- | --- | --- | --- | --- | --- | --- | --- | --- |
| Industrial | | | | | | | | |
| Japan | 24.8 | 35.6 | (8.7)[a] | (10.8)[a] | 16.9 | 19.6 | (13.9)[a] | (19.0)[a] |
| NIEs | | | | | | | | |
| Singapore | 15.4 | 20.0 | 8.7 | 9.4 | 15.7 | 14.6 | 16.9 | 18.4 |
| Taiwan | 34.3 | 48.8 | 13.1 | 10.5 | 27.8 | 23.0 | 30.4 | 29.3 |
| S. Korea | 30.2 | 36.0 | 25.4 | 15.8 | 25.9 | 22.5 | 33.5 | 24.9 |
| Developing | | | | | | | | |
| Malaysia | 16.1 | 13.5 | 14.4 | 22.8 | 10.7 | 6.1 | 20.1 | 26.3 |
| Thailand | 11.1 | 17.2 | 27.6 | 13.0 | 14.8 | 13.5 | 32.4 | 26.9 |
| Philippines | 29.2 | 38.0 | 37.8 | 19.4 | 22.1 | 27.4 | 27.2 | 13.6 |
| Indonesia | 26.3 | 20.6 | 40.0 | 47.3 | 17.4 | 18.4 | 30.9 | 23.8 |
| Giant | | | | | | | | |
| China | 2.7 | 9.3 | 24.1 | 20.8 | 5.1 | 14.8 | 37.9 | 31.0 |

*Sources:* World Bank, *World Development Report, 1985* and *1986*; Asian Development Bank 1986; and national statistical yearbooks.

[a]The figures in parentheses are Japan's share of total U.S. exports and imports.

excluding China; Japan's shares were 9–44 percent in 1975 and 9–47 percent in 1984. As for their imports, the United States provided 11–28 percent in 1975 and 6–27 percent in 1984, whereas Japan provided 17–38 percent in 1975 and 14–31 percent in 1984. The United States was the market mainly for Japan and the NIEs; Japan was the principal market for the developing economies, and eventually for China as well. For the region as a whole, the United States offered primarily the market and secondarily capital goods, whereas Japan supplied primarily capital goods and secondarily the market. Thus, the United States and Japan have been the locomotives that have pulled the industrial freight trains of the other Asia-Pacific countries. In addition, the United States and Japan have been the major direct investors in the region and also have extended the largest amount of loans.

The success of Japan and the NIEs, which have pursued export-led growth policies with the most vigor, has been extraordinary. The growth rates of exports of these economies have far exceeded the growth rates of value added in their manufacturing industry (tables 1.6 and 1.7). They have thus been advancing their stage of industrialization, a fact that is reflected in the increasing importance of machinery imports and the declining significance of other manufactured imports.

Such export-led growth is not obvious in the past experiences of the resource-rich developing economies. But the fact that even they are successfully industrializing

Table 1.6

**Average Annual Growth Rates of Industry in the Asia-Pacific Region, 1965–86**

|  | 1965–80 | 1980–86 |
|---|---|---|
| Industrial |  |  |
| Japan | 8.5 | 5.0 |
| NIEs |  |  |
| Singapore | 12.2 | 4.4 |
| Taiwan | 10.9 | — |
| S. Korea | 16.5 | 10.2 |
| Developing |  |  |
| Malaysia | 10.3 | 6.0 |
| Thailand | 9.5 | 5.0 |
| Philippines | 8.0 | –3.5 |
| Indonesia | 11.9 | 1.8 |
| Giant |  |  |
| China | 10.0 | 12.5 |

*Source:* World Bank, *World Development Report, 1985* and *1986.*

is demonstrated by the declining weights of primary goods in their exports and of manufactured goods in their imports. This points to the simultaneous development of import-substituting and export-oriented industries in these countries between 1974 and 1986, and it is also reflected in the increasing share of manufactures in their own exports over the whole period from 1965 to 1986. In China, too, industrialization has been progressing successfully. Taking the form mainly of import substitution, in 1982 the share of manufactures in its exports (55 percent) even exceeded those of the other developing economies in the region. These data demonstrate the fact that all of the Asia-Pacific economies in our sample are industrializing themselves in one stage or another.

On the other hand, the requirements of international linkage presented different problems for each development model and in practice were met with different mechanisms and with varying degrees of success. These differences are reflected in part in the rates of growth and the changing composition of exports and imports as indicated in table 1.6. Among the NIEs, South Korea moved most rapidly up the industrial ladder, first building light industry and proceeding rapidly thereafter to enter production requiring heavy infusions of capital and technology. (For the differential rates of sectoral growth of each economy, see table 1.8.) Taiwan, on the other hand, at about the same level of per capita income, opted for a more balanced structure of light industries, intermediate goods, and capital goods industries. Only in recent years has it begun to move into the more capital-intensive and technology-intensive sectors. Singapore relied more heavily than either South Korea or Taiwan on government leadership. Nevertheless, being a small economy, it had no choice

Table 1.7

**Average Annual Growth Rates and Composition of Exports and Imports in the Asia-Pacific Region, 1965–86 (percent)**

| | Growth rate of exports | | | Growth rate of imports | | | Shares of | | |
|---|---|---|---|---|---|---|---|---|---|
| | 1965–73 | 1973–83 | 1980–86 | 1965–73 | 1973–83 | 1980–86 | Primary exports 1965–86 | Machinery imports 1965–86 | Other manu-facturers 1965–86 |
| Industrial | | | | | | | | | |
| Japan | 14.7 | 7.4 | 6.4 | 14.9 | 1.3 | 3.5 | 9.2 | 9.11 | 11.24 |
| NIEs | | | | | | | | | |
| Singapore | 11.0 | 7.1 | 6.1 | 9.8 | 7.8 | 3.6 | 65.33 | 14.37 | 30.30 |
| Taiwan | 26.0 | 10.2 | — | 19.1 | 5.2 | — | — | 28.00 | 27.00 |
| S. Korea | 31.7 | 14.8 | 13.1 | 22.4 | 7.5 | 9.3 | 40.9 | 13.34 | 52.41 |
| Developing | | | | | | | | | |
| Malaysia | 8.0 | 4.9 | 10.2 | 4.4 | 7.2 | 5.1 | 94.64 | 22.51 | 32.30 |
| Thailand | 6.9 | 9.0 | 9.2 | 4.4 | 3.3 | 2.0 | 95.58 | 31.34 | 49.40 |
| Philippines | 4.2 | 7.5 | -1.7 | 3.1 | 1.3 | -6.0 | 95.40 | 33.22 | 30.51 |
| Indonesia | 11.2 | 1.4 | 2.0 | 13.9 | 9.8 | -1.0 | 96.79 | 39.39 | 50.38 |
| Giant | | | | | | | | | |
| China | (5.5) | | 11.7 | | (8.0) | 16.8 | 3.16 | 31.00 | 56.00 |

*Source:* World Bank, *World Development Report, 1986.*

but to keep its economy open, imposing no tariffs and no restrictions on capital transactions.

The success of the strategy of the resource-rich developing economies has depended, of course, on securing favorable terms of trade, because export earnings depend not only on the development of new export industries, but also to a great extent on the relative prices of primary commodity exports and imported capital goods. One of the characteristics of the prices of primary products is that they tend to fluctuate widely and to decline in the long run. The oil bonanza greatly contributed to raising the growth of Malaysia and Indonesia. Thailand, the Philippines, and Malaysia also benefited from an increase in the prices of agricultural and forest products in the early 1970s. The same price hike did not occur, however, after the second oil shock, forcing them in the late 1970s and early 1980s to rely heavily on borrowings from abroad to sustain the pace of rapid growth. These unfavorable terms of trade for the developing economies after the second oil shock required them to speed up their industrialization and increase their export of light manufactured goods or such processed primary industrial products as plywood.

As for China, an import-substitution policy was able to achieve more than has usually been the case in smaller and less well-endowed countries. Nevertheless, the fundamental requirements for sustained development obtain for large countries as well as small. Despite the success of inward-looking policies for a considerable period, even giant economies must eventually open up—especially before the vested interests of established enterprises become insurmountable—if they are to avoid becoming locked into isolation from the progressing world. It was the failure to open up earlier that forced China to begin to explore the road of radical economic reform following the death of Mao Zedong.

Obviously, this is a very fluid picture as each economy over time attempts to move up market, reducing the ratio of labor-intensive goods and increasing the ratio of capital-intensive and technology-intensive goods in its exports. The impression given by this process is that the Asia-Pacific economies are engaged in a multistage catch-up competition with each other (Watanabe and Kajiwara 1983). In this competition each strives to move up market by constantly absorbing more and more modern technologies and restructuring its industries as required by its stage of development. Singapore, Taiwan, and South Korea strive to catch up with Japan; the ASEAN 4 try to catch up with the three ahead; and, in a variety of industrial products, China looms up from below to challenge the ASEAN 4.

Why is it that the countries in our sample have been relatively so successful in meeting the demands of development? How is it that they have been able to keep their resilience in the face of the two oil shocks in the 1970s and the world recession in the early 1980s? Why is it that, even so, they remain differentiated in three stages of growth? A number of factors would seem to be important.

Table 1.8

**Average Annual Growth Rates of Production by Sector in the Asia-Pacific Region, 1965–83 (percent)**

| | GDP | | Agriculture | | Industry | | Service | |
|---|---|---|---|---|---|---|---|---|
| | 1965–73 | 1973–83 | 1965–73 | 1973–83 | 1965–73 | 1973–83 | 1965–73 | 1973–83 |
| Industrial | | | | | | | | |
| Japan | 9.8 | 4.3 | 2.1 | -1.6 | 13.5 | 5.5 | 8.3 | 3.8 |
| NIEs | | | | | | | | |
| Singapore | 13.0 | 8.2 | 5.7 | 1.5 | 17.6 | 8.5 | 11.5 | 8.1 |
| Taiwan[a] | 9.0 | 10.3 | 0.8 | 2.5 | 12.0 | 13.5 | 8.1 | 9.1 |
| S. Korea | 10.0 | 7.3 | 2.9 | 1.5 | 18.4 | 11.2 | 11.3 | 6.9 |
| Developing | | | | | | | | |
| Malaysia | 6.7 | 7.3 | — | 4.4 | — | 8.7 | — | 8.2 |
| Thailand | 7.8 | 6.9 | 5.2 | 3.8 | 9.0 | 9.0 | 9.1 | 7.6 |
| Philippines | 5.4 | 5.4 | 4.1 | 4.3 | 7.4 | 6.4 | 4.8 | 5.2 |
| Indonesia | 8.1 | 7.0 | 4.8 | 3.7 | 13.4 | 8.6 | 9.6 | 9.0 |
| Giant | | | | | | | | |
| China | 7.4 | 6.0 | 1.9 | 3.5 | 9.1 | 8.4 | — | 4.5 |

*Sources:* World Bank, *World Development Report, 1985* and *1986*; and national statistical yearbooks.
[a]The periods for Taiwan are 1971–75 and 1975–80.

## Increasing Capital Accumulation and Saving

A high rate of capital accumulation and a high rate of saving are characteristic of most countries in the region. In addition, as can be seen from table 1.9, those rates increased as per capita incomes went up.

A steady increase in the rate of capital accumulation is a characteristic of Japan's history for the past one hundred years. The prewar Japanese rate of capital accumulation did not exceed 15 percent of GNP, but in postwar years the ratio rose from 14.6 percent in 1953 to a high of 32 percent in 1965, and it leveled off at 29–30 percent in the early 1980s. In the Asia-Pacific NIEs and the developing economies, the ratio of capital formation to GNP increased from somewhat below 20 percent in the 1960s to nearly 30 percent or even higher in the early 1980s.

The rates of saving in our sample countries have also been very high. The saving ratio went up quickly from about 16 percent of GNP in the late 1960s to over 20 percent in the early 1980s. In Taiwan and Singapore, it has been even above the Japanese gross saving ratio of about 30 percent, special policies of government in these two countries having played an important role. In Singapore, forced saving through a device called the Central Provident Fund is responsible, whereas in Taiwan it is government saving that is particularly high. Apart from this, however, the household saving rates also are very significant in most of our sample. This steady increase in the rates of capital accumulation and saving with rising per capita income over the past three decades is the most fundamental characteristic of the Asia-Pacific economies. It is also the most fundamental cause of the acceleration of their growth rates.

## Efficient Use of Capital and Technology

Even if the rate of capital accumulation is high, rapid growth may not result unless capital is efficiently utilized. The so-called incremental capital-output ratio (ICOR)—the amount of additional capital required to produce an additional unit of Gross Domestic Product—is an overall index of efficiency in the use of capital; the lower the rate, the more efficient the use. A relatively low rate, especially compared, for example, with South Asia and Latin America, characterizes most economies in our sample. Even in economies of relatively high GDP per capita, where one would expect that larger amounts of capital would be required to bring about incremental increases in output, the increase in the ratio is relatively mild (table 1.10). There are, however, anomalies. In the 1973–83 period, for example, South Korea, with a per capita income slightly lower than Taiwan's, nevertheless had an ICOR slightly higher; this was mainly because it adopted deliberate policies to emphasize heavy-chemical industries. Malaysia and Singapore have high ICORs corresponding to their high and rising per capita incomes; but the Philippines, with a far lower per capita income, has an ICOR as

Table 1.9

**Average Annual Rates of Capital Accumulation and Savings in the Asia-Pacific Region, 1965–86**

| | GNP per capita (U.S. $) 1986 | Rate of capital accumulation[a] | | | | Rate of saving as % of GNP | | | |
|---|---|---|---|---|---|---|---|---|---|
| | | 1965–72 | 1973–78 | 1979–83 | 1986 | 1965–72 | 1973–78 | 1979–83 | 1986 |
| Industrial | | | | | | | | | |
| Japan | 12,480 | 31.9 | 35.9 | 32.0 | 28.0 | 30.8 | 33.6 | 36.8 | 32.0 |
| NIEs | | | | | | | | | |
| Singapore[b] | 7,410 | 36.7 | 34.9 | 40.4 | 40.0 | 23.6 | 32.8 | 35.6 | 40.0 |
| Taiwan[b] | 4,000 | 26.2 | 30.6 | 32.4 | — | 23.1 | 29.3 | 37.0 | — |
| S. Korea | 2,370 | 24.1 | 29.0 | 30.0 | 29.0 | 14.9 | 24.9 | 23.7 | 35.0 |
| Developing | | | | | | | | | |
| Malaysia | 1,830 | 19.6 | 25.7 | 33.4 | 25.0 | 20.8 | 27.2 | 26.3 | 32.0 |
| Thailand | 810 | 23.8 | 25.4 | 25.3 | 21.0 | 21.3 | 23.6 | 20.5 | 25.0 |
| Philippines | 560 | 20.9 | 28.6 | 29.6 | 13.0 | 17.1 | 23.9 | 23.3 | 19.0 |
| Indonesia | 490 | 12.6 | 20.6 | 23.0 | 26.0 | 6.9 | 18.8 | 20.1 | 21.0 |
| Giant | | | | | | | | | |
| China | 300 | — | — | 33.6 | 39.0 | — | — | 33.2 | 36.0 |

*Sources:* World Bank. *World Development Report, 1985, 1986,* and *1988;* and national statistical yearbooks.

[a]Net capital formation expressed as percent of GNP.

[b]Figures for Singapore are for 1982 instead of 1983, and those for Taiwan are for 1970 instead of 1965.

high as Japan's, while Indonesia's relatively low ICOR must in fact be considered relatively high for a country with such a low per capita income.

As for technological innovation during the period under investigation, the most remarkable was the Green Revolution, which introduced high-yielding varieties of cereals, including rice, the most important crop in the region. With the use of land already intensive and the potential for extensive expansion of production limited, the new grains had a dramatic effect on agricultural productivity. Table 1.11 shows the spread of this revolution. Introduction of high-yielding varieties of rice required additional investments in fertilizer and irrigation. Such complementary investments were made possible by the conscious efforts of the governments to expand agricultural investment, as increased food self-sufficiency became a national goal. If the Green Revolution had not made it possible not only to increase production but also to absorb the enormous surplus labor in the rural areas in the Asia-Pacific region, the distribution of income and social stability would have been much worse.

## Highly Qualified Human Resources and Declining Fertility Rates

All Asia-Pacific countries have emphasized education and thereby improvement in the quality of workers, engineers, salaried persons, executives, government officials, and intellectuals (table 1.12). The result is that the majority of workers in these countries now have some secondary education, and there are enough middle managers and engineers to facilitate the transfer of higher technologies. By way of comparison, in South Asia only Sri Lanka and Myanmar have made such an extraordinary education effort and thereby achieved such high literacy rates.

The health of workers also has improved substantially. As the last column of table 1.12 shows, calorie intake differs among the four types of economies; nevertheless, the majority of workers in every country in our sample now get more than the required minimum daily amount of calories.

Another important feature contributing to the improvement of the quality of labor and sustaining economic growth in the long run is the demographic transition. Fertility rates have been declining throughout the region. Here again, however, the four groups of states show significant differences (table 1.13). As one might expect, there is a high correlation between the level of per capita income and the decline in the fertility rate, with the exception of China, where a population control policy has been particularly aggressively pursued.

## Relatively Sound Fiscal and Monetary Policies

Fiscal policies in the Asia-Pacific countries have not always been sound in the sense of keeping the national government budgets balanced. As table 1.14 shows, the revenue and expenditure of each country's central government have usually left a considerable amount of deficit. If, however, these budgets are

**Table 1.10**

**Average Annual Incremental Capital Output Ratios in the Asia-Pacific Region, 1965–83 (percent)**

| | 1965–73 | | | 1973–83 | | |
|---|---|---|---|---|---|---|
| | Growth rate of GDP | Rate of accumulation | ICOR | Growth rate of GDP | Rate of accumulation | ICOR |
| Industrial | | | | | | |
| Japan | 9.8 | 30.0 | 3.1 | 4.3 | 22.7 | 5.2 |
| NIEs | | | | | | |
| Singapore | 13.0 | 36.7 | 2.8 | 8.2 | 37.6 | 4.6 |
| Taiwan | 10.1 | 26.2 | 2.6 | 8.5 | 31.5 | 3.7 |
| S. Korea | 10.0 | 24.1 | 2.4 | 7.3 | 29.5 | 4.0 |
| Developing | | | | | | |
| Malaysia | 6.7 | 19.6 | 2.9 | 7.3 | 29.1 | 4.0 |
| Thailand | 7.8 | 23.8 | 3.1 | 6.9 | 25.4 | 3.7 |
| Philippines | 5.4 | 20.9 | 3.9 | 5.4 | 29.1 | 5.4 |
| Indonesia | 8.1 | 12.6 | 1.6 | 7.0 | 21.8 | 3.1 |
| Giant | | | | | | |
| China | 7.4 | 28.3 | 3.8 | 6.0 | 31.9 | 5.3 |

*Sources*: World Bank, *World Development Report, 1985* and *1986*; Asian Development Bank, various years; and national statistical yearbooks.
*Note*: The ICOR is the amount of additional capital required to produce an additional unit of Gross Domestic Product—an overall index of efficiency in the use of capital—derived by dividing the rate of accumulation by the growth rate of GDP.

Table 1.11

**Average Annual Growth Rates of Cereal Yields in the Asia-Pacific Region, 1967–84**

| | Average annual growth rates of yields | | | Cereal imports (billion tons) | |
| | 1967–73 | 1973–80 | 1980–84 | 1974 | 1986 |
|---|---|---|---|---|---|
| Industrial | | | | | |
| Japan | 0.4 | −2.6 | 2.1 | 19,557 | 27,119 |
| NIEs | | | | | |
| Singapore | 0.0 | 0.0 | 0.0 | 682 | 829 |
| Taiwan | 0.6 | 1.4 | −0.8 | — | — |
| S. Korea | 2.4 | 1.9 | 2.0 | 2,679 | 7,408 |
| Developing | | | | | |
| Malaysia | 3.2 | 2.5 | −0.9 | 1,017 | 2,067 |
| Thailand | 1.1 | 1.5 | 1.9 | 97 | 191 |
| Philippines | 3.3 | 4.0 | 2.1 | 817 | 1,094 |
| Indonesia | — | 4.7 | 5.4 | 1,919 | 1,752 |
| Giant | | | | | |
| China | 3.9 | 2.4 | 6.2 | 0.0 | 290 |

*Sources:* World Bank, *World Development Report, 1985* and *1986*; Asian Development Bank, various years; and national statistical yearbooks.

compared with those of Latin American or South Asian countries, the general soundness of fiscal policies in the region cannot be doubted. On the expenditure side, despite in some cases the heavy burden of defense, most of these governments—in particular, Japan, the NIEs, and Thailand—have spent the higher proportions of their budgets for education and economic services (table 1.15). This clearly distinguishes them from the pattern in Latin America, for example, where, despite relatively negligible defense expenditures, the governments have spent the largest amounts for social welfare and personnel. Among the economies in our sample, it is only in Indonesia and the Philippines that a Latin America–like pattern is found. Malaysia is somewhere in between.

The monetary policies pursued by these countries also have been relatively sound (Tan and Basar 1983). As a result of these sound fiscal and monetary policies, the rate of inflation in each country in the region has been relatively minor, China currently being an exception, and far more amenable to control than most other developing countries in the Third World.

## Tolerable Income Distribution

As a consequence of all these factors, one of the most remarkable achievements of the economies in the Asia-Pacific region has been in the distribution of income. If we define an index of inequality as the average income of the richest 10

Table 1.12

## Social Indicators in the Asia-Pacific Region, 1965–85

| | Literacy rate (% of total population) | | Newspaper circulation (per 1000) | | School enrollment (% of age group) | | | | | | Daily calories (per capita) | |
| --- | --- | --- | --- | --- | --- | --- | --- | --- | --- | --- | --- | --- |
| | | | | | Primary | | Secondary | | Higher | | | |
| | 1970 | 1980 | 1970 | 1984 | 1965 | 1985 | 1965 | 1985 | 1965 | 1985 | 1965 | 1985 |
| Industrial | | | | | | | | | | | | |
| Japan | 99 | 99 | 520 | 562 | 100 | 102 | 82 | 96 | 13 | 30 | 2,669 | 2,695 |
| NIEs | | | | | | | | | | | | |
| Singapore | 72 | 84 | 200 | 277 | 105 | 115 | 45 | 71 | 10 | 12 | 2,214 | 2,696 |
| Taiwan | 85 | 90 | — | — | 97 | 100 | 38 | 91 | 7 | 13 | 2,411 | 2,874 |
| S. Korea | 88 | 93 | 136 | 138 | 101 | 96 | 35 | 94 | 6 | 32 | 2,255 | 2,806 |
| Developing | | | | | | | | | | | | |
| Malaysia | 58 | 60 | 75 | 323 | 90 | 99 | 28 | 53 | 2 | 6 | 2,249 | 2,601 |
| Thailand | 79 | 86 | 20 | 42 | 78 | 98 | 14 | 30 | 2 | 20 | 2,200 | 2,399 |
| Philippines | 83 | 75 | 14 | 21 | 113 | 106 | 41 | 65 | 19 | 38 | 1,936 | 2,260 |
| Indonesia | 57 | 62 | — | 28 | 72 | 118 | 12 | 39 | 1 | 7 | 1,792 | 2,476 |
| Giant | | | | | | | | | | | | |
| China | 43 | 69 | — | 33 | 89 | 124 | 24 | 39 | 0 | 2 | 2,034 | 2,620 |

*Sources:* World Bank, *World Development Report, 1985, 1986, 1987,* and *1988;* Asian Development Bank, various years; and national statistical yearbooks.

Table 1.13

**Correlation of Income Levels and Fertility Rates in the Asia-Pacific Region, 1965 and 1986**

| | GDP per capita 1983 | Fertility rate[a] 1965 | 1986 |
|---|---|---|---|
| Industrial | | | |
|   Japan | 10,120 | 2.0 | 1.8 |
| NIEs | | | |
|   Singapore | 6,620 | 4.7 | 1.7 |
|   Taiwan | 2,612 | 4.8 | 1.7 |
|   S. Korea | 2,010 | 4.8 | 2.2 |
| Developing | | | |
|   Malaysia | 1,870 | 6.3 | 3.5 |
|   Thailand | 820 | 6.3 | 3.0 |
|   Philippines | 760 | 6.8 | 4.6 |
|   Indonesia | 560 | 5.5 | 3.6 |
| Giant | | | |
|   China | 300 | 6.4 | 2.3 |

*Sources:* World Bank, *World Development Report, 1985*; and national statistical yearbooks.
[a]Average number of children born alive per woman during her lifetime.

percent divided by the average income of the poorest 20 percent, we find that in most instances inequality has remained within tolerable limits (table 1.16). This may not be immediately apparent, since the indexes of most economies in the region (excluding Taiwan) appear high in comparison with that of Japan. But Japan's is extraordinarily low by world standards. If one compares the income distribution of the Asia-Pacific countries other than Japan with other developing countries, one finds those in our sample to be unusually equitable. The income share of the richest 10 percent in the Asia-Pacific economies is in the 30 percent range, whereas that in Latin America, for example, is 40–50 percent. The income share of the poorest 20 percent in the Asia-Pacific economies ranges from 3.5 percent to 6.6 percent, whereas in Latin America, with the exception of Argentina, it varies from only 1.9 percent to 2.9 percent.

The Philippines and Malaysia seem to be exceptional among the Asia-Pacific countries in their relative inequality. It is also true that the inequality in the Philippines and also Indonesia may be underestimated by these data (Ichimura 1987). One should not imagine, therefore, that income distribution poses no problems in the Asia-Pacific region. Nevertheless, even with these qualifications, one cannot escape the conclusion that in general the income distribution in the societies of our sample is much more egalitarian than that in the societies of, say, Latin America.

One determinant of income distribution is the level of per capita income. As Simon Kuznets has observed, the relationship between economic growth and income equality seems to follow an inverted U-shaped curve: in the early stages

Table 1.14

**Central Government Budgets in the Asia-Pacific Region, 1971–85 (percent of GDP)**

| | Expenditures | | | Tax Revenues | | | Balance | |
|---|---|---|---|---|---|---|---|---|
| | 1971–75 | 1976–80 | 1981–85 | 1971–75 | 1976–80 | 1981–85 | 1971–75 | 1976–80 |
| Industrial | | | | | | | | |
| Japan | 22.3 | 27.7 | 17.4 | 20.1 | 20.8 | 12.6 | −1.9 | −4.9 |
| NIEs | | | | | | | | |
| Singapore | 24.4 | 29.6 | 26.5 | 25.8 | 17.4 | 27.0 | 1.3 | 2.0 |
| Taiwan | 19.4 | 22.9 | — | 15.6 | 17.8 | — | — | — |
| S. Korea | 18.6 | 18.9 | 17.8 | 12.7 | 16.0 | 18.8 | −3.9 | −0.1 |
| Developing | | | | | | | | |
| Malaysia | 27.6 | 33.9 | 36.6 | 18.7 | 22.1 | 29.3 | −9.8 | −7.2 |
| Thailand | 15.4 | 16.9 | 21.7 | 12.1 | 12.7 | 16.3 | −4.3 | −5.6 |
| Philippines | 13.1 | 14.2 | 10.8 | 10.2 | 11.4 | 11.5 | −2.0 | −1.9 |
| Indonesia | 18.7 | 24.6 | 26.9 | 14.8 | 19.8 | 23.1 | −2.5 | −3.9 |
| Giant | | | | | | | | |
| China | — | — | — | — | — | — | — | — |

*Sources:* World Bank, *World Development Report, 1985-88*; and national statistical yearbooks.

of industrialization, equality usually suffers as per capita income rises; but at some level of income, the relationship is reversed; from then on, equality tends to improve as income rises. The Kuznets hypothesis appears to hold for most countries in the region. There are only two exceptions. The trend toward greater equity in Japan, the most advanced economy in the region, seems to be reversing, suggesting that the relationship hypothesized by Kuznets may not continue after a certain critical point has been passed. Taiwan would seem to be a special case, its income distribution being more equitable than would normally be expected at its level of development; the explanation may be in its pattern of small landholding by farmers who obtain a significant share of the fruits of industrialization from the rising prices of land and rent.

Other factors also would seem to be important in explaining variations in the relative degree of equity achieved in income distribution. At least one notes that in the countries of our sample, equity seems to improve as fertility rates drop, the share of employment provided by agriculture declines, and the level of education rises—all correlated with the level of income.

## Fairly Reliable Public and Private Institutions

Kuznets has also pointed out, as have others, that "modern economic growth" depends not only on the meeting of certain economic requirements, but also on the prior or concomitant development of certain social and political frameworks and ways of thinking that are compatible with the economy's evolution (Kuznets 1966): a strong and stable government, an honest, efficient, and technically trained bureaucracy, imaginative entrepreneurial talent with freedom to operate, an educated and disciplined labor force, a cohesive social community, and a social ethic placing a high priority on growth. These and other, similar factors unfortunately are not generally susceptible to reliable statistical measurement, nor is the weight each should be assigned in the total development equation known. But of their importance there can be no doubt, and at least impressionistically their development seems to be a significant part of the explanation of the degrees of economic success enjoyed by the economies in the Asia-Pacific region as well as of the variations in pattern among them.

At the same time, there would appear to be a certain reciprocity of influence at work, for no one can doubt also that the existence and development of these very institutions and attitudes are at least partly reflective of the economic development they impede or support—which prompts the central concern of this study: precisely how does the process of economic growth impact the social and political system? To what extent, if at all, can the four patterns of development we have identified, the country-specific variations within them, and the differences in level of income achieved serve to explain the varieties of political regimes that have been evolving in the region?

Table 1.15

**Central Government Expenditures in the Asia-Pacific Region, 1972 and 1986 (percent of total expenditures)**

| | Defense | | Education | | Health | | Welfare | | Economic services | | Other | |
|---|---|---|---|---|---|---|---|---|---|---|---|---|
| | 1972 | 1986 | 1972 | 1986 | 1972 | 1986 | 1972 | 1986 | 1972 | 1986 | 1972 | 1986 |
| Industrial | | | | | | | | | | | | |
| Japan[a] | 6.0 | 6.2 | 11.1 | 9.1 | — | 1.3 | 18.2 | 20.3 | — | — | — | — |
| NIEs | | | | | | | | | | | | |
| Singapore | 20.1 | 20.2 | 9.0 | 21.6 | 4.5 | 6.5 | 2.2 | 5.7 | 5.7 | 17.7 | 58.6 | 26.0 |
| Taiwan[b] | 43.3 | 35.3 | 17.3 | 20.5 | — | — | 14.8 | — | 10.3 | — | 67.4 | 27.7 |
| S. Korea | 25.8 | 29.2 | 15.9 | 18.1 | 1.2 | 1.5 | 5.8 | 7.2 | 25.6 | 16.2 | 18.1 | — |
| Developing | | | | | | | | | | | | |
| Malaysia | 18.5 | — | 23.4 | — | 6.8 | — | 4.4 | — | 14.2 | — | 32.7 | — |
| Thailand | 20.2 | 20.2 | 19.9 | 19.5 | 3.7 | 5.7 | 7.0 | 4.6 | 25.7 | 22.6 | 23.5 | 27.4 |
| Philippines | 10.9 | 11.9 | 16.3 | 20.1 | 3.2 | 6.0 | 4.3 | 1.6 | 17.6 | 44.9 | 47.7 | 15.6 |
| Indonesia | 18.6 | 9.3 | 7.4 | 8.5 | 1.4 | 1.9 | 0.9 | 1.4 | 30.5 | 19.3 | 41.3 | 59.6 |
| Giant | | | | | | | | | | | | |
| China[c] | 20.8 | 8.6 | 8.1 | 16.3 | — | — | — | — | — | — | — | — |

*Sources*: World Bank, *World Development Report, 1985* and *1986*; Asian Development Bank, various years; and national statistical yearbooks.

[a]For Japan, the data given under "education" are those reported for "education and culture."

[b]For Taiwan, the data given under "Defense" are those reported by the ROC for "defense and general administration," including security and police expenditures; and the data given under "education" are those reported by the ROC for "education, science, and culture."

[c]For China, the data given under "education" are those reported by the PRC for "culture, education, science, and public health."

Table 1.16

**Income Inequality in the Asia-Pacific Region, Various Years (percent)**

| | Year | Percentage of private income received by households | | | |
| | | Lowest 20% | Highest 20% | Highest 10% | Degree of inequality[a] |
|---|---|---|---|---|---|
| Industrial | | | | | |
| Japan | 1979 | 8.7 | 37.5 | 22.4 | 5.1 |
| NIEs | | | | | |
| Singapore | 1975 | 5.4 | 48.9 | 28.7 | 10.1 |
| Taiwan | 1979 | 8.6 | 37.5 | 22.0 | 4.4 |
| S. Korea | 1976 | 5.7 | 45.3 | 27.5 | 9.6 |
| Developing | | | | | |
| Malaysia | 1973 | 3.5 | 56.1 | 39.8 | 22.7 |
| Thailand | 1976 | 5.6 | 49.8 | 34.1 | 12.2 |
| Philippines | 1985 | 5.2 | 52.5 | 37.0 | 14.2 |
| Indonesia | 1976 | 6.6 | 49.4 | 34.4 | 10.3 |
| Giant | | | | | |
| China | — | — | — | — | — |

*Sources:* World Bank, *World Development Report, 1985, 1986,* and *1988*; national statistical yearbooks; and *TDRI Newsletter*: 89.

[a]A ratio derived from the average income of the richest 10 percent divided by the average income of the poorest 20 percent.

To set the stage for country-by-country studies of this relationship, we turn now to an overview of the nature of these polities and the changes they have been experiencing.

## Political Change

For identifying major changes in each of the Asia-Pacific political systems as well as making comparisons among them, it is useful to think of each at any one time as approximating operationally one of three generalized models: democratic, Leninist, or authoritarian. Joseph A. Schumpeter (1942: 269) long ago pinpointed the "democratic method" as "that institutional arrangement for arriving at political decisions in which individuals acquire the power to decide by means of a competitive struggle for the people's vote." Robert Dahl (1971: 7) has refined this to distinguish two elements: "public contestation," by which he means the selection of government officials by public competition in an atmosphere of free choice, and "inclusiveness," his word for the extent to which all citizens enjoy "the right to participate in elections and office." The Leninist model is almost a polar opposite. We shall define it as a model in which there is one-party rule, an absence of choice, Marxist-Leninist ideological conformity, and extreme mobilization of society under party direction. Authoritarianism falls somewhere in between. Juan Linz (1973: 185) captures its essence best in defining such regimes as "political systems with limited, not responsible, political pluralism; without an elaborate and guiding ideology (but with distinct mentalities); without intensive or extensive political mobilization (except at some points in their development); and in which a leader (or occasionally a small group) exercises power within formally ill-defined but quite predictable limits."

It will be important as we go along to qualify these three generic designations to indicate the peculiar qualities of a particular regime. For some purposes, for example, it will be useful to point out that Japan is a dominant-party as opposed to a multiparty democracy; or Singapore, a civilian as opposed to a military authoritarian system. Moreover, no regime fits any one of these models perfectly. In some the discrepancy is so great that we shall feel compelled to introduce a hedging prefix, for example, using the term quasi-democratic if the regime is of a mixed democratic and authoritarian character (e.g., Malaysia, Taiwan, and Thailand) or applying the qualifier "eroding" to the identification of China today as Leninist to indicate that its Leninist features are weakening but are not yet undergoing substantial change. In most instances, however, we shall try to identify the central character of the regime by one of our models in an effort to pinpoint when a transformation of the political system may have occurred or be occurring.

With these understandings, we turn to an overview of the regimes and their changes that we shall be seeking to explain. Figure 1.1 attempts to represent these changes.

As the figure indicates, each regime type has exhibited a capacity for stability or relative stability in at least one society. Democracy has survived continuously in Japan, and Leninism in China—although it is now eroding, and authoritarianism in Taiwan, while now liberalizing, has had a long history. Each of these regimes, of course, has been challenged by opposition groups. The Communist party in Japan, for example, at one time sought to upset the democratic system by violence. In China, dissident intellectuals have erupted whenever coercion has been relaxed, most recently in 1989. In Taiwan, the "nonparty" (that is, the non-Kuomintang) movement has increasingly attacked mainlander controls and has at last gained electoral legitimacy, revealing a serious erosion of the KMT's authoritarian foundations.

Three other states have made relatively stable choices, though not without brief alternative experiments: Indonesia and Singapore for authoritarianism, and Malaysia for a quasi-democracy. In the Indonesian case, democracy was one of the rallying cries in the war against the Dutch; and when independence was secured in 1949, a parliamentary democracy was installed. For seven years the country was ruled by shifting coalitions of nationalist, Muslim, and socialist parties, but by 1957 factional rivalries and regional revolts were so severe that martial law was proclaimed. The experiment with parliamentary democracy was dead. Two years later, amid growing disorder, the new system was formalized as

Figure 1.1
**Regime Types and Regime Changes in the Asia-Pacific Region, 1945–90**

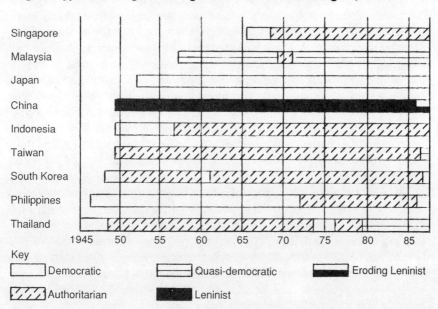

Key

☐ Democratic    ☰ Quasi-democratic    ▬ Eroding Leninist

▨ Authoritarian    ■ Leninist

"Guided Democracy." Sukarno consolidated his authoritarian control with the support of the armed forces and the Communist party (the PKI), but in the mid-1960s he himself was swept aside, following the massacre of about half a million PKI supporters, by the army leadership under Suharto, who assumed the presidency in 1967.

Authoritarian "Guided Democracy" was replaced by the even more authoritarian "New Order." *Pancasila*—an ideological code first enunciated by Sukarno and embracing the five principles of monotheism, humanitarianism, nationalism, democracy, and social justice—was elevated as the main ideological theme of the regime. Opponents of military domination were repressed while other social organizations were coopted under the banner of Golkar, the Joint Secretariat of the Functional Groups, which serves the regime as its political party. The army, being deeply involved in civil administration as well as national security, has given its staunch support, and with the polls managed in such a way as to ensure Golkar's repeated success, Suharto has been returned to office regularly with overwhelming victories.

Singapore began with the Westminster system. Unlike Indonesia, it did not have to wrest power from its imperial masters. The British extended the franchise in 1948, autonomy in 1959, and independence in 1963 as part of the Federation of Malaysia. Independence as a republic came in 1965 with its separation from Malaysia, by which time Singapore had had fairly extensive experience with at least limited electoral politics.

The early years were marked by a tumultuous confrontation between Communist and non-Communist elements for ascendance in the nationalist struggle for the colony. One result was that when the moderate faction in the leading party, the People's Action party (PAP), finally overcame the internal party split engendered by the left in 1961, it determined never to let power slip from its grasp; and it has not. By 1968 most significant opposition leaders had been detained, and it had won total control of the parliament. Democracy as an open, competitive system was ended. In the years that followed, while the legislature was selected by orderly elections, the PAP extended its influence over the society by appointing or coopting the leaders of most significant interest groups in the republic. Overt opposition virtually disappeared as Lee Kwan Yew and the PAP consolidated their control with a high degree of technocratic efficiency and apparent popular support.

Malaysia has followed a different path. It too began life fundamentally as a democracy—on the Westminster model derived from its British colonial heritage, with a constitutional monarchy under an unusual system of rotating kingship and an elected parliament in which most real power ultimately resided. This system was broadly accepted by parties representing Malay, Chinese, and Indian ethnic groups, although the Communists continued their violent insurrection, which had originally been directed against British colonialism. The outcome, however, has not been the Singapore solution.

Malaysian democracy has indeed had its limits and interruptions. From the beginning it has constrained dissent, the Emergency proclaimed by the British in 1948 continuing to 1960 and the Internal Security Act preserving many of its arbitrary provisions thereafter. Within these limits it has further sought to close the deep cleavages in society by a corporatist strategy, reaching a social understanding among the elites of the primary ethnic groups, then pulling their major parties into a National Alliance or Front (today the Barisan Nasional), which has engaged in relatively free elections and always won. While this quasi-democratic solution has shown remarkable resiliency, it has on occasion had its difficulties. Notably, the racial rioting surrounding the national election in 1969 was so intense that the government suspended parliamentary rule for nearly two years until a National Consultative Council could work out a new ethnic compact and set state policy in a new direction.

During the 1970s and 1980s the government resorted to increasingly authoritarian means of rule as the system appeared to be unraveling. A bitterly contested election within the dominant UMNO party in April 1987 ushered in a power struggle that not only disrupted the party and its coalition but threatened judicial independence and fed into a serious clampdown on dissension. In the fall of that year, under the plea of restraining racial tension, the government closed several newspapers, banned public demonstrations, and arrested numerous individuals, including party leaders. While some months later the newspapers were allowed to reopen, most detainees were released, and parliamentary politics appeared to be reviving, uncertainty continues to hover over the future of Malaysia's quasi-democratic regime.

The political experiences of the other three states have been more checkered. They too, like Indonesia and Singapore, started out as democracies only to turn to authoritarianism, but, unlike Indonesia and Singapore, ruling elites have faced stronger challenges, with the result that regimes have changed once, and in some cases, two or three times.

Thailand has oscillated the most. Since the absolute monarchy was abolished in 1932, it has gone back and forth between authoritarian and democratic models a number of times. The military rule of the 1930s was interrupted by a democratic experiment in the mid-1940s, but by 1948 Colonel Phibun Songkram, who had ruled in the predemocratic days, had returned to power. Parties and public expression were liberalized briefly in 1955–57 and 1968–71. During these years the parliament was given more constitutional authority as well; democratic influences were soon stifled again, however, so that in general from 1948 to 1973, the country may be said to have been ruled by military officers, replacing each other by coups d'état and ruling without serious opposition from outside the military. In October 1973 a popular uprising led by the students, at a time when the military itself was seriously split, again drove the military from power, temporarily. A new, liberal constitution was adopted; civilian party leaders, first Kukrit Pramoj, then Seni Pramoj, were elected to power; and freedom reigned in a heady environment of increasingly disorderly participation. In 1976, however, the military, who had encouraged antigovernment disorder, took the opportunity to reassert itself. A coup was followed by a period of suppression, and this in turn, from 1977 to the present, by a period of relatively stable rule.

A new constitution was adopted in 1979. For the next twelve years, governments were supported by coalitions of political parties, first under General Kriangsak, then General Prem, and finally General Chatichai Choonhoven. Military factionalism appeared to have been contained: coups were attempted in 1981 and 1985, largely by junior officers, but they failed. Moreover, there was some sharing of power with the monarchy, the technocrats, and the business community. Thus, although the parties remained weak and divided, subject to military manipulation and unable to challenge the ultimate power of the army, authoritarianism seemed to have been transformed into a quasi-democratic system. Whether the successful coup, led by General Suchinda Krapayoon in February 1991, represents a temporary or a long-term reversion remains to be seen.

The Philippines has had extended periods of both democratic and authoritarian rule. In 1946 it set out on its independent course with a presidential system on the American model, and although attacked by a powerful insurrectionary movement headed by the Communist-led Hukbalahaps between 1946 and 1952 and challenged after 1968 by a new Communist party and its guerrilla arm, it persisted on the democratic path, not under a dominant party as in several other countries in the region, but, until 1972, with changes of the parties in power in response to popular elections.

In 1972, on the plea that the power of certain politically strong families, identified vaguely as "the oligarchy," constituted an obstacle to the reforms that were needed to meet a growing Communist movement, Ferdinand Marcos proclaimed martial law and had the constitution revised, enabling him to rule under emergency powers and virtually by edict. In 1981 martial law was lifted and a "New Republic" was proclaimed, but real authority was not returned to the National Assembly and such measures did not appease the opposition. The assassination of Benigno Aquino, the principal opposition leader, on his return to the Philippines in 1983 touched off a massive opposition movement, which eventuated in the flight of Marcos in 1986 and the return of democracy for a second trial.

Finally, South Korea, which in 1987 also decided to give democracy another chance, has a similarly checkered history. The first experiment with democracy began in 1948 with the establishment of the Republic of Korea on the American model. It did not go well. Political competition was crushed as Syngman Rhee, pleading the Communist menace, assumed the powers of an autocrat. A widespread student rebellion challenged the system in 1960. Rhee was forced to flee and, much as in Thailand a decade later, democracy was restored, only to have it swamped in a melee of political activism. A coup in 1961 brought General Park Chung Hee to power. A national emergency was proclaimed and a new *"Yushin"* (Revitalizing) Constitution was brought forward, restoring the regime to authoritarian patterns.

The assassination of Park in 1979, followed by the assumption of power by General Chun Doo Hwan, brought little change in the fundamental nature of the regime, but Chun did seem to recognize that the pressures for democratic reform were building again. In an unusual step for an authoritarian leader, he lived up to his promise to resign after a seven-year term. Under heavy pressure from opposition parties, Chun permitted a democratic constitution to be devised in 1987, ushering in a return to democratic forms, and the selection of a new president in a hotly contested but peaceful election later that year.

## Is There a Correlation?

At first glance the variety of the Asia-Pacific regimes under consideration is bewildering. Despite the high rates of growth achieved by all, there would seem to be little common political experience. Some have taken the democratic road, some the authoritarian, and one the Leninist; and while some have achieved a remarkable stability, others have changed course a number of times. No pattern appears immediately to emerge. But are appearances deceiving? Our first cut at the problem is to investigate more deeply the history of each individual country, seeking to explain its economic growth and the changes in its political system in all their diversity and apparent uniqueness. As one country after another is analyzed, however, it will be apparent that certain generic forces exert impacts on most of our sample, albeit at different times, in different strengths, and in different combinations. Our second cut, therefore, at the conclusion of these essays, is comparative, an exercise that reveals a striking correlation though with exceptions to be sure: generally those Asia-Pacific countries with low levels of economic growth tend to have autocratic governments, and those with high levels of economic growth tend to have democratic. Is this accidental? We believe not and propose a model to explain it.

# Part I
# A Giant Economy

# 2

## China: Change in a Marxist-Leninist State

### Thomas P. Bernstein

AN APPRAISAL of the impact of economic development on the political system of Marxist-Leninist party-states must begin with a paradox. On the one hand, over long periods Communist states have shown an impressive degree of immunity from the effects of economic development, an immunity that stems from the defining characteristic of such systems, namely, that politics is in command. A Leninist party is one that requires its members to disaffiliate from social interests; it is a party of mobilization, not a party of representation. It is the leadership of the Leninist party that shapes, or rather reshapes, the society and the economy. It is the political elite that deploys its resources for the goal of building a new society. These include the party apparatus; the hierarchically controlled network of party branches and cells in nonparty organizations; mass organizations that function as transmission belts, penetrating all sectors of society and mobilizing the population; a monopoly of communications and propaganda; and a security apparatus. It is the political elite that controls the means of production, decides on the proportion of the nation's income to be invested, allocates resources according to plan, and determines the country's development strategy.

Their power gives such regimes an impressive capacity to insulate themselves from societal influences. Indeed, so great is the power of such regimes that they are able, if they wish, for long periods of time to prevent even the most normal of social changes that accompany economic development from occurring. Take urbanization, for instance. For over twenty years and to a significant degree even today, the Chinese state has been able to prevent migration from the rural to the urban sector. Moreover, for over a decade, Chinese leaders were even able to engineer a massive countermigration of urbanites to the countryside (Bernstein 1977). Marxist-Leninist regimes have been known also to accomplish remarkable feats in accelerating change. Normally, the birth rate declines with development over the long term, but in China, once the Chinese regime had made up its mind to do so, it was able to reduce the birth rate from 37 per 1,000 in 1970 to 21 per 1,000 in 1978 by employing its organizational capacities, including those of the public health sector, as well as positive and negative incentives (Banister 1984: 117–24). Marxist-Leninist regimes have accomplished great feats of societal reorganization, as in the case of agricultural collectivization. No wonder that scholars writing on China have spoken of the "political conquest of society" and of the replacement of society by organization (Vogel 1969; Schurmann 1966).

On the other hand, Marxist-Leninist regimes are by no means permanently immune from social change, social tensions, social pressures, as well as protest and resistance from below. A simple-minded assumption of immutable totalitarian control will not do. At best, the facade of monolithic unity conceals a very different reality. Outward solidarity may lead both outside observers and the ruling elite to overestimate the degree of real and lasting change that has been brought about. Thus, many observers believed in the 1970s that the Chinese commune system had come to be accepted by the peasants. Yet, once the lid was taken off after 1978, peasants embraced the return to family farming with an enthusiasm that came as something of a surprise even to the leadership. Underneath the facade of monolithic unity, spontaneous forces for change are likely to be at work, which at some point or other may undermine and even render ineffectual the preemptive systems of control, especially when divisions among the leaders reduce the party-state's capacity to rule.

How then should the relationship among politics, economics, and society in Marxist-Leninist systems be analyzed? A useful approach is to distinguish between the stages through which Communist regimes typically move. The first is the stage of revolution and consolidation of power. The second is that of mobilization and transformation, during which the regime seeks to remake the society and forced-draft industrialization is the core economic task. It is during this stage of building socialism that the suppression of autonomous societal and economic forces is pursued most vigorously. The third stage is that of adaptation to the more complex society that has emerged from industrialization, urbanization, the spread of education, and other changes (Huntington 1970: 1–43).

During the second stage, that of mobilization, economic and social factors impinge on politics primarily as natural constraints to be overcome and as constraints that result from mismanagement of the development process by the political leadership. This mismanagement has two systemic roots. One source is the enormous power of such regimes, which enables them to plan and carry out changes on a grand scale. But since adequate knowledge to plan is not available, the results are changes made with "strong thumbs and no fingers," to use Lindblom's expressive metaphor (Lindblom 1977: 65ff.). The Chinese Great Leap Forward is only an extreme example of the high cost of ill-thought-out programs. Setbacks lower the morale of the public and cause leadership conflict over planning errors. But even if there are no gross mistakes, the bureaucratization of planning and management exacts costs in terms of lowered initiative and the stifling of innovation.

A second source of mismanagement lies in the ideological commitments that animate these regimes. To be sure, the goal of building socialist and ultimately Communist societies can be used instrumentally to inspire hard work and sacrifice. But sometimes these regimes attempt to incorporate the values of the future Communist society, such as egalitarianism, into their current practice, resulting in a conflict between "utopia and development," to use Richard Lowenthal's formulation (Lowenthal 1970). When utopian aspirations become dominant, setbacks occur that in turn lead to declining work morale and declining economic performance, as well as to conflict among elite members over policy. Popular pressures thus make themselves felt during the mobilization phase, but they are more likely to be the consequences of poor planning on the part of the political leadership than the product of social change as such.

In the third stage, that of adaptation, society has become more complex. Consequently, the party finds it more and more difficult to maintain its all-embracing control without paying an increasing price in effectiveness, especially in innovation. In the economic sphere, the issue that arises is the extent to which nonbureaucratic economic coordination, namely, the market, should be introduced in order to reduce the inefficiencies that inevitably arise from bureaucratic management of an increasingly complex economy. Specialists must have their recognized sphere of autonomy, and the proliferating interests of an increasingly differentiated society and of increasingly complex decision-making tasks must somehow be accommodated, as must pressures from society for more "authentic" forms of participation. The party-state, in other words, must redefine its relation to society.

During the third stage, if the party does what analysts believe to be functionally necessary, it will transform itself from a "general staff" directing the transformation of society to a policy-making and coordinating agency (Huntington 1970). Whether the party makes this transition, however, and whether it undertakes the social and economic reforms necessary to adapt to the new circumstances is not simply the product of social and economic change as such. At least in the short run, it is the product of conscious leadership decisions. The record shows that it is quite possible for a country's leadership to delay even for decades adjustments and reforms that would appear to be necessary on functional grounds. Czechoslovakia from the Prague Spring of 1968 to the autumn of 1989 is one example; another is Kim Il-sung's North Korea. In the light of Mikhail Gorbachev's perestroika, Leonid Brezhnev's eighteen years of rule now appear as an era in which accumulating social and economic problems, including falling growth rates and rising rates of alcoholism, did not elicit a serious response from the leadership but were essentially swept under the carpet. As will be discussed in the last part of this chapter, it is doubtful that the Chinese regime's effort to reconsolidate a system of orthodox rule in the wake of the Tiananmen demonstrations will have similar staying power.

Even when Communist states have taken major adaptive measures in the economic realm, they do not necessarily make the transition to political liberalization, defined as the recognition of the legitimate role of contending interest groups, not to speak of democratization, that is, open contestation for control of the government. But even short of such fundamental change, the adaptation phase of Marxist-Leninist regimes can bring a significant reduction in the extent to which the state dominates society; and the fundamental lesson of Communist reform seems to be that halfway political and economic changes are inherently unstable and that pressures build for a full-scale transformation to political democracy (Z 1990).

## The Era of Mobilization

The Chinese Communist government that came to power in 1949 was the first national government to have full control over the entire mainland since the nineteenth century. A hundred years of rebellions, civil wars, foreign encroachment, and international war had sapped the strength of the various governments. The political stability essential for economic development was largely absent. Industrialization took place in a few relatively secure localities such as Manchuria or Shanghai. The revolutionary achievement of the Communists was that they established full control over the entire mainland and effectively organized the country for development. Their goal was to make China not only into a socialist state but also into a great industrial and wealthy power, thereby realizing the old dream of *fuqiang* (rich and powerful). In a largely agrarian society, building socialism meant industrialization. The two goals were congruent. The goal of rapid industrialization was reinforced by the threatening international environment, in which China had only one friend, the Soviet Union. The Americans, Mao once remarked, will talk to China when it has nuclear weapons, but in order to have nuclear weapons, China must industrialize (Mao 1956: 68; Lewis and Xue 1988: chap. 3).

China committed itself to the Stalinist model of industrialization, that is, to priority for heavy industry, a high investment rate, and a centrally planned, bureaucratically administered economy. Although the Chinese became dissatisfied with the Soviet model—Mao's first public criticisms date from 1956—key elements of the Stalinist model were retained throughout the period 1953–78. For instance, accumulation rates remained at high levels. They reached 23.1 percent of national income in 1953, rose to an extraordinary 43.8 percent in 1959, dropped to 10.4 percent in 1962 during the retreat from the Great Leap Forward, rose again above 20 percent by 1964, and stayed above 30 percent for all of the 1970s, reaching a peak of 36.5 percent in 1978 (*Zhongguo tongji nianjian* [*ZTN*] 1987: 59). As Chinese now stress, the peasantry paid for much of this accumulation—Lin Yifu, deputy director of the Development Institute of the Agricultural Research Center of the State Council, estimates from 26.7 percent to 35.7 percent of all of China's investments between 1952 and 1986—in the form of low farm prices and high prices for industrial products (*Renmin ribao* [*RMRB*] June 29, 1988: 55; *ZTN* 1987: 59). This illustrates the point made earlier concerning the power of such regimes. In China, the Communists came to power with peasant support, yet they were able to squeeze them to a substantial extent.

In accord with the Soviet model, the Chinese party-state also gave absolute priority to heavy industry. The bulk of investment went to this sector, and far smaller shares went to light industry and agriculture. Growth rates throughout the mobilization period were heavily skewed in favor of industry as a whole, which grew at an average annual rate of 10 percent, versus 2.4 percent for agriculture. The commitment to rapid industrialization was maintained throughout, even during such periods as the Cultural Revolution, when the economy was disrupted because of campaigns of ideological revitalization. The commitment to industrialization, at the expense of growth in living standards, especially between 1957 and 1978, was a key indicator of the regime's capacity to implement its preferences.

The mobilization era can be broken down into three subperiods: the First Five-Year Plan of 1953–57; the Great Leap Forward of 1958–62; and the Cultural Revolution of 1966–76. The first period was by far the most successful and is in retrospect seen as a golden age of Communist rule. Peace, the restoration of order, land reform, economic recovery, and the cleansing of society of the corruption of the old provided a basis for mass support that helped infuse the new organizational structure with authority and a sense of common purpose. Opportunities for rapid upward mobility, the opportunity to move to towns, and improvements in the standard of living also contributed to support. The regime effectively and smoothly reorganized society along socialist lines, culminating in the collectivization of agriculture and the socialization of industry and commerce in 1955–56.

But even during this successful period, fundamental questions about the stifling effect of state dominance came to the fore, provoking debate and conflict among the leaders, particularly in 1956–57. First, centralized control of industry, a characteristic of the Soviet model, proved to be difficult to sustain in China because of the large number of small enterprises. Beijing ministries could not adequately coordinate their activities, and in 1957, a substantial proportion of enterprises were handed over to provincial and subprovincial administrative units. But this meant that the same problems of planning were replicated locally. The consequent accretion of economic power in the hands of local party and government officials led to periodic efforts to recentralize control, resulting in a cycle of decentralization and recentralization. A workable combination was not found, in part because Mao refused to resort to the market as an alternative coordinating mechanism (Solinger 1984).

Second, the party-state's enormous power to secure support and compliance had been used, as noted, to collectivize the peasants. But the "High Tide" of 1955–56, in which a hundred million peasant households were organized into

750,000 higher-stage producers' cooperatives, while demonstrating the CCP's enormous mobilizational capacities, was not a success in economic terms because overcentralization caused difficult problems of incentives and management. The incomes of a good many peasants dropped, leading to withdrawals from the collectives in the winter of 1956–57, as well as to attempts by some leaders to reduce the size of the collective and increase the scope open for private and market activities. But these efforts were overridden, and today the High Tide is regarded in China as signifying the onset of a fundamentally erroneous agricultural policy.

Third, the CCP failed to utilize fully the country's scarce pool of technical experts. Most had lived in cities controlled by the Nationalists and some were U.S. educated. Most wanted nothing more than a chance to do their jobs and to serve their country and the party (Yue and Wakeman 1985). They were cowed by reeducation campaigns and subordinated to ignorant party secretaries. In 1956 the regime recognized the problem and called for giving the experts a more effective voice. Mao Zedong saw the alienation of the intellectuals as part of a broader issue of the stifling effects of bureaucracy and of the lack of authentic participation. He recognized that without some opportunity for people to speak out, "contradictions," that is, conflicts of interest, which he acknowledged existed between the party and the masses, could not be satisfactorily resolved. In 1956, strikes and student disturbances had occurred, to which Mao, in an unpublished speech made in February 1957, gave his approval: "If the people insisted on creating disturbances . . . let them go ahead" (Schoenhals 1987: 19). Mao attributed them to "bureaucratism." By letting "a hundred flowers bloom" and permitting nonparty people to criticize the party, unity could be reestablished, and the kind of crisis in party-society relations that had led to revolution in Hungary avoided. But when students and members of small parties normally controlled by the CCP spoke out in May 1957, criticizing the party monopoly and demanding a real voice, Mao treated them as threatening and subversive "rightists," resulting in a massive purge of the country's educated elite. Using quotas, each work unit was required to find rightists, who were sent to the countryside or imprisoned, many not to reemerge until 1978 (Yue and Wakeman 1985). Mao's effort to deal with the central issue of Communist rule—unchecked bureaucratic power—led to the crushing of expertise, paving the way for the irrationalities of the Great Leap Forward.

## The Great Leap Forward

The Leap was a quintessential case of mismanagement, stemming both from the excessive use of state power and from ideological goals. The Leap originated as an attempt to escape from the problems that had surfaced by 1957. Industry had grown at 18 percent during the First Five-Year Plan but agriculture only at 4.5 percent, and at a declining rate. Population and cities were growing rapidly.

Much of industry depended on agricultural raw materials, and Soviet aid was being phased out. One solution to these imbalances was to slow down the rate of industrial growth. Mao instead opted for a breakthrough on all fronts, relying on mass mobilization and maximum use of China's seemingly unlimited manpower. The attempt at a breakthrough was based on the suppression of expertise during the antirightist campaign, the generation of intense pressures on officials to come up with dazzling results, and the generation of utopian expectations that a breakthrough could be reached virtually instantly and that the country could leap forward into communism even ahead of the Soviet Union. Innovations were indiscriminately adopted, ranging from "deep plowing and close planting" and the continuous operation of machines to the mobilization of schoolchildren to wipe out the "four pests." Mobilization took on truly stupendous proportions, as ninety million peasants went "into battle" to build the famous backyard steel furnaces (Mao 1959: 143). New organizations sprang up, most notably 25,000 people's communes, the result of the merger of 750,000 higher-stage cooperatives, a change justified by the scale of labor mobilization of peasants building irrigation works. The immense exertions of the Leap were underwritten by an unprecedented rise in the investment rate, which reached 43.8 percent of national income in 1959 and 39.6 percent in 1960.

The Leap was not simply a case of the sacrifice of developmental for utopian goals. It was the harnessing of utopian means to attain a breakthrough in development. What Chairman Mao dreamt about was instant modernity as expressed in tons of steel. The sprouts of communism that appeared in 1958, in the form of the multifunctional communes or the egalitarian reward system, were supposed to push the country forward, not simply into a trouserless communism, as Khrushchev scoffed, but into modernity. China's leaders, in their eagerness to catch up with Britain, and eventually with the United States, were at least for a brief moment willing to believe that utopian methods worked. Post-Mao Chinese writers have pointed to the agrarian origin of the party, including Mao's own peasant background, to explain egalitarianism as a surge of peasant utopianism, and perhaps there is some truth to this. In any event, once Mao sobered up, he repudiated the foisting of Communist practices on the peasants, and he admitted his own lack of expertise: "Coal and iron cannot walk by themselves; they need vehicles to transport them. This I did not foresee" (Mao 1959: 142).

After several surges, the Leap burned itself out in the summer of 1960, brought to a halt by overextension, dislocation, the abrupt withdrawal of Soviet advisers, and the plummeting of agricultural output from 195 MMT of grain in 1957 to 143 MMT in 1960. The Leap caused an immense famine—the death rate rose from 18.12 per thousand in 1957 to 44.60 per thousand in 1960—the consequence not only of declining harvests but of excessive requisitioning of grain, based on the false reports that far more grain had been produced than was actually the case (Banister 1984: 740–41; Bernstein 1984). Economic indicators plummeted and a major depression ensued. In the face of these disasters, the leaders rallied and took decisive steps, including drastic curtailment of capital construction, import of grain, scaling down of the communes to manageable size, restoration of incentives, and giving experts a stronger voice.

The man-made economic crisis profoundly affected the country's political elite. Its self-confidence was shaken, in that many key leaders, not just Mao, had supported the Leap. Mao's own authority was seriously impaired. Already in 1959, Peng Dehuai, the minister of defense, had charged him with "petty bourgeois fanaticism." Mao succeeded in beating back this attack and in purging Peng, but the episode was a watershed in Chinese politics, for in purging Peng, Mao had violated long-standing rules of intra-elite conduct (Teiwes 1984). The bitter conflicts of the Cultural Revolution can be traced to the disputes generated by the Leap, including the handling of the Peng case, as well as conflict over the extent of the concessions to private initiative necessary for recovery.

The political implications of the GLF disaster for state-society relations are not very clear. To be sure, popular morale declined sharply, as did morale in the military. Risings in remote parts of the country occurred, and the collective system collapsed for a time in several provinces. Some Chinese informants speak of having heard peasants voice open outrage against Mao, but others suggest that peasants reacted along traditional lines, blaming bad officials rather than the emperor who at the time of Liberation had given them land (Bernstein n.d.). Some intellectuals, protected by powerful patrons, satirized Mao's follies, but there is little evidence of long-term disillusionment, for example, in the memoir literature. Ignorance about the true scope of the crisis, combined with the rapid regime-sponsored retreat from GLF excesses, may help explain the apparently short-lived impact of the Leap on state-society relations.

## The Cultural Revolution, 1966–76

The Cultural Revolution was an example of how utopian political and ideological goals shaped state-society relations. The main goal of its initiator, Mao Zedong, was to save Chinese socialism from the threat of "revisionism" by purging his lieutenants who, as in the case of Deng Xiaoping, attached greater importance to economic efficiency than ideological purity ("it does not matter whether a cat is black or white, as long as it catches mice"). In addition, the socialist system would be revitalized by rearing "revolutionary successors." This goal was to be accomplished by giving young people an experience in substitute revolution, encouraging them to "drag out" those "in authority taking the capitalist road." In the name of class struggle, Mao thus took the risk of deliberately destabilizing the regime. University and middle school students became Red Guards. Joined by adult "revolutionary rebels," they plunged the country into chaos, seizing power from party committees and fighting with one another, until the military had to intervene to restore order.

The Cultural Revolution, although unleashed from above by the Maoist segment of the Chinese leadership, permitted a variety of spontaneous societal interests to emerge into public view. Students, workers, and others took advantage of the relative freedom afforded by the upheaval to voice both political and economic grievances. Young people, for instance, wanted redress from the oppressive system of political and class labels, which meant that children of the bourgeois, rightists, and landlords were discriminated against in college admissions. Many youths, including those not affected by adverse labels, resented the narrowing channels of upward mobility that characterized the 1960s, when the ratio of those graduated from senior middle schools greatly exceeded that of those who could be admitted to the higher schools and hence obtain lifetime job security as cadres. Competition and tension generated by these grievances fueled the conflicts among Red Guards during the Cultural Revolution (Shirk 1982). Contract workers, that is, peasants allowed temporarily to work in the privileged urban sector, protested against their treatment.

The Cultural Revolution permitted young people to challenge authority, but it ended up with their deportation to the countryside to be "reeducated by the poor and lower middle peasants." Many of these youths spent years in remote villages, most being allowed to return only from 1977 on. These experiences had a deep impact on them. Most lost their unquestioning faith in the system. Many became political dropouts preoccupied with career and personal advancement. Some became political dissenters, changing from Mao-type critics of bureaucracy to believers in Western-style democracy. Former Red Guards, for instance, were active in the Democracy Movement of 1978–79. These changes among youth meant that the old transmission-belt methods of mobilization of the Youth League no longer worked as well in the 1980s as they had in the 1950s. How to reach young people politically became a serious problem, but the origins of the problem were not so much social change as the effects of the political choices made by Mao and his allies. Moreover, the phenomenon of political burnout, that is, growing indifference to the radical Maoist political message and increased resentment toward endless political campaigns, was by no means confined to young people.

The Cultural Revolution also helped lay the foundation for the economic reforms that began in 1978, namely, the onset of the stage of adaptation defined earlier. As noted, the intent of the Cultural Revolution was to purify the superstructure of society rather than to change the economic system. But Maoists believed that this purification would give a push to economic development in that bureaucrats would engage directly in production rather than sitting at their desks, and the masses, imbued with revolutionary ideals, would exert themselves on behalf of collective undertakings. The agricultural model of Dazhai and the industrial model of Daqing exemplified these ideals. As a study of a village showed, when peasants' personal incomes rose as a result of effective collective undertakings, they were not unreceptive to Maoist ideals, but in this village, the association between dedication to the collective and personal payoffs was only short-lived (Chan, Madsen, and Unger 1984). The reason was that unpopular egalitarian policies were imposed on peasants, as leftist "winds" swept through villages, resulting in curtailing of private plots, free markets, and other collectivist measures (Zweig 1985).

Despite the egalitarian objectives of the Cultural Revolution, inequalities often increased rather than decreased. In agriculture, for instance, although there was a high degree of equality within villages, regional disparities also grew, a change traceable to Mao's insistence on "grain as the key link." Everyone should be self-sufficient in grain, Mao proclaimed—probably in reaction to the Great Leap Forward famine—but this policy impoverished entire regions whose comparative advantage lay not in growing grain but in cotton or other specialized crops. In industry, bonuses and regular wage increases were not given out during the Cultural Revolution era in the name of equality, thereby penalizing younger workers who, as they married and had children, found themselves earning little more than apprentices, in contrast to those workers whose seniority dated to the early 1950s. The decline of the work ethic in industry, manifested in stagnant productivity of labor, can be traced to such policies (Riskin 1987: chap. 10).

Irrational economic practices were an outcome of the sharp decline in the quality of economic planning and management during the Cultural Revolution. The political campaigns forced officials to play it safe and diverted time and energy from planning. Moreover, information available to planners was sharply reduced by the virtual dissolution of the State Statistical Bureau. Indices of lowered efficiency abounded. Each one hundred yuan invested in the First Five-Year Plan yielded an increment of thirty-two yuan of national income; in the Fourth Five-Year Plan (1971–75), the increment dropped to sixteen yuan (*ZTN* 1987: 66). If it had taken five years to complete a capital construction project, it took eleven years in the 1970s. In one instance, the government imported a modern steel mill at great expense but without giving thought to the electric power required to run it. China ended up in 1976 with neither efficiency nor equity.

## The Reform Era

Two years after Chairman Mao's death, China, now led by Deng Xiaoping, dramatically changed course. The Deng group sought drastically to reform China's economic and political systems. They did so because they were deeply dissatisfied with the progress that had been made in the preceding twenty years. They spoke of "ten lost years" or even "twenty lost years." They were ashamed and chagrined by the fact that socialism had produced only meager results in comparison with the other nations of East Asia. They were aware of the extent to which China had fallen behind internationally. There was not only Japan, which had forged ahead with stunning speed, but the "four tigers" of Hong Kong, Taiwan, South Korea, and Singapore, all of which had outdistanced China with regard to rapid modernization. They understood that if China was truly to become a great power, a change in course was essential. And they felt themselves to be under pressure from below to adopt policies that would finally provide a payoff for society. Riots in Beijing in April 1976 had already signaled deep popular dissatisfaction with leftist policies. Some leaders, notably the economic planner Chen Yun, worried about peasant uprisings if nothing were done to improve peasant lives (Chen 1979).

The reform impulse in post-Mao China did not, it is important to note, simply grow out of a lack of economic growth. China's industry had grown at about 10 percent per annum since 1953. A substantial industrial foundation had been established by 1978. The China of 1978 was not the China of 1953. It was capable of producing a wide range of industrial goods, ranging from bicycles to automobiles to missiles. Agricultural growth had kept up with population growth. Grain output rose at an average per annum rate of 2.4 percent between 1953 and 1981, while population grew at 1.9 percent. A Green Revolution had occurred in rice growing, and modern inputs such as chemical fertilizer and pesticides were in use.

What disturbed the leaders were immense imbalances, inefficiencies, and poor results. These included disparities in growth rates among the three major sectors of heavy industry, light industry, and agriculture, and the neglect of services, which sharply lowered the quality of life. For instance, in a city such as Beijing, whose population moved about on bicycles, there were fewer bicycle repair shops in 1978 than there had been in 1957. China's sprawling industrial setup was, as already noted, extremely inefficient. The country relied on extraordinarily high investment rates, which were financed by keeping consumption low and exploiting the agriculture sector via price scissors between such modern industrial products as chemical fertilizer, bought by the communes, and the low prices paid by the state for agricultural produce. Living standards in both town and country had more or less stagnated since 1957. Rural poverty was an acute problem thirty years after the CCP had come to power with peasant support. According to the Central Committee, about 150 million peasants out of 800 million lived in dire poverty in 1978. State relief was inadequate, and begging during the spring months was widespread (Bernstein and Anonymous 1983). Thirty years after the onset of Communist rule, 80 percent of the country's population continued to live in villages. Peasants were essentially bound to the land. On this count alone, the country had barely begun the transition to modernity. Education had made major quantitative advances at all levels, but during the Cultural Revolution a qualitative collapse occurred, especially in higher education, which cost the country over a decade of trained manpower. One-fourth of the population was illiterate, according to the 1982 census. Because the urban sector was unable to absorb young people needing jobs, in part because of the neglect of services, millions were sent to the countryside, their talents largely wasted. Socially, China was in a state of stunted or even frozen development, in which popular energies could not be fully unleashed and in which there was a great deal of suppressed frustration.

China, moreover, lagged far behind the other states of East Asia technologically. During the 1950s, China's industrialization effort had been based on Soviet technology, which to some extent offset the adverse effects of the American-sponsored economic blockade. After the break with the Soviets, the Chinese began to import technology from Japan and Western Europe. But the xenophobic Cultural Revolution largely halted these imports, and although they resumed in the early 1970s, China's economic ties with the outside world were modest at best. In 1978, China's leaders concluded that economic isolationism under the slogan of self-reliance had been a fundamental error, and indeed, an error that dated back to the eighteenth century. In sum, as the economist Robert Dernberger (1987: 5) puts it, China's experience since 1949 has taught us that high growth rates do not necessarily signal successful economic modernization, inasmuch as these growth rates can be accompanied by failures in innovation and technological change, lack of improvements in the quality and variety of output, failure to improve factor productivity and efficiency in production, and retarded growth in the standard of living. The shift to reform thus came because of mismanagement of economic growth. China's post-Mao leaders feared that if new policies were not adopted, the country would fall further and further behind internationally, and that popular dissatisfaction with poor economic results would lead to social unrest and instability.

The reform policies that the Deng leadership adopted were those of the adaptationist stage of Marxist-Leninist states, as defined earlier. They were policies that sought to give more leeway to social and economic forces, by reducing the stifling control of state and party bureaucracies. Since the political system was responsible for the poor economic performance, the first steps in reform had to be political. The reformers began by repudiating the late Chairman's obsession with class struggle and ideological transformation and proclaimed that henceforth, the "central task" of the country would be the "four modernizations" of agriculture, industry, science and technology, and defense. To secure acceptance of the new line by the country's vast cadre force, the reformers embarked on a Chinese version of what the world now knows as glasnost, that is, public exposure of the mistakes of the past, in order to delegitimate past policies and in particular to discredit the infallible leader, thereby making change possible. From 1978 on, the country learned of the costs of radical Maoism in the form of the publication of data on the state of the economy, the atrocities of the Cultural Revolution, the famine of the Great Leap Forward, the evils of egalitarianism ("eating out of the same pot"), the suppression of intellectuals, the foisting of a bureaucratic straitjacket on the peasants, and the damage done to education.

The discrediting of the radical period of voluntaristic political experimentation culminated in a public critique of Mao Zedong's errors from 1957 on. To preserve his reputation as the country's founding father, his earlier activities were not repudiated. But the critique did serve to dismantle the cult of Mao's personality, which during the Cultural Revolution had taken on massive proportions, and which stood in the way of new policies. Criticism of Mao also entailed criticism of the party, which had supported Mao during the Leap. The sacred aura of the party as invariably "correct" was thus implicitly called into question. Exposure of errors was a very important political change, which transformed the country's political climate ("On Questions of Party History" 1981; Harding 1988).

A second political change was a conscious deemphasis of ideology and ideological fervor. The precepts of Deng Xiaoping—"practice is the sole criterion of truth" and "truth through facts"—sanctioned a much more pragmatic approach to policies. The boundaries of permissible discussion were widened greatly. "Forbidden zones" could now be entered, and subjects that had hitherto been taboo could be discussed. Boundaries, however, did not disappear. In 1979, shortly after dissidents had agitated for Western-style democracy, Deng demanded adherence to the "Four Principles"—party leadership, Mao Zedong Thought, the socialist road, and the dictatorship of the proletariat. Deng and other leaders retained the prerogative of deciding when pragmatism had turned to subversion of the "Four Principles." At times, they have concluded that criticisms or demands for change have gone too far. Campaigns against "spiritual pollution" in 1983 and against "bourgeois liberalization" in 1986–87 were signs of this. But these were short-lived efforts and did not have the impact of Maoist campaigns, although they served as reminders of the existence of arbitrarily determined limits; and within this framework, discussion and debate on political, social, economic, and cultural issues has at times been remarkably wide-ranging.

A third change was the rehabilitation of experts and of intellectuals in general. Deng declared them to be part of the "productive forces" and not just part of the base, and hence, indispensable to the modernization effort, even in the absence of overt evidence of "redness." Victims of past campaigns going back to the antirightist movement of 1957 were rehabilitated. Universities and colleges were restored and expanded while academic publications proliferated.

A fourth political change was promotion of rule by law. Rule by law may be contrasted to rule of law, which signifies accountability of the top leaders, whereas rule by law signifies the principle that the party and state bureaucracies ought to act in accordance with the law (Baum 1986). The issue appeared on the agenda as early as 1978, when a reformer asked how it could be that "certain leading bodies" could "order peasants to uproot crops they had planted and grow other crops instead, without being responsible both legally and economically for the ensuing losses" (Hu 1978). Party policies calling for proper behavior toward peasants were not in his view adequate to ensure peasant rights. Special laws and law courts were needed, which would punish violators of peasant rights and enforce contracts. If this were done, peasants could legally demand compensation for losses and be "masters of their own fate."

Legal accountability of officials goes well beyond the concerns of peasants. It is of central significance for state-society relations. It is also crucial for economic reforms, which include private enterprise, for entrepreneurs cannot easily function without legal predictability. But calling for legal accountability was one thing; bringing it about, another. A great many laws and law codes have been enacted since 1978, but there is an enormous shortage of lawyers, and enormous difficulty in making the principle of accountability stick, the central problem being that powerful officials continue to be beyond the reach of the law. Nonetheless, the principle of legality has been put in place as a goal to be striven for.

A fifth political change designed to increase the level of competence in government and party was promotion of the technically trained to leadership positions. Mao had sought to forestall this by promoting "revolutionary successors." Deng has emphasized recruitment of political leaders who are educated and technically trained. This has entailed retirement of many members of the pre-1949 generation, especially those resistant to change, whose formative experience was revolution rather than economic construction. Those with some higher education, technical training, and experience now constitute a large fraction of the leadership (Lee 1988). Premier Li Peng, a Soviet-trained electrical engineer, is a good example. These more technocratic leaders are also being assisted by staff and research agencies associated with the State Council and the party's Secretariat, thus bringing to bear expertise on the analysis of policy issues. A related administrative reform aims at streamlining the bureaucracy by developing a modern civil service and rationalizing cadre policy. The impact of all these changes is still limited, however. Thus, Chinese "technocrats" are not nearly as well educated as their counterparts in Taiwan's economic agencies, and reform of the bureaucracy has not made much of a dent.

## Economic Reforms

The political changes just outlined, although incomplete, have provided something of a framework for economic reforms. These sought to "enliven" the economy by introducing market relations. The idea of the market—vehemently rejected during the Maoist era as symbolic of the profit motive and of exploitation and as leading to anarchy—has been given legitimacy. The market is seen as an alternative to a bureaucratically administered economy. To be sure, reformers do not intend to abandon planning or public ownership but hope to arrive at a mix of plan and market, in which some economic activity is carried on by the state as of old, some in the form of indirect state guidance, and some purely by market-based supply and demand. As thinking on the subject has evolved, the idea of marketizing even state-owned industry has taken hold. The central thrust of these ideas is to liberate the economy from as much state control as possible, using the profit motive, thereby unleashing the initiative, energy, and drive so lacking in the previous system.

The most striking manifestation of the policy of reducing state control may be found in agriculture. There, the main structural reform was decollectivization, which permitted the reemergence of China's most important entrepreneurial unit, the family. Under the new system, the lowest level of the commune system, the production team, has disappeared, and the next highest, the brigade, has become the village committee. The village committee contracts land out to families, collects a tax and a payment to finance collective undertakings such as irrigation, and administers sales to the state, which were compulsory until 1985 and have since been based on contracts. Peasants are free to market their surpluses, to develop sidelines, and to engage in a range of economic activities previously forbidden. The village now leases out village-owned factories or other businesses, usually on a profit-sharing basis.

Party and state cadres have by no means ceased playing a role in village affairs, but peasant autonomy from the tight grip of political authority has increased substantially. For instance, household contracting largely eliminated cadre power over the deployment of peasant labor and gave peasants sources of income over which cadres have no control. The right to engage in private or contracted (leased) enterprise and to participate in markets, as well as to go to work outside their villages, gave peasants still further opportunities to seek gain relatively independently of bureaucratic authority. On the other hand, although compulsory state procurement of grain, cotton, and other key commodities was abolished in 1985, the contracts that have replaced them have in fact retained their compulsory character.

A second reform is the encouragement of urban and not just rural individual entrepreneurship. By the end of 1986, China had about 12 million private businesses in town and country, with a total employment of 18.5 million persons. The latter statistic indicates how tiny most of these establishments are. Still, as of early 1988, 115,000 private entrepreneurs employed more than 8 workers each, for a total of 1.85 million hired workers. Most employed somewhere between 8 and 30 workers; only a very few boasted 100 or more (*RMRB*, overseas ed., March 16, 1988; *China Daily*, March 17, 1988). As of 1986, private enterprise accounted for less than 1 percent of industrial output value, suggesting that most of this enterprise was in the service trades and in commerce. But the existence of private business is an important sign of the retreat of the party-state from full domination of society. Numerous accounts, however, suggest that private entrepreneurs are often harassed by party-state cadres. In 1988, a constitutional amendment sought to legitimate their status (*RMRB*, overseas ed., March 7, 1988).

Collective enterprise has also undergone significant change in that much of it is now run for the benefit of its members or of the locality that owns the enterprise, rather than for the benefit of the state. The growth of urban and rural collective enterprise has been responsible for absorption of a great deal of surplus labor. In the villages, for instance, nonagricultural employment, mainly industrial, has risen from twenty million to eighty-five million laborers, thus contributing to a substantial shift of manpower out of agriculture. Indeed, enhanced mobility is a key characteristic of the economic reforms. Most peasants who leave agriculture go to work in nearby small towns on the principle of "leaving the soil but not leaving the village," thereby reducing, it is hoped, the costs of urbanization. But peasants market goods nationwide, and they may work temporarily in large cities, resulting in a huge increase in the country's floating population (Xinhua, December 9, 1988: 53). Shanghai, for instance, is said to have 1.6 million temporary peasant residents.

Still another economic reform is *kaifang*, or opening up to the outside world. As already noted, the reformist leaders concluded that interdependence rather than self-reliance was essential if development was to be achieved. Kaifang meant reversing Maoist principles that forbade foreign investment, joint ventures, and long-term borrowing. As of 1985, China had borrowed about sixteen billion dollars, and six billion had been invested by foreigners, partly in Special Economic Zones. Foreign trade, which had rarely accounted for more than 10 percent of national income, doubled its share by 1985 and rose to an unprecedented 33.1 percent in 1986. One result of kaifang is a sharply increased foreign presence in China. My research in China has revealed that images of foreign life have penetrated into the far interior. Interactions with Hong Kong have deeply influenced the neighboring province of Guangdong, leading to a substantial degree of economic integration even before Hong Kong joins the PRC in 1997 (Vogel 1989). Another part of kaifang is academic and cultural exchange. To offset the losses of the Cultural Revolution, China has sent thousands of students abroad, particularly to the United States, thereby giving them intense exposure to foreign values and ideas.

The most problematic area of economic reform is the state-industrial sector. Reform of enterprises aims at turning them into independent entities responsible for their own profits and losses. To this end, profit retention schemes have been adopted, and managers have been allowed to sell above-quota output on the market and to acquire inputs on the market as well. In addition, a variety of experiments are under way to allow managers to raise funds in new ways, as by issuing stocks. A contract system is being implemented, according to which managers will be held accountable for meeting targets. The power of the managers is to be greatly strengthened and that of the party secretaries correspondingly reduced.

State enterprises, however, have not become accountable entities. One reason is that the price system does not provide appropriate yardsticks. Some prices have been adjusted to reflect actual scarcities, but many continue to be arbitrary, so that an enterprise can be profitable not because it is efficient but because the inputs that it uses happen to carry a low, state-determined price tag. Moreover, if enterprises were held to account, many would go bankrupt—one-fifth have been losing money—and the result might be an unacceptable level of social turmoil if mass unemployment leads workers to protest the loss of their "iron rice bowl." But the main reason is that the "umbilical cord between enterprise and the state has not been severed" (*RMRB*, January 15, 1988: 22; Solinger 1987). Enterprises maintain long-established relations with their bureaucratic superiors, who bail them out, since these higher-level officials have a stake in the success of the enterprise. The finance, tax, price, and industrial bureaus have discretionary authority to provide loans, raw materials, price and tax exemptions, or subsidies. Managers must cultivate ties with their bureaucratic and political superiors for flexible, that is, favorable, application of the rules.

The reforms have strengthened rather than weakened the old networks of administrative and personal relationships. The central authorities have not found a way of coping with a situation in which local authorities and the enterprises under their jurisdiction have used the power that the center has granted them in ways not corresponding to central goals. As part of the reform, the central government transferred to the localities control over tax revenues from industry and enterprise profits turned over to government. Not only did their resources greatly increase, but so did the interest of local officials in promoting investment, since this generated further resources for local use. Local officials, together with enterprise managers, continue to focus on growth rather than on efficiency, resulting in highly inflationary local investment rates. The macroeconomic instruments with which the central government hopes to keep the economy in check, such as interest rates and taxes, are not in place or are subject to political manipulation. The result of the expansion of local economic power has been massive inflation. In September 1988, the central leaders took steps to regain control over local spending, but whether they will be successful is not as yet clear (Zhao Ziyang 1988: 13ff.). In sum, the reforms are incomplete. Indeed, it is not at all clear what a fully "reformed" Chinese economy would look like; for example, just what ought to be the most appropriate combination of plan and market.

The reform policies have led to remarkable successes. In 1984 and 1985 foreign trade and local industry leaped forward at 68 percent and 59.6 percent, respectively, and domestic trade and services grew substantially (Wong 1988). Overall growth in the post-Mao decade continued to be rapid but was much more balanced, with agriculture growing at 7 percent per year between 1979 and 1985. Productivity also rose very substantially in agriculture, though far less so in industry. Individual incomes also rose substantially during the reform period, as did consumption. Real per capita consumption of peasants rose at an annual rate of 6.7 percent between 1975 and 1986, and that of urbanites at a rate of 5.5 percent (Dernberger 1987: 23–24). The improvements in the standard of living became clearly visible in the urban and rural housing boom and in rapid increases in ownership of televisions and other appliances. The acute poverty of a segment of the peasantry was significantly alleviated, but pockets of poverty and regional poverty in the Northwest remained.

The reforms were not as successful in industry as in agriculture and services.

The country's industrial growth continued to be based on extremely high rates of accumulation. In 1980 the investment rate stood at 31.5 percent of national income. It declined to 28.3 percent in 1981 but rose again to 35.3 percent in 1985 and 34.6 percent in 1986. The transition from extensive growth (the addition of factors of production characteristic of the mobilization phase) to the stage of intensive growth (characterized by the more efficient utilization of existing factors of production) did not take place.

By the mid-1980s, new problems arose. Grain production began to stagnate as the gains from the reform of the commune system exhausted themselves. Peasants could also make more money in nonagricultural enterprise, because agricultural incentives were increasingly affected adversely by new price scissors between industrial and agricultural goods. The former rose with inflation, which became an increasingly serious nationwide problem, whereas the price of the major agricultural commodities was kept at the level set by the state in 1979–81, when procurement prices were increased as part of the effort to revitalize agriculture. The government absorbs the difference between the prices paid to peasants and the prices charged urban consumers, greatly burdening the budget. It has not been willing significantly to increase agricultural prices further, particularly as long as inflation besets the urban consumer. The resulting price scissors have reduced peasant willingness to expand agricultural production. Overall, according to official reports, prices rose by 8.8 percent in 1985, 6 percent in 1986, 7.3–9.7 percent in 1987, and 20 percent in 1988. Inflation in major cities reached 30 percent in 1988, and unofficial estimates went even higher (Lin 1988; *Guangming ribao* [*GMRB*], December 20, 1988; *China Daily*, December 15, 1988). As already noted, when inflation assumed crisis proportions, the leadership decided in 1988 to postpone further efforts at economic reform, particularly price reform, giving priority to the fight against inflation. In their view, this required that the central government regain effective fiscal and monetary control over the economy (Zhao Ziyang 1988: 13ff.).

## Impact of Reforms on Attitudes

During the reform era the popularity of the regime increased greatly simply because Maoist class struggle, mass political campaigns, and the attendant dislocations ended. Mass support also increased greatly as a result of major improvements in living conditions. As incomes rose, vastly more housing was built, and more and more consumer durables such as televisions, washing machines, and refrigerators became available, together with a far wider range of foodstuffs. By the mid- and late 1980s, however, it became apparent that the support for the reformist program was not permanent and that it was adversely affected by the increasingly difficult economic situation. By 1988, the existence of widespread popular discontent, grumbling, and anger were widely reported (*GMRB*, December 4, 1988: 22–23). Five explanations can be offered for the appearance of such attitudes.

First, the reform era has been based on rising expectations, which were consciously stimulated by the central leadership anxious to broaden its base of popular support. Deng Xiaoping promised that the goal of the reform was to make everyone prosperous. Rising expectations were stimulated by the reality that in fact incomes did rise and that many people were able to acquire goods that had hitherto been unavailable or beyond reach. Moreover, the social environment openly and explicitly encouraged acquisitiveness. Advertising on television, for instance, which increasingly reached peasant homes, undoubtedly helped stimulate appetites for modern goods. Broadened access to information about the outside world, particularly Hong Kong and Taiwan, with which ordinary Chinese could easily identify, further stimulated aspirations for a better life.

But as economic difficulties increased in the mid-1980s, particularly inflation, the promise of ever-increasing affluence lost some of its credibility. Worry about price rises replaced confidence that life would steadily improve. Panic buying occurred in 1988, and in spite of the government's action in pegging to the price index bank interest rates on personal deposits kept for three years or longer, many people withdrew low-interest savings (*China Daily*, September 5, 1988). Fear of social turmoil was a major reason for the decision of September 1988 to take new and drastic steps to check rampant inflation (Zhao Ziyang 1988). Even if social disturbances are kept in check, the Communist regime pays a heavy price for inflation, because of memories of the hyperinflation under the Nationalists in the late 1940s, which helped cause their fall. The capacity of the Communist government to restore and maintain price stability had been an important source of pride and support. The uncertainty as to whether the party-state can bring inflation under control is thus highly significant politically.

The regime had not adequately prepared the country to expect that ever-rising incomes could not necessarily be sustained, because so much of its authority and legitimacy had come to rest on economic performance and on its capacity to fulfill the promise of a better life. By the late 1980s, economic problems made it necessary for the leadership to tell the country that prosperity would be realized more slowly and that wages could not be raised faster than productivity ("Be prepared for two or three hard years" (*RMRB* 1988: 26–27). The result is lowered morale and a sense of frustration. Reportedly, many people on the mainland feel that they have no real prospect for catching up with their brethren on Taiwan, whose per capita income had reached U.S. $3,400 in 1986, while that of the mainland was under $500. This sobering of expectations is a reflection of the immense economic development problems faced by the country, which restrict capacity to expand incomes and consumption.

A second explanation for popular discontent relates to mobility and insecurity. The reforms have had an impact on life-styles. People have more choices. Mobility opportunities have increased. During the Maoist era, there was little spontaneous mobility in Chinese society. Mobility was by direction, as when urban youths were sent to the countryside. Peasants were essentially bound to the

land and urbanites to their work units, their *danwei*, upon which they depended
not only for a lifetime job, but for housing, health care, rations, and other essential services. During the reform period, mobility opportunities have increased
and will increase further as the lifetime tenure system in the bureaucracy and the
"iron rice bowl" system in the enterprises are abolished. Peasants can move to
smaller towns, and although they cannot settle permanently in larger ones, they
can work there. The extent of mobility is uneven. Many urban Chinese, including workers, government functionaries, and teachers, are still tied to their units,
although the hold of the units is eroding in that alternative sources of supply of
scarce goods hitherto distributed through one's unit are increasingly available,
while policy also encourages job mobility. As choices expand, young people
may decide not to compete for entrance to higher schools but instead to go into
business and make money, while peasants go into industry or commerce rather
than till the land. The capacity of the state to control the lives of people has
eroded, as shown by increasing juvenile delinquency, crime, and divorce.

The new era has brought new opportunities for enrichment but also new
insecurity. Thus, workers in the state sector worry about unemployment and the
consequent loss of state welfare benefits such as medical care and social security
not available to those working in the collective and private sectors: "Many of the
[newly] unemployed are not at all prepared for the sudden loss of their jobs. . . .
Unemployment raises fundamental ideological issues as well as social problems.
. . . The concept that the superiority of socialism lies in providing everyone with
a secure job has been deeply engraved in the Chinese mentality" (Xinhua, September 5, 1988; see also Xinhua, August 18, 1987).

Inflation is also a powerful source of insecurity, particularly for those whose
livelihood depends on fixed incomes or who, as in the case of peasants, may
have to buy industrial goods the prices of which keep on rising even while state
prices for their commodities do not.

Fourth, relative deprivation. Some have benefited more than others. The extent to which inequality has actually increased is a complex question, if only
because inequality in the Maoist period was greater than many observers had
presumed. In the post-Mao period, policy sanctions inequality; Deng Xiaoping
has explicitly stated that it is legitimate for some to get rich ahead of others, but
common prosperity is still the goal. Incomes generally have risen, and the acute
poverty that beset a section of the peasantry has been alleviated for a substantial
proportion. Thus, the income floor has risen for most; it is the extent of the
increase and the extent to which it offsets inflation that are sources of concern
and of popular grievance. At one end of the spectrum, a relatively few nouveau
riche entrepreneurs earn unusually high incomes (Zhao Lukuan 1988). In between, the intellectuals have benefited least in material terms. They and the vast
cadre force, which lives off fixed incomes, often feel deprived and resent those
who have more flexible ways to make money and offset inflation. Sayings such
as "the experts who make missiles earn less than the peddlers who sell eggs"

express this resentment (*China Daily*, November 5, 1988). Belief that the newly rich make their money illegally or in unfair ways is evidently quite widespread, fed by the still inadequate legal framework within which the new entrepreneurs must operate. For their part, entrepreneurs complain about their lack of security, lack of state welfare benefits, and low prestige. The rates of improvement differ in other ways as well, as with respect to urban-rural incomes: urban wages have risen less rapidly than rural incomes, and workers envy peasants carting refrigerators home on their bicycles. Yet urban earnings are still about twice as high as those of the rural inhabitants (*ZTN* 1987: 669). The new fluidity in income distribution, arising from differential opportunities to benefit from the mixed economy, causes many people to feel disadvantaged and to complain about the fairness of the existing situation.

Fifth, the reform era has seen a major increase in the actual incidence of corruption as well as in the perception of corruption by the public at large. The reforms have created numerous opportunities for party and government officials to "use power for personal gain" (*yi quan mou si*). Party leaders have been known to use influence to give their children opportunities to study abroad or have enabled them to use their family connections to establish lucrative businesses in Beijing or Hong Kong (*Far Eastern Economic Review* [*FEER*], September 18, 1986; *Ming pao yue-k'an* [*MPYK*], July 1986). Officials are often in a position to enrich themselves because of access to foreign currency, because they control scarce inputs monopolized by the state or because they are able to exploit the complex price system of state, market, and "negotiated" prices (*FEER*, October 13, 1988: 96–97). Partial economic reform has given rise to numerous interlocking official and unofficial economic relationships and interests. The possibility of making deals between administrators and factory managers or entrepreneurs is ever present and is often a necessity if anything is to be accomplished. As elsewhere in the Third World, corruption can serve a positive end in that it allows entrepreneurs to get around bureaucratic obstacles, but this is not an argument readily understood by the public.

Like inflation, corruption was a major failing of the Nationalist regime on the mainland, and Communist success in stamping it out was a major source of support. The puritanical revolutionary ethos so noticeable among cadres in the 1950s was bound to erode with the passage of time, but legal norms have not replaced revolutionary values, and legal sanctions appear to be ineffectual. Popular disaffection with the "commercialization of power" has become a central problem for the Chinese party-state's authority (Wang 1988). The suspicion of corruption affects the personal authority of leaders all the way up to Deng Xiaoping (whose son has been involved with a Hong Kong business). Respect for the party-government bureaucrats has sharply declined. One poll, for instance, reported that 41.9 percent of a student sample described cadres as "contemptible, hateful, and detestable" (Rosen 1988).

In 1988 and early 1989, public disillusionment with the country's situation grew to crisis proportions. The negative aspects of China's rapid economic development and of partial reform, particularly inflation and corruption, were felt more widely, while postponement of further reform in September 1988 gave people a sense that the leaders had no answers. The result was a crisis of popular confidence that formed the backdrop to the mass demonstrations in Beijing and many other cities in May 1989. As a foreign academic visitor wrote: "The lack of faith, trust and confidence in the Party leadership by people of all ages and occupations would have alarmed the authorities of any regime. There was a widely held view that the Party and government leadership was incompetent, corrupt, and completely out of touch with the interests and wishes of the population over whom they rule" (Forster 1990).

## The Issue of Political Reform

In 1986, Deng Xiaoping and other leaders diagnosed their country's situation and concluded that political reforms going beyond those initiated in 1978 were necessary. Reformist leaders appeared to understand that new channels relating the party-state and society were needed in order to cope more effectively with the emerging demands from below. Speeches by Deng were circulated internally in 1986 in which he attacked the unlimited power of "patriarchal" party secretaries to whom everyone "has to be absolutely obedient" and even "personally attached." Without political reform, Deng added, "our party will be in a position antagonistic to the masses. Such a situation has already emerged in some localities and units" ("Confidential Document" 1986). Encouraged by such language, the media extensively discussed political reform in the second half of 1986.

Two schools of thought emerged (Dittmer 1987: 12–13). One was uncontroversial. It called for more thorough rationalization of the political system, including separation of party and government, autonomy of factory managers at the expense of the power of the party secretaries, establishment of a proper division of labor in the bureaucracies, and legal delimitation of functions. This school argued strongly for the expansion of legality, viewing rule by law as the best way of holding bureaucrats accountable.

The more controversial school of thought included some leaders such as Hu Yaobang, the general secretary, and Hu Qili, a member of the Secretariat, but consisted mainly of intellectuals. Su Shaozhi, for instance, then director of the Institute of Marxism-Leninism, Mao Zedong Thought of the Chinese Academy of Social Sciences, wrote that CCP rule reflected China's long history of feudal despotism. He argued that the party should be placed under the rule of law, and that legislative and judicial organs should be independent. Mass organizations should not be treated as "conveyor belts" but "should represent the interests of the masses." Various social strata, groups, and organizations, which are becoming increasingly differentiated and which have distinct economic and political interests, should have an opportunity to express their interests in the political realm.

Su suggested that "democratic centralism" was not a concept used by Marx. Lenin had invented it to suit the specific needs of the Russian Revolution, and Stalin later distorted it. " 'Democracy' under centralized guidance means that the people are not the masters, but the ruled." The feudal tradition of trust in wise leaders and "upright officials" merges into this Leninist practice and must be repudiated. Su thus challenged established orthodoxy ("Su Shaozhi" 1987).

Fang Lizhi, an astrophysicist and university administrator, spoke out for meaningful elections, arguing that the people's congresses should be turned into real centers of power. Liu Binyan, a famous journalist known for exposing corrupt officials, also called for freedom of expression on the grounds that a press free to criticize official misconduct would actually help the government improve itself. Fang and Liu, it is worth noting, who argued for expansion of freedom of speech and in the case of Fang also for freer elections, harbored elitist views, arguing that the intellectuals should rightfully be the country's leading group and should become an independent social force. Fang justified this on the grounds that science and technology had become the most important productive force. Fang thus voiced agreement with a statement once made by Deng Xiaoping that China would not be ready for full elections for twenty to thirty years, since peasants were too backward and only wanted upright officials who would look after them (Tanner 1988; Nathan 1985). A philosopher, Wang Ruoshui, put forth a more principled argument, stating that "freedom of scientific study, freedom of creative work, and academic freedom are citizens' basic rights bestowed by the Chinese Constitution and are inalienable freedoms" (*Ming pao*, October 21, 1986). The idea of basic rights rather than of privileges bestowed by the party was a theme alien to the established order.

The articulation of these ideas was cut short by the student demonstrations that broke out in late 1986 and that were supported by academic officials such as Fang Lizhi. The political climate abruptly cooled. Hu Yaobang was dismissed from his post, Liu Binyan and Fang Lizhi were expelled from the party, and Su Shaozhi lost his directorship. A brief campaign against "bourgeois liberalization" indicted those who were allegedly advocating "wholesale Westernization," meaning importation not just of science and technology but also of Western political ideas. But repression was limited and discussion of political reform was only briefly interrupted.

This episode reflects the dilemmas faced by China's leaders as they grapple with the consequences of change. On the one hand, many understand the need to adapt the political system. As noted above, Deng himself called for sweeping changes in the way in which the party monopolizes power. Yet, at the same time, Deng also fears change. To him, the party is the key to the country's unity and stability, and the goal of reforming the excesses of party dominance is to "maintain and further strengthen Party leadership and discipline, and not to weaken or relax them" ("On the Reform of the System" 1984: 324).

Deng, in other words, wants to have his cake and eat it too. He wants the party to adapt, but not to adapt to the point of endangering its power. His motivation is not simply keeping power. Deng and many of his colleagues are afraid of chaos (*luan*). This fear is rooted deeply in Chinese political culture (Solomon 1971). It is also rooted in the experiences of the pre-1949 period, and especially in those of the Cultural Revolution. Deng believes that it was his achievement to have brought the country out of chaos. Deng distrusts autonomous political action from below. He believes Mao made a big mistake by encouraging such action during the Cultural Revolution. Deng abrogated the so-called four greats of that era, namely, rights that included putting up critical wall posters and going on strike, because of their association with disorder. Fear that China might return to the condition once described by Sun Yat-sen as a "dish of loose sand" leads Deng and other leaders to believe that a strong authoritarian regime of which the party is the core is essential to hold China together. These views are undoubtedly strengthened by the very process of reform. While Deng believes that controls must be reduced if reform is to succeed, he is also aware that various social or political forces might become uncontrollable. Hence, he attempts to steer a path between loosening (*fang*) and periodic tightening (*shou*). If reform requires adoption of unpopular policies, for example, with respect to control of inflation, Deng and his colleagues opt for more tightening, as indeed occurred in the fall of 1988 when the central leaders sought to restore control.

At the Thirteenth Party Congress held in November 1987, Party Secretary Zhao Ziyang sought to reconcile the dilemma. On the one hand, he stated that China would stick to party leadership and to democratic centralism: "We shall never abandon them and introduce a Western system of separation of the three powers and of different parties ruling the country in turn." He stressed the need for stability, for a "peaceful social and political environment," and for "proper" management of the "relationship between democracy and stability and between democracy and efficiency." Zhao also seemed to be agreeing with analysts of the adaptation phase of Marxist-Leninist systems, who believe that the main task of political leadership should henceforth consist of coordination of interests rather than of transformation: "The government should work to coordinate various kinds of interests and contradictions; the party committees must be even better at the coordinating work."

On the other hand, Zhao also acknowledged that modernization was giving rise to "complicated social contradictions." Different groups of people may have different interests and views, and they too need opportunities and channels for the exchange of ideas. Zhao identified the "reconciliation of various social interests" as an important task, to be accomplished through a system of "consultation and dialogue," including "the opening of new channels," and the improved utilization of existing ones, including those of the media. "There should be channels through which the voices and demands of the people can be easily and frequently transmitted to the leading bodies."

Zhao Ziyang apparently did not mean that interest groups would be able to pursue their interests in the political arena by pressuring party leaders. Instead, the focus was on helping the party-state gain a better understanding of social cleavages and grievances. Zhao and other writers on the subject seem to assume that conflict can be handled simply by attentively listening, an assumption that is not new. It is found in Mao's 1957 theses on the handling of contradictions among the people, and it is part of the CCP's "mass line" definitions of elite–mass relations. Thus, the idea that policy might be the outcome of the open clash of diverse interests did not gain acceptance at the Congress (Zhao Ziyang 1987).

Press comment since the Congress has spoken of the "steady diversification of interests in society" and of the growth of conflicts among the people over material interests. Such conflicts are said to exist between various occupational groups. Cadres, for instance, opposed gains made by entrepreneurs, while workers opposed salary increases given to intellectuals. Middle-school students want more job mobility, while cadres want a rise in social status. Clashing interests could lead to "unrest," and, therefore, a system of social consultation is necessary to help the government understand the scope of the problem, to provide timely advice and criticism to the government, thereby contributing to the resolution of conflict (Luo, Zhu, and Cao 1987; *GMRB*, December 17, 1987).

In the period after the Thirteenth Congress, ideas directly contrary to democratizing ones also gained attention. These bore the label of the "new authoritarianism," meaning that China should have a strong and dictatorial but technocratic government able to solve its problems, on the order of the regime of Park Chung Hee in South Korea in the 1970s. This reflected the weakening of the Chinese government in the reform period, as manifested by its apparent inability to keep control over key aspects of the economy, such as inflation, and fear of political instability (*Zhongguo qingnian bao*, February 17, 1989).

The main thrust of intellectual discourse in 1988 and early 1989, however, was in favor of democratization as the way out of the growing difficulties in effective governance, the management of the economy, and the accompanying drop in popular confidence. Intellectuals asserted themselves more vigorously. In late 1988, forty-four leading scientists and scholars drew up a petition in the form of a "Letter of Opinion," which they sent to the Standing Committee of the National People's Congress asking for structural political reform. Others petitioned Deng Xiaoping to release political prisoners, especially Wei Jingshen, a democracy activist sentenced to prison in 1981, whose antiregime radicalism had not hitherto been supported by establishment intellectuals (Dittmer 1990; Nathan 1990). In addition, there was wide-ranging, often frank discussion in liberal newspapers and in a "democratic salon" organized by Fang Lizhi with students at Beijing University of the need for political pluralism, for checks and balances, free speech, and independent social organizations (*Wen hui bao*, Shanghai, December 2, 1989; *RMRB*, overseas ed., July 25, 1989). The salon met for a year from May 1988 to May 1989. After the Tiananmen protests of May 1989, such discussions of "bourgeois liberalization" were condemned as having constituted preparation for a "second revolution" (*GMRB*, July 22, 1989). The intellectuals, however, saw themselves not as subversives agitating for the overthrow of the government, but as appealing to the authorities to live up to their own professed ideals by taking seriously the formally democratic provisions of the State Constitution. These demands, in other words, took their cue from the ancient Chinese tradition of the remonstrating official, who, at the risk of his life, appeals to the moral sense of the ruler (Nathan 1990).

## Popular Protest

The immense popular protest movement on Tiananmen Square in May 1989, which for over a month held the world's attention, was a culmination of recurring but small-scale protests in the reform years. During the early phase of reform, most ordinary people probably became less rather than more involved with politics. Many undoubtedly welcomed the opportunity to withdraw from the compulsory and oppressive mobilized participation of the Mao era. People became preoccupied with private concerns, with family prosperity, with making money, and with careers. But as the negative aspects of the reform era, such as inflation, impinged more and more on people's lives, roughly from 1985 on, raising the level of popular dissatisfaction, motivation to express oneself in the public arena increased. Scattered protest had occurred already before the Tiananmen events. Peasants in several locales, for instance, staged vociferous and even violent demonstrations against local government abuses, including refusal to fulfill purchase contracts or to protect them against pollution (*Agence France Press*, July 17, 1987 and June 30, 1988; *Hong Kong Standard*, April 9 and 11, 1988; Cheng 1988). Strikes and slowdowns by workers have been reported, including a case in the winter of 1986, when Beijing bus drivers staged a slowdown to protest the freer opportunities to make money that cab drivers have. A similar case occurred in Shanghai, where, an informant told me, workers reportedly staged a slowdown to protest raises given to teachers.

Students and intellectuals had always been the most protest-prone groups in China. Their political involvement goes back to such watershed events as the May Fourth Movement of 1919. Survey data show that students' "unquestioning loyalty toward the Communist Party [has] been replaced . . . by independence of thought and judgment, respect for talent, and a patriotism which does not always take its cues from party leadership" (Rosen 1988: 8).

Prior to Tiananmen, during the reform period, some students were active in the Democracy Wall movement of 1979 and in efforts to democratize the 1980 elections. They staged major demonstrations in 1985 and 1986, and to a lesser extent in 1988. Protests focused on three themes: One was difficult economic conditions, which led students and teachers collectively to protest the state's underfunding of education, the low pay of teachers, and the poor living conditions of students (*GMRB*, March 29, 1988: 63–64; *RMRB*, overseas ed., July 4, 1988). A second theme was nationalism. Students protested the visible Japanese presence in China, the whitewashing of Japanese wartime conduct, and the management of Chinese territorial claims on Diaoyu Tai (Senkaku). But nationalistic students also protested against African students dating Chinese women, while minority Chinese, such as Uighurs and Tibetans, protested against abuses by the Han government (*New York Times*, December 23, 1985; *Los Angeles Times*, December 28, 1988). Han nationalism, it is worth emphasizing, is likely to be of increasing integrative importance as a substitute for the declining appeal of Marxism.

Most important, students demonstrated for democratizing changes. In 1986, they demanded that the party open itself up to criticism, since it had been responsible for the Cultural Revolution. They protested against party dictatorship and its monopoly of decisions. Posters demanded checks on the party's arbitrary power in the form of law and a free press (*FEER*, January 15, 1987: 9). Students were inspired by the overthrow of Marcos, the democratizing changes in Taiwan, and the student movement in South Korea. Chinese students abroad, most notably in the United States, became involved, writing a letter to the leadership signed by a thousand students—some four hundred used their real names—in which they voiced concern over the campaign against bourgeois liberalization and the dismissal of Party Secretary Hu Yaobang (*Zhong bao*, January 21, 1987). These students, who wrote of their "deep sense of mission about the motherland's future," exemplify the dilemmas of reform: opening up to the outside world is in the leadership's view absolutely indispensable if the country is to modernize, but doing so unleashes forces difficult to control.

The protest demonstrations of 1989 were a watershed in China's political development. They lasted for almost six weeks. They were extraordinarily large. The Beijing demonstrations brought a million and perhaps even two million participants to Tiananmen Square. They expanded into at least eighty other cities. It was not only students who demonstrated, but literally millions of urban residents who rallied to the students, cheering them on as they marched, providing food and other help, and, in the end, seeking to restrain the military as it moved on the square. It was not a movement organized by workers, but many did participate, as did intellectuals. Government employees took part, marching under the banners identifying their units. Only one major social group—the peasants—did not participate, with the exception of some who worked on construction in cities and towns. Peasant nonparticipation was a major weakness, if only because China is still a predominantly peasant country, and because peasants still make up the bulk of the army, which obeyed the order to shoot on June 4.

The party and government leaders responded to the demonstrations in a hesitant and vacillating way. This was due largely to deep internal cleavages between hard-liners and those who took a conciliatory approach. Hard-line approaches included an April 26 *People's Daily* editorial, reportedly written on Deng

Xiaoping's instructions, condemning the demonstrations as a counterrevolutionary disturbance. Hard-liners favored reliance on threats, the deployment of troops, the declaration of martial law on May 20, and finally the use of naked force. But until force was actually used on June 4, threats were not made good, and demonstrators freely defied orders to stop, causing the party-state to look weak and impotent. An "exhilarating sense of popular power" and liberation from the stifling control system greatly contributed to the mushrooming movement (Walder 1989: 39).

General Secretary Zhao Ziyang, apparently in a bid for power over the hard-liners, adopted a conciliatory approach in early May. He called for talks with the students and empowered the media to report realistically on the demonstrations. The resulting extensive and sympathetic reporting on the protests, including the student hunger strike, was an important factor in causing the demonstrations to spread. His revelation of a secret leadership agreement in 1987 that permitted Deng Xiaoping to have the final word on policies even after his retirement—a revelation designed to blame Deng for the country's woes—exposed the emptiness of the formal rules at the top of the hierarchy. The public was well aware of the deep divisions among the top leaders. The split encouraged a variety of officials, including university presidents, the head of the official trade union, and others, to appeal to the government to negotiate in good faith with the students. Military officers, including generals, petitioned against the use of force, while 57 members of the 135-member Standing Committee of the National People's Congress called for an emergency session of the NPC to repeal the declaration of martial law (Dittmer 1990).

The demands of the demonstrators were modest but actually included a challenge to the core principles of Leninism. Students demanded that the hostile April 26 editorial be repudiated; that a genuine struggle against corruption be waged—hatred of corruption was perhaps the key theme that united all of the various participants; that the press report the truth, for example, by exposing corruption of high-ranking cadre children; and that leaders be upright and moral. These themes of moral purity were traditional rather than democratic, and similar to those that underlay the demands of older intellectuals (Solinger 1989). Demonstrators insisted that it was not their goal to overthrow the Communist party, as the singing of the "Internationale" indeed implied.

As the demonstrations gained momentum, however, and as the government began to hold talks with students, an issue arose that did indeed cut to the core of system change. One of the student demands was for representation by student autonomous organizations rather than by the established transmission belt student organizations. This demand, as Nathan notes, implied acceptance of "the first completely independent political organization in PRC history, and the effective negation of Deng Xiaoping's four principles, as they were understood by Deng" (Nathan 1990: 25). This theme was symbolized by the statue of the Goddess of Democracy built in Tiananmen Square, a symbol deeply offensive to conservative leaders.

The hard-liners, under Deng Xiaoping and Yang Shangkun, the head of state and a military leader, and including Premier Li Peng, succeeded in the third week of May in ousting Zhao Ziyang and other, more liberal politicians. They resolved to use force because they viewed the demonstrations as a threat to their system. As Deng put it in June, the demonstrators were manipulated by a counterrevolutionary clique that sought to overthrow the party "and topple the socialist system. Their goal was to establish a bourgeois republic entirely dependent on the West" (Fourth Plenary Session 1989: 13). The establishment of autonomous organizations of students and workers was indeed a threat, conjuring up the example of Poland's Solidarity, although workers' organizations were actually quite small. But after the crackdown workers were punished much more severely than students. And they used force to restore the image of the party-state as capable of ruling. Violent suppression of the "counterrevolutionary rebellion," as the demonstration was labeled, thus ended this largest protest movement in the history of the People's Republic, but at the price of an enormous loss of legitimacy and trust. (For an evaluation of these events, see Fincher 1989.)

## The Prospects for Revived Orthodoxy

The Tiananmen massacre was followed by a major effort at political reversal in order to bring about the restoration of an orthodox Marxist-Leninist system. To this end, a siege mentality was conjured up, symbolized by Deng Xiaoping's post-Tiananmen speech, in which he said that "we must never forget how cruel our enemies are" (Fourth Plenary Session 1989: 15). Efforts were made to halt and reverse the erosion of the political control structure in the reform years. The hard-line leaders took steps to strengthen controls over the media and the publishing houses, to reinvigorate transmission belt organizations such as the Youth League and the system of indoctrination and political study for the student population. Maoist symbols such as the selfless model youth Lei Feng returned. Anything smacking of "bourgeois liberalization" became a target of criticism. The party, many of whose members had demonstrated, became the object of a purge. (On the purge, see speech by Song Ping, head of the Central Committee's Organization Department, in Xinhua, August 22, 1989.)

Scattered reports suggest that the regime has not been successful in reindoctrinating the urban population. Alienation of many citizens, particularly students, but including many others as well, has not been overcome. The regime has been able to restore control, that is, to secure outward compliance, using the material and coercive sanctions at its disposal. But some people have been willing to talk openly with foreigners about their resentment at having to write confessions for their participation in the demonstrations. They did not maintain a facade of compliance, as used to be the case even during the height of political relaxation. (For a perceptive report by a German Sinologist, see Wagner 1989; also *Los Angeles Times*, December 10, 1989. My own conversations in China

around the turn of the year 1989–90 also revealed the existence of defiant attitudes.) There is, in other words, a discernible gap between pretense and reality.

The central dilemma for the country's hard-line leaders is that a mobilization
system as it once functioned cannot be easily restored because conditions have
changed. Communications, for instance, developed rapidly in the 1980s, including access to radio broadcasts and contact with foreigners. Although major efforts were made in the aftermath of Tiananmen to tighten access to information,
the Chinese population cannot be fully protected from news of the outside world.
The momentous events in Eastern Europe and the Soviet Union in the fall of
1989 were particularly important in this regard. Gorbachev's "surrenderist"
stance and the downfall of Rumania's Nicolai Ceauscescu were, by all accounts,
a shock to the leaders and a source of satisfaction to the students and intellectuals
(Luo 1990). Awareness that other Communist states have done precisely what
Deng and the hard-liners sought forcibly to prevent is apparently widespread and
contributes to the hopes in China that the country will at some point go through
similar changes. This is one example of inability to control access to news with
potentially dangerous consequences for the regime.

Most important, the goal of revitalization contradicts the goal of continued
adherence to the policies of the "open door" and economic reform. Deng Xiaoping insisted on continued commitment to these policies, even though most of
the conservatives in control prefer plan to market. To be sure, in the post-Tiananmen period, restrictions on the open door were imposed, as on students going
abroad. Moreover, new economic reforms are not contemplated for several
years. The focus of economic policy is on combating inflation and strengthening
central control over the economy. To some degree, the balance between plan and
market did swing in favor of the former (*FEER*, October 19, 1989: 47–48). But
the most important existing economic reforms, such as foreign investment,
household contracting in agriculture, and a limited amount of private enterprise,
have not been reversed. China, in other words, continues to have something of a
mixed economy.

The commitment to the open door, for example, to investment from Taiwan,
Hong Kong, and the West, means that outside influence, however unwanted, will
continue to make itself felt directly in China. Similarly, the continued existence
of private enterprise and household farming means that the social interests associated with individual and private enterprise will continue to have an indirect
effect, through the "back door," if public expression of interest is prohibited, and
a direct effect if the regime takes a more relaxed attitude.

One example illustrative of the impact of the diversity of social interests is
that of private entrepreneurs and the Chinese Communist party. Private entrepreneurs are those who employ eight or more workers, and as of 1988, 115,000
businessmen fell into this category, some operating very large factories. Fifteen
percent of them were party members. The idea of "exploiters" joining the party
of the proletariat caused debate, especially in the case of millionaires. After

Tiananmen, the party leaders sought to reassert the proletarian character of the CCP, and these entrepreneurs were apparently expelled (speech by General Secretary Jiang Zemin at a meeting of organization departments, in *Zhongguo tongxun she*, Hong Kong, March 31, 1989; and in *RMRB*, overseas ed., October 17, 1989). To attempt to purify the party, however, is to act like King Canute. About half of the country's forty-seven million party members are peasants, (small-scale farmers), and a good many of them are entrepreneurs who lease businesses from the collective or open their own. Their mentality is no different from that of the legally defined private entrepreneurs. Yet to expel all of them would destroy the party's rural base. All the leaders can do is to insist that such entrepreneurs do some good for the community instead of only chasing after money. In other words, unless the regime returns to full collectivization, it is simply not possible to restore a cohesively mobilized Communist party able to impose its conception on society rather than representing diverse social interests. The social changes stemming from economic reform and economic development are not reversible.

What, then, has China's political system in the reform era and in the post-Tiananmen era become? Has China become a "consultative authoritarian" state, as one study suggests (Harding 1988: 200)? Before the forcible repression of mass demonstrations in 1989, decision making within elite political institutions had been based largely on consensus building and debate; hence, the term "consultative authoritarianism" was not inappropriate. But in a crisis situation such as that of the spring of 1989, intra-elite struggle unconstrained by rules replaced consultation. The events of 1989 laid bare the low degree of institutionalization that China has achieved, as manifested by the lack of procedural constraints, the continued power wielded by nominally retired party elders, the unique status of Deng Xiaoping, and the renewed salience of the military in Chinese politics. (For a trenchant analysis, see MacFarquhar 1989.) All this suggests that elite-level politics in China will be unstable in the next few years, meaning that a comfortable term such as "consultative authoritarianism" is not really very helpful.

Even before Tiananmen, China had not made a transition from Leninism to authoritarianism. The concept of "authoritarianism," used in Juan Linz's sense as consisting of limited political pluralism, was not descriptive of the Chinese case. Interest groups, such as those of business, church, and labor that typically exist in authoritarian regimes, have not been legitimized in China, although some interest group activity did emerge, including by organizations that used to play a preemptive role, such as the trade unions, some by the National People's Congress (Xinhua, January 12, 1988: 24, and April 4, 1988: 16–17; O'Brien 1988). But the process of liberalization was far from complete before the hard-liners took power in June 1989, and it is not likely to gain renewed momentum until there is a change in leadership.

If authoritarianism is not an appropriate label, Leninism is also problematic. Formally, China is still a Leninist system. The party still monopolizes power: it still defines itself as the embodiment of historical truth and it is still a vanguard party. Other organizations are still formally the instruments of the party's will, and the ideology still lays claim to providing an all-embracing explanation of past, present, and future. By the time the hard-liners took power, however, the formally Leninist character of the Chinese political system had come to conceal a much more complex reality, as a result of ten years of rapid economic development and reform. The party monopolized power, but there was a big distinction between central power and local power. "You have your policy and we have our counterpolicy" was the complaint ("Yi hao wenjian" 1984; *Xinhua* Commentator, December 18, 1985). There was the claim of ideological monopoly, but the meaning of "socialism" had been relativized and the hold of the ideology had dramatically weakened, particularly among intellectuals and students. Ideology had lost its appeal and was no longer the driving force it once was. Formally, the country was marching in step toward socialism, but in fact, people were marching in all sorts of directions, many of which could not by any stretch of the imagination be called socialist. There was a great deal of unauthorized political discussion in pre-Tiananmen China, which included advocacy of democratization and, at least verbally, a multiparty system. There were even unauthorized publications, though, to be sure, any attempt at establishing an independent political organization was always swiftly repressed. Mass organizations were not really able to play their preemptive mobilizing role, and the Youth League did not effectively reach students. The range of uncontrolled, politically relevant behavior in China had widened dramatically.

As noted, in the wake of the Tiananmen massacre, the Chinese regime has attempted to revitalize the Leninist system. But because of the social and economic diversity engendered by ten years of reform and economic development, the staying power of reestablished Marxist-Leninist orthodoxy is to be doubted. The formal networks of control, including a strengthened public security apparatus, can probably keep assertiveness from below in check, but it is wholly unlikely that the dynamism of the old system, which was based not only on control but also on belief, can be recaptured. The current situation is one of stalemate between the party-state and major segments of society. If a succession crisis occurs, accompanied by a major split in the leadership, in which some contenders see their interests served by mobilizing public support, the present arrangement could speedily collapse, all the more so if the economy were also in major difficulty. Because of the vulnerability of China's formally Leninist system to societal pressures, it seems appropriate to label the Chinese political system of 1990 as one of "soft Leninism," meaning that the formal Marxist-Leninist system has been eroding under the impact of an increasingly complex society and will in due course undergo further change.

# Part II
# Developing Economies

# 3

# Indonesia: Economic Growth and Depoliticization

## Jamie Mackie

INDONESIA is one of the most conspicuous examples in the Asia-Pacific region of a low-income country whose rapid growth seems to have been pushing its political system in the direction of a deepening authoritarianism rather than toward democracy. The quite impressive economic development that has occurred under President Suharto's "New Order" since 1966 has greatly strengthened the power and capacities of the state at the expense of previously vigorous society-based forces. It has created a patrimonialist regime in which both key policy-making authority and the allocation of the most crucial resources have become concentrated at the apex of the political system in the hands of the central government—and increasingly in the hands of Suharto himself (Crouch 1979; Liddle 1985). This has enabled the state authorities to reduce to near impotence the very few independent clusters of countervailing power in the society, such as the regionalist or Muslim groups discontented with government policies, that might in other circumstances have been capable of opposing or disregarding the power of the state, as they had frequently done before 1965, or simply of exerting some influence upon its decision-making processes through the more or less representative or corporatist institutions set up.

These institutions can hardly be described as very democratic or participatory, or even as effectively corporatist (the government's rhetoric about a highly integralist "Pancasila democracy" notwithstanding). The New Order political system could perhaps be categorized as a case of bureaucratic authoritarianism, since it has some of the features of such a regime in the O'Donnell sense, although it is still essentially agricultural rather than industrial in its economic structure (O'Donnell 1978). But it is best described as patrimonialist. Its middle class is much weaker than those in the other ASEAN countries or the NIEs, and neither a propertied bourgeoisie nor strong socio-economic interest groups are yet politically influential there (Crouch 1979, 1984; and Mackie 1989b).

Things were very different before 1965. The power of the state was very weak in the early years of Indonesia's independence and societal forces very strong. The growth of the nationalist movement and its success in mobilizing mass support in the struggle for independence between about 1910 and 1949, when the Dutch were finally forced to bow out, owed a great deal to various social changes taking place during the late colonial era. These changes resulted in part from the economic transformation of the colony in the first half of the twentieth century through the processes of commercialization, urbanization and education. They were also due in part to the challenges those changes represented to traditional status systems and the beliefs that sustained them. Thus new elements were thrown up in the society—teachers, journalists, lawyers, and new-style politicians, the "intellectuals" or educated groups in general—who provided the leadership of the nationalist movement. Political parties began to take shape in the last decades of colonial rule. They were suppressed for some years by both the Dutch and the Japanese, but in spite of their shallow roots, they were able to blossom vigorously in the years after World War II as they sought to mobilize popular support for the Republic of Indonesia in its struggle for independence between 1945 and 1949. They continued to play a crucial part in the politics of the "parliamentary" phase of Indonesia's post-independence history between 1950 and 1959.

Even in the more authoritarian "Guided Democracy" phase under President Sukarno's personal rule (1959–65), political parties remained active and important because Sukarno needed to preserve them as a counterweight to the growing political influence of the armed forces. The Indonesian Communist party (PKI) in particular was able to expand steadily at this time under Sukarno's protection. The highly competitive mobilization politics of the early 1960s culminated in the tumultuous socio-political conflict of 1965–68 and the destruction of the PKI. It was sparked off by the "Gestapu" coup attempt of September 30, 1965, which brought the Sukarno regime to an end and Lieutenant General Suharto, as he was then known, to center stage in the Indonesian political drama. Largely because of widespread fears of a recurrence of such an upheaval if the state authorities should ever prove unable to maintain effective control over societal forces, the armed forces leaders have been able since then to suppress potentially radical political movements and carry out a process of sweeping depoliticization with relatively little difficulty.

State power has become steadily more concentrated in Indonesia under Suharto, in striking contrast to the situation that prevailed under his predecessor, Sukarno, when it was still highly diffused. The various political parties and other movements or organizations based within the civil society, which were active and remarkably influential before 1965, have been dramatically weakened since then. Altogether, the political system has become more authoritarian, far less participatory and rather less pluralistic than it used to be. The social and political chemistry of these changes has owed a great deal, moreover, to the success of the Suharto government in bringing about an unprecedentedly sustained and rapid rate of economic growth since

1966–67. Another factor of great importance in all this, however, has been the personality and political philosophy of President Suharto himself, for unlike Sukarno (or Marcos in the Philippines) he has played a crucial role in getting the growth process under way and keeping it on track, with the aid of the technocrats among his ministers, the so-called "Berkeley Mafia."

There have been some indications recently that the tide may be starting to turn slowly towards a strengthening of at least a few elements in the society vis-à-vis the government, in somewhat the same way as in other countries of the region. Especially since the sharp decline in oil revenues in 1986, the Indonesian government has become less able to disregard the changes and pressures for reform or deregulation that are developing (MacIntyre 1988). But the evidence on this is still sketchy, and no significant political consequences have yet resulted from these incipient changes.

Thus, the Indonesian story is very different from those of South Korea, Taiwan, or even Thailand. Why should this be so? Why has Indonesia been moving in a more authoritarian direction during a period of rapid growth whereas some of its neighbors during similar growth periods have becoming more pluralistic and more democratic?

Is there something peculiar about the growth process itself in Indonesia that helps to explain this? Is the fundamental difference, for example, that Indonesia did not attain the same level of income as its more democratizing neighbors? If so, just how does the level of income impact on the political system? Or should the answer be sought in deep-seated structural conditions? It may be argued, for example, that the overwhelming dominance of the state over society today is the product of a long history and is deeply ingrained in the country's value systems, socio-cultural make-up, and organization of the economy. But, if so, how is one to account for the dramatic mobilization of societal leaders between 1945 and 1965? Or is it to the contingent and coincidental—the rise to power of the person of Suharto, for example, that offers the most satisfying explanation? Or had Suharto no choice but to build the monolithic authoritarian regime that he did?

We shall be reflecting on these and other explanations; but, first, an answer to that question may be sought by examining the course of political and economic development in four distinct periods over the last forty years:[1]

1945–65: The period of political upheaval and social activism under Sukarno

1965–74: A transitional phase when the Suharto regime began to take shape

1974–86: A period of rapid growth accompanied by a deepening authoritarianism

1986–90: A time when a few pluralist tendencies have become observable.

## Political Upheaval and Social Activism, 1945–65

When the Republic of Indonesia was proclaimed on August 17, 1945, just after the Japanese surrender, it could hardly be called a state in any real sense of the word. In fact, the very idea of an Indonesian nation as an independent entity could only be conjured up on the basis of the anticolonial nationalism that had been generated over the previous forty years or so, for no such unit had ever existed prior to the twentieth century. Soon after the proclamation of independence, the government of the Republic moved briskly to take over the former machinery of state left behind by the Dutch and Japanese regimes after their abrupt downfalls. It appointed its own men to key administrative posts, proceeded to build up an army by mobilizing local armed bands of volunteers to fight the Dutch, and sought to win popular support by calling for political parties to be set up as a means of creating organized popular support for the nationalist cause throughout the country. In the early stages, the government's effective power to exercise the normal attributes of statehood, for example, to levy taxes and to pay civil servants' salaries, was very limited. Hence, the strength of the state depended on the degree of active cooperation it could win from the numerous political and social groups that were springing up mushroom-fashion throughout the society.[2] During the struggle for independence, it was about as far from being autonomous as one could imagine. By far the most important sociopolitical development of those early years was the degree of social mobilization and political participation brought about by the necessity to wage a "revolutionary" struggle for independence. It was a struggle conducted in the name of "the people," partly against those "feudal" (i.e., aristocratic) elements who chose to cooperate with the Dutch to preserve their privileged position. There was a strong emphasis on popular sovereignty and social equality (kerakyatan) and a strongly egalitarian character to the nationalist ideology, which continued for twenty years or more after 1945. Many of these ideas were to change in the very different ideological climate of the New Order, when even the use of the word "revolution" was dropped in reference to the struggle for independence.

In 1949–50, after achieving independence from the Dutch following four years of intermittent conflict and negotiations, Indonesia won general international recognition as a state in its own right. Then during the 1950s it proceeded to rebuild the machinery of state inherited from the colonial power on the basis of a parliamentary form of government modelled on the Dutch system.[3] The political parties that had come into being in the early years after 1945 played a key part in the politics of the next decade. The general elections in 1955 were the country's first and still most fully democratic elections; and parliament functioned as the main arena of political contestation until 1958–59. Yet neither parliamentary democracy nor the concept of electoral competition to win voters over to particular parties was very congenial to the more traditional village societies, which were still committed to older ideas of social harmony and organic unity (Feith 1962). Disillusionment with the parliamentary regime developed also because the country's level of economic performance was at best mediocre and often poor in the 1950s. In the tug-of-war between the "administrators" and the "solidarity makers" among the political leaders, to use Feith's illuminating dichotomy, the latter tended to win out as time passed and only slow progress toward national development was achieved. In no way could the early governments of independent Indonesia be categorized as either strong or autonomous, nor the state apparatus as anything but ramshackle and ineffective.

There were two main reasons for this. As Soedjatmoko noted, one was that "political power in this country seems to be quite diffuse . . . widely distributed among the political parties, the government bureaucracy, the army, all diffuse within themselves, and outside these institutions, over large, often inarticulate bodies of opinion or emotion, often of a regional, or local character" (1956:135). Neither the cabinet nor the parliament was the exclusive repository of power. Hence the legal and moral authority of the central government was not sufficient to ensure that the policies it devised could in fact be carried out in all parts of the country. This was particularly the case in the Outer Islands, where the writ of the central government was barely recognized, if at all, at a time when intense regionalist hostility toward the centralizing tendencies of Jakarta officials was building up.[4]

The other reason was that party politicians came to be widely regarded as self-seeking if not downright corrupt (as many were, although on a modest scale by later standards), while the coalition governments that were essential under the multiparty system then prevailing had to be based on a process of horse-trading that generated disillusionment with civilian politicians and increasing calls for strongman rule. Thus, when a series of regional revolts came to the boil in 1956–58, raising problems that neither the government of the day nor the parties and parliament could resolve, there was a crisis of confidence in "liberal democracy," which President Sukarno (at the time a mere titular head of state) castigated as unsuited to Indonesian conditions and the national identity. But when the army leadership backed Sukarno and crushed the regional rebels by force in 1958–59, the hand of the now strongly authoritarian central government was much enhanced. Regional dissidence has posed no real threat to the authority of Jakarta since the early 1960s.

The events of the late 1950s brought about a decline in support for both parliament and the parties, whereas the authority of President Sukarno and the armed forces leaders was greatly enhanced. In 1957, the power of the latter in civilian matters was much extended by the declaration of martial law. Sukarno seized the opportunity in 1959 to decree a "Return to the 1945 Constitution" (i.e., to a presidential style of government) and the inauguration of a system of "Guided Democracy" and "Socialism à la Indonesia" with a highly regulated economy. The state sector of the economy had also been vastly expanded shortly before this by the nationalization of all Dutch enterprises during the course of the wrangle between the two countries over the status of West Irian. This meant not only that the commanding heights of the economy were now under direct state control but that private enterprise was in eclipse and excluded from many lucrative fields of activity. The state–society relationship seemed to be tilting sharply toward the strengthening of the former. But in fact, the inability of the government to avoid budget deficits had disastrous inflationary effects on the whole economy during the years of Guided Democracy, creating conditions in which the state enterprises proved utterly incapable of operating effectively. As inflation spiraled to reach 100 percent per annum by 1963 and over 400 percent by 1965, production declined and living standards fell. The effective power of the government to carry out its grandiose development plans, or even the most basic functions of government, gradually crumbled, and its basic regulatory mechanisms progressively atrophied (Mackie 1967). Meanwhile, as hardships increased, social and political tensions mounted steadily.

Although state power had been formally increased and political parties much weakened by the return to the presidential-style 1949 Constitution in 1959, the reality was that the parties retained their roots in various societal constituencies. Sukarno took various measures to rein in the political parties, postponing elections indefinitely, banning two parties opposed to his policies, purging the elected parliament to an arbitrarily predetermined number of representatives from nine approved parties, and prohibiting civil servants from joining parties. Yet he still needed the backing of the parties in his wrangles with the army leadership, so the process of depoliticization was far from complete. In particular, Sukarno increasingly had to rely on the PKI, the largest and best organized of the parties, for the purpose of organizing mass rallies to demonstrate support for his increasingly radical foreign and domestic policies, to which the army leaders were strongly opposed. The result was that party conflict continued to be fought out vigorously between right- and left-wing forces between 1959 and 1965, producing a degree of social and political polarization that brought acute tension throughout the country by mid-1965. In this highly volatile atmosphere, the *Gestapu* (September 30 Movement) coup was merely the spark that produced the subsequent explosion of right-wing hostility to the PKI and Sukarno and brought about the demise of both.[5]

## The Transition to the New Order, 1965–74

The 1965 coup attempt was a major turning-point in the history of independent Indonesia. It led to a massive backlash of violence against the PKI throughout much of Indonesia, mainly in rural areas, followed by the killings and arrests of hundreds of thousands of Communists and suspected Communists who were henceforth excluded from further participation in political life. It also brought about the drastic ideological and political *bouleversement* that followed over the next twenty years, with the army-backed New Order regime gradually wresting power from Sukarno's hands in 1966–68. The coup attempt itself was a relatively minor affray, quickly suppressed by army units in Jakarta commanded by the then obscure Lieutenant General Suharto, who soon assumed center-stage in the political drama over the next two years, which led him to the presidency in

1968 and to four subsequent terms of office. But the episode left the country hovering for many months on the brink of civil war between various pro-Sukarno and anti-Communist elements, as the once powerful PKI, which Sukarno initially hoped to save from annihilation, was banned and destroyed in one region after another by its old enemies, Muslim extremists and the army. The power struggle left the way open for a brief phase of highly participatory political conflict between right- and left-wing elements in 1966–67, before the army leadership achieved sufficient control over the machinery of state to impose its will on the political and social forces thrown up by the affray. The hopes, disappointments, and disillusionment that were generated in those early years of the New Order have had a continuing influence upon its subsequent development.

The social upheaval in the rural areas was the culmination of intense conflict, frequently associated with disputes over land reform, which had been conjured up by twenty years of almost continuous mass mobilization. The attacks on the Communists were carried out mainly by their old enemies, generally local-level vigilante groups settling scores in the dark of the night frequently with army backing. (Contrary to a common misconception, the number of ethnic Chinese killed or jailed was not disproportionately large, for the PKI had recruited very few of them to membership since 1951.) The origins and character of the entire episode are still too controversial to be briefly summarized here (Crouch 1989:97–189), but there is not much disagreement about its consequences.

The impact of that great social convulsion on the political and social character of the New Order has been far-reaching. For it not only validated the army's claims to a dominant voice in government as the guardian of national security, but it gave legitimacy to an almost universal hostility to communism that has prevailed since then (and, by association, other Marxist or left-wing ideas) as a dangerous, potentially treasonable ideology. It also gave rise to persistent fears about the dangers of any return to a 1965-type breakdown in law and order that have persisted strongly among the better-off and middle classes generally. That is why the Indonesian middle classes, for all their dislike of the arbitrariness and heavy-handed repressive measures of the army-backed regime that came to power under General Suharto, have never been very willing to risk precipitating a return to the instability of the late Sukarno years and the naked violence of 1965–66. Memories of that trauma have been a major factor behind the underlying conservatism of the Indonesian elite since then, its distrust of ideas deemed to be at all "radical" or subversive and its rejection of so much of the old populist and leftist ideology of the Sukarno era.

The final overthrow of Sukarno in March 1966 was brought about not just by the actions of the army itself but through the joint actions of a diverse collection of anti-Communist and anti-Sukarno elements, student activists, middle classes, many intellectuals, and Islamic militants who came together briefly to achieve that goal. They formed what one can loosely call the original "New Order coalition." Throughout 1966–67, these groups were allied with the new army leadership in the political struggle to isolate and then topple Sukarno, purge his supporters in the bureaucracy and the armed forces (particularly in the air force and navy) and to devise a new set of political institutions that would be more democratic yet ensure that the Old Order groups would not be able to make a comeback several years later. That was the essential dilemma of the New Order activists: they wanted to ensure that the excesses of the Sukarno regime would not recur. They hoped for a return to more democratic institutions, which Suharto himself initially advocated; yet they could never ignore the awkward fact that their enemies still had a substantial following in the society and might still outnumber them in a completely free election. And having gone along with a partial depoliticization of Indonesian society on the left, they were to find later that the same process of exclusion would be applied also to them, in lesser degree, as non-Communist (and frequently strongly anti-Communist) dissenters and critics of the regime came to be silenced. They had seen themselves initially as "partners" of the armed forces in the struggle for a more democratic society oriented toward development and modernization. They gradually found themselves relegated to the role of very junior partners at best—and later on regarded as dissidents, almost as enemies, rather than partners.

Suharto himself did not at first appear to be in a very secure political position, for the army leadership itself was far from united about how best to proceed in 1966–67. Pro-Sukarno elements in the armed forces and the regional bureaucratic machinery remained a potential source of trouble. He therefore needed evidence of popular support from the society and the mass media, which was provided by the New Order activists in the student action groups, the Islamic militants, the middle classes, professionals, and intellectuals who were in favor of the new government's more pragmatic goals of modernization and development rather than Sukarno's empty nationalist slogans. He initially had limited economic resources at his disposal even to keep the machinery of government running, let alone embark on ambitious development expenditures; he thus had to rely heavily on slush funds from what were euphemistically called "unconventional finances" to supplement the meager government revenues or buy off disgruntled officers and reward loyal supporters. This inevitably aroused much criticism of the corruption and misuse of funds involved. Even though the Suharto regime had strong patrimonialist features of this kind from the outset, it did not at first have substantial resources to distribute. That was later to change as the economy picked up steam under the stimulus of much increased foreign aid from 1968 on and of steeply rising oil revenues in the 1970s. The success of his economic stabilization program was clearly apparent by about 1970–71, with annual growth rates of around 7 percent being achieved even before the oil bonanza of 1973–74 had occurred. This helped the regime to gain broader acceptance and support, what might be called "performance legitimacy," even among groups initially opposed to it. Yet it was not until the end of the 1970s that the benefits of the new development strategy he had inaugurated came to be widely distributed throughout the society; and even then, there were many skeptics who were opposed to it on doctrinal grounds.

Both the causes of this transformation and its socioeconomic consequences are relevant to our concern here with the effects of economic growth on the political system. The Suharto government initially inherited most of the political and bureaucratic weaknesses of the Sukarno regime, including a desperate lack of funds and taxing capacity in its early years, so that it had to rely not just on the army but also on the "New Order coalition" of civilian elements mentioned above. It was also heavily dependent on international support in the form of foreign aid, loans, and investment funds to finance its rehabilitation and development programs. Until about 1973 the political system was relatively pluralistic, open and competitive, very different in character from the rather heavily authoritarian, monolithic structure that it became over the next decade. The years immediately after 1965 were a period of ebullient political activity and remarkably free expression of ideas and opinions (apart from Communist doctrines) after the oppressive constraints of the Sukarno years. The leadership came initially from the student activist movements but soon extended across much of the political spectrum, except the extreme left, which had to lie low to avoid any charges of complicity in PKI activities prior to the coup (Crouch 1978; Feith 1968). And yet within a few years all this was to change radically. During the 1970s, Suharto's government became vastly stronger and more secure than Sukarno's had ever been. Gradually, many of the society-based forces that had supported the army to bring about the defeat of Sukarno and the left found themselves increasingly alienated from the New Order. As the regime became increasing patrimonialist in character, they found themselves consigned to the political wilderness and loss of influence, unless they were willing to work within the system on the terms demanded of them.

During the years 1967–74, the twin processes of a steady strengthening of the political, financial, and administrative muscle of the state apparatus, the army in particular, and the progressive exclusion from power of many of the earliest and most active supporters of the New Order were essentially two sides of the same coin. The first steps in that direction were the government's actions in barring from active political participation various old anti-Sukarno political leaders who were likely to prove difficult to control, then the reining in of various New Order activists who were too critical of abuses of power by the armed forces and sought to build up an independent political base. The next step was a more systematic marginalization of various civilian elements of the original New Order coalition (and some military officers supporting them) and their plans for the restructuring of the political system along more democratic and participatory lines. This was followed by the government's decision to rely primarily on Golkar, a new form of state party, as its chief standard-bearer in the forthcoming 1971 general elections rather than any of the old parties. A great deal of pressure from the governmental apparatus was brought to bear to ensure victory for Golkar in the elections (its 62 percent vote was almost a case of overkill, which weakened the other parties disastrously), and the roughshod methods that worked then have been continually repeated in all three subsequent elections. Over the next two years, several measures were pushed through which completed the subordination of the political parties and ensured the continuing supremacy of Golkar. Notable among them were the forced amalgamation of the nine political parties into two, which then found themselves highly susceptible to manipulation by the government; the introduction of the doctrine of the "floating mass" (i.e., the isolation of the villages from party politics except during the month prior to each national election); and the dragooning of all civil servants into a monolithic government organization that became a key pillar of Golkar.[6]

The reduction of the once-numerous political parties to a mere two has effectively paralyzed them as effective sources of opposition to the government by generating constant factional conflicts that the government has been able to manipulate easily. The PDI (Indonesian Democratic Party) has polled badly in all elections since 1977. The Islamic party, PPP (Development Unity Party) has been more successful in retaining solid support in many of the old Nahdatul Ulama strongholds, despite vigorous attempts by the government to entice Muslim leaders and organizations into Golkar. Because they have been rendered virtually incapable of upsetting the government, they are tolerated as a safety valve, although in the national parliament and regional assemblies they are rarely able to push through significant amendments to legislation. While the outer forms of a constitutional democracy are preserved--elections, parties, parliament—the system is far from democratic in essentials.

Two important changes within the state apparatus itself helped to tilt the state–society balance more decisively in favor of the former around this time. One was a reform of the armed forces command structure in 1970 to achieve a degree of centralization of control over regional units and their commanders that greatly reduced any possibility that they might act independently of the Jakarta neadquarters staff, as had frequently happened in the past (McVey 1971, 1972; Sundhaussen 1977). The other was a gradual reinvigoration of the overbloated bureaucracy (partly through purges of alleged Communists and political appointees, but largely through better training courses and appointment of better-qualified officials), which made it by the early 1970s a vastly more effective instrument for carrying out government policies than it had previously been. The technocrats who were advisers to Suharto on economic policy from the outset were able to exert some influence in this sphere, although never enough to override the many vested interests entrenched in the bureaucracy. Neither of these reforms had been achievable under the Sukarno regime, and both were critically important first steps in the strengthening of the state apparatus that has been going on continuously since then.

In the early 1970s, much disillusionment developed among the more independent-minded of the New Order activists who had supported the Suharto regime in its early years. Their hopes of active participation as partners with the armed forces in the processes of democratization, modernization, and development, upon which the New Order's rhetoric had initially put such store, turned to cynicism after 1970–71 as they witnessed the corruption and high living of many leaders of the government, reaching right up to the president and his family. Their criticisms were combined with growing concern about the apparently adverse effects of the government's development strategies, which seemed to be favoring foreign capital and the richer and well-connected elements in Indonesian society at the expense of the poor. Not until much later in the 1970s did the fruits of the new development strategy begin to emerge in the form of significant trickle-down effects. The inflow of foreign capital, especially Japanese, in large quantities in the early 1970s, was blamed for much of what was felt to be wrong. It had a great deal to do with the atmosphere of tension that was building up over a host of issues in 1972–73, which culminated in the street riots in Jakarta that occurred during the visit of Prime Minister Tanaka of Japan in January 1974, generally known as the Malari riots. Although of very limited scope and duration, they posed a threat to the stability of the Suharto government because behind them, whether as a directly causal factor or merely indirect, was an element of intra-elite rivalry between two of the President's principal subordinates, Lieutenant General Ali Murtopo and Lieutenant General Sumitro, the latter looking for support outside the inner circle of the regime among the students and Muslims, the former relying more upon its international backers, particularly in Japan. Whatever power plays either man was up to at the time came to nothing, however, and in the aftermath, Sumitro was dismissed and Murtopo relegated to the background for several years. But the riots led to a severe crackdown on the press and dissenting voices, which ushered in a new and far more authoritarian phase of the New Order's development, involving a very different set of political dynamics (Crouch 1974).

## Deepening Authoritarianism, 1974–86

The Malari riots can be seen in hindsight as a watershed in the development of the New Order regime, marking an abrupt end to the previous phase of relatively "open" and competitive politics that had characterized the early years of the New Order, and ushering in a new, more repressive phase in which authority came to be concentrated more and more tightly in the hands of President Suharto himself. Their most immediate outcome was a wave of arrests of various leaders of the student movements involved, followed by the most severe crackdown on dissent, civil liberties, and press freedoms yet seen under the New Order. And because they coincided with the first round of OPEC oil price increases in 1973–74, which at first almost quadrupled, then in 1979–80 further trebled the oil revenues received by the Indonesian government, the political system that has developed since that time has been characterized by an unprecedented strengthening of the financial power of the state and a considerable weakening of the political influence and civil rights of societal forces.

Both developments gave an increasingly patrimonialist character to the entire regime. The resources available to the government for purposes of repression and co-optation were now vastly greater, while it was able to exercise much more control than previously over the allocation of licenses, subsidized credit, and the opportunities for access to the most lucrative business opportunities generally. Key policy decisions also became centralized at the apex of the political hierarchy to a greater degree than ever. The next decade also saw a considerable enhancement of the personal authority of President Suharto himself, after a few shaky years between 1975 and 1978, culminating in a curious flutter of speculation about whether he would even be nominated by the army leadership for a third term in 1977–78. Thus, by the mid-1980s the political system grew to be very different from that which had emerged so tentatively in the uncertain early years of the New Order. Suharto has been virtually immune from any effective challenge since 1980, whether from left-wing radicals (such few as there still are), Islamic militants, political parties, or ambitious generals.

Those changes took time, however, and Suharto had to deal with several challenges to his leadership before he succeeded in shunting aside all potential rivals in the higher echelons of the government and armed forces. One of the most important results of the Malari episode was that it brought home to all New Order leaders just how dangerous it could be for the stability of the regime if mass protests of that type were to be exploited by any of them to serve their own interests in the internal power plays constantly going on within the leadership circle. Sumitro's abrupt dismissal served as a clear warning to other members of the circle that they would not in future be permitted to make any bids whatever for popular support outside it, particularly among dissident Muslim groups, or others in the wider ranks of society.

The course of events between 1974 and 1985 seems to bear out the theoretical proposition posed earlier that rapid growth has strengthened authoritarian tendencies in Indonesia rather than promoted demands for democracy or social groups with a strong interest in pluralism, openness, and competitive economic or political institutions.[7] Society-based groups and forces had been in a much stronger position to push demands for democracy and more open government before 1974—and were more strongly disposed to do so—than they have been since then. An important reason why Indonesia differs from, say, Taiwan, South Korea, or even Thailand in this respect appears to be the relative weakness of its middle class and its private business community. A few such groups may have begun to gain some strength and capacity for independent action in the late 1980s, but only to a minor degree so far.

It has become increasingly clear since 1974 that whereas the New Order regime had started out with a fairly broad base of popular support from anti-

Communist, anti-Sukarno elements in its early years, that base has been narrowing considerably throughout the 1970s as many of its former supporters have moved into critical or overtly opposition camps, leaving the Suharto government reliant mainly on the armed forces, the bureaucracy, and Golkar, hence on coercion or grudging acquiescence rather than the stirring mobilization politics of earlier decades. The story of Indonesian politics since 1974 has mainly to do with the restructuring of the system of "Pancasila democracy" and a "Pancasila society" around these three pillars, allowing little scope for independent political action outside the narrow bounds laid down. The one sphere of life the government could not fully control, however, was Islam, despite various efforts to contain or co-opt Islamic leaders and organizations.[8] Hence, in part, it constantly fears Islamic extremists as a potential source of *kekacauan*, confusion and social disruption, and remains nervous about threats to security and the tranquility of society.

The Suharto government has relied on four main strategies since 1974 to curb any effective opposition to its monopoly of power: exemplary repression (on a selective basis); co-optation into the patrimonialist system; ideological indoctrination to induce conformity instead of dissent; and winning acceptance by delivering the goods economically. It was greatly assisted on the economic front by the dramatic success of its development policies throughout the 1970s and by the windfall bonus of the oil boom. The way these have been utilized can be seen from a survey of the major highlights of Indonesian political developments from Malari to the present.

The three years after Malari were an edgy period of apprehension and uncertainty, dominated at the government level by the unfolding scandals of the Pertamina crisis[9] and among its critics by the fear of arrest or reprisals for their dissenting views as had befallen the alleged ringleaders of the Malari riots. There was a good deal of speculation that the army leadership might soon decide to jettison Suharto because of the magnitude of the Pertamina debacle, which more than negated the benefits of the oil price rises for several years. All this culminated in a strange semimystical plot to displace him in 1976, later known as the Sawito affair, a storm in a teacup that a more self-confident government could have laughed aside (Bourchier 1984). Islamic alienation from the regime was causing it serious concern, however, as the 1977 elections drew closer. In those elections the PPP not only increased its vote marginally but proved to be by far the most effective vehicle for expressing opposition to the government as well as the most stubborn rival to Golkar. The latter suffered a slight decline in its vote (62.8 to 62.1 percent, hardly a disaster), but only after strong protests against intimidation and vote-rigging. The months between the election and the 1978 session of the People's Consultative Assembly (Indonesia's highest constitutional body, MPR), proved to be yet another period of student demonstrations against the regime and strong rumors that some elements in the army leadership were reluctant to nominate Suharto as president for another term. He was finally nominated and duly elected, but the session was tense and troubled, despite a strong attempt by the government to portray its forthcoming socioeconomic program as one devoted to greater equality and welfare (Anderson 1978).

Suharto responded by taking a much tougher stance against student dissent both on and off the campuses, appointing a hardline minister of education to bring the student unions to heel. Other intellectuals of critical bent were also forced into line, and the pressures toward ideological conformity intensified. An indoctrination program based on Pancasila, the five-point Indonesian state ideology, was set up. At first only key officials were required to attend, but increasingly almost all other categories of people were involved, with accusations of any lack of commitment to *pembangunan* (development) or "Pancasila democracy" an increasingly damaging charge against one, just as charges of involvement in PKI organizations or the Gestapu affair had been in the early years of the New Order (Morfitt 1981). Nongovernment organizations found themselves increasingly hemmed in. It all amounted to a subtle rather than blatant form of repression, constantly fluctuating in intensity in a way that kept everyone guessing just what the limits to free expression of alternative views might be, hence promoting caution and self-censorship in public utterances. At a time when the economy was booming and employment opportunities expanding for the skilled and educated, it worked very effectively. Dissenting voices grew weaker, becoming increasingly incapable of mobilizing significant popular support behind their causes.

New challenges to Suharto's authority arose in 1979–81, however, from two unexpected quarters. One was from the reinvigoration of Islam in Southeast Asia in the wake of Ayatollah Khomeini's victory over the Shah of Iran. Paradoxically, the associated movements gained far less support among the well-established mainstream Islamic organizations in Indonesia than they did in nearby Malaysia, except in various small fringe movements, such as a Komando Jihad group that bombed a police station and hijacked a Garuda aircraft in 1981. Such episodes actually helped the authorities to manipulate the sense of potential threat from Islamic extremists in a way that kept the PPP leaders very much on the defensive; they also served to justify the need for a strong security apparatus at a time when there was no longer the remotest threat of a Communist resurgence. The government took advantage of this situation to push through the MPR and parliament in the early 1980s measures requiring the acceptance of Pancasila as the sole ideological basis (Azas Tunggal) of all recognized political parties, a stipulation that caused deep offense to many Muslims since it implied the subordination of their religion to another system of moral values. The PPP ultimately decided it had no choice but to accept, although the decision caused deep rifts in its ranks and substantial defections that took a heavy toll on it in the 1987 elections.

A more serious challenge to Suharto personally arose in 1979–80 from a number of retired senior armed forces officers involved in various study groups set up to reexamine the theory and practice of the "dual function" of the armed forces in Indonesian society. Some of the country's most respected and eminent soldiers were involved in these meetings (Jenkins 1984). Under various names, the best-known being the Petition of Fifty group, they focused attention on the ways in which the good name of the army was being damaged by too close an involvement with the more dubious political and business dealings of the Suharto family and its closest associates. The president finally cracked the whip at them in a major speech to army officers in which he warned them that if they continued to criticize him or his policies they would put themselves outside the system of privileges and rewards for past service, whereas if they were willing to work within its constraints they could expect to go on enjoying them. Not much has been heard from these groups since then.

After defeating these two challenges, Suharto found himself in a position of unprecedented personal preeminence in the early 1980s, completely dominating the political system and imposing the stamp of his own personal style upon it increasingly from then on, barely constrained at all directly by outside forces. Decision-making authority came to be concentrated more than ever before in and around the palace circle of the president and his immediate associates. The 1982–83 elections and MPR session posed no problems for him, and both passed off smoothly. So also did the same set of processes five years later, with only one minor upset over army objections to his choice of a vice-president.[10] The political preoccupations of the 1980s have been more to do with the bureaucratic politics of office and access to the president's ear than with mass politics. Attention became focused for several years on the leadership changes within the armed forces as the last of the old "1945 generation" officers handed over the reins to the much younger academy-trained generation of senior officers, a process in which Lieutenant General Benny Moerdani came to play a crucial role. He came to be seen henceforth as the strongman and potential "king maker" in speculations about who would ultimately succeed president Suharto, with all senior officer heavily beholden to one or the other of them, so that the armed forces too were tightly under Suharto's control.

There has not been much disagreement among observers of the Indonesian political scene about either the main events of this period or their overall significance; yet there have been quite sharp differences about how the Suharto regime in its later form should best be categorized. Some have regarded it as essentially a military regime, others as either a bureaucratic polity along Riggsian lines or as "bureaucratic authoritarianism" in the O'Donnell terminology, or even as, in Feith's term, "repressive developmentalism." There were issues of substance behind these debates about names, and in part the arguments reflected the changes perceived to be occurring in the character of the regime.

In the earliest years of the New Order, Indonesia could in some respects have been described as a bureaucratic polity, for the state sector was very large and big state enterprises like Pertamina, the oil empire controlled by Lieutenant General Ibnu Sutowo, the state plantation companies, and BULOG, the huge rice-purchasing organization, seemed to control the commanding heights of the economy. Private enterprise, be it foreign-owned or indigenous or Indonesian Chinese, was still not at all strong, economically or politically. All that changed during the 1970s, as the state corporations became relatively less important, the private sector much more so (including a great deal of foreign capital), and the financial resources available to the state apparatus from oil revenues, other taxes, foreign aid, and government borrowing vastly greater. Hence, the term "patri-monialist" seemed in many respects to be more appropriate than "bureaucratic polity" by the end of the decade (Crouch 1979).

Since then the debate has become focused more on the extent to which the Indonesian state apparatus can be regarded as monolithic and all-powerful, or as still rather loosely jointed and pluralistic in its structures or modes of operation. Emmerson (1983) has argued that it is not just monolithic but should be regarded instead as a case of "bureaucratic pluralism," partly in reaction to Anderson's emphasis on the importance of the "state qua state" as the fundamental determi-nant of the course of Indonesian politics and decision making. The latter ap-proach represented in its most extreme form the view that the state was essentially autonomous, that societal forces counted for very little in the overall scheme of things in Indonesia. Opposing that line of argument since has been also a Neo-Marxist view of the problem from Robison (1986), providing a "con-stitutive" rather than instrumentalist interpretation of the relationship between the state and social classes, seeing the state as creating the conditions for the development of a capitalist society and capitalist classes, not as the mere tool of those classes; and a "restricted pluralist" interpretation from Liddle.[11] Indonesian observers have offered their own more eclectic interpretations, without being so strongly committed to any one viewpoint. But the divergences of opinion among these various theorists are really not as striking as the convergence, "the underly-ing consensus that the state is largely unfettered by societal interests in its deter-mination of policy" (MacIntyre 1988: 27). All these approaches, except Liddle's, in part, tend to be heavily state-centered, allowing little scope for the role of extra-state actors. They give little attention, as MacIntyre has since done, to the question of interest intermediation. The theoretical significance of these argu-ments is that they underline the fact that the politico-economic system has been by no means static since 1966 but steadily changing in character, albeit not very rapidly (compared to Taiwan or Thailand, for example), nor in any one direction.

The nature and causes of the economic transformation brought about by the Suharto government since 1966 also deserve comment at this point since inter-pretations of the nature of the political system tend to be strongly colored by views about the role of the state in Indonesia's development achievements. Rapid growth has certainly had the effect of strengthening the state enormously and the private business sector to a lesser extent, although the latter tended to be heavily dependent on the former during the era of abundant state funds for development projects. The oil boom of 1973–86 had such a dramatic effect upon the Indonesian economy that the extent and nature of its impact on economic growth are frequently exaggerated, as also have been some of the gloomier predictions about the "crisis" said to be facing the country after oil prices declined sharply in 1986–87. In fact, rapid progress was already being made in other sectors of the economy in raising levels of export commodities and in increasing rice production through the spread of the new rice technology, generally known as the Green Revolution, long before OPEC pushed the world oil price up from around U.S. $3 to $12 per barrel in 1973–74 (and, later, to over $33 in 1979–80 after the Khomeini revolution in Iran). The 1967–73 rate of growth was actually well above that of 1973–81, the trend rates being 8.68 and 7.48 percent respectively, according to Sundrum (1986: 42). The most important effect of the oil boom was not the boost it gave to national income (for it also had a "Dutch disease" effect, hurting other export industries) so much as its effect on government revenues and the balance of payments. For the first time since independence, the government was no longer tightly constrained on those fronts and had abundant funds at its disposal to pursue ambitious development plans out of domestic resources. Whereas public expenditure had been a mere 4 percent of GDP in 1965 and no more than 10 percent in 1968, it rose to 25 percent by 1980. This meant that in place of the poorly paid and ramshackle bureaucratic machine that had become almost incapable of implementing any development policies in the 1960s, the apparatus of government became increasingly well equipped to do its job effectively from the mid-1970s onwards. Instead of having to gouge tax revenues out of the reluctant citizens, the government was now in a position to allocate quite lavish development expenditures, contracts, and cheap bank credits on regional authorities and private firms prepared to cooperate with it. In both respects the power and patrimonial character of the state were greatly enhanced. The economic transformation of Indonesia in the 1970s was due not only to increased oil revenues, however, but also to the Green Revolution (with rice production doubling between 1967 and 1980) and to the overall boost to economic activity, employment, and incomes resulting from the increase in public expenditures under the government's development plans. Sundrum (1986: 65) has argued that the high growth rates of the 1968–81 period were due more to factors other than the improvement in the terms of trade (i.e., the oil price rises), in particular to the increase in purchasing power and demand, higher labor productivity, technological progress, increased employment, and capital deepening. These trends should in principle have been strengthening the private sector of the economy, generating structural changes and thereby helping to tilt the balance in favor of societal forces as against the state, but this seems not to have happened to any significant degree. One of the more surprising features of Indonesia's recent economic development is how little structural change has occurred so far rather than how much. Manufacturing output increased from 8 percent to 14 percent of GDP between 1965 and 1985, while agriculture declined from 54 percent to 24 percent, but these were not especially dramatic changes in comparison with those of other ASEAN nations.

In any case, the oil bonanza lasted little more than a decade. Indonesia experienced three boom years around 1979–81, when the combination of very high oil prices, record rice harvests, and lavish budget expenditures produced high purchasing power all around and even the hitherto unknown phenomenon of labor shortages in many parts of Java. But when oil prices started to decline in 1982, the government had to cut back hard on its budget expenditures, thus compounding the effects on aggregate demand, employment, and incomes. An ambitious program of large industrial construction projects was the first casualty. Growth rates declined to below 4 percent through most years of the mid-1980s, then almost to zero after the serious oil price falls in 1986. This led some observers to conclude that the Suharto regime was facing a major sociopolitical crisis that would expose deep structural contradictions within its ranks (Robison 1987), but in this they underestimated its capacity to cope with the revenue problems confronting it. By 1988, the economy was recovering with more strength and resilience than anyone had previously expected.

## Pluralist Tendencies, 1986–90

Significant changes in both the political system and the economy have begun to unfold since oil prices fell sharply in early 1986. These changes may in due course alter the "terms of trade" of the state–society relationship in important ways. How much they have yet done so is far from clear, however. There are a few straws in the wind suggesting that the patrimonialist character of state power is diminishing somewhat and that private business firms are now more capable and more willing to assert their own interests independently of the government than was the case in the early 1980s, but it is too early to draw confident conclusions about the extent of either process. We can, however, note the coincidence of three tendencies that may together be working to strengthen slightly the hands of societal forces vis-à-vis the state in the final years of the 1980s.

The fall in oil revenues is, of course, the most dramatic of these. Oil prices started to decline from their 1982 peak of about U.S. $36 per barrel to around $28 over the next several years, then plummeted to as low as $11 at one stage in 1986, although they have fluctuated around the $15–19 level at most times since then. The economy suffered a sharp recession in 1986–87 as a result of a drastic reduction in government expenditures, although it managed to recover gradually over the next two years. But just as we should be careful not to exaggerate the causal significance of the earlier oil boom, the same can be said of the 1986 oil price slump. The government had in fact already been forced to cut back development expenditures severely from 1982–83 on; and in the Fourth Five-Year Plan (1984–89) it abandoned the previous assumption that public-sector investment would account for the bulk of the country's development effort, looking instead to the private sector, including Indonesian Chinese businessmen, who now included several dozen extremely wealthy tycoons, to invest more. Even before 1986 a considerable change in the economic climate was occurring, with the private sector now appearing to become "for the first time in her post-independence history . . . an engine of growth for the national economy" (Booth 1986: 24). The government now began to grapple seriously with the problems of over-regulation, monopolies, protection, and "the high-cost economy" resulting from all those sources of inefficiency. A series of deregulation "packages" resulted over the next few years (Hadi Soesastro 1989), and the economy was gradually made a good deal more competitive and efficient. Threats to privatize the notoriously inefficient state enterprises had some effect in prodding them toward profitability, although there has been more talk than action on that front. Unfortunately, much of the benefit deriving from all these reforms has been undermined by the persistence of favored palace-connected business groups with new types of special privileges and corners on the market, the main sources of "the high-cost economy," which has damaged other private-sector firms severely and discouraged private entrepreneurial initiative. In short, this aspect of Suharto's patrimonialist state system is holding back vigorous development of the private business sector, except by his cronies.

A second development of significance is the gradual strengthening of the larger private-sector firms and of the capitalist class in general as a result of nearly twenty years of economic growth. While it is still premature to expect that any of these firms has yet achieved the sort of independence of government that one would expect to find in a more conventionally capitalist socioeconomic system, many of them are now large enough to be far less dependent than a decade ago—the big Chinese conglomerates in particular, but also a handful of up-and-coming indigenous business firms. Some of these are starting to learn the techniques of lobbying and using pressure group tactics to influence government policies, according to MacIntyre (1988), in a way that they would hardly have dared to do a few years ago. The big Chinese corporations still rely heavily on connections with government leaders and officials, but the terms of the bargaining relationship are slowly swinging in their favor as the economy matures and diversifies. There is still a long way to go before the Indonesian capitalist class will catch up even with its Thai counterpart, but changes are clearly occurring and may be expected to enhance the strength of that class vis-à-vis the state apparatus in the course of the 1990s.

The third tendency that may be reducing the dominance of the state over society is the incipient erosion of the solidarity of the elite group around Suharto as the "politics of the succession" comes into the foreground. The succession to an authoritarian ruler has proved a complex and slippery problem in most authoritarian countries. There is no reason to believe that Indonesia will be an exception. A few years ago many observers believed that the institutionalization of the power structure there had been so successfully handled that no great problems would arise when Suharto departed the scene, whether through death or voluntary retirement, for the ABRI (armed forces) leadership would promptly arrange the succession smoothly (Liddle 1985). That could still be the case, but it is now far less certain than it seemed earlier in the decade. The previous convergence of interests between the president and the ABRI leadership is becoming questionable—and may well become more so if he is determined to remain in office for yet another term as he has recently been hinting he might. The rift between him and the ABRI leadership at the 1988 MPR session was a small portent of the change that has occurred. In some respects, divergences of interests between them are now discernible, particularly over the vexing question of the extensive business interests of the president's children, which has aroused a great deal of dissatisfaction since the economy took a turn for the worse in 1986. If significant rifts were to develop within the New Order power structure of a kind that could be exploited by society-based forces, the dangers that were so narrowly avoided at the time of the 1974 Malari riots could easily recur. It would be foolhardy to predict whether this will or will not happen. But one can say with some confidence that the conditions that made possible the emergence of a highly monolithic power structure in the early 1980s, when the state was easily able to subordinate societal forces, are becoming modified or even transformed.

That system owed a great deal, moreover, to the peculiarly personal stamp President Suharto himself was able to impose upon the state system and to his extraordinary success in outmaneuvering and negating pluralist elements in the society. It also depended heavily on the persistence throughout the first twenty years of the New Order of a close congruence of interests, institutional, political, and personal, between the president and senior members of the ABRI leadership, something that has not always been the case in Indonesia over the last forty-four years. But if these two conditions are becoming questionable, the stability of the regime cannot be taken for granted quite as much as previously. If rifts within the power elite start to open up over the succession issue as the end of Suharto's fifth term as president comes nearer, with all the speculation and politicking that will engender, the relationship between state and society could tilt back quite sharply in favor of the latter. Whether it does or not would seem to depend largely on the place of the armed forces in Indonesian society and the nature of their relationship with whoever is head of state at any particular juncture. Above all, the curiously enigmatic factor of President Suharto's personality and style of leadership has to be taken into account in this. But before turning in conclusion to that most elusive element in the equation, let us look briefly at one other aspect of the problem that has not been mentioned so far.

## The Flaccidity of Social Organizations

Why have social classes or interest groups based on the country's major industries or productive sectors not developed as significant actors on the political stage in Indonesia, operating politically as pressure groups do in most capitalist or industrialized societies? Or, to put it differently, why have organized, society-based movements or groups of all kinds (apart from some Islamic organizations) proved so puny and ineffectual vis-à-vis the state? Neither rice producers as a whole (too large and diverse a part of the entire rural population to form a coherent bloc) nor sugar or rubber farmers, nor any others have ever been effectively organized to advance the common interests of their commodity, even of their regions, vitally important though their activities and concerns have always been to the health of the national economy. The reasons why farmers are rarely able to organize effectively in Third World countries have been well described by Bates (1981) for Africa, and many of the same considerations would apply in Indonesia. But large private business enterprises have also been incapable of playing significant political roles since independence. The same holds true for KADIN (Chamber of Commerce and Industry), the quasi-corporatist peak organization for the many rather ineffectual trading and industrial associations (MacIntyre 1988). They have all tended to rely, instead, on personalistic political connections rather than on the kinds of organized lobbying activities and institutions found in many other countries.

Westerners accustomed to socioeconomic systems in which such interest groups and lobbying are taken for granted as a normal feature of political life might have expected that at least the large plantation enterprises established by the Dutch, which were nationalized in 1957–58, might have been able to play some such role within the Indonesian bureaucratic polity, or have been capable of exerting some degree of influence on the formulation of government policies. Yet there is little sign that any has ever done so, except on the basis of personal and particularistic ties, as in the case of Pertamina, the state oil company, in its heyday under Ibnu Sutowo between 1966 and 1975. That was a quite exceptional case, however, made possible by the close relationship between Ibnu and the president, by the dramatic (and largely fortuitous) expansion of the oil industry at that time and the uniquely flamboyant personality of Ibnu himself. No other head of a state enterprise has ever attempted to play anything like the same independent role within the system, and they are not likely to do so as long as they need the government more than the government needs them, as was the case during the oil boom years.

One can find explanations of the failure of interest groups to develop in Indonesia on various planes. The pattern of distribution of property clearly has a lot to do with it, underlining Soedjatmoko's point that power is highly dispersed in Indonesia (economic rather than political power, in this case); hence, it is not conducive to the effective use of political power by particular groups of property-owners or producers (Mackie 1989b). Second, political organizations along class or interest group lines have been strikingly absent there; political parties have not made bids to mobilize support along those lines (apart from the PKI to some small extent, prior to 1965) or proved responsive to pressures from them.[12] The political culture may have been partly responsible for that, having traditionally been strongly collectivist rather than individualist in orientation, antipathetic to the notion that the interests of the community might best be advanced by the pursuit of private gain; hence, it has inclined Indonesians of most ethnic and cultural groups toward strongly paternalist and corporatist notions of the rights and responsibilities of rulers and subjects respectively (Reeve 1985). Modern Western ideas of property rights and civil liberties are not yet at all strongly entrenched there, and until they become so the authority of the state is likely to be given precedence over the rights of citizens, even of wealthy property owners. Finally, on the one plane where economic interests and political pressures have on occasion come into conjunction—regional discontent with central government policies—the balance of power between the central and regional authorities has swung so heavily in favor of the former since the late 1960s that even the interests of, say, the main timber-producing regions or of the smallholder rubber growers concentrated in a few parts of Sumatra no longer find any effective voice, as they had previously done on occasion. I will expand briefly on these four points with an eye to the question of why these potential sources of societal pressure upon the government have been so ineffectual hitherto.

On the matter of the distribution of property, the first point to notice is that land is still the most important and widespread source of wealth and income in the country. Most of the land is held in very small plots by millions of landowning families with diverse economic and political interests, relatively little of it by large landowners, apart from the big plantations once owned by the Dutch and nearly all still in the hands of state enterprises. Indonesian rural society has nothing remotely like the sharp social stratification and class of large landowners found in the Philippines or Latin America. The few score large capitalists who have emerged in Indonesia in recent years owe little or none of their wealth to land. In fact, there can be few countries in the world where landownership has so little to do with the exercise of either political or economic power.[13] In the still rather rudimentary nonagricultural sectors—commerce, finance, services and industry—the distribution of wealth is again not conducive to well-organized agglomerations of producers. Dutch capital dominated these sectors up to the 1950s; and Chinese capitalists have played far more important roles there since independence than have indigenous capitalists, who have been emerging only in a small way thus far. Commercial roles tend to be dominated now by the Chinese, as have much of industry and many financial and services activities (other than banking, where state enterprises have predominated until very recently). The emergence of several dozen new large-scale capitalist corporations since the 1970s, mostly Chinese and many of them operating in collaboration with members of the palace circle or the "politico-bureaucrats" among the indigenous elite, does indeed represent a process of concentration of ownership of much modern-sector capital in the hands of a small, wealthy group of capitalists, although it has not gone very far yet, not nearly as far in Indonesia as in the other ASEAN countries or the NIEs. But even these men exercise whatever political power or influence they do through informal and personal contacts rather than in any structured way as either a self-conscious capitalist class with common class interests or producers or traders with well-organized commercial interests to advance (MacIntyre 1988: 49–70).

On the political level, it is striking that even in the heyday of political parties, prior to 1965, no parties made deliberate bids for political support from interest groups of this kind, or even from particular social classes, except to the extent that the PKI pitched its main appeal toward the poorer peasants and workers, in a gingerly fashion, for class-struggle slogans did not make good politics (Mortimer 1972). Parties have tended to avoid making "categorical choices between one or another type of person, or . . . one or another social class," as Lande (1965: 43) put it of parties in the Philippines, relying more on the primordial loyalties identified by Geertz (1963) and *aliran* solidarities (i.e., "streams of religious belief") as a basis for political mobilization (McVey 1972; Soedjatmoko 1956). And since 1965 any hint of appeals to class consciousness or the terminology of Marxism has become increasingly suppressed, so both PPP and PDI have relied mainly on the broader ideological appeals of Islam and nationalism as weapons to manipulate discontent with the government. Golkar, of course, aims to make a universal appeal to all classes in the society and avoids the discourse of class almost entirely.

Yet it is a little surprising that even among the emerging bourgeoisie and middle class one encounters so little sense of common class interests or class solidarity, least of all in any organized political form. The *aliran* and ethnic cleavages still tend to be the most salient ones. And one of the most basic reasons for that is the fact that ethnic Chinese form such a large part of both classes, the former in particular, and there is still a good deal of feeling against them, or at the least ambivalence, which leaves them with a strong sense of being a beleaguered minority, more inclined to resort to personalistic and particularistic political action than class-oriented affiliations. That may be slowly changing as the corporatization of large-scale business slowly brings about interethnic collaboration and partnerships, but the process has not yet gone much beyond the most rudimentary stages. So it is premature, in my view, to be looking for evidence of any strong sense of class interests, except insofar as demands are being heard from some elements in the educated middle classes for the rule of law, less arbitrariness on the part of government agencies, and stronger civil rights. Paradoxically, the people calling for these things tend to be regarded by the government as its critics rather than its supporters, although in other respects the middle classes have been the principal beneficiaries of the Suharto regime's economic policies.

The political culture inevitably reflects this feature of the sociopolitical system quite strongly and, in turn, affects political behavior accordingly. And because it does so in ways that are still so strongly influenced by traditional Javanese (and other) attitudes of deference to authority, to one's ruler or his officials, and hence also to the latter-day state, the political culture tends to reinforce attitudes and behavior patterns that strengthen the state vis-à-vis society and militate against anything like rugged individualism (Reeve 1985). Only in some parts of the Islamic community are more individualistic attitudes and values being inculcated— which helps to explain why the Suharto regime is so uncomfortable with the maverick elements in the Muslim community. The value systems incorporated in the political culture are also more strongly conducive to collectivist and almost corporatist notions of the common good than to capitalist notions of private self-interest as the basic building blocks of the public interest, which means that the rhetoric of a quasi-state party like Golkar commands a degree of ideological legitimacy that others find it hard to challenge. So here, too, the odds are stacked on the side of the state rather than that of dissentient elements in the society. It takes a lot more courage to buck the system in Indonesia than in most capitalist societies.

Finally, what I referred to above as the regional factor can best be explained by comparing the pre-1965 pattern of relations between the Jakarta authorities and their regional counterparts, when the latter were able to behave with a high degree of independence of the center, with the very different patterns prevailing today. Broadly speaking, when the central government has been weak, the regions have been more autonomous, and vice versa. (That seems to presuppose a zero-sum equation; yet there is no reason why it should be like that if the central authorities could bring themselves to be less frightened of devolving more power to the regions and letting them develop in their own way.) The weakness of the central government in the 1950–65 period was due in large part to the fact that Java, including Jakarta, depended heavily on the Outer Islands for the foreign exchange earnings from which the major tax revenues in the central budget were derived; yet it was becoming increasingly incapable of providing the regional authorities with the resources they needed to maintain the basic functions of government. So inevitably they resorted to smuggling and various other forms of unofficial local taxes, outside the national system, defying central government orders to desist from such practices. To that extent, the unitary state was crumbling toward a system that by the early 1960s could well be described as "de facto federalism," or a set of complex bargaining transactions between central and regional authorities—in effect: "We will only obey your orders if you will provide us with this or that." Since the central government became better funded in the early 1970s, however, that situation has changed radically, to a point where the regional governments have become highly dependent on Jakarta for funds since they lack the taxing powers to strike out on their own. Hence, the power relationship between the center and the regions has changed fundamentally in favor of the former and is not likely to change very radically even with lower oil prices. Yet if the balance of power between central and local power, or state and society (not quite the same thing, but not very different), is so heavily stacked in favor of the former even on this plane, one can easily imagine how much more so it is on others.

## Conclusion

From this account of how the political system in Indonesia has changed over recent decades, it seems clear that economic growth has strengthened state power to a far greater extent than any societal forces, classes, or groups, at least up to 1990. While a persuasive case can be made that the middle class—and perhaps an incipient bourgeoisie—has become stronger as a result of the Suharto-era growth process, they are still the weakest such classes in the ASEAN region so far, whereas the autonomy and power of the state vis-à-vis society is almost certainly stronger in Indonesia than in any other ASEAN country. It may well be that over the next decade or so the socioeconomic power of these classes—and possibly also their political power—may become very greatly strengthened as the core elements in an increasingly capitalist society if moderately high rates of economic growth can be maintained. But we shall have to wait and see.

A further question, however, is whether the difference between Indonesia's tendency to move in a more authoritarian rather than a democratic or pluralist direction is due solely or primarily to the fact that it is a poorer country than the others in the ASEAN–East Asia region. The weakness of the middle classes, the private-sector business firms and the professionals, who would normally be the strongest proponents of more democratic or pluralist tendencies in the political system, is undoubtedly due in large part to the fact that Indonesia is still a relatively poor country—and certainly was so until late in the 1970s. These elements have been growing in strength recently, but from a very low starting point. Yet Thailand and the NIEs were not so far ahead of Indonesia twenty years ago that we can confidently conclude that this alone is the full explanation of our puzzle. Somehow the momentum of growth has generated demands for more democratic institutions in those other countries but has so far barely begun to do so in Indonesia.

One could point to various reasons why Indonesia seems to be out of line with the other countries of the region in this respect. Its low-income status may be one factor—or, more precisely, the widespread perception throughout the society that Indonesia is still too poor a country to be able to afford the luxury of such democratic institutions and freedoms as the industrialized nations enjoy—for Indonesia's governments have rarely been free from an overriding preoccupation with financial constraints of various kinds, foreign-exchange and revenue shortages in particular. But the other countries have had similar problems, and I doubt that the explanation is quite as mechanistic or unicausal as that. Another factor in the equation has surely been the highly patrimonial character of the Suharto regime, even in the early 1970s, and the way the oil bonanza made it much more so between 1974 and 1984. Taken in conjunction with the fact that Indonesia already had a huge state sector encompassing what in the 1960s were still the "commanding heights" of the economy, but only a puny capitalist class that was predominantly ethnic Chinese and hence politically vulnerable, it is hardly surprising that the Indonesian political system developed in an increasingly authoritarian direction from the mid-1970s on, at just the same time as Thailand was moving in a more democratic direction.

I am reluctant to believe that there was anything preordained about that. One might say the odds were stacked more heavily one way in the Indonesian case and the other way in Thailand, as I think they were. It may have been the case that Thailand was lucky that it did not have oil to fall back on, like Indonesia and Malaysia, which both have suffered "Dutch disease" effects for their good fortune. It could even be argued that events in Indonesia might have turned out very differently if the outcome of the Malari affair had been other than what it was, or if Suharto had not triumphed over his rivals as completely as he did in the next ten years. The political system might have remained less monolithic than it became in the 1980s. Attributing the explanations entirely to oil money and the patrimonialist character of the regime, highly important though they certainly were, means leaving out of account other elements that also deserve attention. One of these is the personal factor, the way President Suharto himself has imposed the stamp of his own distinctive style and personality upon the regime, both for better and for worse.

Any explanation of what has happened in Indonesia since 1965 must take into account the immense personal influence of Suharto himself in bringing about the extraordinary concentration of power that has occurred there, the rejection of "liberalism" and individualism as alien Western concepts, and the very impressive success of the development process generated under the New Order. Just as Lee Kuan Yew, Park Chung Hee, and Ferdinand Marcos put their own personal stamp on political and economic developments in Singapore, Korea, and the Philippines (and a host of other national leaders around the world, in this modern age of worldwide presidential leadership styles), Suharto has done much the same, less flamboyantly than his predecessor, Sukarno, but a great deal more constructively.

It used to be argued that the New Order was essentially a military-backed regime of which Suharto was little more than the titular head, a characterization that may have been broadly true until about 1980. But Suharto has personalized the system to an extraordinary degree since then. In fact, the interests of Suharto and his family are no longer entirely congruent in the short term with those of the armed forces, or the bureaucracy, or Golkar, and they may be starting to diverge significantly from theirs. This is where the significance of new social forces or pressures of the kind mentioned by MacIntyre may conceivably become important over the next few years, particularly if there are significant cleavages within the elite over the succession to Suharto that they can exploit politically. It is a moot point whether such cleavages, even if they develop to a level of assuming political significance in the years immediately ahead, will be structured primarily by the socioeconomic interests of the people concerned, or simply by the politics of the succession issue; probably there will be elements of both involved, with varying mixes. The political domain still has a logic of its own in Indonesia, only loosely related to the socioeconomic domain.

That could all change a good deal in the 1990s, particularly if oil revenues decline severely (as is quite likely) and the government has to rely more than in recent years on whatever other tax revenues it can levy from the Indonesian people. If so, the state–society relationship might be altered considerably. But whether or not anything of the kind will happen, or how, cannot be foretold on the basis of any deterministic theory of the state or of state–society relations, either of a general nature or specific to Indonesia. Theories, in matters like this, can be helpful for heuristic purposes as pointers to future possibilities, or as guidelines in the investigation or explanation of past events, but rarely as much more than that. And the truth about Indonesia, as Geertz once observed, lies generally in the nuances, impervious to theories.

## Notes

1. The most basic studies of post-independence politics that best throw light on the first three periods are Kahin (1952), Feith (1962), and Crouch (1978). For the economic side, see Glassburner (1971) and Booth and McCawley (1981).

2. For illuminating low-level studies of the ways in which national political organizations mobilized grass-roots support during the struggle for independence, see Smail (1964), Anderson (1972), Reid (1974), and Kahin (1985).

3. The most authoritative account of the politics of 1950–59 is Feith (1962).

4. Regional discontent with the central government arose mainly out of the disadvantageous effects of a highly overvalued currency and cumbersome multiple exchange rate system on export producers. The best general account of the problem is in Feith (1962: 487–591); an illuminating regional case study is Harvey (1977).

5. A well-balanced account of the coup attempt and its aftermath is given by Crouch (1978): for the official Indonesian version and the best-known of the dissenting versions (the "Cornell paper"), see Nugroho and Ismail (1968), and Anderson and McVey (1971), respectively. The background of social tension between PKI and anti-Communist elements in rural areas over land reform issues, which was almost beyond the government's capacity to control by 1965, is well described in Mortimer (1972).

6. The best account of the origins and development of Golkar as both a concept and an organization is given in Reeve (1985): the events of 1966–74 are well covered by Crouch (1978). Good accounts of the 1971 elections, the most revealing of the four New Order elections about party strength and support in different areas, are Ward (1974) and Oey (1974).

7. The rate of growth of GDP was actually a little higher in the less authoritarian period 1967–73 than over the following eight years, according to Sundrum (1986: 42), but the differences are hardly sufficient to modify the general proposition advanced here.

8. A balanced assessment of the reasons why "an Iran-like Islamic revolution" is unlikely in Indonesia although "there is Islamic extremism in Indonesia," and the view that Indonesian Islam is "more relaxed and tolerant" than Islam elsewhere is given by Johns (1987).

9. The financial crisis in the state oil company, Pertamina, developed in 1974–75 when the company's inability to meet its most immediate loan repayments led to the first

thorough investigation ever made into its accounting procedures, which revealed the extremely offhand expenditures and borrowings undertaken by its free-wheeling head, Lieutenant General Ibnu Sutowo. The government had to take over Pertamina's debts amounting to more than U.S. $12 billion (McCawley 1978). The close personal and financial links between Ibnu and President Suharto were by then notorious: although Ibnu had to resign from Pertamina soon after, no disciplinary action was taken against him (McCawley 1978).

10.  The rift between the president and armed forces leadership over the vice-presidential nomination in 1988 (a matter that had never previously aroused controversy) at the 1988 MPR meeting was the first sign of substantial disagreement between the two. For varying interpretations of its significance see Anderson (1988) and Mackie (1989a).

11.  The categorization of Liddle's various writings on state society interactions in Indonesia as "restricted pluralism" is not his own term but has been coined by MacIntyre (1988) to summarize his theoretical position; I am much indebted to Dr. MacIntyre for many of the ideas woven through this part of my study.

12.  Reasons for the PKI's inability to mobilize mass support on a class struggle basis are set out by Mortimer (1972); for the absence of a strong propertied class and any sense of class solidarity on the right, see Mackie (1989b).

13.  Landownership is far from universal in Indonesia and landlessness is now widespread, while it is becoming common in Java for a large part of the arable land in most villages to be owned or controlled by a small minority of landowners, often as much as 60–75 percent held by 10–20 percent of the total number, with the rest retaining only minuscule holdings. But that does not alter the fact that holdings in excess of fifty hectares are still very rare in Java (conditions elsewhere may be different), and the economics of rice farming are not conducive to large-scale production. The richer farmers are starting to become intertwined socially with local-level officials in both villages and subdistrict towns in a way that may have important socioeconomic consequences over the next few decades, but so far it is hard to discern any common pattern of change of this kind.

# 4

# The Philippines: An Unusual Case

## Jamie Mackie and Bernardo M. Villegas

THE RAPID growth that the Philippines has sustained throughout most of its history since independence might suggest that social pressures generated by that growth are chiefly responsible for the overthrow of the martial law regime of Ferdinand Marcos and the establishment of democratic institutions under Corazon Aquino in February 1986. But in fact the "miracle" at EDSA was the product not so much of dynamic new societal forces as of the stagnation and failing of the authoritarian regime itself, and it represents not so much a break-through to something new as a reclamation of a fundamentally democratic heritage, one rooted in a colonial history, social structure, and state tradition, quite unlike those of the other states in the Asia-Pacific region.

### The Inclination Toward Democracy

The Philippines differs from most other countries in Southeast Asia, with the exception of Singapore, in having been "modernized" and commercialized much longer and more deeply than they were. It also experienced the various impacts of colonial rule less disruptively than, for example, Indonesia or Malaysia, while benefiting more from some of its developmental effects, especially the relatively high levels of education its people received (Steinberg 1987; Wurfel 1989). For decades the life-styles of much of its urban population at the upper levels have been middle-class, almost *haut bourgeois*. Since the time of Spanish colonial rule it has had an entrenched elite of landowning families of a kind not found anywhere else in the region and that, except during the Marcos era, has wielded considerable power both in the provinces and in the Manila political arena. Moreover, the nation has had longer exposure to democratic institutions and modern legal processes than most other nations in Asia, with a long preparatory American tutelage and a working democracy from 1946 to 1972. Hence, the 1986 return to democracy came more naturally to the Philippines than might otherwise have been expected.

The fundamental factor here, which so distinguishes the Philippines from other

Asia-Pacific states, is the historical weakness of its state apparatus in contrast to the strength of the forces and institutions rooted within its society. That was true even of the Marcos regime. Marcos never succeeded in creating a very efficient or effective bureaucratic machine. Initially he attempted to purge and reform it, but gradually he came to treat it as little more than a traditional patrimonial mechanism for buying support with money and jobs. Although he could count on solid backing from the military and a battery of repressive legal powers in the early years of martial law, he was never able to crush the steadily growing insurgency of the National People's Army (NPA) or the Muslim rebellion in the south (the only two such society-based movements able to pose serious and persisting challenges to any government in the ASEAN region since the 1960s), so that by the time he left, large areas of the country were outside the effective control of the government. At the other end of the social spectrum, the entrenched oligarchical elite proved to be remarkably resilient in resisting Marcos's assaults upon it. The church, too, remained largely beyond his control, an island of potential criticism, refuge, and dissent almost unique in the ASEAN world. For a "strongman" regime, the Marcos government was remarkably limited.

A more generalized description of the state's relative weakness might be given using the analytical framework of Eric Nordlinger (1987: 353–90). In his analysis of the factors affecting the autonomy of states and the degree of societal support they enjoy, Nordlinger lists four variables: malleability, insulation, resilience, and vulnerability. States that are highly malleable (i.e., "shaped by the known interests of societal actors" to a high degree) or more highly vulnerable than others (less able or willing to act upon their policy preferences out of nervousness about societal reaction) are likely to have a low level of autonomy, he argues. Conversely, those that are more highly insulated (able to act on their own preferences, not much in need of political support from civil society) and those that are resilient (able to counteract potential or actual opposition) are likely to be more autonomous.

In table 4.1 these criteria are applied to the Philippines over the three phases of political development since 1946.

These various assessments, which are purely subjective, are based on the relative strengths of the elite and mass-based social movements vis-à-vis the state, which have been the crucial determinants of state autonomy at various periods. In the years 1946–72, the old landed families were able to exert a high degree of influence over state policies and their implementation, both directly through Congress and indirectly through the processes of local administration. Conversely, while popular forces were able to exert strong pressure on the government during the early years of the Huk rebellion, they were relatively powerless after it was defeated in 1952–53. During the years of Marcos rule, the old elite was deprived entirely of its political power in Congress and was much reduced in its economic power; initially, popular forces were suppressed, although at the end they were reasserting themselves more strongly. Under the Aquino regime, the pendulum has swung back toward a much higher degree of malleability and vulnerability, with the elite growing stronger politically as time

Table 4.1

**State Autonomy and Its Determinants in the Philippines, 1946–88**

|  | 1946–72 | 1972–85 | 1986–88 |
|---|---|---|---|
| Malleability | Very high (4–5) | Low (1) except in last years of mounting "crony" influences (2–3?) | High during People Power phase (4–5); later subject more to elite than popular pressures |
| Vulnerability | Very high (4–5) | Very low in 1970s; higher after 1983 | Low, but fluctuating (0–1), as government is more susceptible to elite pressures through Congress (2–3) |
| Insulation | Low (0–1) | High initially (4–5), but declining after 1982–83 (3–4) | Low (1–2) |
| Resilience | Moderate at first (3–4), but lower in 1960s (2–3) | Very high initially (5), but falling rapidly at end | Low (1–2) |
| Overall— autonomy | Low | High, except after 1983 | High at first; later declining |

*Note:* Ratings range from low (0) to high (5).

passes and the scope for popular forces to influence government policy becoming weaker. But the overwhelming impression that emerges is that while the Marcos regime was stronger than the previous and subsequent regimes in certain respects, it cannot be ranked as strong across the board, and it does not fit the Guillermo O'Donnell definition of bureaucratic authoritarian (hereafter called BA) regimes with which it has often been classified (O'Donnell and Schmitter 1986).

## The Working of Democratic Government, 1946–72

Why was the power of the state so weak and that of the old elite so strong in the early years of Philippine independence? The answer must be given partly in political and constitutional terms, partly in terms of the country's socioeconomic structure. The executive arm of the government was severely constrained in its capacity to provide strong or decisive government by the extreme flaccidity of the political party system. This system was based on two loosely structured, nearly identical parties, with the president virtually unable to mobilize his own party in support of his programs against a recalcitrant legislature. In addition, both houses of the Congress tended to be resistant to strong presidential leadership, being dominated throughout these early decades by members of the elite families who exercised considerable de facto power locally as well. (On the Philippine political system see Grossholtz 1964; Lande 1965; Simbulan 1966; Wurfel 1979; Doronila 1985.) The autonomy of the state was bound to be rather low in such circumstances. Its effective power was further weakened by inadequacies of the nation's bureaucratic institutions, which were organizationally ramshackle, highly politicized, and intensely personalistic in their basic loyalties. It was not a formula for strong government.

When Marcos declared martial law in September 1972, he asserted that the country's political system was in a state of crisis and that the former party-based system of government, dominated by "the old oligarchs," had proved incapable of giving the country the kind of strong government it needed to overcome its various problems. There was some degree of truth in the latter claim, but the notion of a crisis was grossly exaggerated, except insofar as he himself had stirred up an atmosphere of tension and fear over the previous three years. In fact, in terms of both its economic performance and the working of its representative institutions, the system of government seemed to operate fairly successfully throughout the first two decades of independence. The Hukbalahap insurgency of 1946–53 was reduced to insignificance by a combination of military and political measures under the legendary Magsaysay (Starner 1961). The military never posed any threat to civilian government during those years, although Marcos did, during his first term in office (1965–69) begin to politicize the armed forces' leadership and curry its personal support. The Green Revolution was launched. Economically, the country was making reasonably good progress, with GDP growth rates of around 6 percent and manufacturing industry expanding more impressively than anywhere else in Southeast Asia (albeit behind the protective barrier of an overvalued exchange rate and foreign exchange control regime until 1962 [Golay 1961; Carroll 1965]). One result of this progress was a considerable diversification of elite business interests out of land into industrial and commercial activities. At the same time, food production rose, a well-educated and skilled work force was developing, and mobility was steadily improving across the social spectrum.

On the other hand, in the late 1960s, the country began to run up against various problems to which the old political leaders, Marcos included, seemed incapable of providing solutions. A sense of popular disillusionment with the entire sociopolitical system began to develop, which Marcos blatantly exploited between 1969 and 1972 in his efforts to maintain his hold over the machinery of state and strengthen his power vis-à-vis his political opponents.

In November 1969, Marcos was reelected president at the end of his first term after a campaign marked by unprecedentedly lavish pork-barrel expenditures of government funds to ensure his victory. This precipitated both an economic crisis (resulting in an unpopular devaluation of the peso just after the election) and a political uproar: the "first-quarter storm" of student demonstrations against Marcos in early 1970. This new wave of student unrest and economic nationalism provided a raucous background for the buildup of political tensions in 1970–72. It also reflected a cluster of broader concerns that had been developing through the late 1960s. The most serious of these came from the new manufacturing firms that had grown up behind the protective barrier of exchange controls in the 1950s but were now beginning to feel the effects of being exposed to competition from imports made possible by the decontrol measure introduced in 1962. Concern was also rising about the likely effects of the ending of the Laurel-Langley Agreement in 1974, under which Philippine sugar and other commodities enjoyed preferential access to the U.S. market. This was an issue that touched on all the most sensitive nerves of nationalist sentiment. Moreover, the country's growth rate, while still remaining close to the quite creditable average annual figure of over 6 percent maintained between 1950 and 1968, was starting to decline. To be sure, those years had represented the "easy" phase of development, "based largely on the exploitation of previously unutilized natural resources and the policy of import substitution . . . [but] not accompanied by the difficult, dynamic and surely indispensable changes associated with successful development" (Hicks and McNicol 1971: 228). Productivity had been increasing rapidly in some modern-sector activities, but it was beginning to slip in others, as the extension of the land frontier, on which much of the earlier growth of production had largely depended, ran up against its natural limits in the late 1960s. Clearly, changes in economic policy were needed if the rate of GDP growth was not to decline further.

It is not surprising, therefore, that political debate in the late 1960s became intensely ideological and issue oriented for the first time since independence (Doronila 1985). The debate was still too unstructured and incoherent to provide any clear lines of political party division, however, being essentially an expression of vague discontent with the entire socioeconomic structure rather than of support for any specific program of reforms. As the debate proceeded, the "old oligarchy" and its domination of both Congress and regional economic power came increasingly to be regarded as the root cause of many of the country's ills. Another main target of criticism was "U.S. imperialism" and "neocolonialism," to which the old elite was now widely regarded as the handmaiden, because it was the prime beneficiary of the Laurel-Langley Agreement. In this atmosphere of mounting tension, a Constitutional Convention (popularly called the Con-Con) was assembled late in 1970 to discuss constitutional changes. It contributed substantially to the ideological ferment and tensions of 1971–72 since it focused attention on the failures or inadequacies of the existing political system and thus on the need for remedies. The Con-Con stimulated debate on all that was felt to be wrong with the country while arousing hopes of reform that were often naively idealistic. One of the most contentious issues on its agenda was the question of whether the constitutional restriction on the presidency to two terms should be altered. This was strongly resisted by Marcos's opponents. An alternative proposal that was more strongly supported was to switch from the congressional to the parliamentary system, a change that would in fact have suited Marcos's purposes very well, since he could then aspire to remain in power indefinitely as prime minister. In fact, the constitution promulgated under the martial law regime in 1973 did provide for a parliamentary form of government after a transition period, but Marcos continued to behave as if he were still head of a presidential regime, utilizing executive decree-making powers until 1985.

A good deal of apprehension had developed by 1971 that Marcos was determined to hold onto power after the end of his second elected term in 1973 by fair means or foul. An atmosphere of uncertainty and crisis was steadily building up, partly because of the growth of the NPA and partly because of the armed conflicts that were now developing in Mindanao between Muslim and Christian Filipinos. Most alarming of all to Marcos's opponents, however, was the unusually blatant and brutal bombing attack in September 1971 on the leaders of the opposition Liberal party during the course of an election rally at the Plaza Miranda, where Benigno Aquino, then emerging as Marcos's arch rival, was to have spoken. Marcos promptly took advantage of the opportunity to put the blame on the Communists. He suspended the writ of habeas corpus, thus heightening the sense of emergency. It matters little how far he was personally implicated in that episode, for he was able to take advantage of the sense of crisis it created to spread the belief that the times were out of joint; hence, the safety of the nation could be ensured only through his strong leadership.

## Martial Law and Authoritarian Rule, 1972–86

Marcos signed the long-expected proclamation of martial law on September 21, 1972, following an alleged ambush attack on Defense Secretary Enrile that was later admitted to have been bogus. He made as his pretext "a conspiracy to overthrow our duly constituted government by violence and subversion," essentially by the NPA, although the new wave of violence in Mindanao and Sulu was also cited (Noble 1987; May and Nemenzo 1985). All Marcos's main opponents were arrested; tight control over the press and media was established; demonstrations, rallies, and strikes were prohibited; a curfew was ordered; and the carrying of firearms in public without approval was forbidden. The combined effect of these moves was that there was almost no way in which opposition to these radical changes could be mobilized. Marcos also announced his intention to introduce various long-overdue reforms, including an immediately proclaimed land reform measure, as a means of creating a "New Society" (Abueva 1979).

By doing so, he at least won some degree of acceptance for the new regime among fence sitters who were willing to wait and see if it would live up to its promises. This did not mean that his Liberal party or radical opponents suddenly abandoned their opposition to him or that he was successful in dissipating the still widespread cynicism about his motivations or the validity of his claims about the Communist insurgency. But there was little that any of his opponents could now do about it, unless they were prepared to join the NPA and adopt the revolutionary path, which did not appear to be a promising alternative until well after 1980. So most people acquiesced. The power of the state apparatus had triumphed at last over the forces rooted in society.

For the first few years of Marcos's authoritarian rule, his regime seemed to be very successful and overwhelmingly strong, both vis-à-vis his political opponents and on the administrative and economic fronts. By the time of Benigno Aquino's assassination in August 1983, however, the regime was so seriously weakened that it was rapidly losing control over events. From then until his overthrow in February 1986, Marcos was never able to regain effective control over the economy nor reassert his political authority as forcefully as in previous years. He was merely clinging to office precariously, as the country slid downhill toward disaster.

The reasons why the Marcos regime was so strong initially and so ineffective by the end can best be seen by tracing the life cycle of the regime through four distinct phases of development (Noble 1986). The first three or four years after September 1972 could be called a "reformist" and rural-oriented phase, during which Marcos took a number of strong measures to remedy the ills he said he would eliminate when he declared martial law. During the second phase, 1976–80, that initial momentum of reform slowed down as the development emphasis shifted away from the countryside toward grandiose urban construction projects, reflecting a major change in Marcos's political and economic strategies. Elections were held in 1978 to a legislature of sorts. This is the most baffling period to explain satisfactorily, since it is not easy to pin down just why he departed from his earlier course. He may have felt that the long haul toward national development through the gradual raising of rural production by the bootstraps could be short-circuited by resort to large construction projects, financed by the foreign loans so easily available after the first oil boom. It was in this period that the seeds of later troubles were sown. The country's foreign indebtedness increased to a dangerous level, while "cronyism" (along with Imelda Marcos's influence as the free-spending minister of human settlements) became a serious problem. In the third phase, between the onset of the second oil crisis of 1979–80 and the assassination of Benigno Aquino in August 1983, oil prices and interest rates rose suddenly and unexpectedly, causing the economic situation to deteriorate sharply. Marcos still felt he was in a strong enough position vis-à-vis his political opponents to introduce further political and economic reforms, but in fact by 1983 his difficulties were multiplying fast. His power was slipping, and rumors of his declining health were stirring new hopes among his opponents. The final phase, from Aquino's assassination onward, was marked by the rapid erosion of Marcos's power in the face of massive demonstrations of popular hostility toward him, although in the end it was his own action, the calling of early presidential elections in 1986, that sparked the extraordinary events that led to his downfall later that month.

The political strategy Marcos followed during the first three years of martial law was both ruthless and skillful (Abueva 1979; Race 1975). He crushed his opponents completely, while winning over to his new regime some potentially valuable rural allies who soon acquired a strong stake in its continuance. Immediately after declaring martial law, he introduced by presidential decree a number of measures that were long overdue and generally very popular, most notably his new land reform program, confiscation of all firearms, and the disbanding of "private armies." These were all portrayed as parts of the drive toward a "New Society" by means of his "Revolution from the Center" against the "old oligarchy." Marcos seemed to be making a bid for support from the rural beneficiaries of his new policies in those early years. At the same time he relied heavily on his team of technocrats to cut through the administrative and political tangles previously obstructing the executive. Business confidence and increased investment, particularly foreign investment, were quickly stimulated, and for several years in the mid-1970s the GDP growth rate rose quite sharply (Hill 1982; Hill and Jayasuriya 1985).

Both the political and the development strategies pursued by Marcos in those early years of martial law gave considerable emphasis to the rural sector and the role of the barrios (villages) in his drive to break the power of the "old oligarchy." Rice production was stimulated by a greater extension of rural credit facilities and the use of new rice varieties, but land reform was the main plank in this development strategy. While the land reform program, confined only to corn and rice lands, had severe limitations as an instrument for breaking the power of the rural elite, it has generally been regarded as the most effective of the three postindependence attempts to tackle the tenancy problem. And there is evidence that the beneficiaries did constitute a significant source of rural support for Marcos thereafter, right down to 1986 (Kerkvliet 1977; Wurfel 1979; Fegan 1985). At the political level, too, Marcos seemed to be reaching out to the barrios, for example, through the use of *barangay* councils as instruments for mobilizing plebiscitary expressions of support on various occasions between 1973 and 1976. Much of this outward concern for the ordinary villagers, however, amounted to little more than a rhetorical flourish or a pious hope. Many, particularly the sugar and coconut producers, suffered severely under the exactions of the new sugar and coconut marketing agencies he set up in the mid-1970s under the control of two of his most notorious "cronies," Roberto Benedicto and Eduardo Cojuangco (Hawes 1987).

In the second phase of martial law between about 1976 and 1980, the reformist or technocratic momentum of the early years gave way to several new and more problematic tendencies. Corruption and cronyism became far more blatant than previously, while the power of Imelda Marcos increased substantially at the expense of the technocrats (Sicat 1984). Large urban construction projects financed with funds borrowed from abroad now replaced rural infrastructure development at the forefront of the development plan. Some of them, Imelda's in particular, were indefensibly grandiose and capital-intensive for such a poor country. Foreign banks were then awash with funds from recycled oil revenues and were eager to disburse them at low rates of interest to any government willing to borrow. Marcos proved to be a willing customer. It may well have been that the temptation to take this easier path of borrowing heavily for highly visible urban construction projects rather than the long, hard slog of raising rural productivity at the grass-roots level was the essential reason for the shift in development priorities around this time. (Such projects also generated enormous rake-offs for the Marcos family and the cronies, which was no doubt also an important consideration.) But the outcome proved later to be disastrous, for the huge increase in the country's indebtedness occurred just at the time when agricultural incomes began to fall across most of the country. The decline in rural incomes meant that over the last decade of Marcos's regime the expansion of demand for domestically produced manufactured goods, on which the success of his urban-biased development policies depended, simply did not occur (Hackenberg and Hackenberg 1987). Hence, the manufacturing sector became stalled in the early 1980s while interest rates also began to rise sharply.

Marcos also changed tack politically in these years. After 1976 he never again made use of the various plebiscitary devices he had employed in the earlier years. Instead, under pressure from the U.S. government under the Carter administration, he called for a national election in 1978 to create an Interim National Assembly (Batasang Pambansa) (Bonner 1987). The election was held under conditions so blatantly rigged that most voters abstained in protest, giving Marcos an easy victory. He became so convinced of the ease of this source of apparent legitimation that he held six other electoral exercises over the following years, likewise rigged so as to make it virtually impossible for the opposition to win. The Kilusan Bagong Lipunanan (KBL, New Society Movement) was brought into being as his vehicle for mobilizing support. It functioned not so much as an electoral party as a vast, state-controlled patronage machine, buying votes even more blatantly than the pre-1972 parties had done. Nevertheless, the changes after 1978 enabled the opposition politicians to surface again and become more active (Machado 1978; 1979). Thus, by the time the adverse effects of world economic trends began to hit the Philippines in the early 1980s, the life cycle of the regime was already entering a new phase.

The years 1980–83 were marked by the "normalization" of the political system. Martial law was abolished in 1981, and in that year a presidential election of sorts was held (which the opposition parties boycotted). While Marcos seemed to be at the peak of his power, he could not ward off the increasingly adverse effects of world economic trends. The political climate began to change, too, as signs of a deterioration in his health drew attention to the explosive issue of who would succeed Marcos if he died. A struggle for power intensified within Marcos's palace circle. On the one side was Imelda Marcos in alliance with General Fabian Ver, the new armed forces chief; on the other was the ambitious defense secretary, Juan Ponce Enrile. While this struggle had no political consequences at the time, it was symptomatic of a change in the morphology of the regime. The Marcos court was more and more preoccupied with merely hanging onto power and accumulating more and more wealth. Corruption became blatant, and a fin de siècle atmosphere of public disillusionment and cynicism began to envelop the country.

Opponents of the regime now became more active. The specter of Benigno Aquino, in spite of the fact that he had been in jail from 1972 to 1980 and was then in virtual exile in the United States, began to haunt the regime.

Meanwhile, economic conditions worsened. Commodity prices fell sharply during the world recession of the early 1980s. A crisis of business confidence was precipitated by the Dewey Dee loan scandal and the collapse of several of the largest crony firms in 1980–81. Foreign indebtedness reached fourteen billion dollars by mid-1981 and then ballooned to nearly twenty-four billion dollars by February 1983. Pressures from the World Bank and other creditors now compelled Marcos to attempt a restructuring program by means of various decontrol measures, but with only partial success. By 1983 the magic of "the Marcos miracle" was fast disappearing, and for most businessmen sheer survival had become the order of the day (Hill and Jayasuriya 1985).

Aquino's assassination on August 21, 1983, sparked off the last phase of the regime's life cycle, throwing both the economy and the political system into a tailspin, which lasted until the overthrow of Marcos in early 1986. The factions making up the opposition were still unable to agree on a common strategy to bring about his downfall, but opposition became widespread and open. The New People's Army (NPA) began to increase rapidly in both size and the extent of its operations as a steady stream of opponents of the regime opted for the revolutionary path. This new trend finally led the U.S. government to reassess its earlier policy of almost unconditional support for Marcos and put pressure upon him to liberalize or reform his regime, pressure he resisted tenaciously until late 1985.

No one of these factors alone was responsible for his downfall, however. All contributed to it. But in the end the Marcos regime simply fell apart from its own internal weaknesses. Marcos had aspired to build a strong state, but his aims grossly exceeded the government's capacity to achieve them. Initially he did strengthen the state machinery, for example, eliminating congressional interference in administrative matters and raising government revenues from a very low fraction of GDP in the late 1960s to a more respectable 13.3 percent in 1979. This was, however, no more than a mediocre level of performance by international standards. It was far less impressive than that of the NIEs. Political and socioeconomic power was simply too widely dispersed in the Philippines, and the entire governmental structure too mired in local patronage relations and corruption to be efficiently "developmentalist." The Marcos regime ended up behaving as a patronage machine writ large, a "patron state" in Doronila's terms, in place of the old elite-controlled patron-client relationships (Doronila 1985).

If any one word can be used to summarize Marcos's socioeconomic thinking and goals, it is mercantilism. He believed in a strong state as the means toward creating a stronger, more vigorous, dynamic economy. But the most striking feature of his economic performance was his profligacy in the use of public funds for both public and private purposes. As time passed, the line of distinction between them became blurred outrageously.

The innovations Marcos introduced into the machinery of government to carry out his grandiose plans were neither far-reaching nor enduring (Rosenberg 1979). Four features stand out: the prominent role he gave to "the technocrats" among his advisers in the early years of martial law, the very large increase in the public sector, the centralization of administrative control and the disbursement of public funds, and the creation of various highly influential public corporations and ministries through which the slush funds of the government were handled. In the last category were the Ministry of Human Settlements, headed by Imelda Marcos, with its huge budget allocations and licensing powers over most construction and developmental activities; the National Development Corporation; and Philsucom and Unicom, the two notorious crony corporations controlling all sugar and coconut marketing, respectively, throughout the archipelago. Twelve other large industrial conglomerates of a similar type were planned, although only three ever got started. Between 1973 and 1984, the public sector grew enormously from less than 50 to more than 260 public-utility companies, financial institutions, and other public corporations. Most of them incurred huge losses. Public revenues tripled between 1971 and 1977, then doubled again over the next six years. While initially the influence of the technocrats as the chief advocates of economic rationality in the regime was quite considerable, it diminished severely in the early 1980s, when they found themselves constantly engaged in battle with the president's wife and cronies over the latter's blatant disregard for official policies.

The development ideology proclaimed by Marcos was always more rhetoric than reality. For all his talk about building a strong Philippines and creating an efficient industrial structure capable of selling on world markets like the NIEs, the actual outcome of his policies bore very little resemblance to what was achieved in those countries. The Philippines under Marcos did not develop either the efficient private-sector light industries of Taiwan or the large-scale heavy industrial sector dominated by the *chaebol* of South Korea,[1] nor Singapore's

---

[1]One conscious attempt to imitate the chaebol was the huge Construction and Development Corporation of the Philippines, part of the Hardis holdings, but it collapsed in 1981.

unique combination of a strong public sector plus heavy reliance on foreign investors at the expense of local capital. Nor did it have much in common with Brazil's development pattern, one of the most successful in Latin America. Any notion that Marcos was really bent upon translating his expressed admiration for the South Korean and Singapore models of development into reality (by which he seems to have meant little more than tough law-and-order measures and "social discipline") simply does not stand up to close scrutiny of the facts. There was really very little of an NIE-style "powerhouse state" about the Marcos regime. It resembled more Mussolini's bombastic theater state in Italy and Franco's inefficient dictatorship in Spain.

If Marcos really had in mind to create a strong "insulated developmentalist state" along the lines of the NIEs, based on a business-state alliance with backing from his technocrats, the army, and foreign capital, the classic BA formula, he only partially succeeded (Haggard and Cheng 1987: 128–29). These groups did initially constitute the main pillars of support for his regime, along with a large part, though not all, of the traditional elite. In the beginning, both the middle classes and the business community were also generally prepared to go along. But over the years they became increasingly disillusioned by the capriciousness and arbitrariness of the regime and its denial of long-established legal and civil rights; and it was primarily their disaffection that prompted Benigno Aquino in August 1983 to return to Manila, where his assassination at the hands of armed forces personnel marked the beginning of the end for Marcos.

## The Fall of Marcos

Although Aquino's murder provoked a tremendous burst of popular emotion against Marcos, which led ultimately to his downfall, his removal was not accomplished quickly or easily. The great outpouring of anger and sympathy for Aquino expressed at his funeral and the various demonstrations in Manila during the weeks after his death were things Marcos could not suppress. And the damage done to his reputation and legitimacy, both at home and abroad, because of suspicions about his complicity, was immeasurable. The symbolism of Aquino as a martyr now became a more dangerous threat to Marcos's authority than the threat from Aquino alive had ever been (Ileto 1985). The press began to criticize the regime more uninhibitedly, and neither the president nor the army leaders could do much to curb it.

For all that, demonstrations alone could not topple Marcos directly, nor could they open up serious divisions within the ruling circle. Nor did the severe outflow of capital that occurred, nor the mounting pressures from foreign creditors, immediately undermine his position. Marcos was determined to tough it out, and, despite the rampant economic decline, he succeeded for more than two years. His opponents were too divided to present a united front against him; in fact, he was even able to make some moves back toward apparent normalcy, holding parliamentary elections (entirely rigged, in the customary way) in 1984. But two time bombs were now ticking away beneath him. One was the Agrava Commission investigation of the murder of Aquino, which was revealing evidence of complicity, if not of the president himself, at least of individuals at the highest levels of the military hierarchy. Suspicion fell particularly on General Ver, who had to stand down as armed forces chief of staff during the inquiry. The other was the rapid growth of the NPA between 1982 and 1985 from about six thousand to sixteen thousand armed men (Rosenberg 1984; Porter 1987). This was due in part to the brutalities perpetrated by the military in the course of their counterinsurgency actions and in part to a growing despair that nonrevolutionary solutions would suffice for the country's snowballing problems. Support for Marcos in the United States also was steadily eroded on both these counts.

What finally precipitated Marcos's downfall was his abrupt decision in October 1985 to call a snap presidential election early in the following year. Evidently he hoped that by winning it he would be able to stem the mounting pressure for reforms to which he was being subjected by the United States Congress and, more hesitantly, the Reagan administration. He seems to have believed that because of the continued disunity of his opponents, which consisted of Laurel's UNIDO and the loose-knit LABAN grouping centered on the Aquino family, he would have no difficulty in winning with a minimum of fraud and coercion. He turned out to be badly mistaken. A united Aquino-Laurel ticket was cobbled together, quite literally in the final hours before nominations closed and only after the personal intervention of Cardinal Jaime Sin of the Roman Catholic Church; and Corazon Aquino, the widow of the martyred Benigno, proved to be an immensely popular candidate. At first it appeared unlikely that she could defeat the amply financed Marcos electoral machine with all its local KBL branches behind it. She lacked funds and the extensive media apparatus he controlled. But she was able to make up for this by drawing huge crowds at her election rallies and generating the massive upsurge of "People's Power" that finally contributed so much to Marcos's downfall.

Marcos's second miscalculation occurred because the election attracted such intense international media scrutiny (along with foreign observers sent by the U.S. government and various others), and it was difficult to get away with the customary methods of fraud and stuffed ballot boxes. And when, several days after the polling, the computer technicians walked out of the election tally room in protest against the blatant cheating that they had witnessed, the credibility of Marcos's claim to victory was shattered. Even then, however, it was he who still held power, and despite the call by Aquino for a campaign of massive nonviolent protest against the official election count, it was not yet clear how the newly mobilized masses of Aquino's "Yellow Coalition" could proceed to remove him.

At this point two new and crucial factors came into play. One was the first open defection of senior armed forces officers against Marcos. The other was a belated but critical switch in U.S. support from Marcos to Aquino between

February 22 and 25, bringing the crisis to a point where Marcos himself finally decided that he had no options left but to step down. Serious divisions had been developing in the armed forces. One group of increasingly disaffected officers was the Reform Armed Forces Movement (RAM), who had been discussing possible political action since 1985. This consisted mainly of regular army officers from the Philippines Military Academy who had become concerned at the damage they felt was being done to the army by the large number of reservist officers ("integrees") brought in by General Ver, himself an integree (Nemenzo 1986). They gained unexpected support from a crucial quarter at the last moment, when Defense Minister Enrile and General Ramos threw in their lot with them on February 22, bringing the crisis finally to a head. The movement was inclined toward a coup of its own but decided to wait out the election results. This triggered two actions. The first was their denunciation of the election results as fraudulent. The second was to put into execution their own coup plans. When word of this got back to Ver and Marcos, they moved quickly to order the arrests of the RAM officers involved, as well as of Enrile and Ramos, who then took refuge with several hundred troops in Camp Aguinaldo, on the EDSA Boulevard. This was the first step in the dramatic but tangled chain of events of the next three days that later became known as "the miracle of EDSA." Cardinal Sin then spoke out openly against Marcos in support of the rebels, using the church's Radio Veritas to call for a massive demonstration of "People's Power" around the camp entrances. Hundreds of thousands of unarmed demonstrators, headed by nuns and schoolgirls with rosaries, poured into the streets. The tank units sent to crush the rebels were unwilling to force their way through the crowds. Over the next two days, with other army and air force units defecting progressively to the side of the rebels, Marcos came to realize that he could not launch a successful attack on the rebel headquarters.

His last remaining hope, U.S. support, now evaporated, and Marcos gave up. After having himself symbolically sworn in as president on the 24th, two hours after Corazon Aquino had been sworn in at a rival ceremony across town, Marcos allowed himself to be flown by U.S. aircraft out of Manila to Clark Air Base and then to exile in Hawaii.

To summarize, the murder of Aquino in 1983 and the subsequent withdrawal of support for Marcos by the Manila business community were critically important factors in starting the process of disintegration that the regime suffered over the next two years, but they were not sufficient to unseat him. The growing strength of the NPA and the mounting economic pressures of 1983–85 accelerated the process, but even they were not in themselves sufficient to force him out. Far more serious in the long run was the alienation of substantial elements in the church, the middle class, and the armed forces, as well as the withdrawal of U.S. support (Bonner 1987). And yet, if Marcos had not committed the egregious blunder of calling the snap election in the hope of restoring his tarnished image, events might have taken a very different course.

## The Character of the Democracy Reclaimed

Outwardly, the Aquino regime may seem to have returned to the pre-Marcos pattern of political and social order in the Philippines, but the question of how far the removal of Marcos simply put the clock back to 1972 involves complex issues. Is the old elite really back in the saddle to the same degree as it was before, or are popular forces now strong enough to check its power to some degree? Or has it changed in character since then? Have the events of February 1986 weakened or strengthened the power of the state?

Despite the widespread euphoria generated by the victory of "People's Power" over Marcos in February 1986 and the immense personal popularity of Corazon Aquino over the next several years, she did not use state power at all vigorously to restructure Philippine society, nor did she seize the historic opportunity to restructure the Philippine political system along radically new lines. Several interpretations are possible. One is that if she had institutionalized the "People's Power" mass movement that swept her into office into a new-style political party, attracting support on the basis of forward-looking issues, policies, programs, and a reformist ideology, rather than the traditional patronage-based networks of the past, the return to democracy might have resulted in a more dynamic party system and a more effective state structure. Another is that in any event the state machinery in the Philippines is not strong enough to sustain an activist and interventionist political strategy; hence, it is wiser to limit the role of government to a minimum, relying instead on markets and private enterprise to resolve the country's economic problems. The latter seems to be closer to the strategy President Aquino adopted. Consequently, the political system appears to have resumed many, though not all, of the almost laissez-faire characteristics it had before 1972. The left gained very little in substantive terms under the new regime, which came to rely less on the original "People's Power" coalition and far more heavily on support from the armed forces, the business community, and the old landowning elite families, who were again dominant in Congress.

Constitutionally, President Aquino appeared to face an initial choice, either to exercise power on the basis of the 1973 "parliamentary" constitution devised by Marcos, thereby implicitly acknowledging its legitimacy and having to face a hostile KBL majority in the National Assembly, or to declare a "revolutionary" constitution and call upon emergency powers to push through a vigorous reform program (Turner 1987). Her instinctive caution and conservatism made her disinclined to take either course. Instead, she disavowed the 1973 constitution, choosing to govern by decree until a new constitution could be drafted and ratified, but did not take this opportunity to advance serious reforms. The constitutional commission held public hearings throughout mid-1986 before recommending a return to bicameral congressional arrangements very similar to those under the 1935 Constitution. The constitution was ratified by a 77 percent majority in a national plebiscite in February 1987. Soon after that, congressional elections were held. The loose pro-Aquino coalition of candidates won all but two seats in the Senate and about 70 percent of the seats in the lower house. The president then surrendered her emergency powers and proceeded to govern in accordance with the new constitution. Since that time, attention became focused increasingly upon the ambitions and political strategies of the would-be presidential hopefuls in the Congress, who were looking toward the 1992 elections, almost as much as upon the president herself, while the legislative arm of government again became an independent agency with which the president had to share power as in the pre-Marcos era.

The constraints upon President Aquino's freedom of maneuver after she assumed power in early 1986 were difficult ones. She had to take account of the large numbers of well-entrenched Marcos loyalists in the armed forces and throughout the country, most of the latter being KBL leaders and local governors with strong, patronage-based followings, and she could not afford to antagonize the armed forces' leadership by leaning too far to the left in her efforts to induce the NPA to agree to enter into cease-fire negotiations, which many of her "Yellow Coalition" supporters of February 1986 were then urging. That was presumably why she opted against the alternative course of capitalizing on her immense popularity to build up a strong center-left political force. If she had done so, she might have brought about a major realignment of political forces in the Philippines. By declining to take that path, and then associating herself only in a very indirect way with LABAN, the political party of her main supporters in the 1987 election campaign, she allowed something rather similar to the pre-1972 pattern of highly personalistic parties and electioneering styles to reemerge. LABAN, a loose coalition of half a dozen groups, represented the pro-Aquino forces and had the backing of the government. Opposing the government was a ragtag array of former KBL and UNIDO elements and old Nacionalistas calling themselves the Grand Alliance for Democracy (Robson 1987). A third force, the left-wing Alliance for New Politics, which was made up of the left-wing elements that had boycotted the 1986 election and thus had not been an integral part of Aquino's "Yellow Coalition," was critical of both, but primarily opposed to the right-wing forces. It won insufficient support, however, to gain any Senate or House seats and may prove to have been no more than a transient phenomenon.

Aquino was similarly disinclined to use her immense popularity in pursuit of an activist and reformist socio-economic program. If she had been a different sort of person and had chosen to follow a more radical path, the overall political outcome in the Philippines in 1987–88 might subsequently have been very different. It was not something preordained by broad structural forces so much as a matter of the choices she made between various options. Her handling of the land reform issue is revealing in this respect, for it shows that she not been willing to invoke the political resources of the presidency and the state to resolve it at the expense of the landowners. She probably could have done so with impunity in the aftermath of the "People's Power" revolution of 1986, had she so chosen. Although she initially seemed willing to respond to the widespread calls for energetic government action to complete the implementation of the Marcos 1972 land reform regulations and to carry them further, she was not prepared to use her extraordinary decree-making powers to do that before the election of a new Congress in 1987, after which the old landowners were bound to have an effective veto power. While she did issue a land reform proclamation in the last days before the Congress met soon after the May 1987 elections, various key provisions were left to be determined by that body, which subsequently emasculated the regulations, very much as it had done on previous occasions before 1972 (Tadem 1988). There is little evidence in all this of any inclination on her part to use state power vigorously to remedy social ills, even to the extent that Marcos had purported to do in his early years.

Her economic strategy was rather to back away generally from the interventionism of the Marcos era. The crony corporations and their monopolies over sugar, coconut, grain, and other product-marketing arrangements were dismantled, and new fields of economic activity were opened up. The market was made more competitive, and, although the Aquino regime still has a long way to go in abolishing all the structures of protection and subsidy it inherited from its predecessors, it made significant progress. More important, the technocrats among its chief policy makers were not frustrated by cronies to the extent their counterparts under Marcos were. So the economy began picking up momentum, attaining a 6 percent growth rate in 1987–88 in sharp contrast to the 11 percent cumulative decline in the preceding four years. The inflation rate, which had been 50 percent in 1984, fell to less than 4 percent in 1987, while interest rates were significantly lowered (stimulating an urban construction boom in 1987), and the depreciating peso stabilized. Significant tax reforms were introduced and revenue collection improved. Free marketeers might argue that it was essentially because the Aquino government chose to rely on the market mechanism and did not try to play the "strong government" role that Marcos attempted unsuccessfully that this recovery was brought about so dramatically. On the other hand, it is less clear how far the benefits of this initial spurt of rapid growth percolated down to the poorer rural villagers and urban workers in terms of generally increased employment or rising wages (except in a few particular places), or of any overall recovery from the fall in living standards that occurred in the later Marcos years—though decline in support for the NPA may be a sign that socioeconomic conditions were at least no longer deteriorating.

In her handling of relations with the NPA on the one hand and the armed forces leadership on the other, President Aquino moved from a slightly left-of-center position in early 1986 steadily toward the right, taking an increasingly tough line against the insurgents as time passed. At first, she responded positively to the various calls being made for a policy of national reconciliation and negotiations with the NPA (as also with the other armed insurgency by the Muslim MNLF in the southern provinces). The military were unhappy with this policy. They felt that the cease-fire needed to get negotiations started was beneficial only to the NPA, not to the government forces, but the president was able to get her way on this matter, and in late 1986 a truce was agreed upon so that negotiations toward a more enduring cease-fire could begin. These talks occurred during the lead-up to the constitutional plebiscite of February 1987. But the "Mendiola Bridge massacre" of leftist peasant group leaders by army units, only a few days before the plebiscite, led the NPA to call off further talks, and thereafter there was no return to a more conciliatory policy on the president's part (Porter 1987). Both sides became more unyielding. Throughout 1987 the NPA developed a new and alarming strategy of selective assassinations by "sparrow units" in urban areas, directed largely against armed forces personnel, often in retaliation for their "provocations." This was countered by the growth of various anti-Communist vigilante groups, often extremely right wing and almost entirely outside the control of the armed forces, some of which were in fact quite successful in giving NPA units a hard time in various parts of the country. By late 1988 the situation was becoming disadvantageous to the NPA. As it became aware of the damage being done to the organization's popular support by the sparrow units, it gradually scaled down those activities almost to nothing. In fact, the relative quiescence of the NPA has been interpreted in some quarters as a sign that it has lost a lot of the momentum it was building up in the later Marcos years and, at least for the moment, was at a strategic impasse (Porter 1987).

The main threat to the survival of the Aquino government throughout the years 1986–88 came, in fact, not so much from the NPA insurgents of the left as from within the military itself. Initially, this was due in large part to the actions of Defense Minister Enrile, who had been irked by the fact that the spoils of victory in the events of February 1986 went not to himself, despite the key role he played at one stage in precipitating military units to rebel against Marcos, but to Aquino, who had become the popular favorite. With his considerable personal and factional support within the armed forces, former KBL elements, and some Marcos loyalists, as well as in parts of his own Ilocano-speaking region, Enrile played his hand remorselessly to weaken Aquino's position. He condoned acts of outright disloyalty, such as the Manila Hotel incident in July 1986 and the acts of the RAM leaders who had turned against Aquino and were now plotting against her. Finally, she summoned up the courage to dismiss Enrile and replace him with General Ramos, who subsequently ensured more solid army support for her. But the RAM activists remained a continuing source of concern, culminating in a major coup attempt by Lieutenant Colonel Gregorio (Gringo) Honasan in August 1987, which came perilously close to success and cost many lives. That episode marked something of a watershed, for the president moved much more decisively in the following months to reassert her authority. She reshuffled her cabinet to get rid of several ministers who were distrusted by the army leadership and generally put an end to her earlier mild flirtation with the left. The personal influence of Ramos also increased considerably, and he began to enter into considerations for the presidency in 1992. Thus, over the course of 1987–88, the political center of gravity seemed to shift perceptibly toward the right, back toward the 1960s' pattern of wheeling and dealing in Congress, with strident rhetoric and attitudinizing over the U.S. bases displacing social and economic issues from the policy agenda.

The relative balance of power between the state and civil society also had now become quite different from that of the Marcos years. The military had become a far more important actor on the political stage, although it was still the president herself who finally called the shots on most issues (Hernandez 1985). The repressive powers of the state were still very much in use against individuals sub rosa by the armed forces, but they were not being utilized to constrain society-based movements and organizations to anything like the degree they were under Marcos. The corruption and abuses of the bureaucratic machinery of the Marcos era had been cleaned up in large part, and the government was in many respects more effective, for example, in the tax collection system, than in Marcos's final years. The huge crony empires established under Marcos and the local KBL patronage machines had been dismantled. Broadly speaking, however, the state had become much weaker, and various society-based forces or organizations a good deal stronger. The old landed families had achieved some degree of veto power, through their dominance of Congress, on issues like land reform, but to a lesser degree than in the pre-Marcos years. At the same time the restoration of civil rights in early 1986 had given the left more "democratic space" in which to operate. Above all, the Aquino government had depended at crucial moments upon popular support as part of its raison d'être in a way that Marcos never did.

## The Impact of Economic Growth

Throughout this analysis we have stressed the political dynamics behind the two major regime changes in the Philippines since 1946, without much reference to the immediate impact of long-term socioeconomic trends. This is not because there was little growth.

As table 4.2 shows, during the first twenty-six years of postindependence democratic government (1946–72) when the political regime was for the most part stable and unchallenged (after surviving the early years of the Hukbalahap rebellion from 1949 to 1953), the country experienced one of the highest rates of growth in Southeast or East Asia. It averaged over 6 percent per annum in the 1950s, and it dropped slightly to about 5 percent in the 1960s as it began to run up against the limits of available arable land, untapped forest resources, and domestic markets. It was at this time that the Philippines began to fall behind the other ASEAN nations in the growth stakes, although still maintaining quite a creditable rate overall.

In the early years of the martial law regime, the rate of growth picked up

Table 4.2

**Average Annual GDP Growth Rates of ASEAN Countries at Constant Prices, 1950–85 (percent)**

|  | 1950–60 | 1960–65 | 1965–70 | 1970–75 | 1975–80 | 1980–85 |
|---|---|---|---|---|---|---|
| Philippines | 6.1 | 5.21 | 5.09 | 6.03 | 6.27 | –0.5 |
| Indonesia | 3.2 | 2.01 | 7.02 | 7.94 | 7.91 | 3.5 |
| Thailand | 6.3 | 7.24 | 9.14 | 6.27 | 7.55 | 5.1 |
| Malaysia | 4.7 | 6.87 | 6.09 | 7.12 | 8.59 | 5.5 |
| Singapore | 5.5 | 5.75 | 12.84 | 9.51 | 8.74 | 6.5 |
| Middle-income developing countries (average) | 5.3 | 6.3 |  | 5.5 |  |  |

*Source:* World Bank 1983; Riedel 1988.

slightly, attaining a 1970–80 average of 6.2 percent, about the same as the pre-1965 rate. This was due partly to a sharp rise in foreign investment in 1973–74, then to high levels of government borrowing from foreign banks. In the last five years of the Marcos regime, however, the rate of growth plummeted sharply. The GDP declined by over 5 percent annually in 1984–85. The causes are to be found initially in the adverse terms of trade and rising interest rates. Although the decline was partly due to the deteriorating international environment, it cannot be attributed solely to that, since various other Third World countries, notably Thailand, managed to lift their performance during those difficult years. It was due in far greater part to the profligacy and poorly conceived economic priorities of the Marcos government itself, as unresolved battles raged over the execution of government policies between the "cronies" (including Imelda Marcos) and the "technocrats," and to the economic crisis and capital flight brought about by the assassination of Benigno Aquino. Since the overthrow of Marcos and the advent of the Aquino government in February 1986, the economy has recovered quite remarkably, reaching an average growth rate of about 6 percent in 1987–88, despite continuing political uncertainties and various coup attempts.

That certain economic changes were set in motion by the economy's growth seems also undeniable. The most important of them can be summarized broadly. First, there has been a considerable increase in the size of the urban middle class, mainly in Manila, and a great expansion of education. Second, the old landowning elite has strengthened its base, diversifying its investments out of land into commercial and industrial ventures, urban real estate, and finance. Third, some moderate structural changes in the economy and work force have occurred as the manufacturing and service sectors have expanded, and there has been a shift

from subsistence toward commercial farming generally, resulting in the proletar-
ianization of much of the rural population and an increase in landlessness.
Fourth, a continuing erosion of patron-client relationships in the rural areas has
been evident, along with sharper rural social stratification. But the industrial
proletariat has remained very small in size and strength. The middle ranks of
urban and rural society may have been growing in both size and political influence, but not enough to have had much significant impact on overall power
relations. There has been in fact little change in the basic social pattern of
domination of the economy, society, and political system by a landowning oligarchy. No doubt they did help generate unfulfilled demands that contributed to
the political unrest that Marcos exploited. This may also help explain why so
many members of the middle classes in the beginning tacitly accepted or even
welcomed martial law, hoping that the country's unresolved problems would
now be tackled more vigorously. And surely Doronila (1985: 99) is correct in
thinking that the gradual transformation of the old-style patron-client relations
into a "paternalistic state authority" that accompanied the underlying economic
changes does help to explain the growth of executive power. One may also
recognize that the slowing down of growth in the 1969–72 period did create
concerns, but Marcos's authoritarianism was hardly propelled by that development—nor by a conflict between mounting economic nationalism and foreign
(American) capital as suggested by Stauffer (1979). Nor did the economic decline in the last four years of his presidency compel his flight, although it did
indeed weaken his position. Similarly, it would be difficult to advance a persuasive argument that the overthrow of Marcos owed much to the growing strength
of the urban middle classes even though their withdrawal of support for him
between 1983 and 1985 was indeed one among many factors that led to his
downfall; nor can it be demonstrated that changes in the character of the elite, let
alone a "revolutionary" upsurge of support for the NPA from impoverished
peasants, were directly responsible for it. All of these phenomena would have to
be ranked as of relatively slight causal significance among the various factors
leading to Marcos's downfall.

Thus, while long-term social changes induced by or accompanying economic
growth played a part in both the seizure of autocratic power by Marcos in 1972
and his overthrow in 1986, the changes were too small for their influence to have
been more than slight and indirect. They could hardly be regarded as precipitating factors directly responsible for bringing about either crisis. The main precipitating factors were political and arose out of the intra-elite power struggles going
on in both 1971–72 and 1983–85. The reasons why growth has had only a weak
impact on this polity would not seem to be hard to find. While the economy was
expanding, so was the population. With the highest fertility rate in the region, the
Filipino people's per capita income has remained one of the lowest in the region,
with the result that relatively little mobilization of Philippine society has taken
place.

What of the future? Will the Ramos regime that came to power in the spring of 1992 be better able to improve the "fit" between the forces of society and the apparatus of the state than was Aquino, Marcos, or their predecessors? Is democracy now here to stay? This remains to be seen, but the long-term prognosis is not very promising. Much depends on the new regime's handling of the entrenched elite. While the economic basis of the elite's power and influence has been shifting from land toward modern-sector economic activities, the political basis is still the localized power that the elite derives from extensive landownership. Industrialization and modernization have not yet gone far enough to break that nexus. Marcos interrupted it for a few years, setting up the KBL and the crony empires in its place, but he did not really destroy the "old oligarchy" as he threatened to do, and he failed to create a really strong state apparatus as a counterpoise to it, as the other strong leaders around the region have done. So the return to democracy under the Aquino regime represented something of a triumph—at least temporarily—of the old elite within that regime. But in the long run, the stability of democracy will depend largely on the handling of the macroeconomic consequences of economic growth, most of which have yet to be felt.

# 5

# Thailand: Liberalization Without Democracy

## Chai-Anan Samudavanija and Sukhumbhand Paribatra

LITTLE is known about government and administration in the early Bangkok period (1782–1873), although in the later years Thailand came in closer touch with the modern world through its relationships with various European powers. In 1855 Thailand signed its first treaty with Britain, known as the Bowring Treaty. After that, several treaties were made with other European powers. These foreign treaties had a tremendous impact on the Thai economy because they released commerce and destroyed monopolies. Before 1855, Thailand's fiscal autonomy was unimpaired, but the Bowring Treaty imposed a ceiling of 3 percent on import duties and also established export taxes on almost all major and minor products.

## An Economic Overview

Economic historians use the signing of the Bowring Treaty as the beginning of the modern Thai political economy. The first century after 1855 was marked by a very slow growth of the GDP, estimated to have averaged between 1.3 and 2.2 percent per annum. Only after World War II did the Thai economy begin to grow at a faster rate (Sompop 1988). The slow growth of the economy before World War II was due to the traditional financial conservatism of the state and a low level of government spending, which characterized the fiscal policy pursued by both monarchical and constitutional governments. Government spending on education and agriculture from 1892 to 1931, for example, was never more than 5 percent of total expenditures, compared with that on defense and interior, each of which received sizable shares of about 20 percent annually (Chai-Anan 1971: 38). After 1932, the new constitutional regime promised to bring happiness, welfare, and prosperity to the people by "creating jobs for all people" and to support the extension of education. By 1935 the Ministry of Education was receiving about 12 percent of the national budget, "nearly double what it had been allocated in the last year of the absolute monarchy (Ingram 1954: 380). The ministries of Defense and Interior, however, continued to get the largest share of the national budget.

From 1948 to 1955, the pattern of government expenditure changed. Infrastructural services were given tremendous increases, the 1956 value added to the infrastructure and social overhead services being ten times as large as that in 1948 (Chattip 1970: 33). This made a great impact on the economy since it increased the ratio of capital expenditure to total government expenditures from 13 percent during 1935–39 to 30 percent in 1953. Between 1954 and 1958, for example, 3,629 kilometers were added to the national highways, making the total length of national highways 8,191 kilometers in 1958 (International Bank for Reconstruction and Development [IBRD] 1959). Although this changing pattern of government expenditures gave the Thai economy a new dimension, economic growth before the First National Economic Development Plan (1961–66) was relatively low, compared to the period under the First Plan, due to a low level of national saving (Sompop 1987).

Economic growth in Thailand, therefore, may be said to have begun during the 1960s, when the average growth rate of GDP was nearly 8 percent. During the 1970s, economic growth was sustained at 6–7 percent, and in the first half of the 1980s at 5 percent, even though during this latter period the world economy was undergoing a big recession. Hence, since 1961, in terms of growth, the Thai economy has performed well relative to most countries of the Third World, despite major disruptions brought about by the first and second oil crises in 1972–73 and 1979–80, respectively (table 5.1).

During this process of economic growth, the structure of production was also transformed. The agricultural sector, the mainstay of the Thai economy, grew at lower rates than other sectors, especially during the 1975–83 period (table 5.2). As a result, the share of agricultural production in the country's total GDP dropped dramatically from some 40 percent in 1960 to just over 23 percent in 1985. At the same time, the manufacturing sector, with a much higher growth rate, saw its share of GDP increase from 12 percent in 1960 to 21 percent in 1985. This increase, together with the development of the oil and gas sector, boosted the industrial production share of GDP in 1985 to 29 percent. The service sector has also steadily expanded, with its share amounting in 1985 to over 47 percent.

Although agriculture has accounted for a declining share of GDP over the last three decades, the agricultural sector has by no means been static. While the share of crops in agricultural production in the 1980s remained at 70 percent as in the 1960s, a good deal of diversification has taken place (table 5.3). "New" cash crops such as maize, sugar cane, cassava, and tapioca, have expanded rapidly, thus lessening the country's traditional dependence on rice and rubber, particularly for export earnings (*1987 Year-End Economic Review* 1987: 32–34).

Table 5.1

**Average Annual Growth Rates of GDP by Sector in Thailand, 1960–85 (percent per annum–constant prices)**

|               | 1960–70 | 1970–75 | 1975–80 | 1980–85 |
|---------------|---------|---------|---------|---------|
| Agriculture   | 5.5     | 5.1     | 3.2     | 3.9     |
| Crop          | 5.0     | 5.1     | 3.5     | 4.3     |
| Industry      | 11.0    | 7.1     | 11.4    | 5.0     |
| Manufacturing | 10.8    | 9.5     | 10.5    | 5.4     |
| Construction  | 10.0    | -0.4    | 14.3    | 1.4     |
| Service       | 8.5     | 6.7     | 7.9     | 6.2     |
| GDP           | 7.9     | 6.3     | 7.6     | 5.3     |

*Source:* Thailand NESDB.

The manufacturing sector expanded mainly to satisfy the domestic demand especially during the 1960s and 1970s, encouraged by the government policy of import substitution implemented during this period. The major import-substituting industries were textiles, construction materials, and consumer products in chemical and engineering industries. Another group of industries was resource-based and processed commodities such as paddy, sugar cane, timber, rubber, and tin into semifinished products. In the 1980s, however, manufactured goods began to play an increasingly important part in the country's drive to expand exports, their share of total exports being raised from 1.4 percent in 1960 and 18.7 percent in 1972 to 39.7 percent in 1985 (Thailand Board of Trade). Major manufactured exports now include textiles and garments, gems and jewelry, integrated circuits, footwear, plastic products, furniture, ball bearings, steel pipes and fittings, and artificial flowers (*1987 Year-End Economic Review 1987*: 13).

The oil and gas and lignite sector was a late starter but has made good progress. After the second oil shock the government accelerated the effort to replace imported energy with domestically produced oil and gas, and in 1985, 40 percent of Thailand's modern energy requirement, representing 2.4 percent of GDP, was produced at home (Thailand National Economic and Social Development Board [NESDB]). An attempt now is being made to promote more purposefully the country's petrochemical industry, especially through the initiation and expansion of the Eastern Seaboard Project ("The Petrochemical Industry in ASEAN" 1988).

During the last nearly three decades the Thai economy also has been increasingly linked with the global economic system. Where trade is concerned, in the 1970s export growth rates substantially exceeded GDP growth rates (table 5.4), and, as pointed out above, exports now include a very high proportion of manufactured products. Thailand's major trading partners are Japan (20.8 percent of total trade in 1985) and the United States (14.9 percent), with others' shares being less than 10 percent

Table 5.2

**Share of GDP by Sector in Thailand (percent)**

|  | 1960 | 1970 | 1975 | 1980 | 1985 |
|---|---|---|---|---|---|
| Agriculture | 40.2 | 32.2 | 30.5 | 24.9 | 23.2 |
| Crop | 31.2 | 23.7 | 22.4 | 18.5 | 17.6 |
| Industry | 18.3 | 24.1 | 25.0 | 29.9 | 29.4 |
| Manufacturing | 11.9 | 15.5 | 18.1 | 20.7 | 20.8 |
| Construction | 7.2 | 5.8 | 4.2 | 5.7 | 4.7 |
| Service | 41.5 | 43.7 | 44.5 | 45.3 | 47.4 |
| GDP | 100.0 | 100.0 | 100.0 | 100.0 | 100.0 |

*Source:* Thailand NESDB.

(Thailand Department of Business Economics). Where foreign investment is concerned, the country's links with the global capital system have also increased dramatically. Foreign investors are now involved in enterprises totaling over 23 billion Baht in registered capital, which is distributed over a range of key sectors, most notably banking and finance, commerce, services, construction and textiles ("Foreign Investments in Thai Firms" 1987: 19; *1987 Year-End Economic Review* 1987: 3). Thailand's major investment partners are Japan (nearly 3 billion Baht in registered capital), the United States (nearly 2 billion Baht), Taiwan (1 billion Baht), and the United Kingdom, Hong Kong, and Singapore (0.7, 0.6, and 0.5 billion Baht, respectively) (Thailand Board of Investment).

Economic growth beyond doubt has contributed to a higher level of income and a higher standard of living for the Thai people. Thailand's population has more than doubled to number now more than fifty million. Rapid urbanization has taken place. In 1960 just over 10 percent of Thais lived in cities and towns, but by 1983 the percentage had increased to nearly 25 percent. The level of education also has risen fast, the percentage of Thailand's population enrolled for higher education increasing from 2 percent in 1960 to nearly 15 percent in the early 1980s (Thailand, NESDB). One estimate was that by 1991 universities alone would have one million students (*Bangkok Post*, February 13, 1987: 3). But it is also clear that the fruits of development have been unevenly distributed, with the urban-business-industrial sector in particular gaining by far the larger portion. The facts are telling. In 1976 the average annual income of those working in the industrial, commercial, and service sectors, located mostly in or around Bangkok, was 45,215 Baht, 70,339 Baht, and 32,665 Baht, respectively, while that of farmers was only 7,113 Baht. In 1983 the average personal income of people resident in Bangkok, whose population constitutes some 10 percent of the country's total, was 7.0, 4.4, 3.6, and 2.1 times more than those of people living in the northeastern, northern, southern, and western regions, respectively (Thailand, NESDB; Medhi 1987). Development efforts evidently have been biased against the agricultural sector. Furthermore, government measures, far from being able

Table 5.3

**Agricultural Diversification in Thailand, 1972–85 (constant prices)**

|                          | 1972  | 1978  | 1983  | 1985  |
|--------------------------|-------|-------|-------|-------|
| Average share of all crops in agriculture | 72.0  | 73.9  | 76.0  | 75.9  |
| Rice                     | 42.9  | 39.9  | 38.6  | 38.1  |
| Rubber                   | 4.3   | 4.0   | 4.5   | 4.8   |
| Maize                    | 3.7   | 5.4   | 5.7   | 7.1   |
| Sugar cane               | 4.3   | 5.9   | 7.5   | 8.2   |
| Cassava                  | 4.4   | 9.9   | 10.7  | 10.7  |
| Other crops              | 40.5  | 44.9  | 33.1  | 31.2  |
| All crops                | 100.0 | 100.0 | 100.0 | 100.0 |

*Source*: Thailand NESDB.

to reverse the trend, have served to accentuate it. The public revenue system has tended to be somewhat regressive and thus to make income distribution more uneven. At the same time the public expenditure system has rendered benefits to higher-income, urban families rather than lower-income, rural families (Twatchai and Chaiyawat 1983: 87–90; *Siam Rath,* June 11, 1988: 1).

The effects can be seen in the rapid expansion of the middle class, mainly in but not confined to Bangkok. Numbering only 178,000 in 1960 and 284,000 in 1970, Bangkok's middle class has increased to 1,800,000 in 1986 or the equivalent of 31 percent of the city's population. A similar, but less dramatic, trend has also taken place in other urban centers, where the provincial middle class constituted some 19 percent of the population in 1986 (table 5.5). The middle class now represents 7.5 percent of total employed persons while the working class and farmers make up 23.5 percent and 57.6 percent, respectively (Thailand Labour Research Branch). Although obviously a relatively heterogeneous group, those belonging to the "new" Thai middle class share a number of common characteristics. They are young (mostly in the 25–35 age group); highly educated (bachelor's degrees); exposed to "modern," Western-influenced culture; and employed in the professions as executive, managerial, administrative, or technical personnel. They have small families with a working spouse and a two-bedroom house in either government or private housing estates; like to travel, read, and tune in to radio and television programs, especially those on current affairs; and, if they do not own one already, aspire to have a car and a credit card (*Deemar Media Index,* 1986).

There has been also a rapid expansion of "big business enterprises," that is, business concerns with assets of more than 500 million Baht. According to a 1979 study, the value of capital owned by these amounted to nearly 74 percent of the nation's product that year (Krirkiat 1983: 21). Nor are such enterprises limited to heavy industrial, construction, and manufacturing sectors; they are prominent also in such areas as agriculture, where a giant Thai agroindustrial firm, the

Table 5.4

**The Role of Foreign Trade in Thailand (million Baht)**

|                          | 1962   | 1972   | 1978     | 1983    | 1985    |
|--------------------------|--------|--------|----------|---------|---------|
| Exports, f.o.b.          | 9,497  | 21,750 | 82,251   | 145,076 | 191,710 |
| Imports, c.i.f.          | 11,149 | 30,635 | 109,956  | 234,279 | 253,340 |
| Trade balance            | −1,652 | −8,885 | −27,705  | −89,203 | −61,630 |
| Exports/GDP (%)          | 14.6   | 13.5   | 17.5     | 15.7    | 18.3    |
| Imports/GDP (%)          | 17.1   | 18.9   | 23.4     | 25.4    | 24.2    |
| Exports + Imports/GDP (%)| 31.7   | 32.4   | 40.9     | 41.1    | 42.5    |

*Source:* Thailand NESDB and Bank of Thailand.

Charoen Pokphand Group, has become a multinational company with a turnover of two billion U.S. dollars expected in 1988 (Paisal 1988: 58–59).

In contradistinction to the "successes" of big business and the middle class, there remain many "have-nots," particularly in rural areas, who have been "left behind." Although the poverty problem has been alleviated somewhat and Thailand is a land of plenty where starvation and malnutrition are relatively rare, many people, especially in the rural areas, still live below the poverty line (table 5.6). Moreover, the prospects for improvement do not seem bright. First of all, although Thai farmers have their own land and only 18 percent of the total farming households rent the planted area, the concentration of landholding is relatively high, with 6 percent of landowners accounting for 31 percent of total landholding and 69 percent of landowners possessing less than 20 *rai* (2.5 *rai* = 1 acre) (Thailand, NESDB). Second, off-farm employment opportunities are limited, as reflected in the facts that Thailand's agricultural labor force has remained around 70 percent of the total employment (Thailand, National Statistical Office) and that unemployment has rapidly increased since the early 1970s (table 5.7).

In sum, the overall picture of Thailand is that of a dynamic country that has been able to take advantage of the growth of the world economy and at the same time to cushion itself from the worst impacts of the vicissitudes arising therein, but also a country faced with problems of equity and distribution, of poverty and lack of opportunities for advancement for many of its own people. The question is: what have been the political implications and consequences of this process and this degree of economic growth?

## A Political Overview

Between 1932 and 1973, the Thai political system was what Fred W. Riggs appropriately calls a "bureaucratic polity" (Riggs 1966; Chai-Anan 1989). In 1932 a group of junior military and civilian officials overthrew the absolute monarchy and adopted a formal constitutional democracy as the system of government. But real democracy did not emerge, partly because the extent of popular interest in the revolution was

Table 5.5

**Class Composition of the Thai Population in 1986 (percent)**

| Social status | Bangkok | Provincial towns | Rural |
|---|---|---|---|
| Upper class | 16 | 18 | 12 |
| Middle class | 31 | 19 | 13 |
| Lower class | 53 | 63 | 75 |
| Total | 100 | 100 | 100 |

*Source:* Thailand LRB.
*Notes:* Bangkok: Upper class = family monthly income of 15,000 baht or over.
       Middle class = family monthly income of 8,000–14,999 baht.
       Lower class = family monthly income of 7,999 baht or below.
   Provincial town: Upper class = family monthly income of 10,000 baht or over.
       Middle class = family monthly income of 6,000–14,999 baht.
       Lower class = family monthly income of 5,999 baht or below.
   Rural: Upper class = family monthly income of 4,000 baht or over.
       Middle class = family monthly income of 3,0003,999 baht.
       Lower class = family monthly income of 2,999 baht or below.
   Per capita income in 1986 = 16,091 baht.

limited, and more importantly because the "revolutionaries," the so-called Promoters, were reluctant to relinquish the reins of authority. Thus, bureaucrats replaced princes and nobles as the dominant political group monopolizing the power of the state; and constitutionalism, instead of providing general and neutral rules of the game to regulate participation and competition or guaranteeing real and meaningful popular political participation, became a means for the rulers to justify and facilitate their rule. The aspirations and activities of extrabureaucratic groups were kept stifled. Politics became, as David Wilson aptly puts it, "a matter of competition between bureaucratic cliques for the benefit of the government. In this competition the army—the best organized, most concentrated, and most powerful of the branches of the bureaucracy—[came] out on top" (Wilson 1962: 277). Military coups d'état, of which there were eleven between 1932 and 1973, became an institutionalized means for political leaders to alternate in power and at the same time to keep popular participatory political institutions under control. What took place during most of this period was not only a narrow-based military dictatorship, but also a vicious cycle of politics, whereby military leaders would stage a coup to abrogate the constitution in force, reintroduce participatory institutions of some kind, try but fail to keep control of such institutions, again stage a coup to avert a political crisis, real or imagined, and thus "safeguard the nation's security." Frequent military interventions, furthermore, served to interrupt the development of key participatory institutions, particularly parliament and parties. Significantly, since 1932 only four parliaments completed their terms; the rest were disrupted by coups d'état. Political parties, when allowed to function, never evolved beyond being groupings of individuals or networks of patrons and clients, which had no programs linking them to the masses at the grass roots.

Table 5.6

**Percentage of Households under Poverty Line by Region in Thailand, 1976**

| Region | Percent |
|---|---|
| North | |
| Urban | 24 |
| Rural | 24 |
| Central | |
| Urban | 21 |
| Rural | 13 |
| Northeast | |
| Urban | 33 |
| Rural | 46 |
| South | |
| Urban | 32 |
| Rural | 31 |
| Bangkok Metropolis | 12 |

*Source:* Smith 1980.

Other voluntary participatory institutions were also closely controlled, most notably labor unions.

One of the main reasons why the Thai military was able to retain its political dominance for so long was its organizational attributes. One attribute was its knowledge and monopoly, or at least virtual monopoly of the instruments of violence. Another attribute was institutional cohesion. Although intramilitary conflicts frequently occurred and, as pointed out above, constituted the substance of Thai politics in this period, the military enjoyed a high esprit de corps and a consensus on major issues, most notably the desirability of continued military supremacy. As in the case of other modern military organizations, this spirit was forged by a common recruitment, training, selection, and promotion process, seen to be based upon merit and quality of service, that is, professional criteria; by the disciplines of a tight, hierarchical organization, calling for respect, deference, loyalty to superiors, and, where such was lacking, swift punishment; and by the ease and frequency of professional contacts. In the case of the Thai military, this esprit de corps was strengthened by old-boy ties among graduates of the same classes at the armed forces preparatory schools, the military academies, and the National Defense College. It was strengthened also by specific common service experiences, for example, the 1932 coup, the Korean war, and the Vietnam war; and by intermarriages and memberships on the same corporate boards.

During these four decades, the Thai military developed common perspectives on politics and security, a fact that both reflected and reinforced its institutional cohesion. Security came to be defined in terms of regime-maintenance, and all types of dissent, particularly communism, were seen to be a security threat. The military's professional role was given a wide interpretation. Officers believed

Table 5.7

**Labor Force and Unemployment in Thailand, 1971–84 (persons)**

| Year | Unemployed | Labor force | Percent of unemployed |
|------|-----------|-------------|-----------------------|
| 1971 | 35,280 | 17,493,761 | 0.20 |
| 1972 | 85,470 | 17,151,990 | 0.50 |
| 1973 | 73,890 | 17,499,995 | 0.42 |
| 1974 | 72,500 | 17,981,692 | 0.40 |
| 1975 | 73,600 | 19,155,441 | 0.38 |
| 1976 | 154,630 | 19,953,044 | 0.77 |
| 1977 | 258,300 | 21,198,300 | 1.22 |
| 1978 | 226,600 | 22,276,973 | 1.02 |
| 1979 | 240,000 | 22,191,874 | 1.08 |
| 1980 | 265,200 | 23,013,370 | 1.15 |
| 1981 | 263,500 | 24,579,400 | 1.07 |
| 1982 | 1,058,500 | 25,739,800 | 4.11 |
| 1983 | 665,000 | 25,849,300 | 2.57 |
| 1984 | 1,563,500 | 26,402,700 | 5.92 |

*Source:* Thailand, NESDB and NSO.

strongly that their supreme duty was to maintain order, safeguard the key national institutions, and administer the nation's progress. Politics, to them, was a "game" played only by politicians and could bring about instability, disorder, obstructions to the path of progress, and consequently dangers to the society at large. On the other hand, they believed that their own interventions in politics, whether by force or otherwise, were not political actions per se, but preemptive, manipulative, corrective, supportive, or administrative mechanisms both to protect the nation from those who were playing at politics or harbored ill intentions toward it and to steer it along the path of progress once more.

The propensity toward regime-maintenance in general and anticommunism in particular that the military generated was both reflected in and reinforced by three factors. One was the high prestige attached to a career in the military, which came to represent a much-favored channel of upward mobility, especially for young men of middle-class or lower-class, country backgrounds. The second was the wide acceptance of the military's preference for a "stable and orderly" society and a "strong," "efficient," "no-nonsense," "virile," "patriotic," and "Thai" leadership. And the third was the support given to the military by civilian bureaucrats who also shared many of the former's concerns and aspirations (Chai-Anan and Sukhumbhand 1987: 193–94).

It was clear by the early 1970s, however, that the process of economic growth and development taking place during the previous two decades had brought profound changes. Rapid expansion of the urban-industrial sector and of the educational system fostered greater political pluralism, political awareness, and ultimately political mobilization when it became obvious that the military regime would continue to resist the demands for greater political participation and, if necessary, to continue to rule by force. The student-led uprising of October 1973 against the regime finally brought to an end the military's complete domination of Thai politics. Between 1973 and 1976 the flower of democracy bloomed, with the Thais' political awareness and mobilization reaching heights that were never before or after attained (Morell and Chai-Anan 1981). Reactionary coups of 1976 and 1977 cut short the era of open politics, but the so-called 14 October 1973 Revolution and the experiences of political participation made possible by it had a deep, long-term impact upon the structure and processes of Thai politics. The military could no longer monopolize power. The participatory political institutions that had come into being had begun to develop a life and a momentum of their own. What emerged after 1977 was a "mixed" system, a system with significant liberal characteristics but without Western-style liberal democracy, a system where state–society relations have assumed three separate, yet interacting, dimensions, namely, security, development, and participation. The coexistence and intertwining of these three dimensions are reflected in two key sets of dyadic relationships. One is the military–civilian relationship. The other is the government–private sector relationship.

## Military–Civilian Relations

As discussed above, during the first four decades or so after the overthrow of the absolute monarchy in 1932, the military was by far the most powerful political actor, dominating every facet of Thailand's political life and keeping in place a dictatorial regime that ruled almost unchallenged for most of the period. But from the early 1970s a number of "liberalizing" trends appeared and continued to exist despite the severity of reactions against these trends in 1976–77. (The discussion in this section is mainly based upon Chai-Anan and Suchit 1985: 90–114; Suchit and Sukhumbhand 1986: 52–76; Suchit 1987; Chai-Anan and Sukhumbhand 1987: 187–233).

One manifestation of such trends was the longevity of the 1978 constitutional system which lasted until 1991 and, largely in the same form, survived one attempt at far-reaching, surgical amendment (in 1983) and two failed coups d'état (in 1981 and 1985). Before 1988 three general elections were held in accordance with this constitution, more or less on schedule and more or less trouble-free. For a country that between 1932 and 1988 had seen twelve constitutions, fourteen coups d'état, and forty governments, this was an achievement indeed.

One crucial factor sustaining the life of the 1978 Constitution was the divisiveness within the armed forces, still the most powerful group in the country, with the various factions counterbalancing and deterring one another to prevent precipitate action and, when an attempted coup takes place, helping one another to defeat it. The longevity of those constitutional arrangements, however, was also based on other equally, if not more, important factors, which in themselves reflected longer-term liberalizing tendencies within Thailand's body politic.

The first is the military's acceptance, qualified to be sure, as will be pointed out below, of the principle and practice of popular political participation. In key political questions, especially those related to the stability or survivability of the government, the military continues to exert its considerable influence as the most powerful group within the Thai body politic, but most of the time this process consists of behind-the-scenes maneuvering, rather than a naked demonstration of firepower. The military's acceptance of the principle and practice of popular political participation can be traced to the fact that the present officer corps has been much more exposed to outside ideas and perspectives than its predecessors and consequently has been made aware, not only of the popular demands for political participation, but also of the complexity of the tasks of governance and development that make it virtually impossible for a small group of military leaders to manage the country's affairs unassisted. The espousal of a number of ideas concerning political participation and the cultivation of ties with many nonmilitary groups, especially intellectuals and technocrats, by the former army chief, General Chavalit Yongchaiyuth, reflects this liberalizing trend within the armed forces.

The second is the strength of political parties. Quite clearly, the major Thai political parties have been beneficiaries of the rapidly growing pluralism within the Thai society and of the burgeoning power of the business and financial community. Although, as will be pointed out below, it is not an unmixed blessing, the parties have been able to bring about a close relationship with the business and financial interests. Major banks and companies channel funds into their coffers, and prominent bankers, financiers, and business leaders have become leaders, deputy leaders, and executive committee members of the parties at the national level, with a parallel development taking place at the provincial and local levels. The political parties have also been able to attract younger, better educated people, many of whom have firmly established reputations as able technocrats. The composition of the parliament following the 1986 general election reflected these developments: 25 percent of all MPs came from the business community, 58 percent belonged to the 30–49 age group, and 61 percent received higher education. In the 1980s the political parties and politicians were able to play a more active role in the tasks of running ministries, promoting development programs, legislating, budgeting, and also scrutinizing the executive's performance, not only in money matters, but also in the fields of national security and foreign affairs, empires hitherto run by military officers and civilian bureaucrats to the complete exclusion of politicians.

The third is the strength of the monarchical institution. The revival of the Thai monarchy in the late 1950s and the 1960s, after a long period of eclipse following the overthrow of the absolute monarchy, was due not only to the reservoir of good will and loyalty that the Thai populace has to this traditional institution, but also to the fact that the royal family has been able to benefit from the process of modernization in Thailand and at the same time to "modernize" the institution itself. The rapid expansion of communications and telecommunications technology since the 1960s has allowed King Bhumibhol and Queen Sirikit to gain access to the hearts and homes of their subjects across the length and breadth of the land in a way that their predecessors in a less advanced age had never been able to do. Moreover, the king has been able to make the monarchy a working institution relevant to the needs and aspirations of his subjects by traveling constantly through remote and poor areas, visiting people to hear their grievances and gauge their needs, and also personally initiating many development projects—now numbering more than a thousand—aimed at improving conditions especially in deprived, security-sensitive areas. The king's *barami*, or charisma, gained from meritorious deeds, has given him a special position in the hearts and minds of the people, which in turn has allowed him to exercise a moderating influence in political matters and to preserve the constitutional system. At least five times in the 1980s through personal interventions, proxies, or public gestures, the palace restrained ill-advised moves by the military, which would have either toppled the existing constitutional government or at the very least precipitated unpredictable political crises. The first was during the April 1981 Young Turks' coup; the second was the release of the two Young Turks arrested in September 1984; the third was during the confusing aftermath of the devaluation in November 1984; and the fourth was during the September 9, 1985, coup. The role of the monarchy in promoting development and upholding the democratic form of government is the clearest manifestation of the coexistence and intertwining of "tradition" and "modernity."

The longevity of the 1978 Constitution does not mean, however, that Thailand had become a full-fledged, Western-style, liberal democracy or that the military has submitted without reservation to the principle of civilian authority, which is a key principle underlying such a system. Or, to put it another way, there was liberalization without democracy.

In the first place, it is evident that the October 14, 1973, Revolution did not bring about long-term changes in a number of areas where the military is concerned. The structure of the Thai military's organization has remained the same. Though factionalism and diverse intramural conflicts exist within the armed forces and impede concerted political initiatives on the part of the military, the "revolution" left untouched the organizational attributes contributing to their institutional uniqueness, cohesion, and political strength, actual or putative. The common processes of recruitment, training, selection, and promotion, the discipline, and the facility and frequency of contacts have remained intact. More important, so has the military's monopoly or virtual monopoly of the instruments of violence. In this connection it is highly significant that the key army units and organizations continue to be deployed around the political nerve center, namely,

Bangkok and its environs, the control over which has been decisive in all coups d'état except that in 1981.

Partly because the military still dispose of a great deal of firepower, partly because there is no tradition of parliamentary supervision over it, and partly because there is a traditional acceptance of functional differentiation among the various branches of the bureaucracy, the Thai military has been able to preserve its autonomy or, at the very least, its share of responsibility in areas where its specialized knowledge and expertise are called for. One such area is defense budgeting and arms procurement decisions. Another is preparation for and conduct of security operations. A third is the formation, development, and operation of the security apparatus, paramilitary units, and security-oriented grass-roots programs and organizations. A fourth is the appointment of personnel to key security and security-related positions.

The position of the armed forces in this regard has been strengthened by the fact that Vietnam's invasion of neighboring Thailand had brought a "clear and present danger" to Thailand, thus allowing military leaders to provide more reasons and justifications for continued increases, not only in overall military spending and arms procurement programs, but also in the "secret fund," a budget item earmarked officially for intelligence and undercover security work, but in practice used as military leaders see fit. In 1986 nearly six hundred million Baht were provided for the army's "secret fund." The fact that the annual defense budget now usually constitutes some 20 percent of the national budget and over 4 percent of the country's GDP means that the military has direct and unchallengeable control over a significant portion of the nation's resources.

The availability of such resources allows the military to have greater organized access to the "hearts and minds" of the people than any other institution in the country, governmental or private. It operates 210 radio stations all over the country, 87 of them located in the crucial central region, and also two television channels with a nationwide outreach. The army uses these broadcasting stations for a number of activities: expounding the military's ideas concerning the nation's economy, society, and politics; lauding the army's or individual army leaders' roles in preserving the nation's security; mobilizing the masses to support Royal Thai Army (RTA)–sponsored programs; attacking the army or the government itself, should either prove to be "out of control"; and indeed, when the need arises, summoning "patriotic" Thais to take specific political actions, as was the case in the Armored Corps radio station's call for "all true Thai patriots" to crush leftist demonstrators then assembled in Thammasat University in October 1976.

Moreover, in recent years, as part of the defense programs and also of the army's developmental functions (which will be discussed below), the army has established a number of civic action units, which operate at all levels right down to the localities, including the army's Directorate for Civil Affairs, "Democratic Centers" in villages where reservist organizations are located, the National Defense Volunteers Organization, and the Capital Security Command. Collectively, these serve to enhance the army's presence and influence at the grass roots and to promote "appropriate" knowledge and political awareness, especially among the rural populace. The number of persons attending the various army-sponsored "walkathons" to celebrate the king's and queen's birthdays in the past few years bears testimony not only to the monarchy's continuing popularity, but also to the army's ability to mobilize the masses.

This in turn means that the Thai military's perceptions of security and politics still play a crucial and even decisive role in the formulation and implementation of all security-related policies and programs. Moreover, continuity in terms of organizational structure and functions also means continuity in terms of ideals and beliefs. While today there is some doubt, ambivalence, and disagreement about how and how far the military should act to safeguard the nation's interests, especially in the political arena, the Thai officer corps is at one in holding onto its convictions that the preservation of the three institutions of nation, religion, and monarchy is the sine qua non of national security, that communism constitutes the greatest threat to these institutions and, hence, national security, and that the military have the *right* to take all necessary actions, including political interventions, to suppress any threats to national security.

Indeed, most Thai military officers now reject many of the fundamental tenets of a Western-style liberal democratic system, although they claim to be, and for all intents and purposes are, committed to the "democratic system of government with the king as its head." From their point of view, democracy based on free elections with power concentrated in a house of representatives is not always true democracy because there is no guarantee that these elections will bring competent, responsible, and honest people to the legislature. Nor can political parties be entrusted with the task of governance, for they are basically no more than "trading companies," corrupt, bent on the pursuit of power and self-interest, bickering among themselves, and having no ideals whatsoever. In fact all *voluntary* participatory political institutions and processes ultimately are considered potential channels for Communist infiltration and subversion.

Therefore, the military perceives it to be its duty to play an active "political" role, not only in monitoring and controlling voluntary participation, but also in providing "appropriate leadership for the unity, security, and development of the country at large." This involves the selection and protection of "suitable" premiers and governments; efforts to maintain a strong, appointed upper House and the military's right to take up ministerial portfolios; reorganization of the state apparatus to give the executive more control; and promotion of *controlled* participation through mass-based security-oriented organizations. The role also entails direct interventions in the task of economic development, if and when both the state apparatus and the private sector are, or are seen to be, ineffective, such as recently in the efforts to assist in the rice trade, the national fertilizer project, and the project to develop the poor Northeast by transforming this drought-stricken region into a green belt.

Thus, the military's role-conception in the areas of security, development, and participation demonstrates its rejection of the underlying ideals and political consequences of a Western-style liberal democratic system. It also suggests that its preference is for bureaucratically guided liberalization, expressed in terms of limited participation, which puts emphasis on consensus over competition, a minimal legislature over an active and potent parliament, appointments over elections, and centralization over decentralization or the devolution of power.

In contradistinction to the military's capacity and will to exert influence in key areas, Thailand's political parties continue to be weak, divided, and indecisive. Discontinuity of elected parliaments in the past has had adverse effects on political parties, disrupting their institutional development and efforts to perform interest-articulating and interest-aggregating functions at both national and local levels. Their reach to the grass roots remains limited and badly organized, as reflected in the fact that the Democrats, the party that has been in existence the longest, has only 113 branches and 14,719 members nationwide. Moreover, when allowed to function, as they have been since 1978, political parties suffer from the lack of discipline among members, who are wont to pursue factional and individual interests rather than to abide by party policies and priorities.

Recently the need for campaign funds has led to a closer relationship between parties and business interests. This development, however, has not strengthened parties as political institutions. On the contrary, the involvement in party politics of prominent businessmen and financiers serves to reinforce factionalism, as each "philanthropist" moves to extend influence within the parties and to seek recompense for "generosity" by attaining a ministerial portfolio. The increasing domination of the business and financial community, and the greater propensity toward the pursuit of self-interest that this domination entails, in turn makes it more difficult for the political parties to incorporate new social groups into their structures, to develop programs that can appeal to and articulate the views of a broad cross section of the public, and to stand by their principles or campaign pledges after the battles for votes are over and done.

The Democratic party's experiences after the July 1986 general election demonstrate the predicament into which Thailand's political parties have fallen. During the electoral campaign, the party's leaders successfully presented the Democrats' image as a dynamic, progressive, and united party, willing to abide by its principles. But afterward they immediately violated their own promise to allow only a member of parliament to become the premier, to ensure the party's participation in the Prem government, and consequently fell out among themselves in a conflict over ministerial portfolios. Thus, within a space of a few months the Democrats' fortunes tumbled. From being a powerful bloc of one hundred members of parliament, which arguably could have formed a coalition government of its own choosing, it has become a deeply divided and largely indecisive party. Significantly, when former prime minister M. R. Kukrit Pramoj's house was besieged by some three hundred men from the RTA-commanded Rangers unit for some remarks he made about army chief Chavalit in April 1987, the Democrats, a party that had been distinguished for its willingness to take a principled stand against military dictatorships, failed to develop a common front in an obvious case of military abuse of power.

The continuing imbalance of power between the military and the political parties means that liberalizing tendencies have developed but have not led to the creation of a Western-style liberal democracy. Ultimately this is a reflection of the fact that in Thailand's present political system, the "output structures," that is, the state apparatus comprising military and civilian bureaucracies, are excessively developed in relation to "input institutions," such as interest and pressure groups, parties, and parliaments. The strength of the Thai state structures in turn has been due partly to past and present security and development policies and programs, which allowed and continue to allow the government in general and the military in particular to engage in a wide range of activities from the national to the grass-roots level. Or, to put it another way, the complex interactions among the security, development, and participation dimension in military–civilian relations has brought about a political system that can be characterized as liberalization without democracy.

Let us now turn to the second dyadic relationship.

## Government–Private Sector Relations

The processes of technocratization and liberalization have taken place not only in the political arena, but also in the economic sphere. This is evident, first of all, in the role of technocrats. The growing complexity of the economy puts high premium on the art and science of management of the manifold functional problems that arise as part of the process of development. This in turn precipitates the rise of a class of highly educated and often also very highly motivated "professionals" whose main concern is to apply their acquired knowledge, skills, and experience in pursuit of excellence in their respective fields of competence, preferring in general to disregard the political implications and complications arising therefrom. And because of the complexity of the economy, the bureaucracy often defers to the expertise of these technocrats and even coopts them into the system. Indeed, given the fact that government service is considered a highly valued occupation in Thailand, it is inevitable that many highly educated people with such a "professional," technocratic outlook would join the government or government-related institutions, such as the National Economic and Social Development Board (NESDB), which is responsible for drawing up and monitoring the five-year development plans; the Thailand Development Research Institute (TDRI), which undertakes research projects for the government; and the various agencies directly concerned with banking, trading, and investment.

The process of "liberalization" is reflected also in the more independent position of the private sector vis-à-vis the government. In the past the financial-business community suffered from a number of handicaps. From the earliest days of development of the capitalistic system in the country, this community was dominated by ethnic Chinese, who in turn were dependent upon and controlled during the absolute monarchy period by princes and nobles, and after 1932 by the civilian and military bureaucrats. This position of internal dependence on the part of the Chinese-dominated financial-business community meant that it was vulnerable to the government's nationalistic campaigns, as in the years before and after the Second World War, and also to government leaders' pursuit of self-interest. Indeed, the years between 1947 and 1973 were most notable for the stranglehold that military leaders had on the community. This was the period of "commercial soldiers," when different military factions built up their economic bases by setting up their own companies, securing control over state enterprises and semigovernment companies, and gaining free shares from Chinese-owned private firms; and then used these economic bases to extend further their influence within the body politic (Chai-Anan 1982: 14–22).

The process of economic growth in Thailand helped to transform this quasi-colonial relationship between the civilian-military bureaucracy and the Chinese financial-business community, a relationship that over the long run was becoming less unequal in any case due to intermarriages and the two elites' increasingly similar socialization processes, particularly where education was concerned. Due to vast expansion of the industrial, agroindustrial, trading, financial, and nonfinancial services sectors, and also to rapid increases in the linkages with the outside world, the financial-business community has been transformed from a basically dependent entity into a more independent and organized sector, which is innovative and liberal in its outlook, and dynamic and hardworking in the conduct of its affairs. This transformation is reflected in the present political position and role of political parties, with whom the financial-business community enjoys an increasingly close—some would say symbiotic—relationship. It is seen also in the fact that the government is paying greater attention to the private sector and its needs. One example is the case in June 1988, when eighty major construction companies successfully put pressure on the government to reduce import taxes on steel bars and billets to compensate for losses arising from sharply increased construction matériel costs (*Bangkok Post*, June 15, 1988: 15,30). The government's greater sensitivity to the demands and needs of the local private sector has extended also to those of the foreign private sector. In May of the same year, for example, the government was forced to reexamine the Port Authority of Thailand's policy regarding the use of cranage at the busy Klong Toei Port of Bangkok in response to both local and foreign firms' calls for a more equitable and efficient arrangement (*Phu Jad Karn*, May 16–22, 1988: 1,7,8; *The Nation*, May 16, 1988: 19; and *The Nation*, May 17, 1988: 19).

This process of "liberalization" in the economic arena, however, also has its limits. In some industrializing countries the expansion of the middle class, the "bourgeoisie," or the entrepreneurial class has served as a democratic force, forging an alliance with other forces, gaining control over the state, and democratizing it (Cardoso 1988). In Thailand this has not happened, the Thai bureaucracy having been able to seize the initiative in promoting economic development and having succeeded in coopting first the technocrats and then the private sector.

It was in the late 1950s and early 1960s that Thai military leaders incorporated economic development as an integral part of their strategy to create stability and security for both the regime and the nation. With the assistance of foreign and local advisers, the government promoted what can be termed the "ideology" of development, which helped to transform a faction-ridden bureaucratic polity into a more unified activist bureaucratic state. The Budget Act of 1959 established a central budget office directly responsible to the chief executive. A Budget Procedures Act of the same year gave an appreciable degree of order and coherence to the budgetary process. These reforms in the legal and organizational bases of public financial administration, together with the inauguration of the First National Economic Development Plan in 1961, resulted in the subsequent rise to power of the technocratic elite, which gradually became the power base of a new military-technocratic alliance. The activist role of the state can be seen in the growth of the administrative structure and change in the pattern of government spending after 1957. In that year there were only 90 departments and 550 divisions; in 1979 there were a total of 131 departments and 1,264 divisions (Woradej 1979: 4).

This qualitative and quantitative development of the bureaucracy made it possible for the government to allow the financial-business community to participate in some areas of the decision-making process under terms of reference determined by the state, at the time when the private sector was rapidly expanding. This process of cooptation meant that the latter does not present a real challenge to the bureaucratic-activist, technocratic state but strengthens it because the state's decision-making capacity is enhanced by the private sector's participation as a source of information, expertise, and ultimately legitimacy. Moreover, once the private sector is given this channel, the need for the financial and business community to seek alliances with political parties in order to influence policy decisions is lessened. Although obviously many financiers and businessmen "go into politics" to try to exert control over the nucleus of state power, many more do not, preferring to deal directly with the military and technocrats. For them access to, rather than possession of, political power is a precondition for the accumulation of wealth. In this sense the relationship between politics and economics is essentially one of exchange, rather than one involving the transfer of power from the economy to the polity (Chai-Anan 1988).

The impetus toward cooptation of the private sector was the political situation, domestic and international, in the mid- to late 1970s. The period contained a series of traumatic experiences for Thailand, creating fear and uncertainty among the upper class, the civilian and military bureaucrats, and the financial and business community: the student revolution of October 1973, followed by a lengthy spell of student activism; the fall of Indochina to Communist forces in 1975 and the U.S. military withdrawal from mainland Southeast Asia in 1975–76; the violent right-wing coup of October 1976; border problems with Khmer Rouge Cambodia in 1977–78; and Vietnam's invasion of Cambodia in 1978–79. It was during this period that those in charge of Thailand's security politics came to the conclusions that security was a multidimensional concept and that real security involved not only self-reliance in defense, but also a balance among military, political, and socioeconomic requirements, with priority to be given to economic development (Sukhumbhand 1987b: 84–90). This line of thinking was pervasive among the upper echelon of Thai policy makers, and again it was during this period that Dr. Snoh Unakul, one of the top technocrats in the government circle, developed his strategy of public–private sector cooperation, based on the premise that if Thailand was to survive and prosper, "progressive capitalists" should be encouraged to join hands with the government and "exploitative capitalists" kept under control, to avoid the disarray that political chaos could bring to the market economy (Snoh n.d.).

Significantly, the Fifth National Economic and Social Development Plan (1983–86), drafted by civilian and military bureaucrats in close collaboration with one another, identified as the main objective of Thailand's development strategy the achievement of "national stability," which in turn was to be brought about by the balancing of security requirements with economic development requirements, with priority given to economic development (Sukhumbhand 1987b: 84–90). The Fifth Plan devoted a great deal of attention to the issue of cooperation between the public sector and the private sector. Chapter 6 of the plan was entitled "The Mobilization of Cooperation from the Private Sector," and under the section on "Problems" it stated with uncharacteristic bluntness that the relationship between the two sectors was very poor: "The main problem of the public sector is the inefficiency of the bureaucracy, which makes laws and regulations obstructive to development, while the private sector which has to comply with those laws and regulations, possesses more efficiency in management, but seeks to make profits without being responsible to social justice in society as a whole." It called for the encouragement of the private sector to improve its management capacity in order to respond to increased responsibilities (Thailand, NESDB 1982: 417–19).

At the same time the Fifth Plan identified an urgent need to study the pattern and form of the existing institutions of the private sector, to develop them into effective instruments that could serve the state, and to find ways and means of assisting the private sector. It also went on to propose a system and a mechanism for public sector–private sector cooperation that was to take the form of a high-level joint committee. Clearly, the new wave of thinking was to liberalize and privatize, with the technocratic state shifting its role from that of a controlling and curbing agency to that of a supervisory and promotional body. As the Fifth Plan stipulated, the state would "delegate responsibility and some powers to the organizations (of the private-sector) in order to lessen the burden of the state" (Thailand, NESDB 1982: 418–19).

Accordingly, the Joint Public and Private Consultative Committee (JPPCC) was formed (fig. 5.1), with the prime minister as chairman and the NESDB secretary-general, Dr. Snoh Unakul, as committee secretary. Other members are deputy prime ministers, ministers, and deputy ministers of economic ministries, the governor of the Bank of Thailand, and the secretary-general of the Board of Investment. The private sector is represented by three members from the Thai Chamber of Commerce, three from the Thai Industry Association, and three from the Thai Banking Association.

The creation of the JPPCC at the national level was followed by the development of regional JPPCCs. In 1967 there were only two chambers of commerce, and from 1968 to 1976 not a single new chamber of commerce was established. This was because the government had continuously maintained its policy of control over chambers of commerce in fear of their potential political influence. From 1980 to 1983 only eleven provincial chambers of commerce were registered. After the government-sponsored meeting of regional JPPCCs in Chiangmai in February 1984, twenty-three chambers of commerce were established in various provinces. From 1985 to 1987, another thirty-four provincial chambers of commerce were established with the encouragement and guidance of the government. The administration of a provincial JPPCC is under the office of the governor, who is the chairman of the committee. It is natural that the dynamism, or the lack thereof, of this body is determined by the governor.

The structure of the JPPCC at both the national and provincial levels is basically bureaucratic, with officials numbering more than representatives of the private sector. In a series of interviews conducted by the authors (Chai-Anan and Sukhumbhand 1988), representatives of the private sector all agreed in principle on the utility of the set-up. But some were critical of its effectiveness and thought that the JPPCC was merely a "talking stadium" (one even said that it was a "do-nothing" body), while others were of the opinion that having such a body was a psychological breakthrough for public–private sector relations, which used to be quite antagonistic. Another said the national JPPCC was not a free and open platform but was too much guided by the secretariat. One active member of the JPPCC from the private sector, however, praised the secretary-general of the NESDB for his astuteness and indispensability.

It is evident that the JPPCC is a mechanism created and utilized by technocrats to arrange relations between the state and the private sector. It is a vehicle used by the technocrats, not only to establish a constructive alliance with the industrialists, bankers, and businessmen, but also to put pressure on the bureaucracy to reform, for example, the tax system and the regulation of public utilities. In this sense, the technocrats are taking the role of reformers as well as

**Figure 5.1 The Joint Public and Private Consultative Committee of Thailand**

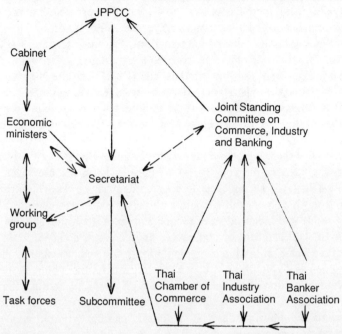

guardians of the "national interest." Through its secretariat the JPPCC established a standard operating procedure, barring matters that are of specific interest to firms and accepting only matters concerning the general interests of a sector or a type of industry.

The establishment of the JPPCC and the keen interest taken by the top leadership can be regarded as an important safety valve that helps reduce conflict and tension among the military, technocratic-bureaucratic elites, and the financial business community. Its existence presents an alternative channel to the emerging economic forces for communicating with the top leadership other than joining or setting up political parties. Professionals in the three associations prefer to go through the JPPCC and are committed to developing it rather than taking the political route. The creation of the JPPCC can therefore be regarded as a nonpolitical, political body that strives to help the public and private sectors reach consensus and work together in the spirit of *krengjai* (deference), instead of going through the process of competition and bargaining via political parties and parliament.

The basic problem of the JPPCC is its composition, which has been criticized as representing only big business interests. The agenda for the JPPCC meetings, for example, is decided by the Joint Standing Committee on Commerce, Industry, and Banking; and since medium-sized and small business concerns are poorly represented on that committee, these businesses have preferred to bypass the JPPCC structure altogether and develop direct contacts with the bureaucracy. On the other hand, there has been a great concern to promote provincial chambers of commerce in order to strengthen the economic base of the Thai capitalist system. Since 1983 the Center for International Private Enterprise (CIPE) of the American Chamber of Commerce has been active in giving funding to the Institute for Management Education for Thailand (IMET) and the National Institute for Development Administration (NIDA) to organize training for provincial businessmen. CIPE has granted ninety-seven thousand dollars for a six-year program aiming at the training of all members of seventy-two provincial chambers of commerce.

It seems that there is a conscious effort to help develop a strong private sector that spreads all over the country. The emphasis is on the provinces, not the center, and in fact, the policy is to assist provincial private enterprises to be independent. This strategy of economic pluralism is an important mechanism in creating stable and independent economic and social forces outside the primary city. Provincial chambers of commerce, once created, could become "instruments of the state," at least in supplying information and articulating and aggregating demands. While these structures are regarded as nonpolitical, they are in fact very political in nature; for whatever the original intention may have been, the JPPCC and provincial chambers of commerce are state-led pressure groups that have made political parties dysfunctional as participatory institutions.

Thus, in the management of the Thai economy there have been liberalizing tendencies, which, however, have not led to democratization. This is reflected in the relationship between the government and the private sector, which, as in the case of military-civilian relations, is based upon complex interactions among the security, development, and participation dimensions. The private sector has become more powerful, capable of exerting pressure on the government directly or indirectly, through ties with political parties; but it has proved incapable of controlling the nucleus of state power and indeed has invariably been reluctant to try to do so. Rather, it has been "coopted" by the bureaucratic-activist state, during which process the latter has demonstrated a great capacity to adjust to new environments and forces and also to provide leadership when appropriate. Or, to put it another way, the private sector, far from being a competitor of the bureaucracy, is no more than a junior partner of it and, when allowed to participate in policy matters, participates under terms and conditions stipulated by the bureaucracy.

The nature of the government–private sector relationship is perhaps well illustrated in the dealings with the People's Republic of China (PRC) and the Republic of China (ROC), or Taiwan, since the mid-1970s. The decline of American power and the rise of Vietnam during this period prompted Thailand to adjust relations with the two Chinas, normalizing, then operating closely with the PRC, and cutting off diplomatic ties with the ROC—while trying to preserve the considerable economic relationship with it. What the government initiated and continued to do for reasons of security and development, the private sector supported and continues to support for reasons of profit. The Sino-Thai financial business community utilizes its ethnic and linguistic ties with the PRC and the ROC to good effect, increasing trade and investment relations with both Chinas and thus helping to strengthen the government's de facto two-China policy (Sukhumbhand 1987a).

## The Challenge of the Future

Thailand demonstrates that in an Asian society, state–society relations can be complex and multifaceted, involving security, development, and participation dimensions, interactions among which constitute the core of the political process in that society. Thailand today is also illustrative of the fact that a liberal technocratic state is not necessarily a democratic state. In Thailand, the politics of liberalization takes place at the upper level of state–society relations, making the bureaucratic polity relax its controls to the degree required to administer the rapidly growing economy more effectively and to utilize the considerable resources offered by it more efficiently. Thus, the process of liberalizing the bureaucracy should not be confused with the democratization of the society, which concerns not only a redistribution of political power, but also the transformation of the values and social bases of the state. The foregoing discussion also points out that the emergence of new social and economic forces does not necessarily weaken the state if the latter can adjust to and coopt these forces. What takes place is not an objective process of synthesizing the "old" and the "new," "tradition" and "modernity," but a subjective, state-induced process of synthesizing to make the two coexist and to gain strength from such a coexistence.

If it is true that in Thailand there has been liberalization without democracy, then the question arises as to how stable such a state of affairs is. Here there is no easy answer. Up to now, with the exception of the 1973–76 period, Thailand has demonstrated a fine capacity to maintain stability; and the infusion of technocratic blood into the aging veins of its bureaucratic polity has proved to be highly beneficial, allowing the kingdom to adjust itself to new internal and external environments. But clearly, Thai society is changing rapidly. New social and economic forces are emerging and gaining strength. The Thai state ultimately has to come to terms with these forces, and coming to terms ultimately means providing more meaningful access to these forces whose participation is presently circumscribed. Or to put it another way, Thailand's future stability may be dependent upon the state's capability to readjust its priorities, attaching greater importance to participation, while preserving the nation's security and promoting its economic development. At some points during the process of readjustment there may be trade-offs among the needs of security, development, and participation. Thus, the task is an unenviable one. But as Thailand approaches the twenty-first century, when a number of unknown challenges await it, the task is urgent, and delay in taking it up may prove highly costly.

# 6

# Malaysia in an Uncertain Mode

## Zakaria Haji Ahmad

ECONOMIC growth has had a complex and contradictory impact on the evolution of the Malaysian political regime, in some ways contributing to the inclination to impose more authoritarian controls and in other ways strengthening the democratic resistance.

Authoritarian impulses in Malaysian society are not rooted exclusively in economic soil. As internal police documents indicate, there were those who felt from the very inception of the state that a strong central government was essential (Zakaria 1977). The notion of a "strong executive" was in fact enshrined in the Malaysian constitution; and the racial riots of 1969 provided the rationale for tilting further the Westminster system so that power in this multiethnic land could be more securely retained in Malay (and, one might add, Moslem) hands.

But concern for economic growth has played a role in these developments. One of the principal instruments of the reforms of 1971, for example, was the New Economic Policy (NEP), which was inaugurated in that year as a twenty-year program of state-led growth. It was intended, of course, to expand the economic pie to the benefit of the entire nation—an objective that has been substantially achieved; but above all it had the very specific objective of using affirmative action to strengthen the economic power of the Malay community vis-à-vis the other ethnic groups, and thereby to consolidate Malay political dominance in the state. Its execution has brought not only a reduction in non-Malay political influence, but also a greater state intervention in the economy than ever before.

This has been particularly evident in recent years, when an augmentation of the power of the state has in part been justified by the need to cope with international pressures, systemic inefficiencies or "deviations" troubling the growth process. It was the state's deep concern to overcome the recession of the mid-1980s, for example, that partly fueled the expansion of executive authority that has occurred in recent years. With the growth rate having plunged from 7.8 percent in 1984 to –1 percent in 1985 (table 6.4) and with social tensions rising, the ruling National Front, the Barisan Nasional (BN), issued a call for general elections, and in an open letter and manifesto in 1986, Dato Seri Dr. Mahathir Mohamad, the front's leader and prime minister, argued that the revival of the economy required "strong government":

> The only way we can ride through this recession is to face it calmly, to plan our moves carefully and to utilize our intrinsic strengths. If we give in to emotions, if we choose the easy way out and wildly accuse each other, we will only compound the damage. . . . It is especially when the going gets tough that we need a strong, experienced and firm hand, to deal with the problems we face. (*New Straits Times*, July 26, 1986)

Overwhelming victory at the polls seemed to be a mandate for change. Accordingly, in recent years, while many of the fundamental, democratic institutions and practices that distinguished the polity in the early postindependence decades have been retained, others have been modified. Political rights, popular participation, and civil liberties, for example, have been more severely curbed, with the result that the Malaysian polity has become less a true or liberal democracy than it was in the earlier years (Mauzy 1983: 4).

It would be far too facile, of course, to attribute the recent strengthening of state power exclusively to what were felt to be imperatives for recovering from recession. The appeal of "Mahathirism" in which, somewhat like "Thatcherism" in Britain, a strong executive takes center stage and by thought, style, and action largely dominates political, economic, and perhaps even social life, draws sustenance from other roots as well. Nevertheless, that rapid economic growth has provided an important justification for an increase in state power and thereby strengthened authoritarian tendencies seems incontrovertible in this as in earlier times.

On the other hand, and paradoxically, economic growth has also had the opposite effect, strengthening also those forces that seek to restrain state power and enliven the democratic process. The economic growth record, after all, has been extraordinary, the per capita GNP rising from U.S. $350 in 1967, a level little better than the low-income states of Africa, to U.S. $1,830 in 1986, a level that provokes debate whether Malaysia should now be acknowledged as one of the Newly Industrializing Economies like South Korea, Taiwan, Singapore, and Hong Kong (World Bank 1989: 20, and 384–85). Relatively brief though this period of growth has been, it has set in motion processes of modernization and pluralization that are transforming Malaysian society. Concomitant with these changes has been the growth of a greater political awareness among the citizenry. The result has been to create an expanding social base for the democratic ideals and institutions that animated the state when it was founded, and a growing resistance to the authoritarianizing trends that growth has otherwise been used to justify.

To understand this ambiguity in the impact of economic growth on Malaysia, one needs to appreciate that economic development is taking place there, not just within parameters set by such elements as its resource base and the international environment, but even more within those set by geographical and racial cleavages that tear open its very heart.

Malaysia is a country physically divided into two portions by the South China Sea. The "Peninsular" portion (an official term replacing the former reference of "West Malaysia") comprises the former Federation of Malaya with the states of Perlis, Kedah, Pening, Kelantan, Trengganu, Pahang, Perak, Selangor, Negeri Sembilan, Malacca, and Johore; the other portion consists of the states of Sabah and Sarawak on the island of Borneo (formerly "East Malaysia"). Integration of the two portions is made difficult not only by physical separation and geographical distance, but also by different histories. Integration is also complicated by differences in the powers enjoyed by the various states. Sabah and Sarawak joined the former Federation of Malaya six years after its founding and were accorded certain special authority, for example, over immigration, which the peninsular states do not have. Thus, in a manner of speaking, Malaysia is actually two countries, physically and spiritually.

Even more salient than these divisions are those along ethnic lines, which are so deep that every political issue tends to be transformed into a communal one and places the society "on the razor's edge" (Mahathir 1985). The Malays, who constitute only 47–48 percent of the population, regard their interests as more than primary because of their indigenous origins. The other major races, namely, the Chinese, Indians, and Pakistanis, who have placed their stakes in the system and therefore demand proportional powers as citizens, are seen as migrants from the outside. The result is that Malay/non-Malay (usually read Chinese) political competition constitutes the major parameter in Malaysian politics. Underlying it is the prevailing conception that the Malays dominate politics while the non-Malays dominate the economy.

It is argued in some quarters that this compartmentalization is not necessarily an exclusive ordering and that "Malay political hegemony" might be further ensured by the creation of opportunities and equity participation for the Malays in the business and economic sectors as spelled out in the New Economic Policy (NEP) adopted in 1971. But increased Malay participation in the economic sector does not necessarily connote that increased non-Malay participation in politics is welcome. The notion exists among sections of the Malay elite and population that the so-called intercommunal bargain struck prior to independence, in which citizenship rights for non-Malays were exchanged for "special rights" for Malays, was in fact too great a concession of power and needs to be rectified.

The ethnic parameter is further complicated by the existence and demands of other ethnic groups, such as the Kadazans, Bajaus, and others in Sabah; the Ibans in Sarawak; and the *Orang Asli* (aborigines) in the peninsula—all of whom are classed with the Malays as indigenous *bumiputras*, literally "sons of the soil." Indeed, the ethnic cleavage is trichotomous: Malay versus non-Malay versus "natives" (non-Malay indigenes). Of late, these divisions have been further accentuated by the rise of religious revivalism, which infuses the traditional ethnic Malay/non-Malay division with a Moslem/non-Moslem cleavage.

In terms of population, the Malays and other indigenous groups comprise about 58.6 percent of the population as compared to the non-*bumiputras*, among whom are about 31.2 percent Chinese, 8.6 percent Indian, and the remaining nonindigenous about 0.7 percent. From 1957 to 1969 this gave rise to the notion of Malaysia as a multiethnic nation. Nevertheless, from the very beginning, when the Westminster parliamentary system was adopted, the Malays were politically favored. The electoral constituencies were drawn so as to give more weight to rural areas, where Malays are dominant, than to urban areas, where non-Malays chiefly reside.

But Malay leadership was severely challenged by widespread racial riots in the May 13 Incident of 1969. In the aftermath, while the Westminster system still attracted support as an ideal, the indigenous community moved to modify the rules of the game to guarantee that Malaysia would henceforth be not a multiethnic state but a "Malay-based" polity in both form and substance. Although guarantees were built into the system for citizenship status and certain non-Malay rights such as the teaching of vernacular languages in the schools, the underlying rationale in nation-building became the creation of an integrated country through the common use of one language, namely, Malay or what is now referred to as Bahasa Malaysia, the "Malaysian language." National and state identification was to be through "Malay symbols," such as allegiance to Malay royalty and the declaration of Islam as the official religion. In addition, Malays were to enjoy "special rights," such as preference in selection in the public services, entry into universities, and gaining of business licenses and scholarships. In the economic realm, the NEP sought to redress the racial economic imbalance by attempting to increase the share of Malay ownership of the corporate sector to as much as 30 percent by 1990 from the 1 percent before 1969 (Zakaria 1987: 122–23).

For a more detailed analysis of the interaction between the forces of economic growth and the evolution of the polity within the parameters of racial politics, I turn now to a sequential examination of the three periods into which Malaysian political history may be divided: the first, from 1957 to 1969, when democratic institutions were tested in a consociational form; the second, from 1969 to 1971, when that test was interrupted; and the third, from 1971 to the 1980s, when the present quasi-democracy was launched. While race is the leitmotiv in all three periods and regimes, the reciprocal relationship of the economy and the polity are clearly revealed in the correspondence of the consociational democratic period with that before the NEP and of the quasi-democratic period with that under the NEP.

## Consociational Democracy (1957–69)

When independence was obtained in 1957, the political practices of the former white rajah were adopted with little or no modification. Flushed perhaps with the ability to obtain *Merdeka* from London so quickly in the terminal colonial period and with the overwhelming election victory (fifty-one out of fifty-two seats) in the 1955 countrywide Legislative Assembly elections that gave indigenous self-government, the leaders seem to have thought very little about the special conditions in the country and whether full-fledged democracy on the British Westminster model could work there. In the effort to present a common front to gain independence, ethnic differences were deemphasized. That politics could and would be left primarily to the Malays and business to the Chinese in the postindependence period seems to have been at least tacitly assumed. How tenuous this "bargain" was became apparent in the years that followed (Zakaria 1989: 352).

The political mobilization that followed independence intensified ethnic loyalties and placed the race qustion in the forefront of the debates about public policy. Indeed, the ruling Alliance party that came to power in 1955 and that also won victories in the three elections in this period (1959, 1964, and 1969) was an amalgam of three components that represented the Malays (in the United Malays National Organization or UMNO), the Chinese (in the Malayan Chinese Association or MCA) and the Indians (in the Malayan Indian Congress or MIC). With the exception of the People's Action party (PAP) party based in Singapore, which was a part of Malaysia only from 1963 to 1965, this intercommunal formula continued even with and after the formation of Malaysia in 1963; in Sabah and Sarawak, parties also were organized on ethnic lines and were linked, *mutatis mutandis*, to the Alliance in Peninsular or West Malaysia. In effect, while the form of democracy was that of Westminster, the reality shared important elements with Arend Lijphart's notion of consociational democracy (Lijphart 1984), in that Malaysian society was organized largely into certain major communal groups, each of which exercised considerable autonomy and each of which participated in central decision making by proportional representation in a grand ruling coalition of the National Front. It was in practice the accommodation between the elites of the participating ethnic groups that allowed for democratic politics (Milne and Mauzy 1978: 352–56).

Until the breakdown of the political system in what is known as the "May 13 Incident" in May 1969, the pattern of consociational democracy provided for both political pluralism, albeit colored by race, and political stability. Security was provided in spite of an ongoing Communist insurgency (the "Emergency" that was officially declared ended in 1960) and an external threat of aggression during the Indonesian "confrontation" of 1963–66. The Alliance formula worked well. It allowed for an airing of views by the various ethnic elites that would be settled within the inner circles of the coalition leadership. The ground rules of interethnic bargaining displayed the features of politics by a directorate or cabal, well described by Karl von Vorys:

> First, the relationship of citizens with the same group would continue to be managed through a semi-autonomous communal hierarchy. Second, the relationship of citizens across communal boundaries or to the government would be

regulated through terms agreed to by an inter-communal Directorate at the highest level. Third, the terms of inter-communal relations would be promulgated in a constitutional contract, then implemented and when necessary augmented by policies secretly negotiated. Fourth, the members of the Directorate would have to possess dual qualifications. They would have to be the leaders of the political organization [party] of their community most capable of mobilizing mass support behind the government in democratically controlled elections. No less important, they would also have to be men who could maintain the confidence of their colleagues by keeping negotiations within the Directorate secret and by refraining from ever mobilizing their external communal mass-support to bring pressure on the secret negotiations. (von Vorys 1975: 14–15)

While cabal-style politics and partial consociational democracy provided stability and vigor in the body politic, the more fundamental issue of the nature of the Malaysian nation-state—whether it was to be "Malay" or "multiracial"—remained unresolved and indeed contentious. That in turn touched on yet another fundamental question of the ethnic sharing of the wealth of the country, which the Malay leadership sought to redistribute. During the period under review, the government's emphasis on increasing the wealth of the Malays was expressed in terms of seeking a "balance" among the races, chiefly by "balancing the interests of the urban and rural areas of the country" (Milne and Mauzy 1978: 322). Thus, government economic policy concentrated on rural development programs and to some extent on helping Malays "play a larger role in industry and commerce."

Meanwhile, under a growth strategy that emphasized the expansion of commodity exports (Rao 1971) but that continued to give some weight to import-substitution, the economy was expanding. From 1960 to 1965 the GNP grew at an average annual rate of 5.7 percent and from 1965 to 1970, 6.2 percent (tables 6.1 and 6.2).

Nevertheless, there was a growing sense of discontent, even despair, that the fruits of growth were not reaching Malays, but were benefiting primarily the non-Malays and foreign business interests. In several *bumiputra* economic congresses held before 1969, suggestions were advanced to correct the racial imbalance in wealth and income distribution and in economic opportunities. Malay leaders feared that inaction would ultimately lead to racial ignominy. Data collected by economists showed that the income differential between Malays and non-Malays was wide. In 1970 the average Malay household income was only about half that of the average non-Malay household. R. S. Milne and Diane K. Mauzy elaborate on how marked the disparities were:

Within each community there were wide differences in income, so that average figures are unenlightening. Poverty was more marked in rural areas, where the majority of the population is Malay. Moreover, inside rural areas, Malays tend to be concentrated in the most backward economic sectors, for

Table 6.1

**Average Annual GNP Growth Rate in Malaysia, 1960–70**

|  | 1960–65 | 1965–70 |
|---|---|---|
| GNP at current prices | 5.7 | 6.2 |
| GNP at 1960 prices | 6.3 | 5.6 |
| Total consumption at 1960 prices | 6.3 | 4.1 |

*Source:* Rao 1980: 6.

example, as cocoanut and rubber smallholders, single-crop padi farmers, tenants and share-croppers in padi and rubber cultivation, and inshore fishermen. In urban areas the gap in income between Malays and non-Malays was not as wide. Before the start of the NEP, from 1957 to 1970, inequality of incomes actually increased. (Milne and Mauzy 1978: 328–29)

At the same time, the high growth rates heightened expectations and thereby also contributed to the weakening of the form of consociational democracy that had allowed for intercommunal bargaining.

## The Interregnum (1969–71)

The racial riots of May 1969 brought about the suspension of democracy (Zakaria 1989: 360–85). In the months that followed, all partisan political activity was banned. Several opposition leaders, including V. David and Lim Kit Siang, were incarcerated. Press freedom was initially curtailed although gradually relaxed, and strong action was taken against paramilitary groups capable of waging organized violence.

Authority was vested temporarily in the National Operations Council (NOC), which, under the leadership of Tan Sri Ghazali Shafie, Tun Abdul Razak, and Tun Ismail, focused its efforts on restoring peace and devising a reformed system that could provide orderly government and racial harmony (Ghazali 1985a). It proceeded in secrecy, sharing its deliberations only with a National Consultative Council (NCC), which was established with a wide range of representation from various groups in society and politics, excluding only the Democratic Action party (DAP) and the Labor party. In 1970 Tunku Abdul Rahman, the fatherly figure who had held the prime ministership since independence, stepped down; with him went the style of affable accommodation that, from an extremist Malay viewpoint, had come to be seen as blessing a collusion of Chinese capitalists and Malay UMNO politicians rather than intervening decisively in business and the economy on behalf of the Malays as was now desired. The country was poised for a new era.

A fundamental choice the council had to make was whether the system of government to follow NOC rule was to be democratic or authoritarian. There

Table 6.2

**Annual GNP Growth Rate in Malaysia, 1961–71**

| Year | GNP |
|------|------|
| 1961 | 0.2 |
| 1962 | 5.2 |
| 1963 | 6.6 |
| 1964 | 6.2 |
| 1965 | 10.4 |
| 1966 | 6.3 |
| 1967 | 5.1 |
| 1968 | 4.4 |
| 1969 | 8.6 |
| 1970 | 6.4 |
| 1971 | 3.4 |

*Source:* Rao 1980: 6.

was every opportunity for the NOC to be arbitrary. Its members could have enriched themselves, but they did not. "Special Measures" were in fact taken to prevent malfeasance (Ghazali 1985). Given the coercive instruments under the council's control and the divisions within the council between "old guard" and younger elements, it or elements within it might have resorted to a coup, but they did not. And while there is oral evidence that the members did debate extensively the merits of democratic versus nondemocratic models of government, it would appear that a return to normalcy was their foremost goal, and normalcy for them meant democracy (Ghazali 1985; see also Mauzy 1983: 46).

But not democracy in a purely liberal style, nor one in quite the same consociational form Malaysia had experienced before the disruption. Malaysian democracy was henceforth to be more restricted. The basic rights of the communities as laid down before 1969 would be maintained, and provision for intercommunal bargaining would be restored, but, as observed by von Vorys:

> the final decision on cultural integration, the appropriate marginal rates of growth in the Malay access to the economy and Chinese access to government would not be resolved by a compromise among more or less equal parties. They would be decided by what the top UMNO leaders considered fair and in the interest of Malaysia. It was, of course, a very much simpler system. (von Vorys 1975: 344)

The rationale for Malay dominance rested on the NOC's analysis of the causes of the May 13 riots (Malaysia 1969). Measures were promptly devised to cope with the grievances that had shaken the system (Ghazali 1985).

First, a new Department of National Unity (DNU) was created. Under the leadership of Tan Sri Ghazali Shafie, it drafted a national ideology, or *Rukunegara*, as follows:

> Our Nation, Malaysia, being dedicated
> to achieving a greater unity of all her peoples;
> to maintaining a democratic way of life;
> to creating a just society in which the wealth
> of the nation shall be equitably shared;
> to ensuring a liberal approach to her rich and
> diverse cultural traditions;
> to building a progressive society which shall be
> oriented to modern science and technology:
> We, her people, pledge our united efforts to
> attain these ends guided by these principles:
> Belief in God
> Loyalty to King and Country
> Upholding the Constitution
> Rule of Law
> Good Behavior and Morality. (Ghazali 1985a: 41–42)

Second, new educational and economic policies were introduced to redress the grievances of the economic imbalance so as to achieve national unity. Most prominently and expressly stated were the National Education Policy under which, among other provisions, the Malay language would be vigorously used as the medium of instruction from elementary school through the university, and which was designed to build the economic basis for the post-1969 political system. The NEP called for a two-pronged strategy of poverty eradication and "restructuring," by which was meant the reduction, if not elimination, of the identification of race with vocation. Rejecting the feature of Malaysian social and economic structure in which non-Malays dominated the business and economic sectors, and Malays the agricultural and nonmodern sectors, the planners called for a deliberate effort to "urbanize" the Malays and assist them in gaining access to the more modern sectors of the economy so that they could, at a minimum, be on a par with the more advanced non-Malays (Milne and Mauzy 1978: 321–51; Ghazali 1985b).

In Peninsular Malaysia in 1970, for example, Malays owned only 1.9 percent of the limited companies, and Indians, only 1 percent; Chinese owned 22.5 percent, and foreigners, 60.7 percent. The NEP set the ambitious twenty-year goal of reducing the foreign share to 30 percent, raising the Malay share to 30 percent, and leaving the rest to the non-Malays. It created or reserved for Malays and other *bumiputras* a certain percentage of posts in the business sector. And under the provisions of the Industrial Coordination Act (ICA), "licenses required from the Ministry of Trade and Industry could be revoked if requirements about *bumiputra* ownership and employment were not met" (Milne and Mauzy 1978: 346).

It is difficult to judge precisely what popular sentiments were. The Chinese and other non-Malays were certainly not happy with the decidedly Malay tilt of the reforms, but they were powerless to resist, and the popular yearning for a return to normalcy following the shock of May 13 generated a mood of acceptance of what appeared to many to be modest and fair improvements of the system, however bold the prescription.

Finally, the elections in Sabah and Sarawak ensured the reform government a two-thirds majority in the newly reconvened parliament in 1971. Tun Abdul Razak, the new prime minister, secured the passage of the Constitution (Amendment) Bill, which branded as seditious any future challenges to the constitution and certain sensitive issues that were entrenched there, specifically Malay rights, citizenship (especially of the non-Malays), the monarchy, and Malay as the national language.

Although this authoritarian period was transitional, it was accompanied, not unexpectedly, by an arrest of economic growth. As shown in table 6.2, in 1969, the year of the riots, economic growth reached the high level of 8.6 percent, but thereafter temporarily dropped off, sliding down to 3.4 percent in 1971. Obviously, the breakdown in the political system had undermined confidence in the economy. But the return of political order restored economic confidence as well. At least among the leaders of the ruling coalition elite there was a belief that the May 13 Incident had been an aberration and that the NEP would prevent the recurrence of such an event.

Now politics would be in command, with an interventionist government taking bold action in a somewhat less than fully democratic structure, but not one that was thoroughly authoritarian. As Donald Snodgrass, a past adviser to the Malaysian Economic Planning Unit (EPU), noted with reference to the Second Malaysia Plan, the new policies had "little precedent in other developing countries" and were "all the more startling for having emerged from what had previously been regarded by many as a 'conservative and pro-free enterprise' government" (Snodgrass 1980: vii–viii; also Lim 1975a: 2–10). One result was to make any subsequent government's legitimacy highly dependent on its success in achieving the central goal of the NEP: advancing the lot of the Malays.

## Quasi-Democracy and the NEP (1971– )

The Malaysian political system from 1971 onward has been a reordered one and therefore differs from the consociational democracy of 1957–69. The difference is reflected in the changed role and attitude of the Tunku, who so largely symbolized the earlier era. In his "As I See It" column, which in later years he wrote in the daily tabloid, *The Star*, he has commented critically on many of the changes. Particularly after the advent of Dr. Mahathir to the premiership in 1981, the Tunku seemed increasingly to side with those opposing Dr. Mahathir's leadership. New ideas and ways of doing things have been introduced in the political system and the society, revealing the will of a strong executive. In their train has emerged a split within the Malay political leadership, specifically within UMNO. Change is taking place also in the economy, with state intervention having become so pervasive that, in the words of one observer, "in order to understand what is happening in Malaysian politics, one must follow stock market activities and try to disentangle the 'paper' companies and subsidiaries and the individuals behind them" (Mauzy 1987: 232).

It is useful to subdivide the post-1971 period into two phases: the first between 1971 and 1981, when prime ministers Tun Razak and Tun Hussein Onn were at the helm; and the second from 1981 on, when Dr. Mahathir has taken charge. The politics of the first phase can now be seen to have been transitional to the emergence of the quasi-democracy that has become so evident during Dr. Mahathir's tenure. In this early transitional period, certain features inherited from the consociational democracy days reasserted themselves, but with modification. Such features, for example, as the grand coalition of communal organizations and the "segmental autonomy" of these organizations were still acknowledged even though the emphasis placed on them depended more than before on the style and nuances of individual leaders.

A very significant feature of the post-1971 political system is the primacy of Malay political power, in contrast to the more multiracial leadership that had been a characteristic of the 1957–69 period. The post-1971 system is still at least in semblance a parliamentary democracy, but since 1969 its basis is that of "Malay political hegemony" within the context of a multiracial coalition government. "Malay political hegemony" refers to the dominance (Malay politicians are quick to note it is "dominance" and not "domination") of the aspirations and wishes of the coalition's senior partner, UMNO, in its format of decision making and the resolution of demands made by its non-Malay components (Vasil 1971: chap. 1). Malay political dominance in the post-1971 system seeks to ensure as well "Malay" symbols of state and nation, the filling of critical posts with Malays in the bureaucracy, police, and armed forces, increasing participation in the public and private sectors, the promotion of a Malay-based national consciousness—all of which provides a sense of nativistic achievement (Zakaria 1987: 119, 123–25; Das 1987). It could be argued, of course, that a Malay-based nation-state and political system had been the prevailing notion of governance from the beginning in 1957 and even before that, but it is the post-1971 system that made such a conception, perhaps once and for all, unassailable.

Malay dominance or hegemony has been seen as essential to the achievement of the NEP, which spanned the twenty years from 1971 to 1990. This emphasis in effect meant that in the post-1971 period, political power had to be concentrated in Malay hands if the Malay-related economic goals were to be achieved. It also meant that the earlier "accommodationist" approach in racial politics was no longer tenable.

Nonetheless, in the first phase, under the leadership of Tun Razak and later

Table 6.3

**Principal Macro Indicators of Economic Growth in Malaysia, 1970–80**

|  | 1970 | 1980 | Average annual growth rate (%) |
|---|---|---|---|
| GNP at purchaser's value | | | |
| (1970 prices in U.S. $ mil.) | 11,953 | 25,444 | 7.8 |
| GNP per capita (in 1970 U.S. $) | 1,109 | 1,784 | 4.9 |
| Savings (as % of GNP) | 26.1 | 27.2 | |
| Gross investment (as % of GNP) | 21.4 | 29.6 | |

*Source:* Malaysia, *Fourth Malaysia Plan*, extracted from Mehmet 1986: 3.

Tun Hussein Onn, although the attainment of regime priorities required the concentration of strong political authority at the center, and although the latter, for example, did not hesitate to apply emergency rule in Kelantan in 1977, the governing style was one of instituting reforms by coopting opposition elites. Their tenure in power was too short to arrive at more definite conclusions of their manner of government, but it is evident that their use of the system was cautious and not heavy-handed. In the second phase, however, the style of Dr. Mahathir has been more direct and more resolute, so that the *quasi*-democratic features of the system have become more apparent.

The economic restructuring in the NEP required not only Malay political dominance, but also an expanding economic pie so that redistribution would not rob Peter to pay Paul. In the event, economic growth was impressive. Economist Ozay Mehmet, who has critically reviewed Malaysia's economic performance, comments: "Its aggregate savings have been extremely high, and during 1970–80 its gross national product grew at an average rate of 7.8 percent per annum. As a result of these favorable circumstances, real per capita income was 60 percent higher in 1980 than in 1970—an average growth rate of 4.9 percent per annum" (table 6.3). In 1984 the Malaysia per capita GNP in current prices reached the record-making high of U.S. $2,040 (World Bank 1989: 384).

This performance depended heavily on commodity exports. It was therefore increasingly vulnerable to international demand and supply conditions, even as diversification into manufacturing was embarked upon. The worldwide slump in the mid-1980s is reflected in the plummeting growth rate in 1985 of –1 (table 6.4). The recession was finally contained, however, and from 1987 the economy resumed its upward climb.

Political stability returned in the first phase of the post-1971 period. During the Tunku's tenure, Tun Razak had been seen as a loyal deputy who worked assiduously to improve the conditions of the rural Malays (Ness 1967). He was therefore viewed positively in the early quasi-democratic years as a prime minister of technocratic or administrative type who would push for Malay modernization. A reduction in politicking became possible because of the broadening of the

Table 6.4

**Real Growth Rate of GDP in Malaysia, 1980–88 (percent)**

| Year | Growth |
|------|--------|
| 1980 | 7.4 |
| 1981 | 6.9 |
| 1982 | 5.9 |
| 1983 | 6.3 |
| 1984 | 7.8 |
| 1985 | −1.0 |
| 1986 | 1.2 |
| 1987 | 5.2 |
| 1988 | 8.7 |

*Source:* Malaysia 1989: 13.

three-party Alliance into the Barisan Nasional or National Front. This "grand coalition" of relatively autonomous communal groups facilitated the mediation of ethnic and other disputes. The enlargement of the coalition also made it virtually unbeatable at the polls, the BN rolling up unbroken victories in the 1974, 1978, 1982, and 1986 elections. The only opposition outside the front came from the Malay-based Parti Islam (PAS), which itself was in the BN before 1974 and 1978, and the DAP, both of which had some regional, but little national, support. Non-Malay political interests became marginalized (Heng 1988), a tight Malay control was maintained over the center, and intra-Malay politics became intensified.

Malay dominance would seem to have been secured; however, a number of incidents occurred in the 1970s and 1980s that seemed to challenge the survival of the regime and, in some instances, the security of the nation itself; for example, the student and farmer demonstrations in 1974, the resurgence of Communist terrorist activities in 1974–76, the fear of a possible invasion from Vietnam following the latter's move into Cambodia in 1978, and the recurring aggravation of communal tensions as a result of the politics of restructuring. All of these, according to Harold Crouch, "constituted a prospect of a further political upheaval" and were seen as justifying "a turn to a more authoritarian form of government" (Crouch 1980: 5–6). Strong if indirect influence was exerted over the press, most of which is now owned by the ruling political parties. The Universities and Colleges Act was amended in 1975 to prevent students from taking part in political activity. In the late 1970s freedom of association was curbed also by amendments to the Societies Act.

The new thrust found expression also in more extensive intervention by the state in the economy. Economic restructuring under the NEP—designed to create a class of wealthy Malays and increase Malay ownership and control—led to what Mehmet terms "trusteeship," a state managerial role exercised by a small group of political decision makers and supported by a larger group of officials and public service staff (Mehmet 1986: 6ff.). Accordingly, the size and role of the bureaucracy, including quasi-governmental and statutory bodies, expanded rapidly. At the end of 1974, there were forty-five public enterprises owned by the federal government in addition to thirty-seven state-owned public enterprises (Mehmet 1986: 10–11). By the end of the 1970s, there were ninety-one federal public enterprises and fifty-six state statutory bodies. The federal public service underwent almost a fourfold expansion, increasing from 139,467 in 1970 to 521,818 by the end of 1983.

Government and quasi-government agencies, most under seconded civil servants, but all playing a role in the NEP under political aegis, spearheaded the necessary activities to achieve a better deal for the *bumiputras*. The public vocabulary became filled with such acronyms as PERNAS (the National Corporation), UDA (Urban Development Authority), ASN (National Unit Trust Scheme), and the various SEDCs (State Economic Development Corporations). Because these agencies sometimes also engaged in business, they provided vehicles for capital accumulation and opportunities for patronage (Gale 1981). The political parties also participated in business. UMNO, the MCA, and the MIC each had an investment arm, introducing a new element of commercial competition into the party arena.

For the success of the NEP, the leadership role of the bureaucracy was deemed especially important. This role, Mehmet argues, has made it possible for the bureaucratic trustees to emerge as a cartel:

> They have effectively cornered economic planning and decision-making to enrich themselves while paying lip-service to poverty eradication. Inter-racial income inequality, historically a major source of conflict in multi-racial Malaysia, is now being replaced by widening intra-ethnic inequality, especially among the Malays. (Mehmet 1986: preface)

Mehmet's thesis of cartelization is well argued. On the other hand, the enrichment of the bureaucracy and the growth of income inequality among the Malays can be attributed as well to the overall growth of the economy. High growth has provided the agencies with resources that these "trustees" have been able to use to subsidize enterprises whether efficient or not, thereby building "distributional coalitions" and creating "vast opportunities for self-enrichment" (Mehmet 1986: 132–54; also Toh 1982).

In spite of these deficiencies, there were sufficient gains in the NEP from the macro view to persuade the general Malay public and the various pro-Malay constituencies that Malay politics in command could ensure socioeconomic success. Malay stakes generally had increased in both the economy and the polity after 1971. Between 1970 and 1985, "the proportion of the Malay work-force employed in middle-class employment categories rose at a spectacular rate from 13 percent to 21 percent" (Crouch 1989: 14). The *Mid-Term Review of the Fifth Malaysia Plan (1986–1990)* noted that, "relative to their population share, the total number [of *bumiputras*] increased at an impressive rate of 11 percent compared with 5 percent for the non-*bumiputras*"; however, it also noted that despite such progress, the "overall disparity" between the two categories "remained clear at 1:3 compared with their respective shares in the population" (Malaysia 1989: 62–68). On poverty eradication, the incidence of poverty measured by household income levels decreased to 30.3 percent in 1983 from a 1970 level of 49.3 percent (Crouch 1989: 18). In terms of corporate ownership and control, *bumiputra* individuals and trust agencies increased their share from 4.3 percent in 1971 to 18.7 percent in 1983 (Malaysia 1985: tables 3–12). Malay urbanization in Peninsular Malaysia also proceeded apace; compared to 14.9 percent in 1970 (Milne and Mauzy 1978: 340), by 1990 it was expected to reach 45.8 percent (Malaysia 1989: 77).

Impressive as the gains were, it was apparent by the time Dr. Mahathir came to office in 1981 that ethnic tensions were growing more acute—partly as a result of the changes that had already taken place and partly from the expectations of changes yet to come. Strains increased during the recession of the mid-1980s, and under these diverse pressures, political contention broke out within the Malay leadership, leading in 1987–88 to a split between the so-called Team A and Team B elements (Shamsul 1988) and finally to a split in the party itself. The recent period has been marked also by financial scandals and public-sector mismanagement, for example, the Bumiputra Malaysia Finance Berhad fiasco in Hong Kong, the receivership of deposit-taking cooperatives, the Employees Provident Fund's activities in dubious share-buying schemes, huge losses among several banks, and alleged corruption and criminal breach of trust among people engaged in public takeovers and illegal corporate loans. Within UMNO itself the charge was levied that "money politics" had taken over (Muzaffar 1984).

That politics in the 1980s was so unstable is surprising. When Prime Minister Mahathir and his deputy, Musa Hitam (dubbed quickly the "2-M" government), took the reins in 1981, many in the country anticipated the beginning of a more dynamic, innovative, energetic, and even liberal administration. Their style of control was evident as they instructed the public bureaucracy to "clock in," asserting perhaps the primacy of politics in what had heretofore been an "administrative state" (Esman 1972; Puthucheary 1978). Two other significant steps they undertook indicated a no-nonsense, more liberal political approach: the release of those detained under the draconian Internal Security Act (ISA) and the closure of ailing public enterprises that had been established in the first decade of the NEP. According to data compiled by Harold Crouch (1989: 3), from a figure of 586 in 1981 the number of ISA detainees fell to only 40 in 1986 before increasing again with the arrest of 106 in "Operation Lallang," following a sharp increase in racial tensions in October 1987.

Dr. Mahathir's policies were not merely slogans, such as the "Clean, Efficient, and Trustworthy" government that he preached, but profound and in some sense revolutionary. In his "Look East" policy he began a search for a development strategy that fused or assimilated the Islamic values of Malaysians with the work and saving ethics of the Japanese and the Koreans. A program of heavy industrialization was begun, one objective being to make Malaysia a top producer of motor cars. At the same time agriculture was not overlooked, and Dr. Mahathir himself was involved in the drafting of the New Agriculture Policy (NAP) that was introduced in the mid-1980s. It was as though a neonationalistic phase had been embarked upon (Zakaria 1988). Compliance from many sectors was demanded, and a heavy dose of investment for the ambitious schemes of industrialization was required. Outwardly, consociational processes seemed to be preserved, but in essential style and operation, the wishes of the chief executive were predominant.

Despite the adverse economic conditions of the mid-1980s and notwithstanding political challenges from his detractors, especially from within UMNO itself, Dr. Mahathir was able to maintain the strength of the BN. In the 1986 elections, the BN won comfortably (Drummond 1987: 93–109; Khong 1986). In nine by-elections in Peninsular Malaysia since then, the BN has won seven (the other two being won by PAS and Semangat '46), albeit with reduced majorities. In the economic arena, however, the continuing attempt to extend privatization and secure better control of "off-budget agencies" did engender political controversy, and when suspicions were voiced that privatization was benefiting Dr. Mahathir's political colleagues and allies, he was even accused of running a Marcos-style administration (Malaysian Bar Council 1987).

Although control of the media served to exclude views and news of events and personalities opposed to the official line, the advent of the Mahathir government did not bring further restriction on political discourse. In fact, the economic growth of the 1970s brought with it an enhanced quality of life. The citizenry became more involved in public issues. In the late 1970s and 1980s public-interest groups began to proliferate, groups like ALIRAN (Friends of the Environment) and FOMCA (the Federation of Consumer Associations) (Khong 1987). These groups cut across racial lines and demonstrated a growing pluralism even as the state became more autocratic.

But criticism of the regime had its limits. In "Operation Lallang" in October 1987, which was meant to prevent certain individuals and groups from inciting another racial incident like that in 1969, political party leaders as well as leaders of public-interest groups were arrested, and three newspapers were shut down. More ominous, perhaps, for the future of liberal democratic politics was the government's attack shortly after on members of the judiciary, including the Lord President, who were accused of wrongdoing and overstepping their lines of authority vis-à-vis the executive. In 1988 the Lord President and two Supreme Court justices were removed (Young 1988; Salleh 1989). The government made much of the doctrine of the "separation of powers," arguing that this imposed serious limits on the judiciary's consideration of executive decisions, especially in cases concerning the regime and national security. In subsequent parliamentary legislation in 1987–88, even recourse to the courts on ISA detentions, which had been the legal instrument for "Operation Lallang," became nonadmissible.

## Race, Growth, and Politics

How will the Mahathir administration develop from this point on? One cannot be sure. Based on Dr. Mahathir's past performance, however, especially in warding off threats to his policies and leadership, it seems possible that he will outlast his adversaries for some time; indeed, in spite of his multiple-bypass operation in early 1989, he and his followers have emerged stronger and more cohesive than before ("Malaysia—In Shape," 1989). Dr. Mahathir has exhorted those split from UMNO to rejoin the party for the sake of "Malay unity," and indications are that support by UMNO (whether in its "new" form or otherwise) will remain a prerequisite for any government, democratic or otherwise, if it is to achieve and satisfy Malay aspirations. The economic recession of the mid-1980s led to a greater flexibility in NEP implementation, but not to its fundamental weakening. The need to reduce racial differentials in economic roles and opportunities remains, and so long as that is true, whatever will be decided in the National Economic Consultative Council (NECC or MAPEN), which has been formed to devise a post-NEP policy, must emphasize the politics of economic development. Under such circumstances, it is as yet difficult to see any weakening of the present quasi-democratic structure.

It is tempting to assert that economic growth in Malaysia has left in its wake a "middle class" that has had a serious impact on the nature of politics in Malaysia. Anders Tandrup (1984), for example, argues that the NEP must be understood as "an important tool in the power struggle between the various cliques and fractions [sic] of the Malay ruling class," with Chinese and foreign capital playing important, but subordinated roles. Similarly, Johan Saravanamuttu (1989) believes that class consciousness has been a "new" political force, one that has been important in the development of a bourgeois democracy and will eventually replace race in Malaysian politics.

But the conclusion seems inescapable that communalism remains and will continue for some time to remain the key to Malaysian politics. The NEP did bring about a differentiation of the society and the economy that has colored politics, but, even when in-fighting erupted within UMNO, it was more of an intra-ethnic struggle than one of class interests cutting across ethnicity. (For a different view, see Shamsul 1988: 173–74). Indeed, among those opposed to Dr. Mahathir after the UMNO split in 1987, none presented an alternative to UMNO's objectives.

Thus, in Malaysia, the all-enveloping cloud of communal rivalry obscures the political direction in which economic growth may be driving, whether primarily democratic or authoritarian. Dr. Mahathir may exhibit an autocratic style, but the powers at his behest have been in place since 1957. It is also apparent that the felt need for Malay predominance in the political system outweighs the urge for a full-fledged, Western-type liberal democracy. Moreover, economic growth has facilitated the expansion of Malay political power, which was necessary to achieve NEP goals, and has allowed for a concentration of power within the Malay political elite, assisted by a subservient, pro-Malay bureaucracy. The felt need to preserve this role and power and be less buffeted by opposition elements of threats to the regime has led to legal and other measures that have made Malaysia seem more authoritarian and less democratic from the late 1970s on.

On the other hand, while economic growth has provided some support for the transformation of the system from a more or less democratic to a more authoritarian or quasi-democratic form, it has also mobilized the society for political action in a way that has prevented this authoritarian trend from going any further than it has. As Crouch (1989: 14) points out, "Malaysia's social structure provides substantial barriers to the adoption of a fully-fledged authoritarian system in that economic and social development has produced social groups with distinct interests which they seek to protect and advance." Race remains a central issue, but the growing pluralism of Malaysian society that economic growth has stimulated has so far ensured that the government remains more or less responsive to the needs and demands of all its variegated societal elements.

# Part III
# Newly Industrializing
# Economies

# 7

# South Korea: Democratization at Last

## Sung-joo Han and Yung Chul Park

IN 1988, after three decades of authoritarian rule backed by the military, Korea managed a peaceful transfer of power through a democratic process. Only a year before, few thought that such a development would be possible. This political change has also come after three decades of rapid growth and industrialization during which Korea has developed into one of the important manufacturing centers and the twelfth-largest trader in the world economy, with per capita income approaching U.S. $3,000. Is there a causal relationship between these two developments? We believe there is—but there are other causal relationships as well.

The nexus of their relationship is to be found in the modernization process, a complex syndrome of social and economic changes involving rational and secularized thinking, political awakening, industrialization, and social mobility, which have accompanied the rapid expansion of the economy. One consequence of these changes has been to destabilize authoritarianism. Secularization has undermined the traditional bases of political authority, and increased awareness has created demands and expectations that could not be met by the government. Industrialization has tended to create new social and ideological cleavages and conflicts. Social mobility and urbanization have made people more susceptible to ideological agitation and disorderly mass action. A second consequence has been to stimulate change toward democracy. Improved communication and greater awareness have made it difficult to maintain an authoritarian government. Rational thinking has made more feasible and necessary the acquisition of government office by election. Economic growth and social development have contributed social groups, such as the middle class, that generally support a democratic system.

Nevertheless, these tendencies have not unfolded smoothly. A number of factors have distorted or delayed their evolution. One such factor has been the nature of the traditional society. Before the process of modernization began in the late nineteenth century, Korea was an authoritarian society ruled by a highly centralized bureaucracy under an autocratic monarch. This was in sharp contrast with such feudal societies as traditional Japan, which, although equally authoritarian, had maintained a pluralistic and decentralized polity. The concentration of power in the central government in Korea was further heightened in the twentieth century during Japanese rule, which imposed on Korea a highly centralized colonial administration. Until the end of World War II, Koreans had experienced only a highly centralized executive authority that was neither checked nor balanced by countervailing power groups, such as regional lords or elected representatives. In South Korea today, there is still a highly unbalanced development of political institutions—that is, an "overdevelopment" of output institutions such as the bureaucracy and the military as opposed to an "underdevelopment" of input organizations such as political parties and interest groups.

A second element that has impeded the political changes that the modernization process might otherwise have engendered is the uncontrolled and indiscriminate way social change has taken place. During the colonial period, the traditional elite lost its power and social status; many of its values were discredited and practices discarded. Moreover, Korea experienced a total dismantling of its political institutional and authority structures. Socioeconomic modernization was introduced to Korea by a foreign elite who had no interest in preserving the country's traditional institutions. Thus, when Koreans had the opportunity to form their own government after their liberation from Japanese colonial rule, they had to build their political structure from the very beginning. They had not preserved any traditional mechanisms by which loyalty to the new government could be generated; this placed excessive burdens on new means of legitimacy, such as elections, which are yet to be fully institutionalized.

Third, the kind of politics a modernizing society is likely to experience at any given time depends on the sequence of its political experiments since the modernization process began. South Korea began its experiments in modern politics only four decades ago. It did not have satisfactory results with either the charismatic leadership of Syngman Rhee or parliamentary democracy during the 1960–61 period. Such an unsatisfactory experience with other systems might be called "legitimacy by default"—that is, the acceptance by the people, albeit without enthusiasm, of a military-backed authoritarian system out of the feeling that the alternatives had not proved more desirable. Now authoritarianism has had its turn—a long one at that—and has been decidedly rejected as a suitable system for South Korea today.

As for the fourth factor, South Korea has been under a constant and acute security threat since 1948. A devastating war took place in 1950–53, leaving the peninsula divided and the South under a continuous threat thereafter by a formidable foe in the North. For this reason, South Korea has had to maintain a large military establishment, a government capable of mobilizing national resources for defense purposes, and a society oriented toward maximizing security against internal subversion and external attack. Such requirements have tended to favor the rise of a "firm" and strong state. Indeed, a substantial portion of the people seem to have felt that a "soft" state would not be able to cope with the security problem or handle the task of economic development, which is deemed necessary for security. A corollary of this argument for much of the postindependence period has been that a strong state is not compatible with a democratic system of government.

Finally, the dilemma of liberal democracy had been especially acute in South Korea because of the serious social and ideological cleavage between the conservatives and the radical left. The division of the country between the Communist-controlled North and anti-Communist South has been primarily responsible for the intolerant, antileft attitude among key groups in South Korea, such as the armed forces, the police, the bureaucracy, and individuals in the "establishment." On the other hand, radicalism has grown, particularly among the students and those who consider themselves belonging to the "deprived" groups, to the extent that it is seen by the conservatives as posing a genuine threat to the survival of the nation, not to mention to the existing socioeconomic order.

Radicalism in Korea exhibits traits of strong nationalistic and egalitarian beliefs (Han 1974: 5). The appeal of radicalism derives from the perception among many of an uneven distribution of the benefits of socioeconomic change and of the country's excessive dependence on foreign powers. Radical activists have thus demanded a complete overhaul of not only the political system but also the socioeconomic structure itself. This, however, hinders the democratization process. As the defenders of the socioeconomic status quo see it, the choice is between revolutionary change and the existing socioeconomic order rather than between liberal democracy and dictatorship. In the past the result has been a vicious circle of oppressive measures and radical demands. Korea has thus undergone a tortured experience on the path to democratization.

## A Cycle of Struggle, 1961–79

Major-General Park Chung Hee came to power in May 1961 after toppling the constitutionally established government of Chang Myon, accusing the latter and the civilian leadership of being corrupt, incapable of defending the country from internal and external threats of communism, and unable to bring about the economic and social transformation desired. Upon taking power, General Park pledged to transfer the government to "fresh and conscientious politicians" when the tasks of the revolution had been completed. During the ensuing two years, Park made preparations to assume the leadership of the future "civilian" government by banning more than four thousand politicians of the previous regime from political activities for at least six years. He consolidated his own position within the ruling group of primarily military leaders by purging recalcitrant elements and potential rivals. He then staged a national referendum that adopted a new constitution providing for a strong presidential system with a weak legislature, and he built a party (the Democratic-Republican party) to aid him and his supporters in presidential and legislative elections.

In 1962, he also launched the First Five-Year Development Plan, staking out a domestic policy strategy that made economic growth together with national security the prime objective of government. Political stability was regarded as indispensable to both these objectives and necessary even if it entailed high costs. Accordingly, the government ensured military backing for its policies and, when it felt the situation required, limited civil liberties and employed repressive tactics to coerce business, financial institutions, and labor to follow its directives. During the 1964–67 period, the government reoriented the economy away from import substitution to export-led industrialization. It devalued the won and doubled interest rates, thereby bringing the prices of foreign exchange and money to their equilibrium values and allowing the market to take over a greater role in making business decisions. It restructured the tariff system, overhauled the tax structure, and improved the tax administration. These reforms constituted an attempt to liberalize the economy. They were to a large extent responsible for Korea's subsequent economic growth.

They also served to broaden the government's public support. Following a series of political crises that resulted from Park's reluctance to relinquish military rule, and under pressure from the United States and political forces at home, a presidential election was held in November 1963. Park, who had formally retired from the military at the end of August to participate in the campaign, won the election, which was considered to have been conducted in a reasonable, fair atmosphere. He received 46.7 percent of the vote. Park's support was weak in the urban areas; he also failed to receive strong support from the so-called military areas along the Demilitarized Zone (Kim 1971: 135). But in the legislative election that immediately followed, Park's party won a large majority—110 seats out of the total of 175, and in 1967 Park was reelected by a more comfortable plurality of 49 percent of the votes cast, over his chief opponent's 39 percent (the anti-Park and antimilitary vote was split between two major civilian candidates). In the second half of the 1960s, all appeared to be going well for President Park's continued stay in office.

Beginning around 1969 and 1970, however, the economic performance started to deteriorate. A high rate of inflation, combined with a slow rate of depreciation of the won against foreign currencies, resulted in a sharp increase in the current account deficit. The deficit and price inflation were then followed by a slowdown in economic growth. These developments were blamed on and precipitated a retreat from liberal economic policies. Increased government intervention followed.

The shift to a policy of economic intervention was also occasioned by a rising concern for the growing power of the private enterprises. Over time, there had emerged several dozen conglomerates (the *chaebol*), which accounted for a large share of Korean exports and were major actors involved in the development of heavy, chemical, and defense industries. These conglomerates had amassed considerable wealth and increasing economic and financial power, which they hoped to use to exert greater influence on government policy. To prevent any further private concentration of economic power, the government felt the need to keep these groups under control. It was considered difficult to do so, however, while at the same time liberalizing previously controlled markets, import restrictions, and foreign exchange regulations. The government decided, therefore, to exert its authority over the conglomerates by retaining control over the financial institutions that supplied a significant share of their domestic credit needs and by strengthening tax surveillance as well.

Another impulse for greater intervention was the felt need to shift exports from labor-intensive to capital- and skill-intensive, heavy industrial products. It was during the Second Five-Year Development Plan period (1967–71) that the government began laying the groundwork for these structural adjustments by introducing a series of laws designed to support investment in heavy and chemical industries. The problems were large. Enormous investments in fixed capital and technology were required with long gestation periods and uncertain rates of return, not to mention the difficulties of cultivating new foreign markets for the products. Understandably, even the large firms were reluctant to take on these risks, with the result that the government had to provide a combination of guarantees, equity participation, tax concessions, and preferential low-interest credits to get these industries started. The dominant view at that time was that the development of heavy and chemical industries could not be left to market forces but required political stability and government intervention in resource allocation to direct investment to those industries. In short, the Park regime drew up a strategy that envisaged a second industrial takeoff directed by government.

A fourth development leading to greater government intervention was the sharp deterioration in the international trading environment beginning with the first oil shock in 1973. This dealt Korea a severe blow. It suddenly made the prospects of the economy unfavorable. Uncontrollable inflation, deceleration of growth due largely to a sharp drop in export demand, and mounting current account deficits awakened the society to the severity of its vulnerability and exacerbated its feelings of insecurity. It is often suggested that a free market system foists insecurities on the population. In a highly open economy like Korea's with a poor resource endowment, the society is likely to feel particularly insecure and vulnerable—more so than those in economies pursuing inward-looking policies. To protect itself, such a society is inclined to invite government intervention in resource allocation and in the business decision-making process. At least that is what happened in South Korea.

These changes helped generate widespread support for the argument that Korea could not afford to lose more time in experimenting with economic liberalization while international markets for goods, services, and capital failed to function in the competitive manner expected. The Korean public became convinced that developed countries on whose markets Korea depended for export earnings as well as resource-rich countries from which Korea imported raw material could use their market power to pursue political objectives unacceptable to it. To protect the economy from these potential foreign political pressures, it was argued that the society should rally behind a strong leader and government even if political ideals had to be compromised.

The crisis in economic policy occurred at the same time as opposition to the government's political tenure began to boil. The student movement, with its opposition to the government's "military" character and the "reactionary" nature of its foreign and economic policies, presented one problem; the constitution, which restricted the presidency to two four-year terms, presented another. The first major outbreak of student demonstrations since 1961 took place in 1964 against the proposed Korea–Japan normalization treaty. Many students believed that South Korea had made too many concessions to Japan and that the treaty was negotiated in a "humiliating" manner. They were demonstrating not only against the treaty but also against what they considered were many failures of the Park government. The government initially attempted to mollify the students by postponing the signing of the treaty and reshuffling the cabinet; however, the protest grew in size and intensity. The government, well aware of the consequences of the April 1960 student uprising, when Rhee was overthrown, sternly suppressed it, declaring a state of martial law and arresting several hundred students.

Large-scale demonstrations occurred many times since then during the Park regime: in 1965 against the ratification of the Korea-Japan treaty, in 1967 against allegedly unfair National Assembly elections, in 1969 against the constitutional revision that permitted a third-term presidency for Park Chung Hee, and after 1972 against the Yushin (Revitalizing Reforms) Constitution. In the face of a mounting threat to the regime caused by student disturbances, President Park tightened the legal ban against student activism. In October 1971, he ordered, among other things, the expulsion from school of the leaders of demonstrations, rallies, sit-ins, strikes, or other "disorderly activities," the disbandment of all nonacademic circles and groups on the campuses, and the prohibition of all "unauthorized" publications by students. A presidential decree of April 1974, later repealed, provided for punishment up to the death penalty against student protest activities. When the 1969 constitutional amendment—achieved through a referendum—enabled the president to run for his third term in 1971, the move became another serious cause of agitation by the students, which in turn brought further and heavier penalties. The 1971 presidential election, in which Park's chief opposition candidate, Kim Dae-jung, received 46 percent of the votes cast, indicated to Park that his continued stay in office could be threatened under the existing electoral system despite enormous advantages he enjoyed in elections as the incumbent.

Except for the Korean Central Intelligence Agency (KCIA) activities and the suppression of student political activism, many of the oppressive features of the regime did not begin to appear in full force until 1972. Before that there was relative freedom of the press, speech, and opposition activities. All three presidential elections held prior to 1972 were rather close ones that could have gone the other way with a little more unity, popular appeal, and astuteness of the opposition. The question arises as to what might have happened if Park had actually lost one of those elections. Kim Se-jin, a student of Korean military politics, pointed out the irony of Korean democracy: "Park's victory [in 1963] was in fact a blessing for the future of democracy in Korea. Had the military lost, it can be safely assumed that the military would have ignored the electoral outcome and continued to rule even though such rule would have meant a total destruction of constitutionalism" (Kim 1971: 136).

During the 1970s, the restrictions on opposition activities and limitations on effective political competition were legally prescribed. Until 1979, when the Park government collapsed following the president's assassination, the key legal instrument for this purpose was the Yushin Constitution, which was adopted in a referendum held under martial law in November 1972. The Park government had proposed the Yushin Constitution assertedly to facilitate national unification, to cope with the changing international situation, and to carry out effectively the country's socioeconomic development. It provided for an indirect election of the president by a National Conference for Unification, which was locally elected and thus more easily subjected to the influence of the government; appointment by the president of one-third of the 219-member National Assembly (the rest of the membership being elected in seventy-three 2-member districts); an unrestricted number of six-year terms for the president; reduction of the powers of the legislature and the judiciary; and curtailment of civil and political rights by presidential decrees (Lee Chae-jin 1973: 99–101). In the face of mounting criticism and protest, the Park government promulgated a series of "emergency measures" in 1974, banning all criticism of the Yushin Constitution and demand for its revision. A March 1975 revision of the criminal code provided for heavy jail terms for any citizen at home or abroad who "insults, slanders, or harms by rumors or other means the government or its agencies." Student demonstrations and rallies were strictly prohibited by law and presidential decrees, under penalty of imprisonment and expulsion from school (Han 1975: 43–45).

Various explanations have been offered for the authoritarian trend in Korea during the 1970s. Neo-Marxist writers argue that the South Korean government had to resort to repressive measures to collaborate with and serve the economic interests of international capitalism led by the American and Japanese multinational corporations (Bix 1973; Breidenstein 1973). Other scholars have pointed out factors of a more general nature, such as the centralizing and hierarchical nature of Korea's social structure and political culture; ideological cleavages between the "rightists" and the "leftists" as well as between the "authoritarians" and the "liberal democrats"; and the unbalanced development of political institutions, i.e., the "overdevelopment" of the output institutions such as the bureaucracy and the military relative to the input institutions such as political parties and interest groups (Henderson 1968; Wright 1974; Han 1974). Still others have emphasized the political leaders' personal penchant for power and the legacy of Korea's recent history, especially the Korean War, which left the society militarized and lacking in civil values (U.S. House of Representatives 1974).

Comprehensive as the above listing of the explanations might appear, it is not quite adequate in two respects. First, it does not distinguish between what might be called, on the one hand, the "permissive" factors, which constitute the general background to authoritarianism and, on the other hand, the "causal" factors, which act as the direct, moving forces in what might be called an "authoritarianizing process." Second, the explanations do not adequately address themselves to the question of why the process of authoritarianization was accelerated in South Korea from around the end of the 1960s.

It seems reasonable to suppose that the general-level factors—sociocultural, ideological, institutional, and historical—provided a permissive environment for authoritarian rule. Particularly influential was the "militarized" nature of the society—the large number of military personnel and veterans, the diversion of huge amounts of resources to defense, the priority given to military considerations in foreign and domestic policy making, and the permanent emergency atmosphere—as well as the support that the Park government received from the military, bureaucratic, and business sectors.

Among causal and timing factors, the crisis in economic policy might seem a logical candidate, occurring simultaneously and calling for greater intervention—or so the government argued. Certainly the intensification of economic controls was consistent with the authoritarianization of the political system and no doubt benefited by it. On close inspection, however, the role played by the change in economic strategy appears to have been more permissive than causal. The causal and timing factors were overwhelmingly political.

The most important and immediate impetus for the emergence of an oppressive regime was the intensification of the opposition and the Park government's realization that elections under the existing system (pre-Yushin) would not guarantee continued victories for the DRP candidates. Moreover, even if a favorable outcome were engineered by illegal means, such a fraudulent victory seemed likely to provide the government's opponents with a rallying point against it, as such an event had provoked Syngman Rhee's opponents to collective action in 1960. The 1969 constitutional amendment enabled President Park to maintain the electoral support necessary to keep the president in office indefinitely. Many of those who had held a reasonably favorable attitude toward the Park government and had a high regard for its achievements were disappointed by its tampering with the constitution to prolong Park's presidency. Since the 1969 amendment permitted a third term only for the incumbent, a further stay in office beyond the term would have required another change in the constitution, which in turn would have cost the Park government more popular support.

It seems certain that, during the several years following his narrow election victory in 1963, President Park succeeded in increasing his support levels, primarily due to the successful implementation of the government's economic development plans. In elections, he and his party were also aided by the availability of disproportionately large amounts of campaign funds, which were of crucial importance in Korea (Chang 1971). As the situation was changing substantially after 1969, however, a significant restructuring of the legal and governing system was deemed necessary if a transition of power either within the government party itself or to the opposition were to be prevented.

On its part, the government argued that, by eliminating for practical purposes the interparty electoral competition, much "waste" of resources and energy that had been an indispensable part of electioneering by both parties could be eliminated; that the government, through its system of so-called administrative democracy—which placed emphasis on the identification, articulation, and representation of interests by administrative means and mechanisms—could more effectively concentrate on solidifying the nation's defense and achieving social and economic development without interference from "politics"; and that the country should not be turned over to a weak government that could easily be toppled by another military coup d'état. Apologists for the government also argued that an authoritarian, but humane and benevolent, government was not adverse to Korea's political-cultural tradition and was therefore not unacceptable to a great majority of the Korean people (Hahm 1974). Regardless of the validity of these arguments, however, opposition to the authoritarian regime was growing at a rapid rate, and the government was losing legitimacy as well as the ability to maintain social stability and effective governance.

That is not to say that the political effects of two decades of Park rule were all negative. As a result of his persistent drive for rapid economic development, he did succeed in creating a substantial middle class, which could become the mainstay of a democratic political system if one were established and if it proved able to provide continued economic growth, social stability, and security from external threats. A related consequence of Park's rule was the regularization of government procedures and the institutionalization of executive power. It is true that these were accompanied by excessive bureaucratization of the government and the proliferation of authoritarian practices surrounding the presidency; this strengthening of the bureaucracy, however, also made the exercise of administrative power by the government and its leaders more economical, predictable, and effective—all qualities useful for providing continuity and stability in the face of the more frequent changes of government a future democracy might require.

But as Park's second decade of power drew to a close, it was the negative aspects of his regime that proved most consequential. One of his most serious failures was not to provide an institutional and political framework within which an orderly succession could take place following his departure from the political scene, voluntarily or otherwise. Park needed the Yushin Constitution to prolong and strengthen his presidency. But it had been tailor-made only for him, leaving the nation after his death with a highly unpopular and unworkable legal framework within which a new leader or government could not be chosen in an orderly way. In addition, he thwarted the development of an institutionalized party system for engaging the various competing forces and interests in the political process or bringing a new generation of leaders to the fore. Park was personally suspicious of both the progovernment and opposition parties. He considered them as a necessary evil at best and a threat at worst. Neither his own Democratic-Republican party nor the opposition New Democratic party was given a proper opportunity to develop the necessary leadership structure and to cultivate grass-roots support. As a result, political parties failed to become the main medium by which struggles for power and influence could be carried out following Park's death.

Moreover, in the course of his prolonged rule, President Park had generated so much opposition to and alienation from not only his own rule but also the sociopolitical system as a whole that, once he departed from the scene, piecemeal changes and a peaceful transition became almost an impossibility. Various individuals and groups sought radical solutions and tried to "settle old scores" immediately. In addition, during President Park's tenure, much of the top elite circulation took place horizontally and within a limited circle of supporters, thus frustrating the power aspirations of ambitious individuals both within and outside of his own party and intensifying the intraparty as well as interparty power struggles.

Another negative legacy was the increased propensity and capability of the military to play a political role. In large part because of the way the Park government came to power and also because it depended heavily on the military for staying in power, the military became prone to intervene in politics when it felt there was the need and the justification. Finally, as Park became increasingly unpopular, he made political use of the security issue with the unfortunate result of weakening its credibility. Many people, particularly the students, acquired the habit of showing cynicism toward South Korea's security problems, which were nonetheless genuine. At the same time, the political involvement of some of the government law enforcement and intelligence agencies compromised their effectiveness in performing their tasks and caused them to lose credibility.

Thus, at the time of President Park's death, Korean society had a potential for acute polarization and power struggle, and its political system lacked the necessary leadership structure and institutional mechanisms by which such struggles could be managed without violence or social disorder. It was this situation that induced and enabled a group of military leaders to step in and take over the reins of power in the political vacuum that followed the death of President Park in

October 1979. The restoration of democracy in South Korea thus had to be postponed until another round of authoritarian politics had completed its cycle.

## The Chun Era: Democratization Postponed

The authoritarian system of Yushin collapsed in 1979 with the assassination of President Park Chung Hee by his chief intelligence aide, who claimed that he acted to save the nation from a revolutionary "bloodbath." It is not certain that the opposition could have succeeded had the assassination not taken place. It is clear, however, that serious strains had begun to appear in the regime and that a major crisis was brewing. Its popularity was at an all-time low, measured even by the results of elections heavily distorted by government interference. For example, Park's Democratic-Republican party had suffered a serious loss in December 1978 when it obtained only 31 percent of the popular vote in the National Assembly election. Large-scale riots took place toward the end of his regime in such major cities as Pusan and Masan.

Park's death was greeted with the popular expectation that authoritarian rule would come to an end and full democracy would be restored. A period of active anticipation and live political activity by various groups and individuals was followed, however, by the declaration of full martial law in 1980. In August, with the support of key military leaders, General Chun Doo Hwan, who had headed the Military Security Command under the Park government, took over the post of acting president, after which the rubber-stamp National Conference of Unification elected him as president. In October, a new constitution, which retained many of the key features of the Yushin Constitution, was put to a national referendum. It was approved by an overwhelming vote. Under the new constitution, Chun was elected president without competition for a seven-year term in January 1981. Chun promptly disbanded all political parties of the previous regime, purged their leaders, and placed under political ban hundreds of politicians and other activists. In addition to his own Democratic Justice party, he allowed the formation of several parties by political personalities and organizations that could not challenge the ruling group in any effective way. Instruments of "power and control" such as the KCIA (renamed the National Security Planning Agency) and the Military Security Command were retained or strengthened. The new National Assembly and the interim Legislative Council that had preceded it in 1978 enacted laws that enabled the government to effectively control the press and the labor movement. In short, another cycle of authoritarian rule devoid of political competition and civil rights began (Lee Chong-sik 1981).

There was nothing inevitable about the fact that in 1980 South Korea's democratization process would face another serious setback and authoritarian rule would be restored. It is possible, however, to offer a few explanations as to why the transition to democracy, which had been so ardently and overwhelmingly

y South Koreans after nearly two decades of authoritarian rule, had to
oned once again.

First, even though Park had died, the power structure—the military, the bureaucracy, and other groups that had a vested interest in the status quo—remained intact. Only the ruling Democratic-Republican party was seriously
weakened, although it did not collapse. This was in contrast to the post-Rhee
period, when few organizations or groups remained supportive of the political or
socioeconomic system that the Rhee regime had left behind. Thus, the remnants
of the Park government, as an organization if not as individuals, including the
interim cabinet of Choi Kyu-Hah (who had been Park's prime minister before his
death and who had temporarily succeeded him), were able to hold off the pressures and demands of the anti-Park forces to implement the democratization
process immediately. They bought enough time for those who had a stake in the
authoritarian system to regroup and render support for a regime that was likely to
be more favorable to their interests than a democratic one.

Second, the party politicians, particularly of the opposition, lacked effective
leadership and unity. The chasm was especially evident between the incumbent
leaders of the New Democratic party (the principal opposition party during the
Park period) and the forces represented by and supporting Kim Dae Jung, who
had been imprisoned and deprived of the right to participate actively in politics.
Being certain that their turn to assume power had come, and preoccupied with
struggle and competition among themselves, the democratic politicians of the
opposition allowed the antidemocratic forces outside party politics to gain control of the events and ultimately supersede the parties.

The radical and vengeful image of certain groups, particularly among dissident students, intellectuals, and progressive Christians as well as the politicians
who were supported by them, also contributed to a certain degree of acquiescence that the general public exhibited when authoritarian rule was restored by
Chun. Even though riots broke out in certain cities such as Kwangju when
martial law was extended throughout the nation in May 1980, citizens began to
show as much concern about the social instability and disorder accompanying
the democratization process as about its delay. Such concern became more poi-
gnant as student demonstrations intensified and after large-scale riots by miners
and steel mill workers broke out in April. The "middle class" had grown during
the Park regime and acquired a vested interest in socioeconomic stability and
continuity. It was still too insecure about its political and economic status to opt
decisively for political freedom and democracy at the risk of sacrificing the
country's continued economic growth and its own newly secured socioeconomic
status.

A fourth explanation for the relative ease with which Chun and his military
associates took power can be sought in the nature of the South Korean military
itself. It was with General Park Chung Hee's military coup d'état in 1961 that the
Korean military began directly intervening in politics. Until then, President Syngman

Rhee had skillfully kept the military under control and away from political involvement. It was only during the last few days of the Rhee government that the military played a decisive role in the political outcome when it refused to use violence against the anti-Rhee demonstrators. But by coming to power by a military coup d'état and by staying in power primarily through the support of the military, the Park government contributed greatly to politicizing the military. Top officers came to believe they had a claim and indeed an obligation to involve themselves in South Korea's politics by virtue of their position as defenders and protectors of a society under constant threat of external invasion and internal subversion. After all, the military was getting a disproportionate share of the national budget and manpower, and the society had been highly militarized in terms of its mentality and way of life. Furthermore, although the Korean military had lacked cohesion among the high-ranking officers and between the higher and lower officers during the earlier (Rhee and Park) periods, by 1980 the core consisted of graduates of the South Korean Military Academy, among whom there were strong senses of camaraderie, shared interest, and responsibility. Thus, it is no mere coincidence that General Chun represented Class One of the Military Academy and that his military colleagues were able to secure the acquiescence, if not the support, of a substantial part of the middle- and lower-ranking officers (colonels and captains) in their takeover of the government.

A contributing factor in the collapse of the democratization process was the absence in South Korean society of individuals, groups, and institutions such as a monarch or respected political elders that could act as a mitigating, mediating, and moderating force among the contending political forces. Political conflicts therefore tended to be of a naked, confrontational, and zero-sum nature. In this normative vacuum, there was no one person or institution that could bestow upon or deprive a person or group of legitimacy. Neither could anyone authoritatively endorse or deny someone else's claim to power even when it was clear that fair and due process was ignored and popular aspirations betrayed.

To make matters worse, the Korean economy was hit by the second oil shock, a poor harvest, rising interest rates that greatly increased Korea's debt servicing burden, and trade protectionism that sharply reduced Korea's export earnings in 1980. The massive investment undertaken for the development of heavy and chemical industries turned into idle capacity and in many sectors had to be scrapped. These internal and external developments came together to result in a negative rate of economic growth in 1980, which was a shocking experience to many Koreans, who had been accustomed to rapid growth for almost two decades.

Knowing that he had come to power without a popular mandate, Chun devised a novel definition of democracy, arguing that its most important ingredient was a "peaceful transfer of power" at the end of the president's prescribed term, something that had never happened in South Korea's post–World War II political history. Thus, he repeatedly stressed his determination to step down at the end of his seven-year term, in early 1988. Clearly, this gesture was far from adequate to mollify the anger and frustration of those who saw their democratic aspiration and struggle nullified by a group of ambitious military officers. The antigovernment, democratic movement in due course picked up where it had left off upon the death of President Park. Only this time it was to be better organized, more forceful, and more widespread than before. As it became clear toward the end of the Chun government that his idea of a "peaceful transfer of power" was to be within the "power group" rather than to the civilian opposition, antigovernment activities intensified to the extent that the Chun government was driven to making a choice between total suppression by mobilizing all the coercive instruments of power, including the military, and substantial concessions to the opposition to begin the democratization process.

Having secured a legal basis of power through the adoption of the new constitution, Chun and his supporters attempted to devise a party system that would give the government an overwhelming advantage over the opposition. They thus tried to establish a multiparty system in which the dominant (government) party would be opposed by several minor parties. Furthermore, there was to be scarcely any competition within the dominant party. Such a scheme seemed to be having some success as, in the first National Assembly election held after the establishment of the Chun government, the ruling Democratic Justice party (DJP) received 36 percent of the votes cast while the rest were shared by twelve other parties, including the opposition Democratic Korea party (DKP), which obtained 21 percent, and the National party, which was formed by individuals with close connections with the defunct Park government and which secured 13 percent of the votes.

This was only a temporary phenomenon, however. As the political ban on former politicians was lifted for the most part, there was a coalescing of opposition forces into a single party. The parliamentary election of February 1985 brought about a basic realignment of political power and parties. In that election, the New Korea Democratic party (NDP), formed largely by politicians who had been placed under political ban in 1980 by the Chun government, made an impressive showing, winning 67 of the 187 elective seats. This compared with only 35 for the existing Democratic Korea party, which, even though it had acted as the main opposition party during the preceding four years, was seen by the electorate as being accommodating to the Chun government. The new opposition party's electoral success led to a mass defection of the DKP members to the NDP, with the result that a virtual two-party system emerged. Now the battle line was clearly drawn—between the government party, which insisted on the legitimacy of the government as well as the existing constitution by which it came to power, and the opposition party, which argued that the government lacked legitimacy and that the system as it stood favored the incumbent party, because in the indirect election of the president, the electoral college was susceptible to government influence.

As the government party had a clear majority in the National Assembly, however, the battle—with constitutional revision as the key symbolic as well as substantive issue—was waged in the streets and on the campuses largely by the *chae-ya se-ryok* (forces in the field), consisting of dissident student leaders, intellectuals, and progressive Christians. Even Stephen Cardinal Kim, who headed the three-million-strong Korean Catholics, joined those who called for a constitutional change. In the face of large-scale demonstrations, mostly by university students, continuing social instability, and pressure from various groups including the church, intellectuals, and lawyers as well as the United States, the Chun government decided in February 1986 that the constitution after all would be revised before the expected transfer of power in 1988. It was perhaps not a mere coincidence that, only a few weeks earlier, the Marcos government was ousted by "People Power" in the Philippines.

As the debate on constitutional revision continued through 1986, it became clear that the opposition was determined not to retreat one step from its demand for a presidential system of government in which the president was to be elected by a direct, popular vote. The government, on its part, proposed a parliamentary system of government in which the chief executive would be elected indirectly by the legislature.

There were several reasons why the opposition rejected the idea of compromising with the government on constitutional revision. First, there was so much distrust of the government by the opposition that any move, even an apparently conciliatory one, was seen as mere maneuvering by the ruling military group to perpetuate itself in power. It was suspected that Chun was simply trying to buy time.

Second, the opposition was divided internally so that a leader could give the appearance of accepting a compromise solution only at the risk of being accused of selling out and betraying the cause of democracy. This was especially true in view of the fact that one of the opposition leaders, Kim Dae Jung, who was technically still under political ban and therefore carried something of a moral authority within the opposition, remained adamant about the proposal for direct popular election of the president. Under these circumstances, even an opposition leader with the stature of Kim Young Sam, who had previously advocated a parliamentary system for South Korea, could not even suggest the possibility of a compromise. In 1987, a leading proponent of compromise, NDP leader Lee Min Woo, paid a heavy price for acting on his inclinations.

Finally, in the Korean political culture and under the existing rules of the game, compromise is seen not as a sign of rationality and goodwill but as a signal of weakness and lack of resolve, not only by one's adversaries but by one's allies as well. This leads the power players chronically to overestimate their own strength and underestimate that of their rivals. Any gesture toward compromise is likely to be met by further demands by the adversary, which tries to take advantage of the opponent's perceived feebleness. Politics in Korea usually takes the form of a zero-sum game in which winning is more important than keeping the game playable and productive. It was for this very reason that the government also refused to entertain the idea of accepting the opposition's proposal. It did so only when it was faced with a massive show of force by student demonstrations, which were often accompanied by violence.

Meanwhile, on the economic front, the Chun regime showed itself to be far more skillful. Like the Park government before it, the new government placed heavy emphasis on economic growth and the maintenance of a deterrent posture against possible North Korean aggression; and once again the need for stability was used to justify political repression. But the Chun government, in contrast to the Park government, did not try to revive the strategy of high growth under government direction. Instead, it chose to distinguish itself from the Park government by changing to a course of liberalization and stabilization. In this shift, it was strongly influenced by the liberal economic thinking then spreading in the Third World. It was convinced that the setback in heavy industries and the associated drain on domestic resources could have been avoided had the management of the economy been left in the hands of the private sector and market forces. It was also concerned by an increasingly unfavorable environment. At home, a rise in unemployment was feared as a serious threat to an already shaky social stability. Abroad, the continued availability of external financing seemed uncertain. It was inconceivable that exports would grow as fast as they had in the 1970s, and any further deterioration in the current account threatened to undermine Korea's creditworthiness and ability to borrow. Given the continuous requirement for external borrowing, the government believed that the best policy was to pursue stabilization policies with the hope of reducing the size of current account deficits. Many policy makers also held the belief that restoring price stability would help restore Korea's rapid growth, improving its international competitiveness by breaking the price–wage spiral and inducing private savings.

Some individual policy makers hoped also that economic liberalization would be the first step toward establishing political democracy, but clearly it was the aim to improve economic efficiency rather than to facilitate political change that motivated the government.

Thus, the years after the inauguration of the new government saw a vigorous implementation of economic liberalization and stabilization. On the liberalization side, efforts were concentrated on dismantling import barriers, reducing tariffs and export subsidies. Financial liberalization also was actively promoted. To restore price stability, the government first tightened fiscal and monetary policy, broke up real estate speculation, restrained wage increases beyond a certain level determined by productivity increases, and curtailed price support programs for agricultural commodities. In some years, the government did not hesitate to freeze national budgets if there were signs of inflationary pressures. The adjustment of government support prices for rice and other commodities was made within limits that would not jeopardize the stabilization program, thereby cutting back agricultural subsidies. Wage increases for government employees were also held in check, and private firms were implicitly pressured to use these increases as a reference point in determining their wages. Labor union activities were not allowed or were suppressed; in particular, those strikes staged for wage increases that appeared to be excessive met with a severe crackdown.

Except in the trade sector, progress in economic liberalization was slow. Several institutional constraints and structural characteristics of the Korean economy may have impeded it, but another factor clearly was the conflict between the efforts to liberalize and those to stabilize. Wage restraint, credit control, and price regulation of real properties were necessary and effective for stabilizing prices, but such policies required a greater government intervention and limited the scope and progress of economic liberalization. Nevertheless, the performance of the Korean economy under the Chun regime was exceptional by any standard. Coming out of the recession and political instability during the 1979–80 period, Korea regained its rapid rate of growth and succeeded in stabilizing prices and in eliminating current account deficits. At this stage, it is difficult to make a full explanation of this achievement, but the combination of economic liberalization and stabilization, helped by a favorable trading environment, would seem to have been the most important factor.

## The Democratic Transition, 1987–88

By any measure, 1987 was a momentous year for South Korean democracy (Han 1988). Running against the political clock with President Chun Doo Hwan's seven-year term scheduled to end in February 1988, and also against the international clock with the Seoul Olympics to occur in the summer of 1988, events moved briskly. The massive protests in the spring produced government capitulation in June. Negotiation for and adoption in October of a new constitution led to the election of a president in December by a direct popular vote.

The year began inauspiciously for President Chun Doo Hwan and his Democratic Justice party. As the deadlock between the ruling party and the opposition New Korea Democratic party on the issue of constitutional revision remained unresolved and antigovernment student demonstrations persisted, the country learned in mid-January that Park Chong Chol, a Seoul National University student, had died of torture under police interrogation. The revelation of the incident, which was confirmed by the government, could not have come at a worse time for the DJP. It was trying to persuade the opposition to accept its proposal for a parliamentary form of government in return for certain democratic reforms. The opposition had been in disarray, split from within between those who were adamant about their proposal for a presidential system with a direct popular vote and those who were willing to compromise. The torture-death of Park Chong Chol not only gave the antigovernment movement within and outside party politics a rallying point but also contributed to strengthening the position of hard-liners within the opposition, who now regarded the government as weak and vulnerable. The actual power and leadership within the opposition NDP were held by Kim Young Sam and Kim Dae Jung. Kim Young Sam insisted that the party's 1985 election pledge for direct presidential elections was the very basis of its existence. As noted above, his political rival for leadership of the opposition, Kim Dae Jung, took an even more hard-line stand. The two Kims succeeded in quashing an initiative by nominal party leader Lee Min Woo, who offered to consider the DJP's constitutional formula in exchange for seven major political reforms, including the release of political prisoners, press freedom, and the restoration of Kim Dae Jung's political rights (*Far Eastern Economic Review*, February 5, 1987: 16). Nonetheless, the squabbling within the opposition did not subside, and in early April the two Kims split from the NDP to form a new party. Sixty-six of the NDP's ninety lawmakers followed the Kims' breakaway lead and, on May 1, formally inaugurated the Reunification Democratic party (RDP) with Kim Young Sam as its president. The humiliated Lee Min Woo, on his part, merged the remnants of his party with the People's Democratic party (PDP), which had split from the NDP in early 1986, to form a twenty-six-seat bloc in the National Assembly.

These events were important, but the origin of the 1987 political drama can be traced directly to President Chun Doo Hwan's declaration on April 13 of his "grave" decision to suspend debate on constitutional reform. Only a few months earlier, the Chun government had seemed quite capable of maintaining its authoritarian system with only modest concessions to the opposition and to democracy. The opposition was split between those who, although silent for the most part, were willing to accommodate and those who were not. Student protest, while continuing, was losing sympathy and support among the general public because of its radical and extremist tendencies. Thus, if it had wanted to do so, the government could have attempted to pass a constitutional amendment embodying its own proposal. The opposition leadership could not and would not have accepted it. But if it had been accompanied by a program of genuine democratic reforms, the passage of a new constitutional draft as required by the existing constitution might have elicited, while not perhaps enthusiastic acceptance, at least a fair degree of acquiescence among the public.

In a classic case of miscalculation, the Chun government decided to push its luck and announced that constitutional revision, after all, would not take place and the next presidential election would be held under the existing, unpopular, constitution. In defending the measure, the DJP argued that the opposition, badly splintered, could not act as a responsible negotiating partner and that time was running out; continuing political uncertainty and instability would hurt the change of government and the Seoul Olympics. Rather than bringing about certainty and stability, however, Chun's decision was met with near universal disapproval by the South Korean public and provided new momentum to student protest, which had been losing ground. The government was placed in an even more embarrassing position following disclosures in mid-May of a cover-up in the Park Chong Chul incident. Chun's cabinet shake-up of May 26 in which three of his closest aides, Prime Minister Lho Shin Yong, Home Minister Chung Ho Yong, and the director of the Agency for National Security Planning, Chang Se Dong, resigned, did little to cool the anger of the protesters.

Street violence reached its peak after June 10 when the DJP, in an audacious act of political insensitivity and imprudence, formally nominated Roh Tae Woo as the party's presidential candidate to become Chun's handpicked successor under the existing constitution, which provided for an indirect election of the  president. Thousands of students poured into the streets, many hurling fire-bombs. The riot police, who responded mainly with massive tear-gas sprays, were hopelessly outnumbered by the demonstrators, with the latter often joined and cheered by middle-class citizens. Several hundred people were injured, and one student died in the clashes.

In the face of massive, prolonged, and often violent antigovernment demonstrations, the choice for the Chun government and the DJP was narrowed, on the one hand, to mobilizing troops to quell the demonstrations, thereby risking large-scale violence and possibly civil war; and, on the other hand, to making a wholesale concession to the forces of democracy and risking the loss of power. Chun tried to mollify the opposition by proposing a meeting with Kim Young Sam. At the meeting, which took place on June 24, Chun indicated to Kim that he was willing to allow a resumption of parliamentary negotiations on constitutional reform. Sensing that support for Chun had weakened, however, Kim rejected Chun's offer, insisting instead that the government should agree to hold an immediate national referendum to choose between a parliamentary system and a presidential system with a direct popular vote; to release all political prisoners; and to restore the civil and political rights of Kim Dae Jung.

In a dramatic turn of events, Roh Tae Woo, the DJP's presidential candidate and a former military colleague of President Chun, surprised both supporters and opponents of the government by announcing on June 29 a democratization plan that embodied a wholesale acceptance of the opposition's demands, effectively ending the "spring of discontent" (*Far Eastern Economic Review*, July 9, 1987: 8). Roh's eight-point proposal, subsequently accepted and endorsed by President Chun, pledged "the speedy amendment" of the constitution, support for direct presidential elections, amnesty for Kim Dae Jung, and the restoration of his civil rights. The opposition, in a rare show of approval, welcomed Roh's action. A democratization process finally began.

The immediate results of the Roh declaration were the restoration of Kim Dae Jung's political rights, release of political prisoners, and the start of negotiations on constitutional amendments. Kim Dae Jung, the man who unsuccessfully ran against Park Chung Hee in the 1971 presidential election, was considered a perennial anathema to the successive regimes of Park and Chun. He had been kidnapped from Japan by agents of the Park government in 1973 and incarcerated until 1979, when Park was assassinated. After a brief period of active politicking in the spring of 1980, Kim was arrested by the martial law command in May 1980 on charges of inciting riots. He was subsequently sentenced to death by the Chun government, which eventually commuted the sentence to a twenty-year prison term. Kim was then allowed to travel to the United States, where he stayed for two years before returning to Korea in February 1985. After the restoration of his political rights in July 1987, Kim Dae Jung became officially an adviser to the RDP while sharing effective power within the party on an equal basis with party President Kim Young Sam.

No sooner did power seem to be within reaching distance than trouble started in the marriage of convenience between the two Kims. Each Kim saw himself as the hero of South Korea's political drama, and each plainly thought the other was behaving unreasonably in refusing to pull out. Kim Young Sam claimed that he appealed to a broad cross section of increasingly middle-class Koreans. This made him not only very electable, in his view, but also a much more suitable figure, once elected, to unite a politically fractious nation. Kim Dae Jung saw things differently: after exile in the United States and repeated jailings and house arrests in Korea over the years, he had suffered more in the cause of democracy, he asserted. His failure to run in the presidential election, he warned, could churn up anger and frustration among his many supporters and reignite the potentially dangerous regional antagonisms that had always bedeviled Korean politics. After meeting a few times, the two Kims failed to agree on a single candidacy, and both of them eventually decided to run, even at the risk of defeating themselves. After the formal adoption of the new constitution on October 22, Kim Dae Jung formed a new party, the Peace and Democracy party, and declared himself its presidential candidate.

The new constitution, which was adopted by a national referendum following a series of negotiations between the government and the opposition parties, was the fruit of a long struggle by the two Kims, who had insisted on direct popular election of the president. But it was also a product of political expediency. The most problematic aspect of the new constitution was that it allowed the election of the president by simple plurality. The three presidential aspirants, particularly Kim Dae Jung and Roh Tae Woo, knew that they would have difficulty obtaining a majority of the votes, and thus their chances of winning would be maximized in a situation of multiple candidacy. The constitution also failed to provide for a vice-president, making it even more difficult for power contenders within the same party to compromise and remain united.

Joining the three-way race of Roh Tae Woo (Democratic Justice party), Kim Young Sam (Reunification Democratic party), and Kim Dae Jung (Peace and Democracy party) was Kim Jong Pil, former prime minister under President Park Chung Hee, who ostensibly wanted the people's vindication of the record of his defunct Democratic Republican party (1963–80). Since each candidate knew he could win by securing firm support from a minority, campaigns were conducted to maximize regional and partisan appeal. Roh Tae Woo, who promised political stability and continued economic growth, had his largest support in the southeastern provinces, among middle-class voters, and in rural areas. Kim Young Sam, who called for an end to decades of military rule in South Korea, also appealed to voters in the Southeast and to middle-class voters, although his support was particularly strong among the urban white-collar voters. Kim Dae Jung, who enjoyed solid support within his native Southwest, tried to maximize this support among the underprivileged and young voters. The role of Kim Jong Pil, who was strong in his native Chungchongdo provinces, was essentially that of a spoiler, drawing votes from the upper middle classes that could have gone to either Roh Tae Woo or Kim Young Sam. Regional rivalries, often expressed in violent disruption of campaign rallies by candidates from rival provinces, were most conspicuously manifested between the Southeast and Southwest. Many of Kim Dae Jung's supporters in the southwestern Chollado provinces felt that their region had been discriminated against by the regimes successively dominated by leaders from the southeastern Kyongsangdo provinces. Citizens of Kwangju, in particular, felt that their city had been the object of regional oppression in 1980 at the time of the "Kwangju uprising." Ultimately, the level of voting support for each of the candidates closely coincided with his regional background; Kim Dae Jung received more than 90 percent of the votes from his home provinces and less than 5 percent from the southeastern provinces.

Localism played an especially important role in the 1987 election because of the particular combination of candidates, which tended to magnify the rivalries and animosities among regions. The strong regional identification of the candidates, particularly Kim Dae Jung, ensured that the campaign was to be divisive and emotional. With the newly adopted electoral system allowing the election of the president by a mere plurality of votes, the candidates were encouraged to conduct parochial campaigns, with the result that each of them alienated a large segment of the general population. By casting themselves as regional champions, they also tended to promote regional rivalries. Although localism will continue to be a salient factor in South Korean politics, its importance will probably decrease in future elections with a change in the composition of the candidates and the emergence of new campaign issues. It is thus unlikely that regional rivalries will constitute a serious obstacle to Korea's future democratization process.

The June 29 declaration by Roh Tae Woo brought about a brief hiatus in student political activities. Soon, however, the activists went back to work, demanding the release of all "political prisoners" and accusing the Chun government of scheming to rig the election. Small-scale demonstrations continued throughout the fall. As the election approached in December, however, the students decided to concentrate on working to ensure a fair election, and they organized themselves into teams of election- and ballot-watchers.

The subject that became a prime issue in the campaign was the controversy surrounding events on December 12, 1979. On that day, several military leaders, including generals Chun Doo Hwan and Roh Tae Woo, had mobilized troops, apparently without proper authorization, to overpower and arrest General Chung Sung Hwa, who was then the army chief of staff and martial law commander. General Chung, it had been stated, was suspected of complicity in Park's assassination. During the election campaign, General Chung joined the Kim Young Sam camp and publicly accused the Chun-Roh group of having carried out a "mutiny." The public revelation of the details of the December 12 incident was a serious setback to Roh Tae Woo's effort to present a nonmilitary image of himself, although the extent of damage done to his election campaign was impossible to ascertain (*Wolgan Chosun*, December 1987).

Despite charges of irregularities, the voting took place as scheduled on December 16, and Roh Tae Woo, the DJP candidate, was elected with 36.6 percent of the votes cast. Kim Young Sam, the more moderate of the two Kims, was second with 28 percent; Kim Dae Jung came in third with 27 percent. Although the losing candidates charged the government with an unfair election campaign and frauds in ballot counting, it was clear that the main reason for the defeat of the opposition was that its vote was split almost evenly between its two major candidates. A divided opposition not only caused its own defeat (despite the fact that the two Kims together received 55 percent of the vote), but it also produced a minority government that would face challenges to its legitimacy.

Nevertheless, the December presidential election and the earlier events of 1987 contributed to resolving, at least in part, the thorny question of legitimacy that had loomed large throughout the period of the Chun Doo Hwan government. Despite the fact that the DJP candidate won by a mere 37 percent of the vote, and notwithstanding the charges of election fraud, most people accepted that the election of the president by a direct, popular vote had passed the democratic test of selection of a government by an open and competitive election that respects the basic freedoms of expression, assembly, and organization. The candidates campaigned unhindered by government restrictions, and each of them, including the government candidate, was subjected to spirited debates and tough questioning.

On balance, what is it that brought about this dramatic political transformation in South Korea? Surely, part of the explanation is to be found in the Chun government's ineptness in dealing with the opposition politicians, its indiscriminate policy of oppression and rigidity helping to unite the very foes it sought to divide. Moreover, it lacked logic and consistency in its approach to the constitutional issue and could not retain existing supporters or convert new ones. The personal unpopularity of the president also helped to strengthen the antiauthoritarian movement. With a more popular and charismatic leader, the authoritarian cycle might possibly have lasted longer. It may also be argued that Chun was hamstrung by his success. He could hardly have saved his regime by calling out the troops in view of the damage that could have been done to the economy and to the Olympic Games, for which the regime took credit and in which it had so much pride.

Part of the explanation is to be found also in the pragmatic attitude and approach of South Korea's military leaders and military-turned-politicians. Faced with an overwhelming show of force by the demonstrators and political opponents, those leaders—including President Chun and the DJP presidential nominee, Roh Tae Woo—decided to accommodate the opposition, rather than to mobilize troops and risk a breakdown of the political system and a resulting plunge in the country's economy and international prestige. It is also possible that the United States, with which South Korea is allied and which counseled prudence and restraint, particularly on the part of the military, was instrumental in their decision to try the democratic route. Equally important, perhaps, was their assessment that, given the factional divisions within the opposing forces, the DJP had at least an even chance of winning the next presidential election even with a direct popular vote. In fact, the DJP made every effort to boost the image of its nominee by giving him the sole credit for the democratization gestures of the DJP and the government. How ironic that the ruling party of an authoritarian government should adopt a democratization strategy to retain power!

Even more of the explanation is to be found in the persistence, strength, and determination of the opponents of the Chun government, including the opposition politicians, antigovernment students, and ideological dissenters whose character and very existence were in large part to be accounted for by the economic growth the Park and Chun regimes so assiduously promoted. Between 1967 and 1987, the South Korean economy grew at an average annual rate of over 7 percent, converting Korea from an underdeveloped, low-income country to a newly industrializing economy (NIE) with a per capita income of nearly $3,000. This rapid economic growth brought about social changes that not only increased the pressure for democratization but also facilitated that process.

First of all, economic growth increased the size of the middle-income group, who are politically conscious, interested, and assertive. A 1987 survey showed that as much as 65 percent of Koreans identified themselves as members of the middle class, indicating the emergence of a social base upon which democratic politics could be built (*Wolgan Chosun*, December 1987).

Rapid economic development was also accompanied by an increasing complexity and pluralization of the society. Social groups and organizations that required, demanded, were capable of, and became accustomed to autonomy in management and decision making proliferated. State involvement in the private sector came to be resented and resisted. Furthermore, industrialization was accompanied by rapid expansion in the means and modes of communication and transportation, facilitating the exchange of information and people. This made it difficult if not impossible to sustain a government that was weak in popular support and legitimacy.

Moreover, as a result of the government's forward-looking strategy, Korean society became thoroughly permeated by outside influences. These influences and outside pressures for democratization tended to favor democratic values and procedures. Thus, rapid economic growth as a national objective came to be replaced by the goal of becoming an advanced society—and in the minds of Koreans such a society had to be not only affluent but also democratic.

Finally, economic advance elevated Korea to a position stronger in defense capabilities than that of North Korea. In the minds of many Koreans, this change greatly reduced the possibility of a North Korean invasion and to that extent raised questions about the national security argument used to justify repressive measures.

## The Prospects for Democratic Stability

There are reasons enough to be uncertain about the future of Korea's democratic transformation. The influence of those primary impediments noted at the outset—the authoritarian elements in Korea's traditional society, the discontinuities introduced in the colonial period, the unhappy experiences with democracy earlier on, the security threat from the North, and the deep political cleavage between the left and the right—still persist.

Whether the leadership required will be forthcoming is also in doubt. The personal ambitions of those in the power game make accommodation and gradual evolution difficult. Corporate loyalties, such as of the military, and regional interests make such cohesion difficult. The ideologically radical nature of significant parts of the opposition provides justification for an authoritarian reaction by powerholders; and the desire for retribution has become more salient as rapid economic growth has provided opportunities for corruption for those in power. Institutionally, the failure of a stable party system to take root presents an especially serious problem for democratic stability in South Korea.

There are several reasons for the weakness of political parties and party systems. First, the serious imbalance that exists between the bureaucracy (including the military) and political parties has hampered the development of the latter. Powerholders in Korea generally tend to favor and depend more on the bureaucracy, which is readily available and generally dependable, than on political parties, which are often hindrances to unquestioned and unchallenged power. The large and well-developed military bureaucracy magnifies the problem of bureaucratic power, which is the result of a long Confucian tradition as well as Japanese colonial rule.

Second, parties have not been able to cultivate a stable following among the voters because, in the post-1948 period, there has been no room for ideological deviation from the officially accepted line on virtually all important issues, including unification, national defense, socioeconomic development, and management of wealth. This insistence on ideological consensus is the result not only of traditional preoccupation with orthodoxy under Confucianism but also, since

1948, of the physical and ideological confrontation with Communist North Korea. Ideological uniformity has thus deprived the parties of opportunities to offer meaningful policy choices and to effectively reach and organize sectors of the society that are yet to be mobilized for electoral support and party activities. This is becoming an increasingly serious problem as the political challenge to the governmental and socioeconomic systems grows among those who are opposed to the government on ideological grounds. Emphasis on economic development and export-led industrialization, it is argued, renders social gaps and contradictions more serious—between the rich and the poor, the industrial and nonindustrial sectors, and the international and national orientations. "Socioeconomic justice" and "national identity" have become catchphrases with which dissenters who oppose the entire system join the antiauthoritarian "democrats" in their antigovernment activities.

A third reason for the weakness of the party system can be found in the many changes of regimes and constitutions that took place usually through extraordinary measures by governments that came to power by nondemocratic means. No party, whether government or opposition, has survived long enough to claim the loyalty and support of the public. Instead, parties and their leaders have often been purged and discredited after one or another of the uprisings, coups, or other upheavals South Korea has frequently experienced.

Still another obstacle to the development of a strong party system is the private nature of South Korean politics. Personal, factional, and regional rivalries are still deeply embedded in Korean political behavior. Factions and personal ties are often formed on the basis of provincial origins, school ties, same graduating class (as in the case of the military ties), other common experience in the past, or a common patron who has assisted the members in financial and other matters. Personal ties (*inmaek*) constitute an extremely important political factor even under circumstances of curtailed political activities. In contrast with political factions in Japan, which in some ways contribute to stable party policies, Korean political factions and groupings tend to be fragmented, amorphous, and often lacking in strong personal leadership.

Finally, the government's occasional banning of existing leaders from active political participation, as happened during the early Park as well as the Chun periods, has made institutionalization of parties extremely difficult. Certain other legal measures, including regulations controlling political activities, have reduced the chances for party continuity and stability.

One may question also how constructive a role the various social and political groups will play. What workers and farmers do depends very much on the government's ability to sustain economic vitality and expansion and to channel their demands and aspirations through an orderly and legitimate process. The serious labor disturbances in the spring of 1980 as well as in the mid-1980s indicate that there is a potential for further problems in case the workers' demands are not adequately responded to and/or there is a limit to the government's ability to control and establish order. With a very young population entering the labor market in large numbers, workers will become increasingly assertive and susceptible to ideological mobilization. Since the early 1960s, successive regimes have limited through legal and extralegal means the organizational activities of the workers. With political democratization, the scope of their organization, activities, and demands is likely to expand radically. Unless institutional means (primarily parties) are found to represent their interests and channel political aspirations, worker participation will take place in large part outside of the regular political process, seriously straining the effort to consolidate democracy.

Because of the large number and concentration of university students in major cities, their political role has been and will continue to be very important for some time to come. Their agitation has made the continuation of authoritarian rule difficult. Similarly, however, student activists will prove to be a major challenge to a democratic government in its consolidation, as their extra-institutional political participation will not only immobilize the government but also give foes of democracy a justification to take over power through undemocratic means. A combination of political, social, psychological, and organizational factors makes and keeps the student situation in South Korea fluid. Student protest is becoming increasingly well organized, ideological, and violence prone.

The military continues to play a crucial role in politics. An unusually large amount of human and material resources continues to be devoted to defense and security, and the military can easily prevail over the civilian sector. The military may have temporarily retreated from active involvement in politics under pressures from the sentiments and forces opposing military-dominated authoritarian government, but it hovers over the shoulders of a civilian regime and is capable of intervening should it feel the need and sense the opportunity.

On the other hand, there is even more reason to believe that the new democracy will take hold. Except for the conflict between the political extremes, most of the impediments to democracy are weakening.

The Korean party system, for àll its unstable and fragile nature, has exhibited an enduring tendency since the 1950s. It is partly due to the presidential system of government that the politicians have been inclined to gather around two major parties, one for and the other against the government. This is exactly what happened in the wake of the February 1985 election. The ruling party had no choice but to accept the situation, although its own preference was obviously for a multiparty system in which the opposition would be divided among several parties. Until the two Kims went their separate ways in the 1987 presidential election, the two-party system survived in its basic form even when the opposition party split between the hard-liners and the "accommodationists," as most of the opposition members then joined the splinter Reunification Democratic party.

Of the major social groups, the farmers are not likely to resort to collective disorderly actions against a democratic government any more than against its authoritarian predecessors. Their inclination has always been to support the party in power so long as it addresses their needs. The Park and Chun governments understood this well. For all the emphasis on economic growth and industrialization, the Park Chung Hee government had a strongly agrarian orientation, emphasizing the need to provide benefits to the rural areas. Even under the Chun government, which has paid more attention to industrial and urban problems, rural areas have been the mainstay of political support for the ruling party. It is one of the many ironies of South Korean democracy that assurance of electoral success in the rural areas has been an important condition for the party in power to implement measures that make possible meaningful political competition, the key element in political democracy.

Although labor relations deteriorated in the early months of 1989, it is highly unlikely that industrial conflict, even if it escalates further, will bring the economy to a complete halt or cripple Korea's major industries. Well before this happens, workers and employers will be likely to agree to at least a transient and very uneasy truce, even though they may not be able to restore industrial peace.

One reason for this optimism is that a relatively large proportion of Korean firms, in particular those in export-oriented industries, have seen a market improvement in their financial positions for the past three boom years. In 1988, for example, deposits held by the corporate sector increased 52 percent, and corporate securities holdings more than tripled. While an increasing number of small and medium-sized firms are being driven by labor disputes into bankruptcy, many of the larger Korean businesses in industries with serious labor disputes are better prepared financially than they would admit to accommodate the unions wage demands. Moreover, a majority of Korean workers, whether they belong to labor unions or not, appear to be conservative in their outlook and would hardly be prepared to trade job security for abstract political causes.

Another reason to believe that labor and management will be restrained from a complete break is the stabilizing pressure of the middle class. Although it is admittedly ineffective and often unreliable, a system of checks and balances has begun to develop in Korean society. If the union movement veers too far to the left to the point of threatening the very existence of Korea's capitalist market-oriented system, public pressures can be expected to build up counterbalancing forces. Over the last two decades of rapid growth and industrialization, the middle class has increased in both size and influence. Whenever it has been driven to take sides on ideological issues, it has made a conservative choice and in so doing played a crucial role in stabilizing the society.

The students are less easy to track, but generally speaking, there are three ways of looking at student political activism in Korea. Some observers regard it as an essentially passing phenomenon at a certain stage in industrial development. According to this view, student activism will run out of steam of its own accord and normalcy will be restored after a period of unrest, as seems to have been the case, for example, in Japan. Others argue that student activism in Korea is a response to a particular combination of socioeconomic and international circumstances, so that no matter what kind of government is in power, it is likely to pose a serious political problem for a considerable period of time.

A more persuasive view is that radical students are able to take advantage of antiauthoritarian sentiments and mobilize the support of a large number of students only when the political system is not democratic. If this view is accurate, with the passage of time and as the democratization process proceeds, radical and activist students will be deprived of the most important justification for mobilizing the support of other students. This will be only a slow and gradual process that will involve many setbacks and detours, particularly in view of the accumulation of grievances of several generations of students who have opposed, and suffered under, successive authoritarian regimes. Nonetheless, in due course, and with improved situations in both the economy and politics, the "student problem," as it is called in South Korea, will become far less serious than it has been so far.

There is reason to believe that the military also will maintain a less interventionist stance. After several decades of activity it is now acutely aware that a government cannot rule in South Korea without the consent of the governed. It is thus not likely that the military will intervene in politics without major provocation. Experience in other countries such as Brazil has shown that the military can agree to take a back seat on its own accord when the civilian sector offers a moderate alternative.

A crucial factor, of course, will be the condition of the economy. Continued growth will be essential to legitimize the transformation and also to strengthen the modernization process on which it depends. Beginning early in 1989, there have indeed surfaced some disturbing signs indicating that the Korean economy is finally slowing down after three consecutive years of double-digit growth with stable prices and current account surpluses. During the first quarter of 1989, export growth fell to below 10 percent in sharp contrast to almost a 38 percent expansion a year earlier, while import expansion remained strong at more than 20 percent. As a result, the trade account recorded a surplus of less than $100 million, down from $1.3 billion during the same period of 1988. The pace of price increases accelerated, speculative transactions in both the stock and real estate markets mounted, and, most important of all, the frequency of labor–management disputes rose markedly. Industrywide wage negotiations that began in March seemed likely to produce double-digit wage increases throughout the economy. As one magazine article puts it, in the late winter of 1989 the debate in Korea was not over whether it would repeat the performance of 1988 but over "how much growth will slow and how much inflation will rise" (*Far Eastern Economic Review*, March 23, 1989). Thus, it is highly unlikely that double-digit growth with stable prices can be sustained. In the spring of 1988 all available forecasts predicted that the GNP growth rate would drop to around 8 percent for the next two years. While this is not so vigorous a growth as in the preceding decades, it is surely impressive by international standards and reflects the fact that economic fundamentals that support strong and stable growth remain largely intact.

As a nation striving for democratization and industrialization, Korea is fortunate in many respects. Over the past two decades, it developed a relatively strong economy, able to withstand much of the political instability Korea has been beset with and to absorb the economic costs democratization may require. Korea has at least a larger pie to slice than before. Korean workers still work harder and longer hours than their fellow workers in many other countries with which Korea competes in the world market. The Korean labor force is well educated, and despite strained industrial relations, has maintained a high degree of work discipline. Korea has also developed a large capacity to absorb foreign technology and to develop its own. As Japan's closest neighbor, Korea enjoys a number of advantages compared to its competitors in penetrating the Japanese market. From Korea's point of view, the more pressing and immediate problem would be the deterioration in the international trading environment.

These considerations do not guarantee that the democratic transformation of 1987–88 will not face setbacks, but they do suggest that Korea is at the threshold of an evolutionary process by which democracy is being restored and will take root. The society's growing complexity and international involvement can be expected to result in increasing demands and pressures for pluralism, openness, and competition in politics. More important, the political public, both in and outside the government, is determined to broaden and deepen the democratization process. There is reason to be cautiously optimistic.

# 8

# Taiwan in Democratic Transition

## Tun-jen Cheng

THE ROAD to political democratization often has been strewn with dramatic tragedy. Explosively violent clashes between students and police have marred South Korea's journey toward democracy. In other countries, such as Burma and the Philippines, the transition toward or restoration of democracy has entailed much worse episodes of violence and turmoil. Fortunately, Taiwan's democratic movement has thus far been characterized by relative political stability and less intensified conflict. Yet political advances have occurred in the context of political continuity. What, then, has changed, and what remains unchanged?

By 1990 the political changes in Taiwan were not insignificant. The democratic movements of the early 1970s culminated in a dramatic breakthrough in 1986. As a result, the thirty-eight-year-old martial law decree was lifted, as were bans on new newspapers and the formation of new political parties. The Kuomintang (KMT) regime also committed itself to reforming the archaic "Long Parliament," which has been dominated by delegates elected in 1947. Once legitimized, organized opposition to the KMT regime challenged every remnant of the authoritarian order, including the extraordinary power vested in the presidency under the special temporary clause attached to the 1947 Constitution. Political contestation at the national level intensified. Competitive politics, in turn, contributed to an embryonic party system. Due to the increasing importance of electoral processes, the Legislative Yuan began to reassert itself vis-à-vis the Executive Yuan. Unlike most privileged but dormant members of the Legislative Yuan, new legislators were actually exercising their lawmaking and investigative powers and were being responsive to constituencies.

At the same time, much remained unchanged. The ruling party was still ubiquitous in the military and state apparatus. Major officeholders with decision-making powers continued to be either elected by the 1947 National Assembly (the case of the president) or appointed (the case of the provincial governor and mayors of two special municipalities, Taipei and Kaohsiung). Two-thirds of the legislators were old-timers who had never had to renew their mandates since 1947. Persuaded and induced, but not forced, to retire, many of these original legislators (and national delegates who elect the president) were unwilling to be pensioned off without unusually large compensation and high honor, which the opposition parties refused to offer and the reformist KMT leaders were reluctant to offer. The broadcasting media—an instrument so crucial to freedom of expression and political campaigning—was still tightly controlled by the government and the KMT. In sum, Taiwan had not opened up sufficient space for full political competition; above all, it failed the litmus test of democracy—power transfer following full political contestation. The KMT regime had certainly become more responsive, but definitely not yet democratic.

Although the extent of change has been somewhat limited, the direction of change is unambiguously toward democracy. Political change in contemporary Taiwan goes beyond liberalization—the process of phasing out repression and guaranteeing civil liberties. Political democratization—the opening up of political space to competition and the establishment of institutions and procedures for political contestation—has also been set in motion, being intertwined with liberalization. Indeed in Taiwan liberalization came *after* the revision of electoral rules, and the restoration and expansion of central-level elections. While the KMT continues to enjoy built-in safeguards of its political power, a "letter of intent" for its removal has been delivered. Reneging on this promise will impose a stiff political price for the KMT. The expectations of further democratization instilled within society and the opposition parties have lowered the level of political tolerance for authoritarian rule. Any activity by the regime that can be construed as intentionally obstructing democratization will have serious political repercussions for the KMT. While security threats, economic adversity, and social tension may put a brake on the process, the cost of reversal is high.

In this essay I shall begin by first placing political change in postwar Taiwan in historical and theoretical perspective, assessing, on the one hand, a popular thesis on the association between authoritarianism and economic transformation and, on the other hand, the modernization theorists' thesis on the association between democracy and economic development in capitalist systems. I shall argue that these theories cannot adequately explain regime dynamics in Taiwan. Taiwan, after all, was a colony of Japan from 1895 to 1945. The establishment of one-party authoritarianism in the immediate postcolonial years resulted not so much from the requirements of its economic development as from the processes of decolonization, regime relocation, and the political learning of the regime from past political failure. On the other hand, the tendency toward democracy in Taiwan in the past three decades has indeed reflected the drastic socioeconomic changes that have subsequently taken place, although certain political conditions, including regime type (party rather than military regime), local elections permitted by the regime, and the pattern of subethnic cleavage, were equally important in "preparing" Taiwan for its democratic transition. I shall then turn to the very process of democratic transition, assuming that democratic transitions are not automatic but in need of political entrepreneurship and that the paths of transition condition the pattern of democratic consolidation. Finally, I shall discuss the configuration of the democracy that may emerge in Taiwan.

## Regime Formation and Economic Development

Taiwan's polity cannot be conveniently placed in any one of the prevailing typologies of political systems: Leninist, authoritarian, democratic, and the various stripes of each. While the consensus among scholars is that the KMT regime is authoritarian (Tai 1970; Wu 1980; Domes 1981; Winckler 1984; Gold 1986; Johnson 1988), if one tries to draw a clear boundary between the state and society, an ambiguous political picture of Taiwan appears. Until the mid-1980s, as a regime, KMT rule approximated authoritarianism in state-society relations; however, as a party, regarding state institutions, the KMT was unmistakably Leninist. Thus, Taiwan's polity in that period is perhaps best identified as quasi-Leninist: an authoritarian regime managed by a Leninist party.

From 1950 to the mid-1980s, the KMT's party structure and relationship to the state were Leninist in nature. A pyramidal party structure paralleled the state; party organs controlled administrative units at most levels of government as well as the military; decisions were reached through democratic centralism; and the party held an effective monopoly on political power. The two opposition parties allowed to coexist with the KMT were marginal, basically functioning as "friendship parties" of the ruling party. A self-conceived elitist party, the KMT sought to mobilize society via mass organization in pursuit of the national goals it defined. Party cadres were trained to be revolutionary vanguards (Chen Sheng-shih 1977; and Chen Chieh-hsien 1977), and, at least in the 1950s, party cells penetrated virtually all social organizations. Intra-elite pluralism was not tolerated. Instead, conformity to party-cum-national ideals imbued the political milieu. The party embraced Dr. Sun Yat-sen's Three Principles of the People, or *san min chu i*, namely, nationalism, democracy, and the people's livelihood (a very moderate form of state capitalism). While eclectic in nature, Sun Yat-senism precluded the articulation of any alternative ideology.

Despite the close affinities to Leninism, state-society relations on Taiwan are characterized more by authoritarianism than Leninism. Two critical features differentiate the KMT from other Leninist regimes. One distinction is its official commitment to the ultimate goal of constitutional democracy. In antithesis to Leninist parties elsewhere, which upheld the Marxist-Leninist principle of proletarian dictatorship and the monopoly of political power by a Communist party, the KMT has, since first gaining national power in 1927, promised Western-style democracy via tutelage. According to the 1947 Constitution, the KMT's role has devolved from a revolutionary party tutoring the government and society to but one of many competing democratic parties, but by 1950, during the party reform, the KMT's role as a "revolutionary-democratic" party was reinstated. Even so, this was accomplished only through so-called temporary provisions claimed necessary due to the technically unconcluded civil war, not the revision of the constitution (January 1989). More important, while its democratic inclinations did not inhibit the KMT from establishing political hegemony, the party did permit democracy at the subnational level. Instituted by the KMT, local and provincial elections have been competitive, authentic, and reflective of local interests. Local elections have subtly changed the primary function of the KMT from one of ideological guardian to electoral machine and, as will be shown, have proved to be a crucial condition for Taiwan's democratization.

The second and perhaps most critical difference between the KMT and other Leninist parties is the former's cautious affirmation of capitalism. Not at all lacking in socialist ideas, the KMT regime was embedded in a capitalist economy. The principle of people's livelihood, one of the three pillars of *san min chu i*, was interpreted as legitimizing a moderate form of state capitalism. It was used, however, to justify not the inhibition of private enterprises, but the maintenance of an ill-defined level of state-owned enterprises as a safeguard against the private sector (Li 1988: 38–39). With private ownership widespread, the distinction between public and private spheres was affirmed. There would be self-circumscribed limits to what the state could do vis-à-vis society. This has been particularly true since the late 1950s, when the state began to reduce its productive and allocative functions; the state sector no longer offered the best employment and career opportunities. A Leninist party in a capitalist society opens up other avenues, other than the party-state, to status and wealth. This also implies that resources are dispersed in society, and the state can exercise control over private ownership and market exchange only at the risk of inefficiency.

The quasi-Leninist KMT regime on Taiwan analyzed above is often associated with the remarkable development of Taiwan's economy. But the KMT regime was not reconstructed in order to adapt to its new economic circumstances on Taiwan. In fact, economics had little to do with its remaking. Three key noneconomic factors contributed to the effective consolidation of the KMT's political power in Taiwan and consequently to its political capability to effect economic change. These three factors were the pattern of Taiwan's decolonization, the relocation of the regime to Taiwan, and the knowledge gained from the KMT's experience of political failure on the mainland.

The indigenous elite was never recruited to the colonial bureaucracy, and thus when Japan returned Taiwan to China in 1945, KMT expatriates quickly displaced the former colonial administrators. An islandwide revolt erupting in 1947 against the mismanagement of a corrupt KMT governor led to the decimation of the local elite. Its inheritance of colonial properties and access to foreign aid—the economic corollary of political-security incorporation into the Western alliance during the cold war—made the KMT regime resource-rich vis-à-vis all other social entities. In the 1950s, the state controlled all foreign exchange derived from aid and state-managed agrarian exports and monopolized the banking sector, while state-owned enterprises accounted for half the island's industrial production. Shaking loose from its dependence on the support of Shanghai capitalists (whose interests it often violated), the KMT now fostered a business class beholden to the state. Finally, after 1945, Taiwan was retroceded to the KMT regime directly, without the mediation of the United States as in the case of Korea or, for that matter, Japan. Consequently, no democratic experiment was introduced.

Defeated by the Communists on the mainland in 1949, the KMT regime was forced to retreat to Taiwan with basically 1.5 million state employees, civil and military. Ironically, regime relocation enabled the KMT to overcome various political constraints on its exercise of state power. As an émigré regime without ties to Taiwanese landlords, the KMT carried out a rapid and thorough land reform, creating a rural social base for the regime. Because of political retreat, opposition parties nearly disintegrated and survived only on KMT largess. Isolated from their constituencies and dependent on the regime for their tenure, legislators and members of the National Assembly were subordinated to executive authorities. Factionalism within the party was eradicated when some factional leaders fled or took the blame for the collapse of the regime on the mainland.

The KMT's resounding defeat on the mainland also ignited a massive campaign for political learning from the past failure. For nearly a decade, "what went wrong" was an automatic question raised in any institutional design and policy choice that it was to make on Taiwan (Kuomintang 1970). Through political reform in 1951 the party apparatus acquired organizational capacity and a semblance of a corporatist structure with which to ensure the power base of the regime. The KMT built a commissar system and rotated commanders in the army, preventing the resurgence of warlordism that had plagued the pre-1949 KMT regime. The KMT also extended its organizational branches into every social organization. The 340 KMT-penetrated farmers' associations enabled the state to maintain extensive control over rural areas. The China National Association of Industry and Commerce, an umbrella organization, functioned as a channel by which government policies were relayed to business. Though it remained moribund until 1975, the Chinese Federation of Labor, composed of eleven national federations, ensured the prominence and leadership of enterprise management and local cadres in union affairs. The Youth Corps was used to guide students' recreation activities. Together with business and farmers, students and labor—two breeding grounds for political instability during the KMT's mainland years—were subsumed under the KMT's corporatist structure (Tien 1989: 44; Zeigler 1988: chap. 6). Its hegemonic presence in the society then led the KMT gradually to open up electoral space for participation at the local level, reversing the top-down political process. Not only did local elections supply political information to the regime, but they also permitted factionalized local elites to compete within KMT-controlled political space without letting factionalism spill over to the central level. Additionally, local elections were a handy device for political cooptation.

The KMT underwent reconstitution primarily in response to security imperatives—namely, the Communist threat from the mainland—and in support of its avowed political objective: the recovery of the mainland. Political consolidation was thus not used to support Taiwan's import-substitution industrialization (ISI) in the 1950s, which was a situational necessity associated with the economic disorder of the immediate postwar period, not a premeditated economic strategy (Cheng 1989b). Nevertheless, although not installed to effect an economic transition, a highly autonomous KMT regime was instrumental in sustaining various stages of postwar economic growth. Facing virtually no political obstacles, the KMT regime, under the persuasion of indigenous technocrats and American aid-giving agencies, reoriented Taiwan's economy toward export markets at the turn of the 1960s, when the early phase of ISI reached a limit. The adoption of an export-led industrialization strategy not only solved the "ISI crisis" but more significantly put Taiwan on a path of rapid and sustained economic growth. In several other developing countries, the "ISI crisis" resulted in a bureaucratic-authoritarian coup by which the military allied with technocrats to entice foreign capital and exclude the popular sector (urban lower middle class and workers) in order to pursue either ISI deepening, as in Brazil, or export-led growth, as in South Korea (O'Donnell 1973; Im 1987: 231–57). Such a regime change was simply not necessary for Taiwan under a KMT that was both politically insulated and omnipresent.

## Socioeconomic Change and Democratic Impulses

The story of Taiwan's economic development is an economist's delight and need not be retold. In Toshio Watanabe's words (1978: 389), postwar Taiwan, like South Korea, achieved a compressed industrialization that took other developing countries a century to accomplish. For two decades since 1960, all indicators show Taiwan's remarkable success in economic development. Its GNP growth rates have been close to double-digit figures since the early 1960s. Inflation rates were 2 percent in the 1960s and low double-digit figures in the 1970s, some of the lowest among developing countries (table 8.1). Income distribution improved rather than deterioriated, contrary to Kuznets's prediction (table 8.1). While Taiwan's economy is extremely external dependent, foreign capital played a much less important role in its development than is the case in most Latin American NICs, which deliberately pursued ISI to avoid dependence on foreign capital (Cheng 1987b: 54–55). Its economy has been flexible enough to cope with external shocks, rebounding faster than most less developed countries, and today is inundated with foreign exchange reserves.

Rapid growth begat liberalizing social consequences that the KMT did not fully anticipate. With the economy taking off, the literacy rate increased; mass communication spread; per capita income rose; social mobility accelerated; the rural sector shrank; a differentiated urban sector—including labor, a professional

Table 8.1

**Economic Indicators of Taiwan (percent unless otherwise indicated)**

|  | 1960 | 1964 | 1970 | 1980 |
|---|---|---|---|---|
| Per capita GNP (U.S. $) | 130.2 | — | 360.4 | 2103.0 |
| Ratio of income of highest fifth to lowest fifth | — | 5.33 | 4.58 | 4.17 |

|  | 1960–70 | 1970–80 |
|---|---|---|
| Average growth rate per annum |  |  |
| GNP | 9.4 | 8.6 |
| Exports | 22.9 | 31.2 |
| Industrial output | 15.8 | 15.5 |

*Source:* Republic of China, Economic Research Center for U.S. Aid.

middle class, and a business entrepreneurial class—came into being (tables 8.2 and 8.3); and an overwhelming majority of the people began to identify themselves as middle class (table 8.4). These features are common to all growing capitalist societies. By the 1970s, economic development in Taiwan had created the socioeconomic setting that modernization theorists of various stripes believe is conducive to the establishment of democracy.

Modernization theorists treat economic development as a prerequisite for democracy. In their original formulation their theories addressed the issue of the functioning, rather than the genesis, of democracy and posited that without wealth, stable democracy would be difficult to sustain (Lipset and Turner 1987; Diamond et al. 1987: 5–20). By extrapolation, one would expect a gradual process of political opening during the process of economic development or after a society has attained a certain level of development. Whether one highlights the incremental or threshold effects that economic development has on political development, modernization theorists predict the inevitable trend toward democracy. In Huntington's words, "[as] one moves up the economic ladder, the greater are the chances that a country will be democratic" (Huntington 1984: 201).

At least four lines of reasoning support the likelihood of democratization with or after economic development. First, economic prosperity allows higher levels of education to expand, raising public awareness of issues related to political rights, which in turn creates popular demand for participation. Political awareness is further heightened by urbanization, modern communication, and increasing attentiveness to noneconomic goods. Second, social interests become more differentiated and potentially conflictual, requiring compromise and reconciliation,

Table 8.2

**International Comparison of Taiwan's Socioeconomic Development**

| Country | Higher education (% of age group) | | Life expectancy (years) | | Urbanization ratio (%)* | |
|---|---|---|---|---|---|---|
| | 1960 | 1981 | 1960 | 1980 | 1961 | 1981 |
| Taiwan | 5 | 19 | 66 | 71 | 30 | 48 |
| South Korea | 5 | 18 | 54 | 66 | | |
| United States | 32 | 58 | 70 | 75 | | |
| Japan | 10 | 30 | 68 | 77 | | |

*Sources:* World Bank 1984; Republic of China,Economic Research Center for U.S. Aid, Republic of China Directorate-General of Budget Accounting and Statistics.
*Ratio of population in cities of more than 100,000 inhabitants to total population.

which often can only be realized in the political arena. Meanwhile, social mobility may lead to a fluid class system that prevents ideology-fueled confrontation (Lipset 1981). Third, more resources become available to compensate losers and hence facilitate political bargaining. David Apter has noted that political struggle in most postcolonial developing nations is brutal, fierce, and uncompromising because political defeat means permanent unemployment (Apter 1961: 154–68). A wealthy society can moderate political tensions and conflict by providing career options for elites that lose political battles. Fourth, economic complexity increases the cost of political control, especially in the case of capitalist economies (Lindblom 1977: chap. 12). The more diversified an economy is, the more difficult it is for a regime to block a political opposition's access to resources in the private sector.

These four general socioeconomic conditions clearly existed in Taiwan during the 1970s, when the democratic movement began to surge. First, thanks to the growth of a meritocratic educational system, the postwar generation now became new social critics. Imbued with knowledge and confidence, but not civil war experience, they began to question the legitimacy of the authoritarian institutions, such as the privileged status of the legislators and members of the national assembly (*Ta hsueh tsa chih*). Second, by the mid-1970s the "grand transition" from an agrarian to an industrial economy was no longer central to social change. Instead, what was noteworthy now was the industrial deepening and diversification, as well as the rise of the service sector, all resulting in complicating sectoral interests. Third, since the early 1970s Taiwan's trade accounts began to register surpluses, and the balance of payments conditions improved. With the exception of the two oil-crisis years, 1974 and 1981, the government's budget has been in surplus since 1965. Distributive issues loomed large in budgetary politics. Fourth, while industrial lines, occupational categories, and private firms

Table 8.3

**Class Structure in Taiwan, 1985 (percent of total population)**

| Categories | | Percent |
|---|---|---|
| Capitalist | | 4.6 |
| Petty capitalists | | 29.3 |
| Agricultural | 17.9 | |
| Nonagricultural | 11.4 | |
| Managerial | | 6.8 |
| Labor | | 59.4 |
| Agricultural | 3.7 | |
| Nonagricultural | 55.7 | |
| Total | | 100.1 |

*Source:* Sheu 1987: 34.

multiplied, the KMT's institutional capacity for mobilization and control, once so effective and well developed, rapidly eroded. This happened in part because the KMT regime no longer entertained the idea of recapturing the mainland through military measures and therefore relaxed the parties' mobilization efforts. Yet by and large, the dynamic capitalist system had simply outgrown regime control. Between 1969 (at the Tenth Party Congress) and 1981 (at the Twelfth Party Congress), KMT membership doubled, thanks to student recruitment (Hsieh 1970). The number of registered companies increased tenfold (Directorate-General of Budget). KMT efforts to reorganize a cadre system based mainly on administrative regions along occupational-functional lines have failed. Dispatching secretaries to all civic (including trade) associations in the 1950s, the KMT could barely monitor, not to say staff, them in the 1970s.

Lucian Pye (1985: 233) regards Taiwan as a paradigmatic case of an authoritarian regime that by successfully navigating economic development generates pressures for democracy in its own wake. Democratic transition in Taiwan, however, cannot be explained simply in terms of the general socioeconomic preconditions identified above. Economic development in Taiwan, as elsewhere, may engender democratic impulses but does not necessarily ensure the making of democracy. Facing democratic movements, some states tighten the clamps of authoritarianism; other states accommodate democratization. The trajectories of political change of those countries going through a democratic transition also diverge. The character of transition is thus a crucial variable bearing upon political outcomes, an issue I shall deal with later. Furthermore, the Taiwan case displays three specific conditions that the modernization literature fails to include, all of which can be instrumental to the initiation and pursuit of democratization.

The first condition that has facilitated democratic transition in Taiwan is a rare balance of social forces that neutralize political domination and mitigate

Table 8.4

**Perceptions of Social Stratification in Taiwan (percent)**

| Strata | Parents | Self | Offspring |
|---|---|---|---|
| Upper | 1.2 | 0.6 | 7.3 |
| Upper-middle | 7.2 | 9.3 | 32.6 |
| Middle | 36.1 | 54.7 | 36.9 |
| Lower-middle | 36.4 | 26.8 | 5.8 |
| Lower | 19.1 | 8.6 | 1.0 |
| Uncertain | | | 16.4 |
| Total | 100.0 | 100.0 | 100.0 |

*Source:* Yung 1982.

polarized conflict. There are three aspects to this condition. First, a postwar land reform eliminated landlords in Taiwan, removing a primary cause for political radicalism, namely the rural class cleavage that reflects the most obvious and blatant form of exploitation. Historically, the European landlord class (and its Latin American counterpart, which was exported oriented), took the staunchest conservative political stand, resisting the extension of enfranchisement. In Latin America, the endurance of democracy in Venezuela and Costa Rica owes in part to the countries' solution of the peasant problem: the former by an oil bonanza, the latter without a sizable peasantry to begin with (Karl n.d.).

Second, the hierarchical nature of Taiwan's preexisting social cleavage was upset, rather than reinforced, by economic development. The Taiwanese-mainlander cleavage (accounting for 85 percent and 15 percent of the population, respectively) was the main social divide in Taiwan. Many ethnically divided societies—especially where the ethnic balance is relatively even as in the case of Malaysia, Holland, and Belgium—have settled on consociationalism, which is one form of democracy (Lijphart 1975). Many others—especially where the ethnic mix is highly lopsided—display political domination by either the majority (Spaniards in Spain, Turks in Turkey, and Anglophones in Canada) or the minority (whites in South Africa), a political equilibrium all too often perpetuated by ossified economic hierarchies. The Taiwan case is intrinsically different. Its social cleavage existed between two subethnic groups that share the same racial-cultural-linguistic origin though differing in their timing of entry into Taiwan and in their command of dialects. For historical reasons explained above, a consociational arrangement was never attempted; instead, the mainlanders monopolized state power, while the indigenous Taiwanese were diverted to pursue economic advancement for upward social mobility. Two decades of economic development thus gave rise to a new structural condition, namely, resource-rich Taiwanese found themselves in a position to counterbalance, if not undercut, political domination by mainlanders.

Third, big capitalists were missing from Taiwan's business sector. In its quest for economic development, the KMT regime avoided grooming "national champions" in order to prevent the formation of big capital. Indeed, the regime also avoided empowering business associations so as to mitigate the bargaining power of business. As a result, small and medium enterprises came to dominate industrial production and exports. These unorganized, flexible (as seen from high entry and exit rates of firms), and export-oriented small and medium businesses were to be beyond the political control of the regime (Cheng 1987a: chap. 3).

The predominance of unorganized small and medium enterprises precludes the confrontation between big capital and big labor, a situation unfamiliar to most developed countries and several advanced less-developed countries such as Mexico and even South Korea, where labor unions are being politically enfranchised. Although labor has become the largest class in Taiwan (table 8.3), only one-sixth of it is employed by big corporations, and hence it is not easily mobilized. Indeed, as Hill Gates (1979) argues, the line between labor and self-employed is often blurred. The "dirty hand" apprentices in small firms are often spun off into independent owners, alleviating urban class conflict.

At the other end, small and medium businesses—especially those firms in exports and modern economic services—are also connected to the intellectual-professionals through various social ties, such as school, regional, and workplace affiliations. I believe that from my reading in dissident journals, and supported by the observations of Hu Fu (1988), it has been the intellectual-professionals who have been the principal feeders to the political opposition in Taiwan. They have stood to gain from a political opening, but they have been most keenly aware of the discrepancy between democratic ideals and the authoritarian realities, and they are well equipped with legal expertise and social mobilizational abilities. Social linkages to small and medium businesses give opposition activists political funds as well as fallback career options. Small and medium businesses may well have permitted opposition leaders to pursue political activities that in light of other economic alternatives many of them might otherwise not have had. If a direct connection between democracy and economic growth does exist, it may be that the political oppositions that wealthy countries generate are precisely those who have benefited from the system and yet retain the propensity and abilities to challenge it.

The second condition of Taiwan's democratic transition is its regime type—a one-party rather than a military or bureaucratic-authoritarian regime. It is not certain whether one-party regimes are more conducive to democratic transformation than military regimes. On the one hand, the military may be more willing than the ruling party to withdraw from politics and thereby accelerate the democratic transition. Facing democratic pressures, economic adversity, or defeat in war, the military, as the case of Argentina illustrates, can just "leave the mess" behind and retreat to its preserved domain of national security. In contrast, a party regime has to figure out a way to democratize while concomitantly retaining power. This suggests that one-party regimes should be more reluctant to give in to democratic pressures than military regimes.

On the other hand, because of its roots in society, its cooptative capability, and its electoral functions, a party regime is usually better informed about sociopolitical pressure than a military regime. A one-party regime is also better poised for political competition than a military regime that hastily organizes a new political party to oversee the process of political transition. Thus, once a party regime has committed itself to democratic transition, either by its own initiative or in response to pressure from the opposition, it is probably more willing and capable of letting democratization run its course. In addition, the exercise of veto power by the military during democratic transition is less a problem for one-party regimes than for regimes previously formed by the military.

Given its pivotal role in the national revolution of 1911 and the subsequent nation-building, in addition to its self-commissioned task of recovering the mainland, the KMT continually resisted strong societal pressures to transform its role from a hegemonic to an ordinary party. As I shall show below, it was the push of the opposition that propelled the KMT to commit to an accelerated democratization in Taiwan. The KMT's hesitancy to pursue democratization contrasted, however, with its ability to implement it. Ever since the turn of the 1970s, the KMT has been adapting to social change, despite its inability to control or even monitor the ever-expanding private sector. Since the Tenth Party Congress in 1969, the KMT began to recruit young cadres, in particular indigenous Taiwanese, turning the party into a mass party (Jiang and Wu 1989). Within its leadership stratum, the KMT began to promote the liberal-oriented, often Western-trained elite, thanks to the expansion of higher education and the opportunities for studying abroad. Located in the Department of Organization (in charge of recruitment, training, and local elections), this "liberal bloc" within the KMT emerged as the "soft-liners," in contradistinction to the "hard-liners" (cadres in the security apparatus and "old guards"), who were preoccupied with social order and with the KMT's historical mission of recovering the mainland and building a strong nation.

The third condition that laid the groundwork for Taiwan's democratization is the praxis of local elections. Unlike bureaucratic-authoritarian regimes, which practice plebiscites, the KMT regime permitted regular elections, albeit controlled and limited. Whereas the KMT regime suspended elections at the national level, executive and council positions at the county, township, and village levels have been chosen by direct and periodic elections since 1950. Beginning in 1959 the Provincial Senate, originally composed of delegates elected by county councils, was turned into the provincial assembly, subject to direct ballot.

Local elections created a bloc of cadres within the party whose raison d'être depends on votes in the political market rather than purely the management of internal, secretive party affairs. Because of the expansion of local elections, KMT cadres were trained not just for "revolution" but for electoral competition as well. As such, the KMT was exposed to conflicting local interests that necessitated harmonization, arbitration, and balancing. Indeed as Yang-teh Chen shows, the KMT has attempted to change its priority in nominations to favor civil service and other, less local-interest-based elite (Chen 1978; Lerman 1978: part 3). Local factions and notables nevertheless remain a major group under the banner of the KMT in local politics. Over time, the Leninist feature of the KMT has gradually eroded in the face of electoral imperatives.

Local elections were equally instrumental for the growth of the political opposition. Despite the KMT's ability to monopolize local elections, it always reserved some spaces for "independents." The arena for independents to compete ranged from 16 percent to 33 percent of local offices (table 8.5). One rationale for granting political space to dissidents was to provide a safety valve for the system. Yet local elections turned out to be a training ground for political dissent, the supply of which eventually proved costly to suppress. In fact, local elections tended to generate an oversupply of political elites beyond the KMT's absorptive capacity and hence frequently resulted in the defection of "surplus" KMT elites to the dissident side.

Furthermore, competitive local elections also gave the political opposition a convincing reference point in the debate on representation in the Legislative Yuan. As the prospects of recovering the mainland became dimmer and dimmer in the 1960s and as the diplomatic isolation became obvious in the 1970s, the legitimacy of the old guard's domination of three national representative bodies was cast in doubt, and the suspension of national-level elections became even more difficult to justify. Once the political arena at the central level opened up, the political opposition fostered at the local elections quickly shifted its field of operation. Indeed, the growth of the opposition and the democratic movement in Taiwan has been election driven.

## Democratic Transition Through Transaction

Taiwan's democratic movement is not a recent phenomenon. In the 1950s a group of intellectuals and dissident political elites first founded a journal called the *Free China Fortnightly* to criticize the regime and later attempted to form a political party to promote liberal democracy in Taiwan. While it was certainly a forerunner, this reformist group did not engender the social forces that are pushing for political liberalization today. The roots of the contemporary democratic movement can be traced back directly to the political stirrings of the newly emerging middle-class intellectuals of the early 1970s.

The democratic forces in contemporary Taiwan started out as a political reform movement undertaken by young intellectuals at the beginning of the 1970s. The triggering events for political reform were a series of diplomatic setbacks, including derecognition by six major Western countries in 1970 and the loss of Taiwan's membership in the United Nations in 1971. Diplomatic defeats created

Table 8.5

**Ratio of Local Offices to Which KMT Members Were Elected Before and After 1970 (percent of total offices)**

| Local office | Pre-1970 (average) | 1977 |
|---|---|---|
| Provincial assembly | 84.2 | 70.0 |
| County magistrates/city mayors | 89.8 | 75.0 |
| County and city councils | 66.8 | — |

*Source:* For pre-1970 elections, adapted from Hsian 1971: 76, tables 4–6.

public concern about Taiwan's future and led the informed public to question the political efficacy of the regime in solving the "destiny" problem. The intellectuals' political discourse soon turned from diplomatic to domestic sociopolitical issues.

The KMT's response came from its new leadership under Chiang Ching-kuo, who, upon assuming the premiership in 1972, initiated a new agricultural policy to correct urban bias in economic policy; coopted young, especially indigenous Taiwanese, technocrats into the government; relaxed the bounds of political discourse; and permitted the soft-liners within the KMT to experiment with supplementary elections at the central level to rejuvenate the aging national representative bodies. Yet the limited scope of political reforms led to the exodus of several new KMT elite, who then convened various streams of dissidents to compete in the 1977 local elections and then transformed a political reform movement into a democratic movement (Huang 1976: conclusion). An accelerated and intensified movement during the critical ten years between 1977 and 1986 finally resulted in a "democratic breakthrough," which began the current stage of democratic transition.

Without doubt, the local election of 1977 was instrumental in the formation of the political opposition's pursuit of democratic transition. In this election, individual non-KMT candidates plus dissident activists, for the first time in Taiwan's postwar history, coordinated their efforts to achieve an astounding result: their seats in the Provincial Assembly doubled, and their number of mayors and county magistrates tripled (table 8.1). The *tangwai* (literally, non-KMT people), a term coined by the media to characterize the emerging collectivity of the opposition, acquired its group identity and, due to the precedent of this collective action in the 1977 election, became a political pole toward which various dissidents began to gravitate. An emerging group identity, successful collective efforts, and impressive electoral performance elevated the new opposition as a credible alternative to the KMT.

The response of the regime to the rise of new opposition was containment.

Even KMT soft-liners were surprised by the results of the 1977 local elections. Due to a violent episode during the election—the first antigovernment riot since 1947—the hard-liners' view prevailed. The hard-liner approach to the new opposition was suppression, quickly reflected in the KMT's harsh attitude toward *tangwai* members in the rovincial assembly. This, in turn, "radicalized" the opposition, who, because of its electoral victory in 1977, had already become overconfident, indulging in radical action. Controlling around one-third of the seats in the provincial assembly, the opposition could only monitor policy but could not prevent, not to say pass, any resolution. To demonstrate their strength and to propagate their political support for democracy and human rights, the majority of the opposition (called the "*Formosa* Group," after the magazine) defied martial law decrees and stormed the streets. The effect was to spur hardliners to employ more police force to stall the opposition's rallying of the masses. In this test of resolve, the opposition escalated mass rallies, hoping that social mobilization would shield them from the police. Eventually the demonstration-police spiral led to violent confrontation between two sides in Kaoshiung in 1979, after which most of the leaders in the radical opposition were imprisoned.

In the aftermath of the Kaoshiung incident, brinkmanship gave way to bargaining. The opposition—now under moderate leadership—avoided street action while occasionally agreeing to behind-the-scenes negotiations with the regime. Its major efforts were directed at four goals: building up electoral strength, exploiting the legislative arena, highlighting the issue of democratization, and seeking "external" allies. To maximize electoral gains, leaders of the opposition recommended candidates, standardized platforms, and formed campaign-support groups. In legislative debates, the opposition members seized every open-question period to publicize their views on democratic transition. Often in tacit collaboration with young turks within the KMT who had to face reelection, the opposition members also reassessed various procedural and substantive issues within the legislature. Via the floor of the legislature and the dissident journals, which were constantly banned, but not the KMT-controlled media, the opposition popularized the issue of democratic transition by identifying concrete steps and logical sequences the KMT regime was urged to follow. Essentially, the opposition proposed the following schedule of democratization: political liberalization including the lifting of martial law and media restrictions, reelection of the three national representative bodies, and direct election of the president and the governors. Finally, beginning in 1982, the opposition cemented ties with overseas Taiwanese associations, which, due to their lobbying efforts on Capitol Hill in Washington, D.C., could provide leverage against the regime. Also beginning in 1982, the opposition began to address foreign policy issues, particularly the most sensitive issue, namely, Taiwan's international status.

Apart from bargaining with the regime since 1983, the opposition has sought to formalize its internal organization. When taking concerted action, the oppositional activities were by and large election driven and legislature centered. Overemphasis on elections and the legislative debates, however, caused a split between opposition leaders holding public office and the "younger" generation oppositionists who advocated social mobilization and radical political change—complete power transfer and constitutional rewriting (Lin et al. 1983–84). A formal organization would give the opposition movement an authority structure to harmonize policy stands and integrate various political groups. Given that political parties were legally forbidden, the opposition finessed the regulation by forming an Association for Public Policy (APP), first established in Taipei in 1984, and then throughout the island despite the KMT's repeated warnings of suppression.

The KMT's response to the mounting opposition movement was a combination of incremental political change and intimidation, reflecting the coexistence of soft-liner and hard-liner groups. The KMT leadership backed the soft-liners in order to balance the hard-liners and to avoid confrontation with the opposition. For each election, the KMT created additional seats in the three national representative organs. In the 1980 election, fifty out of close to five hundred seats were new; in the subsequent 1983 election, there was no increment. So few new seats were added that it would take more than two decades to alter the balance between the old guard and new members. By that time, the old guard will have either passed away or become too old to function anyway. Moreover, despite opening up new space for competition, the KMT made no concessions in political liberalization. Indeed, the opposition faced constant intimidation (and allegedly political killings), even after the demotion of the head of the Department of Political Warfare under the Ministry of Defense in 1984 had weakened the hard-liners.

The KMT's incremental approach to democratization has a number of problems. First, it reverses the logic of democratization. How can a fair election be conducted without ensuring the opposition's rights of expression and association? In nearly all the cases of Third World democratization, liberalization is always the first step the authoritarian regime undertakes. Second, the KMT regime's credibility in enforcing martial law decrees thinned as the scope of public discourse and various organizing efforts of the opposition had defied the spirit, if not the letter, of the martial law decree. Despite internal squabbling, the opposition had been able to advance both electorally and organizationally, giving little excuse for a KMT crackdown. Third, a reform that would take two decades to complete was not a purposive act but a generational evolution. In nearly every round of debates on liberalization and democratization, the opposition and liberal scholars overwhelmed the KMT, whose counterarguments based on national emergency were quickly losing persuasive power.

It was under such an asymmetric condition—the opposition's ever-innovative challenge and the KMT's inflexible response—that a chain reaction of breathtaking moves occurred on both sides. In December 1985 the late President Chiang

Ching-kuo made an explicit commitment to constitutional procedure for political succession, delegitimating military intervention. In the summer of 1986 he appointed a blue-ribbon KMT committee to consider principal issues of political debates. In September the opposition took a blitz action in forming a party, the Democratic Progressive party, or DPP. Then in October, instead of persecuting the DPP, the KMT declared its intention to annul martial law decrees; abolish the ban on newspapers, civic associations, and political parties; and reform the three national representative bodies.

The words were backed by deeds. Since the 1986 political breakthrough, the regime has seized initiatives in the following three areas of democratic transition. First, with regard to liberalization, martial law was lifted in 1987; it was displaced by a national security act that still imposes some restriction on civil liberty. The press was decontrolled. Laws governing civic association are being enacted. Restrictions on political discourse are minimal.

Second, regarding the scope of political competition, the debate on constitutional reform has started, centering on presidential powers. The electoral reform of the three national representative bodies will be based on induced (not forced) retirement, on the one hand, and large-scale replenishment of new blood, on the other, such that new delegates will soon outnumber the old delegates. In other words, the "Long Parliament" will soon be reduced to a "Rump Parliament."

Third, with respect to the recasting of the KMT's role in the political system, its new general secretary, Mr. Lee Huan, upon assuming his position in 1987, indicated his party's intention to compete with organized opposition on an equal and fair basis (*Chung yang jih pao*, August 4, 1987: 2). The KMT has undertaken internal reform, including the adoption of a nonbinding primary—experimented with since 1982—for party nomination, elections for about half the delegation to the Thirteenth Party Congress in 1988, and even open competition for membership in the Central Committee. The KMT is gradually disengaging itself from the state apparatus, especially from schools, the government, and soon from the judiciary, though not from the military. Since 1987 KMT cadres could no longer be transferred to civil service while government subsidies to the KMT were abolished.

Democratic transition in Taiwan is obviously not due to hegemonic intervention after war and conquest as in postwar Japan, nor is it a case of redemocratization as in the Philippines or arguably of popular upheaval as in South Korea, nor is it a case of the authoritarian regime in retreat as in the case of the recent regime change in Argentina. (See Stepan 1986 for an analysis of various paths to transition.) Democratization in Taiwan has been partly propelled by organized opposition in society, partly engineered from above by the KMT. The trajectory of transition can be seen as a function of strategic interaction between the regime and the new opposition ever since the latter emerged as a credible political force in 1977 (Cheng 1989a). To use Donald Share's (1987) analytical category, Taiwan is traversing democratic "transition through transaction," which is rapid and has the consent of the preexisting authoritarian regime. In terms of duration, the ongoing process of democratic change in Taiwan does not appear to be one of long, incremental adjustment or protracted revolutionary struggle that often extends across several generations. In terms of the relationship between the regime and its challenger, the Taiwan case is not "transition through rupture," denoted by elite displacement and institutional discontinuity following a coup, revolution, extrication, or collapse of the authoritarian regime.

But why did the strategic interaction result in "negotiated democratization" rather than revolutionary uprising? Why is Taiwan on a course of transition through transaction rather than rupture? Several points can be made about the democratic transition in Taiwan.

First, the initial experience of violent confrontation had a salutary effect on the very process of democratic transition. In other countries, such as South Korea and the Philippines, democratic transition started with bargaining between the regime and opposition parties, but ended with popular uprisings and confrontation. The stalemate or failure of bargaining thus had the effect of impelling confrontation. The sequence of strategic interaction between the regime and opposition in Taiwan was reversed: it began with a head-on collision between both sides, as signified by the violent Kaohsiung incident, and was then nudged toward bargaining over the terms of the transition.

The Kaohsiung incident discredited, if not ruled out, the confrontational approach to democratization and put a premium on bargaining. In game theory terms, the game of chicken was displaced by the game of coordination. Such a shift in game was crucial to the democratic transition. For one thing, confrontation as an action-driven situation locked the hard-liners of the regime and the radical leaders of the opposition in a self-accelerating cycle of intimidation and defiance. It was only after the Kaohsiung incident that both sides began to debate concrete issues of democratization. For another, once the mode of interaction switched from confrontation to bargaining, the test of skill and the use of discourse displaced the test of will and the use of force. The ascent of the moderate leadership in the opposition was coupled with the recovery of the soft-liners within the regime.

Second, political entrepreneurship of the opposition was decisive in pushing the regime to commit to accelerated democratic transition. After the violent clash with the opposition in Kaohsiung, the regime showed its willingness to pursue political change. This signal was more goodwill than a commitment, however, including neither the content of democratic reform nor a timetable for change. Resisting every major demand for democracy by the opposition, yet continuously increasing the margin of electoral competition, the KMT was at best undertaking an incremental approach to democratization. The KMT had little incentive to do otherwise. On the one hand, by the martial law restrictions—which froze the organizational disadvantage of the opposition—and by the slowness in opening up political space for competition, the KMT ensured the maintenance of its political power. On the other hand, by proceeding incrementally, it was able to avoid having to confront vested interests and the problem of separation between party and state.

The KMT did consent to an accelerated democratic transition later in 1986. In large part, this breakthrough should be attributed to the political entrepreneurship of the opposition. In the first half of the 1980s, the opposition took nonviolent initiatives to press for democratization, to which the KMT barely responded. The opposition made good use of bargaining arenas: it shunned the streets, minimized closed-door negotiations with the regime, exploited the Legislative Yuan, and explored overseas supporters. Before the lifting of martial law, street activities rendered the opposition vulnerable to suppression. Closed-door negotiations were often biased against the opposition, which, lacking hierarchical authority within its leadership, could not make credible commitments. In the Legislative Yuan, members of the opposition could use a guaranteed forum to gather information on policies, publicize their demands for democratization, and create an image of a "loyal opposition." Overseas was the only arena that escaped the government's control. Overseas allies could echo and amplify the demands and cause of the opposition, exerting international pressure on the regime.

Guided by legal expertise, the leaders of the opposition also set the agenda for debate on democratic change. By first raising sensitive issues in the legislature and then elaborating them in dissident magazines, the opposition broadened the scope of political discourse. On democratization, the opposition did not just identify a logical sequence for change, but also pushed for a timetable for change. Equally skillful in its issue identification and agenda setting for democratic change was the opposition's ability to use extralegal devices to finesse martial law and organize itself.

Political entrepreneurship of the opposition increased the costs of inaction on the part of the regime. Extralegal organizational devices, which violated the spirit, though not the letter, of the law, also had the effect of discrediting martial law. As the opposition repeatedly raised the ante and prevailed, the threat of crackdown became less and less credible. On the other hand, as the costs of reliance on built-in safeguards for maintaining power increased, the option of cashing in its depreciable political capital—accumulated through its role in economic development—became very attractive to the KMT. The opposition's ability to reconfigure political parameters altered the cost–benefit calculation of the KMT, and thus induced the KMT to accelerate democratic transition.

Third, the political entrepreneurship of the regime was equally important. The regime received an instant payoff for its widely publicized commitment to democratization: it dramatically improved its international image. This was a great gain for a regime facing international isolation, accusations of human rights violation, and mainland China's diplomatic offensive for reunification. While the actual decision-making process of the democratic breakthrough in 1986 is yet to be studied, one can hypothesize that this "side-payment" permitted the late President Chiang Ching-kuo to override easily the dissent of the old guard and hardliners within the KMT.

Moreover, by refraining from suppressing the illegally formed DPP and by consenting to democratic transition, the regime regained initiative in bargaining position. For example, the KMT was able to attach three preconditions to the formation of new political parties, the so-called three no's: no violence, no advocacy of communism, and no advocacy of territorial separatism (i.e., no advocacy of Taiwan independence). Indeed, playing an active role in the democratic transition, the regime was in a position to steer the course of future change.

## The Appeal and Relevance of the Japanese Model

Democratization can be reversed. History has seen many instances of the breakdown of consolidated democratic regimes or the abortion of fresh democracy under severe economic shocks, social disorder, and external military intervention. But assuming that democratic transition in Taiwan continues, what sort of democratic system is likely to emerge?

Democracy also, as Arend Lijphart (1984) has shown, can assume many forms, such as consociational (or consensual), majoritarian, or consultative. Consociational democracy is not an option for Taiwan, as discussed earlier. Majoritarian democracy with frequent transfers of power, premised on a two-party or multiple-party system, has been established in a polity previously under single-party authoritarianism, such as Turkey. The split within the ruling party, however, was instrumental in the emergence of the majoritarian democracy in postwar Turkey (Ozbudun 1987). Given that the DPP was created in the society rather than within the party-state, and given that this opposition has not been able to break the barrier of 30 percent voting support, majoritarian democracy is not in the making in Taiwan. Consultative democracy—postwar Japan being the paradigmatic case—seems to have tremendous appeal to a political system previously under single-party rule. Under this democratic system, the ruling party continues to hold political power but in consultation with semipermanent yet divided opposition parties, averting the "tyranny of the majority" while deradicalizing the otherwise frustrated opposition. Such a consultative democracy may well be what Taiwan is heading for.

The KMT has both the incentives and capacity to help bring about a consultative democratic system. The KMT is willing to install such a system because it will be the principal beneficiary, whereas the opposition parties will suffer from collective-action problems—including free-rider and defection problems. Prevention of a KMT-dominant system is a public good available to any opposition party irrespective of the level of its effort. This free-rider problem can be alleviated by a "pact" for power sharing among the opposition parties if they succeed in displacing the ruling party. (For costs of coalition making, see Adrian and

Press 1964.) But, similar to a cartel, such a pact is difficult to sustain if newcomers continue to appear. If the pact is remade to accommodate newcomers, the chance of members' defection to the ruling party side becomes greater. The ruling party may offer payoffs to offset the cost of defection. On the other hand, the KMT can appropriate the gain of a consultative democratic system, thus facing no incentive problem.

Because democratic transition in Taiwan has been characterized by transaction, not rupture, the KMT has the opportunity to promote, if not create, a consultative democratic system. Under transition through rupture, "the ability to delegitimate the previous regime is all that gives legitimacy to the emerging regime" (Share 1987: 531). Moreover, the previous regime becomes a target for political opposition, a hindrance to the process. Under transition through transaction, the authoritarian regime consents to and participates in the making of the emerging regime. This suggests that after committing to democratic transition, the KMT can steer the course of change and design democratic institutions in such a way as to ensure its staying on top. There is evidence that the KMT is exercising such discretionary power. Before 1986 the KMT had taken a strong position against any new opposition party. The newly enacted law on civil associations, however, sets minimal requirements for new political parties, which encourage proliferation of small parties. By lowering the entry barriers to political competition, the KMT has weakened the DPP, induced the formation of many small parties, and hence created coordination or coalitional problems for opposition parties as just elaborated. The Workers' party, formed in 1988, drains both the leadership and supporters away from the DPP. Hoping to receive concessions from the government, environmentalists have avoided a close association with the DPP.

The "congressional reform" also testifies to the KMT's abilities to consolidate its power in the emerging democratic system. As mentioned above, the formula that the KMT adopted in 1988 to reform the three national representative bodies was to add new seats sufficient and quickly enough to outnumber the old guard, who were encouraged rather than compelled to retire. The formula evinces the KMT leadership's compromise with the vested interests of old delegates. Yet it also empowered the KMT to control the pace of reform so as to ensure its proportional gain (70 percent as it stands now) in new political space. Relatedly, the government can also alter the electoral system to halt the expansion of the DPP. Taiwan's electoral system, similar to the one for the Lower House in Japan, based on single but nontransferable vote, multiple-seat, large-size districts, has favored smaller parties that can pool scattered resources to support a few candidates. Because of its ability to allocate votes among its supporters, thanks to its local organizations and the residential complex of state employees, the KMT has polled well under this system. In early 1989 the KMT revised the electoral law to trim the size of electoral districts, preventing the DPP from maximizing its winning of seats. The KMT has avoided, however, resorting to the single-vote, single-member system, which would have compressed the living space for small parties altogether.

While its rule-making capacity tends to perpetuate the KMT's political power, the DPP's inflexible foreign policy stance is also conducive to the making of a "permanent opposition," another similarity between Taiwan and Japan. (For the importance of the opposition in one-party-dominant regimes, see Pempel n.d.) The DPP has shown an ideological fervor for applying the principle of self-determination by all residents on the island to solve the sovereignty problem of Taiwan. This policy stance originated in the DPP's use of the subethnic cleavage to galvanize its democratic movement. Democratization was initially cast in terms of the mainlanders' illegitimate monopoly on political power and a process of redistributing political power to the Taiwanese. The DPP soon saw its advocacy for Taiwan's self-determination as a perfectly logical position to take in the light of its demand for democracy: if the majority of Taiwanese could decide their internal affairs, why could they not control their own international status? Whether the DPP's foreign policy stand has the support of the majority of Taiwanese is still unknown (the available public opinion surveys are utterly unreliable given the great stake of this highly emotional issue). The obsession with this foreign policy issue, however, tends to lock the DPP into a politically disadvantageous position.

First, given strong opposition from both the KMT and mainland China, the DPP leadership bears the burden of proof for the feasibility of its creating a new status for Taiwan in the international system via self-determination. While the DPP banks its party's future on this grandiose issue, the KMT is investing heavily in other policy areas where the general public has an immediate, though not necessarily higher, stake. These areas include social welfare, environment, consumer welfare, regional development, and many other issues that are common to a society reaching a higher stage of economic development. The DPP has already lagged behind the KMT in developing expertise and efficacy in socioeconomic policy areas. The disparity can only grow as Taiwanese society becomes more pluralistic and its economy becomes more complex.

After nearly three decades of rapid development, new socioeconomic forces have risen to prominence, weakening the vertical Taiwanese–mainlander cleavage and creating cross-cutting conflicts. These include horizontal cleavage between labor and capital, regional cleavage between environment-conscious rural dwellers and growth-oriented urbanites, and sectoral cleavage between import consumers and local industrial or agricultural producers. As foreign policy issues—whose sunk cost is high and political yield uncertain—drain its political resources, the DPP faces a credibility gap in intricate socioeconomic policy areas.

Second, perhaps thinking that their political capital would appreciate by linking the issue of democracy to self-determination in such Manichean terms, the opposition presented itself as a Taiwanese political force and was regarded as such. This deprives the DPP of support from many liberal intellectuals, especially among the mainlanders, who would side with the DPP for democracy but not for self-determination. Moreover, while the DPP is a Taiwanese party, the KMT is not really a mainlanders' party. The KMT leadership has since the 1970s initiated the process of "Taiwanization." By the 1980s an overwhelming majority of its members and its candidates for public offices (estimated at around 75 percent and 80 percent, respectively)—the latter being a reservoir of new leaders—were Taiwanese. And the Taiwanese representation in the KMT's commanding Standing Committee approached 50 percent in the late 1980s. While the bonds between social forces and political forces in Taiwan remain weak, recent empirical studies affirm that the DPP's social bases are narrow while the KMT's are broad, balanced, and diversified. The DPP's supporters—exclusively Taiwanese—tend to concentrate in the self-employed business sector, working class, and, above all, segments of the population rejecting Chinese identity. In contrast, voters for the KMT are very evenly distributed among various sectors (Lin 1988: 113–22).

Not only is the KMT no longer a party of the mainlanders, but it also ceases to be a party of devoted cadres. If anything, the KMT is evolving into an aggregation of heterogeneous interests, a catchall party managed by professional party workers. While the KMT certainly can internalize conflicting social interests, it possesses resources to reconcile social conflicts, as demonstrated in its mediating role between labor and capital in the enaction of the Basic Labor Law in 1982 (Republic of China, Legislative Yuan 1985).

If one believes that the democratic transition in Taiwan has a teleological dimension, then the Japanese model of a democratic system has both appeal and relevance to Taiwan. History, however, is not always a linear progression and is full of contingencies and surprises. The KMT may engineer from above, but it cannot control the DPP or other opposition parties' responses. Nor can the KMT control an "optimal" pace of democratic reform, one fast enough to satisfy the public while slow enough to allow for the gradual consolidation of its electoral position.

The combined elections for the Legislative Yuan, gubernatorial positions, and the Provinicial Assembly in December 1989 illustrate the limits of the KMT's ability to design the process of democratic transition. Taken together, of the combined elections, the voting share of the KMT dropped from 70 percent to 60 percent while the major opposition party avoided being victimized by internal conflicts and even made significant inroads, capturing six out of twenty-one positions for county magistrates (a net increase of five, including the crucial Taipei County seat). Despite registering only a slight increase in voting share, the DPP's gain was substantial. The minor opposition parties received 10 percent of votes, which came at the expense of the KMT, not the DPP. Except for one position in the Provincial Assembly, minor opposition parties did not win a single seat in any other contest, bolstering the DPP's image as the representative political opposition.

Many factors accounted for the KMT's setback in this election, including the deteriorating law-and-order condition, rising housing costs, and several other policy issues for which voters held the ruling party responsible. But the principal reason for the KMT's electoral slip was its inability to accelerate "congressional reform," as it had promised to, by way of inducing or persuading enough tenured lifetime national representatives to retire. This not only caused the KMT to lose some credibility but also it created a disciplinary problem within the party— many KMT candidates defied party orders and joined in the criticisms of the extremely unpopular old-timers. In contrast, the moderate faction of the DPP skillfully skirted (but dropped) the sensitive subject of Taiwan independence, hoping to defer the issue until after it comes to power.

It would be premature to conclude that the results of the 1989 election signal the advent of a two-party majoritarian democracy in Taiwan. The election was the first since the lifting of martial law and the legalization of opposition parties. If this election represents a secular trend of the changing balance of political forces, then the DPP may stand an excellent chance of gaining political power in the near future, when political space is totally open for competition. Then we shall see the Turkish style of democratic transition. On the other hand, the opposition's advance may well be a one-time gain rather than a long-run trend. The 10 percent drop in the KMT's voting share was only partially absorbed by the DPP, implying an increase in protest votes. Indeed, there are good reasons to believe a one-party-dominant system will emerge.

The radical–moderate conflict within the DPP persists. Pronounced during the campaign period, internal struggles within the DPP could have been alleviated if one of the two factions had been electorally discredited. But both factions performed equally well; hence, factional strife should resurface in the legislative arena. As long as the radical faction continues to advocate a venturesome approach to Taiwan's independence, the DPP will have difficulty in attracting the support of the vast middle class, which is concerned primarily with personal security and prosperity.

Moreover, the majority of voters may attempt to punish the KMT up to a point where the KMT will not be displaced by the DPP, yet will be forced to be more responsive to constituents. Whether 55 percent versus, say, 60 percent of voting share is the baseline for electoral punishment, is both difficult to determine and realize at least initially. Looking after its own political interests, the KMT (assuming it is a rational actor) has evinced the determination to turn the electoral tide by finally addressing the important issue it evaded in the last election, namely, political reform, or, more specifically, the problem of pensioning off lifetime tenured members of the "congress" to make room for new, more competent delegates.

## Postscript

Democratization is a protracted process. The pace of political reform in Taiwan has quickened after the strenuous presidential election in the spring of 1990. The election was made by the first National Assembly, which was predominantly controlled by the delegates elected in 1947. The nomination and endorsement of the presidential candidate and his running mate triggered an acute, high-level leadership conflict within the KMT. To mend the rift within the KMT and to lay the groundwork for an accelerated democratic transformation, President Lee Teng-hui convened a National Affairs Conference in the summer of 1990, collecting advice from, and attempting to build consensus among, political elite of both the KMT and the DPP, opinion leaders, and experts. The first hurdle for democratic reform under President Lee—namely, to have himself electorally validated by those old-timers whose power he was about to neutralize—was overcome. Had that difficult election failed to empower an extremely popular President Lee, a social revolt would have broken out. The National Affairs Conference also legitimized the high-priority task of political reform that he assumed, though the methods of reform remain undefined.

Meanwhile, the senile delegates' sustained resistance to the KMT party center's offer of voluntary retirement with a handsome pension triggered an acute social protest, massive student sit-ins, and nearly universal media condemnation of their intransigence. Against this background, President Lee astutely requested the Grand Justice Constitutional Council for a review of the judicial decree that was used to rationalize the indefinite extension of the tenure of the national representatives elected in 1947. The Grand Justice's reinterpretation of that decree ordered the compulsory retirement of those representatives by the end of 1991. The second hurdle for Taiwan's democratic reform was removed. This "long parliament," which monopolized legislative power as well as the election of the presidency for more than four decades, is finally being phased out without a political revolution. Meanwhile, the president also declared the end of the state of national emergency. This action both put pressure on Communist China to renounce its hostility toward Nationalist China on Taiwan and forced all political actors in Taiwan to turn to the task of constitutional reform.

The third, and probably final, hurdle to the young democracy in Taiwan is to overhaul the 1947 Constitution. Areas for reform include restructuring the power relationship between the Executive Yuan and the president, determining the fate of the Control Yuan, and changing the method of producing a president. The 1947 Constitution has been a potpourri of institutional devices, with more built-in checks and balances than those in the American constitution. That a strong presidency was ever possible under this originally highly checkered constitution was a result of emergency clauses that superceded the constitution. Now that emergency powers of the president are being phased out, the exercise of political power will have to be redefined. Among the three steps of democratic change outlined here, the final one is most consequential; political rules that will be binding for years to come are being rewritten. Moreover, the subethnic cleavage seems to correspond with the political faultline in this constitutional game. To simplify, mainlanders favor a cabinet system, which will allow the mainlander elites to share power, while many Taiwanese favor a presidential system, which, because of population arithmetic, will certainly produce a Taiwanese president. The outcome will be a mixed or revised semipresidential system, à la Finland or France.

The third step was completed in the first half of 1992 by the constitutional National Assembly, whose members were elected in December 1991. The legislative election in December 1992 was the first one held under the refurbished constitution, and one at which all members were newly elected. That was the first founding election. It crystallized the power and set the pattern of electoral politics for many years to come.

This essay is not meant to document and analyze the just-mentioned events, which are widely reported, and the meaning of which can be fully understood only when all is over. Rather, this essay is about the trend toward democratic change and the fundamental forces shaping its process. These events pose no surprise to the conclusion already reached: that a wealthy, middle-class-dominated, and local election-tutored Taiwan was a soil ripe for democratic change, that the subethnic cleavage has not only accelerated, but, complicated the body of change, and that an indigenized but still dominant KMT is shaping the course for a Japanese destination. Democratic transition in Taiwan has not quite been a "velvet" one, but at least it got started, unlike other cases—such as Burma and Communist China—which did not have the luxury of even reaching the point of democratic transition. Democratic transition in Taiwan is not problem free and is intertwined with the turbulent relations with the mainland, but it continues to proceed, and a Japanese-type of one-party dominant system seems to be emerging. Despite this trend, a split of the KMT, a split of the DPP, and consequential realignment among the beleaguered parties remain possibilities.

# 9

# Singapore: Coping with Vulnerability

## Chan Heng Chee

FOR ANYONE wishing to explore the linkage between economic change and political change, there are no better starting points than the contributions of Marx, Moore, and Lipset. Karl Marx was the first to detail the argument that changes in the system of economic production presaged changes in the superstructure of state institutions, ideology, and values and the emergence of new classes. Since then, generations of social scientists of all ideological dispositions have incorporated, over and over again, this thesis into their analytical frameworks in the investigation of political, economic, and social change (Meyer 1960; Fischer 1970: 80–93). In our time, Barrington Moore, Jr., in an ambitious work, *Social Origins of Dictatorship and Democracy*, opened up the scope of comparative history and provided the insight that agrarian transformations and conflicts determined the nature of political revolutions and the shaping of modern political systems (Moore 1966). The accessibility of these two grand theories should be sufficient yeast to stimulate research, but there is a third yet to be considered, the more specific inquiry of Seymour Martin Lipset, who, in trying to establish the social prerequisites of democracy, drew the connection between the establishment of democratic political systems and economic growth and development (Lipset 1963: 45–76). And in recent years, following the phenomenal economic changes and economic performances of the newly industrialized countries of South Korea, Taiwan, Hong Kong, and Singapore, Lipset's hypothesis, if not Marx's or Moore's, begs to be tested in the political laboratories of the Asian-Pacific states.

To be sure, the politics of the Northeast Asian states is passing through an astonishing pace of change, and the democratization of previously authoritarian regimes seems well in the cards. The case of Hong Kong is different as its future is bound up with the developments in China. This leaves Singapore—the island city-state, 621 square kilometers with no natural resources except for its location and people, but an economic miracle nonetheless, and something of a showcase state for development—which progresses at a pace and in a direction that is uniquely its own. Singapore, at the end of an era of rapid economic modernization

219

and growth, has reached a major political transition. The phenomenon of economic growth presupposes a strategy or strategies and ushers in a process that shapes not only the economic but the social and political realms as well. The political-economic equation of Singapore's development is not dissimilar to the two larger Northeast Asian states seen also as exemplars. Economic growth was predicated upon political change, and political change stimulated further growth, which spawned new pressures for greater, far-reaching political change. The central question to be investigated is: What is the link between economic growth and political evolution? A related question that follows naturally is: How and to what extent do culture, leadership, history, and specific environmental contexts impose a powerful framework upon the political evolution?

Economists have periodized Singapore's economic growth in three distinct periods: 1960 to 1965, a period of slow growth (averaging 5.5 percent) that coincided with the transition from self-government to independence; 1966 to 1973, a period of high growth (averaging 13 percent) after separation from Malaysia; and 1974 to 1984, a period of slower growth (averaging 7.9 percent) after the oil shock (Lim et al., 1988: 7). This chapter, however, will discuss the linkage between economics and politics in the development process by using a periodization that is more definitive politically.

Political scientists generally recognize four distinct periods in the republic's political development: 1959 to 1965, which marked the politics of political consolidation; 1966 to 1970, which is best characterized as the politics of survival; 1971 to 1984, the politics of rapid economic growth; and the period beginning in 1985, which opened a new era of political transition.

## The Politics of Consolidation: 1959–65

The singular pursuit of economic growth was not a luxury enjoyed by the People's Action party (PAP) leadership in its early years of office. In 1959, when autonomy was granted by the British, Singapore was a highly politicized society. The PAP, which had achieved its first legislative majority in 1957, was a united front of Communists and non-Communist social democrats and a leading mobilizer in politics. The route to political power for the PAP was via the support of labor and the Chinese-educated constituency, who felt oppressed in the British colonial order. Strikes, street demonstrations, and student activism in Chinese schools were modes of anticolonial political action led by the pro-Communist faction of the party. The imminent political concern of Lee Kuan Yew and his social democrat associates was the assertion of the moderate leadership and the subjugation of the pro-Communist faction of the party. Right from the start, Lee understood that the political struggle could not be fought on political controls alone but that ultimately, economic performance and the efficacy of his leadership were critical considerations.

The first fully elected government of Singapore faced daunting social and economic problems. There was an acute housing shortage after the war. The population growth rate was 3.2 percent per annum, net annual immigration was 0.7 percent, and unemployment stood at a serious 13.5 percent (Tan 1986: 273). The United Nations Industrial Survey Mission, invited in 1960 to advise the Singapore government on its industrialization program, estimated that over the decade 1960–70, 214,000 jobs would have to be found, mostly in manufacturing, to solve the employment problems (United Nations 1961: 11). The existing manufacturing sector was weak. The 1957 census showed that 61,000 persons were engaged in manufacturing, mostly in the processing of rubber and coconut oil, out of an economically active work force of 471,000, and most industrial establishments employed less than 10 workers. The development of manufacturing was an urgent matter as entreport trade was declining in view of the new nationalism in postindependence Southeast Asia. This in turn depended on securing access to larger markets; overcoming Singapore's free-port status; remedying the shortage of trained managers, skilled workers, and entrepreneurs; and disciplining a strike-prone work force.

Thus, a political merger with the Federation of Malaya was seen to be an economic necessity and in the longer run a political necessity. So also was central planning. In fact, the UN Industrial Survey Mission, led by Dr. Albert Winsemius, a Dutch industrial economist, wrote a report that became the blueprint for Singapore's economic development. The UN report (commonly known as the "Winsemius Report"), in addition to identifying the key industries for development, recommended the establishment of an Economic Development Board to undertake the functions of industrial promotion, financing, creating industrial facilities, and providing technical consulting service, a proposal that in effect created the engine of growth.

In a retrospective interview in 1981, Dr. Winsemius recalled his early advice to Lee Kuan Yew on the underlying political requirement for the industrialization of Singapore:

> Number one is: get rid of the Communists; how you get rid of them does not interest me as an economist, but get them out of your unions, get them off the streets. How you do it is your job. Number two is: let Raffles stand where he stands today; say publicly that you accept the heavy ties with the west because you will very much need them in your economic program. (Drysdale 1984: 252)

Prime Minister Lee consequently adopted a two-pronged strategy. At the political level, he sought to domesticate internal party factionalism. The first challenge to the party leadership was mounted by the populist maverick Ong Eng Guan, the minister of national development. The issue at the 1960 Party Conference was the lack of intraparty democracy and the rightist drift of party policies. Ong tabled sixteen resolutions against the party leadership but failed to muster support from the pro-Communist faction as the latter calculated that the time was not ripe for a severance with the moderates, with the result that he was expelled from the party (Pang 1971).

The second challenge, from the pro-Communists, was a more complicated one to handle. The PAP's assumption of power led to the release of eight PAP pro-Communist union leaders detained by the British authorities under the Preservation of Public Security Ordinance. The return of key left-wing mobilizers to the political arena forewarned of the eventual showdown and an attempt by the Communists to take control of the party. In anticipation of this development, Prime Minister Lee and his colleagues opened up a line of defense outside the party by establishing a statutory board, the People's Association (PA), in 1960 to organize an islandwide network of community centers to increase contact with grass roots. At the same time, they moved to regulate the mushrooming "yellow" and splinter labor unions with the enactment of the Trade Unions (Amendment) Bill in 1960, which empowered the Registrar of Trade Unions to refuse registration of unions that did not comply with the established conditions. This step was accompanied by attempts to create a Trades Union Congress to unify and control the labor movement. In fact, it was this increasing governmental control that accelerated the internal party competition.

The Communist challenge came into the open in 1961, after a period of maneuvering with the party and in the union movement, precipitated by the Malaysian Prime Minister Tengku Abdul Rahman's merger proposal of a larger Malaysia including Singapore. The pro-Communist faction in the PAP opposed the party's "independence through merger" stand, thereby drawing the battle lines (Drysdale 1984: 283–324; Sopiee 1974). The battle for merger proved to be the most serious political contest for Prime Minister Lee, leading to the historic split of the left wing from the PAP to form the Barisan Sosialis in July 1961. The party apparatus was captured by the pro-Communists, and almost all the party branches defected to the Barisan Sosialis. The split would have demolished the moderate wing had Prime Minister Lee not been able to activate the network of newly established People's Association community centers as an alternative party apparatus. There ensued an intensification of political struggle in the trade unions. The PAP-led trade union movement, the Trades Union Congress, split along ideological lines into the National Trades Union Congress (NTUC) sponsored by the moderate leadership and the Singapore Association of Trades Union (SATU) backed by the Barisan Sosialis. The NTUC developed a tightly centralized framework by which labor was subsequently disciplined and allowed controlled representation in the political system while the left-wing trade unions were progressively suppressed. Although the NTUC grew from a minority movement to a majority movement between 1961 and 1965, it was after Singapore gained its independence from Malaysia that the existing corporatist industrial relations system was fully expanded.

The second prong of Prime Minister Lee's strategy was the strengthening of the administrative structures. This was to have direct impact on the economy and in the social sphere. Singapore inherited a reasonably strong civil service from the British, one that was familiar with traditions of bureaucratic neutrality and efficiency but disdainful of the nationalist politicians and their objectives. In the developing political struggle, the political leadership shrewdly regarded the English-educated civil service as their natural allies. The Political Study Center, established in 1960 to resocialize a colonial bureaucracy into the thinking and goals of the elected politicians, proved to be the single most important instrument forging the political alliance between the PAP leadership and the bureaucrats to defeat the Communists and enhanced the administrative capacity for Singapore's development (Lee 1959; Seah 1981: 173–94). The shared trust and consensus that emerged from this dialogue formed the underlying basis for the rise of the "administrative state" in postseparation Singapore; it reached its apogee in the 1970s in the frequent recruitment of bureaucrats into the PAP as politicians and subsequently their appointment to the cabinet.

The early decision to use statutory boards to promote national development proved to be both advantageous and effective (Quah 1981). Freed of the cumbersome constraints on government departments, the statutory boards translated political will into immediate effect. In 1960, the Housing and Development Board (HDB) was created as a successor to the Singapore Improvement Trust, the colonial housing authority. The HDB began with the construction of 7,320 housing units in 1961 and constructed between 10,000 and 13,000 units annually in the years 1962–69. And whereas SIT under the colonial government housed only 9 percent of Singapore's population, the HDB by 1975 housed 51 percent of Singapore's population and 85 percent by 1988 (Republic of Singapore, Housing and Development Board 1970; Teh 1979: 98). Viewed from a political perspective, public housing was a major redistributive measure in Singapore, the political equivalent of land reform in an urban situation, laying the broad foundation for economic development. This, together with the mass education program, represented, in Irma Adelman's terms, the redistribution essential to successful economic growth, an approach adopted by South Korea and Taiwan as well (Adelman 1979: 312–22).

In 1961, the Economic Development Board (EDB) was set up in accord with the recommendations of the Winsemius Report, followed by the Public Utilities Board (PUB), the Singapore Tourist Promotion Board (STPB), and the Port of Singapore Authority (PSA) in 1964. The activities and results of the EDB were not spectacular in the initial years even though steps were taken to promote an industrial policy. Politics was in command.

After the party split, the PAP leadership took its fight against the left-wing opposition to a national referendum on the issue of achieving independence from Britain by merging with the Federation of Malaya, Sabah, and Sarawak. On September 1, 1962, it defeated the antimerger forces by a clear margin of votes (Drysdale 1984: 308–12; Bellows 1970). But merger with the Malay states did not provide the economic benefits Singapore had hoped for. Instead, the PAP government engaged in a bitter, tense racial and political confrontation with the Kuala Lumpur government and the politicians of its leading party, the United Malays National Organization (UMNO) (Fletcher 1969).

The common market, which for Singapore was the essence of merger, never materialized. Nonetheless, the experience of Malaysia was important to the island state and the PAP for three reasons. First, the central question of who should govern in a multiracial polity was debated openly and the assumptions of different ethnic perspectives were expounded upon. The Malay leaders asserted a vision of a Malay Malaysia with Malay dominance as the linchpin; from Singapore's perspective, Malaysia should develop as a Malaysian Malaysia with an accommodationist policy toward the non-Malay groups. The outcome of the confrontation saw the termination of an option of a future in a larger political unit for Singapore. But the experience of Malaysia honed Prime Minister Lee's reflexes in the management of ethnic relations, which continue to influence the shaping of domestic and foreign policy. Second, the foreclosure of the Malaysian option for Singapore's development set the republic on a different development path, which resulted in its rapid economic growth. Third, the conflict between Kuala Lumpur and Singapore united the population behind the PAP leadership, paving the way for the emergence of one-party dominance.

Economically, the years 1960–65 were, in terms of Singapore's records, years of slower growth compared to the double-digit economic performances immediately after separation. During this period the GDP growth rate averaged 5.5 percent a year, but it was far lower in 1963–65, the years of Malaysia, and in 1964 was actually negative, due to the Indonesian Confrontation. The basic problems of unemployment remained unresolved. In 1959, the annual census of manufacturers showed 29,199 persons employed in 531 manufacturing establishments. In spite of the EDB's efforts, only 21,000 new jobs were created (Goh 1973). Singapore pursued an import substitution policy directed at the Malaysian market, but tariffs were levied on only 157 items, such as steel bars, plastic products, chocolates, cement, and sugar. Because the policy of import substitution was short-lived, Singapore did not entrench a class of industrial and business interests that were dependent upon the state for protection, nor were there substantial stakes to defend. Thus, the switch subsequently to export-led industrialization did not meet with resistance.

This analysis of the early years of PAP rule suggests that a pattern of control and concentration of power in the hands of the government was introduced right from the start. The justification for this lay primarily in the felt need to counter the Communist threat. Measures were taken in an ad hoc fashion for this purpose rather than in accordance with a blueprint to promote development, even if the link between political stability and economic growth was understood. The realignment of the bureaucracy with the political leadership proved to be a most strategic and consequential alliance domestically, while the triumph over the

Communists in the united front and the domestication of labor unions and radical students drastically altered the political scene.

## The Politics of Survival: 1966–70

The unexpected and traumatic separation from Malaysia on August 9, 1965, was the most significant factor impelling new strategies for Singapore's survival as a political entity. From 1966 to 1970, the newly independent republic went through a dizzying pace of political, economic, and social change (Chan 1971). Indeed, Lee and his cabinet colleagues were forced to reverse fundamentally their orientations about Singapore's future. The identity formation and economic policies of the state were until this time primarily geared for merger with Malaysia. The exigencies of the crisis demanded quick action. In retrospect, the most significant policies that shaped modern postseparation Singapore were laid down in the first five years of independence. It was also in 1970 that the Singapore leadership gained some measure of confidence that the unlikely nation-state was a viable enterprise.

Paradoxically, it was not a testing time for domestic politics. The perception of clear threats and the definition of clear goals predisposed the society for high mobilization by the political elite. The concern for territorial integrity and territorial survival was paramount. At the time of separation, Singapore had no military force except for two battalions of the Singapore Infantry Regiment, which was dominated by Singapore Malays, a discovery that exacerbated the sense of crisis (Chan 1985). The issue of economic survival resurfaced without the fallback of the Malaysian hinterland. Furthermore, the task of shaping a natural identity out of a fragmented immigrant multiethnic population presented formidable challenges.

The PAP leadership's response was to launch a "massive exercise of survival" that accentuated the exhortative and mobilizational style of an earlier left-wing era. Right from the start Lee concluded that for Singapore to survive as a nation it had to be "a tightly organized society" and a "rugged society." In July 1966, he told the country that "Societies like ours have no fat to spare. They are lean and healthy or they die. We have calculated backwards and forwards for eleven months on an independence we never sought that our best chances lie in a very tightly organized society" (*The Mirror*, July 25, 1966, p. 1).

The preoccupation with the fundamental limitations of an island-state and the absence of room for maneuver in a small state situation recur constantly in the speeches and writings of the PAP leaders. Fifteen years later, in 1981, this conviction was still being forthrightly expressed in a National Day Rally speech of the Singapore prime minister: "If you want to know why I am tough, it's because I know what happens. . . . And you know that Singapore has only one chance and that is to go up—tighter, more disciplined, up the ladder. You unwind this and it's curtains for everybody" (*The Straits Times*, August 21, 1981).

The "tightly organized society" found its form in the establishment of multiple networks of para-statal grass-roots institutions throughout the island and in exhortations for "social discipline." The People's Association community centers were increasingly effective in counteracting Communist mobilization. In 1965, PAP political penetration was enhanced through the creation of the Citizens Consultative Committees (CCCs), one for each constituency, to act as contact points for the government to keep its finger on the people's pulse. The CCCs also opened avenues for the recruitment of local traditional leaders to participate in and support government political structures. They thus helped to provide the information and the access, without which, the prime minister has argued, the Communist stranglehold of the political system could not have been dislodged (Lee 1984). This organizational formula was further developed in 1978 by the introduction of Residents' Committees (RCs). As Singapore's population was increasingly regrouped and resettled in the massive public housing programs, the Housing and Development Board (HDB) estates, Lee reasoned that it was essential to detect the housing and environmental problems generated by urban highrise, high-density living before they burgeoned into major political issues, and to proceed quickly to resolve them. Thus, grass-roots institutions such as these, working in tandem with PAP branches, saturated the political ground and served as auxiliaries to the bureaucracy in effecting the government's will.

Tightness was also achieved by marginalizing the opposition. The April 1968 general election returned a one-party parliament for the first time. Fifty-one PAP candidates were elected unopposed. Only seven of the fifty-eight seats were contested, and the PAP won 84.4 percent of the votes cast (Josey 1968). The opposition parties boycotted the election, recognizing the general support of the electorate for the ruling party in a time of national crisis. The Barisan Sosialis committed the strategic error of withdrawing from the parliamentary arena for doctrinal reasons, leaving the entire legislative stage to the PAP. This set the unusual precedent of a possibility of total control of the legislature by one party through a free and fair election and conditioned the PAP subsequently to expect this as a political norm for Singapore.

The decision to secure defense through a citizen army with the passage of the Singapore Army Bill (1968) and the National Service Bill (1967) added to the impression of a regimentation of society. Looking from the outside, not a few writers characterized Singapore as a "garrison state" with a "siege mentality" (Buchanan 1972; George 1973).

An economic strategy that, prior to separation, rested on entreport trade and an industrial policy of import substitution underwent a serious reassessment. Export promotion as a basis for industrialization was clearly adopted in 1968, the impetus for change coming from the British announcement to withdraw east of Suez by 1971. British bases in Singapore had traditionally made a major defense and economic contribution. In 1967, it was estimated that British military expenditure in Singapore annually amounted to 15 percent of Singapore's GNP while giving employment to forty thousand persons directly (Republic of Singapore Information Division 1984: 296).

The most immediate political result of the export promotion industrialization policy was the passage of the Employment Act and the Industrial Relations (Amendment) Act in 1968, which, to use the minister of labor's words, were designed "to rationalize employer-employee relationships with a view to attracting new investments and increasing the efficiency of our trading and industrial enterprises" (Vasil 1988: 142). This was to be done by disciplining the work force and curtailing labor union powers. These two bills, passed in a one-party parliament, were interpreted as the start of an authoritarian trend, a concentration of powers and its corollary, an exercise of tight control. They were justified as functional requirements of economic development. In 1968, the Abortion and Sterilization acts were also passed as part of a population policy package to keep birth rates down in the development process.

In mid-1968, the EDB was reorganized and the Jurong Town Corporation was formed to manage and develop Jurong and other industrial estates. The Development Bank of Singapore also took over financing operations from the EDB. A package of fiscal incentives was offered, ranging from tax relief of up to five years to unrestricted repatriation of profits and capital, to investors willing to launch industries favored by the government. This proved to be a successful formula, and by 1970, an influx of foreign investors entered Singapore. There were 271 factories operating in Jurong with another 103 under construction. Direct foreign investments in fixed assets in manufacturing industries stood at $1,700 million (Republic of Singapore Information Division 1984: 297).

The deemphasis of the traditional role of the labor unions, which was designed to discourage industrial action for higher wages, was accompanied by a massive reeducation of the labor movement. The National Trades Union Congress organized a national seminar on the theme "Labor Goes Modern." It openly recanted its former militant role and explained new, constructive ways to improve the welfare of the workers following the Swedish and Israeli models of trade unions (Pang 1981: 481–97). A number of profit-oriented cooperative ventures that benefited union members in the form of either lower prices or shareholding were launched.

The result was the growth of a powerful and prosperous organization in partnership with the government and the formation of a tripartite decision-making system consisting of employers, the government, and labor that was responsible for determining the wage policy in the country. Tripartism was officially introduced in 1972 with the establishment of the National Wages Council, an advisory body to the government. Its objectives were to recommend annual wage increases, to ensure orderly wage development so as to promote economic and social development, and to assist in the development of incentive schemes to improve productivity.

Between 1966 and 1970, the Singapore economy exploded, the GDP shooting up at an average annual rate of 13 percent and the double-digit growth continuing until the oil recession. Industrial stoppages declined from 116 to 5 between 1961 and 1970, and trade disputes from 1,225 to 486 (Republic of Singapore Department of Statistics 1983: table 3.10). In a study of the Singapore economy in 1987, Lawrence Krause made the point that between 1965 and 1973, it not only performed well but took off from a starting per capita income of U.S. $524, which was high by the standards of developing countries, so that subsequent high growth rates were not statistical artifacts derived from a low base. The average Singapore wage rate in manufacturing in 1965, though low by the standards of industrial countries, was much higher than other developing countries. During this same period, unemployment fell to 6 percent, which was lower than the 10–15 percent figure estimated for 1959–65, and an improvement over the 1966 unemployment level of 8.9 percent (Lim et al. 1988: 11).

In promoting the goal of economic modernization for the city-state, Lee made a critical change in 1970 in the language policy. At independence, he announced an accommodationist strategy of integration, that is, the adoption of multilingualism, multiracialism, and multiple religions. As far as language policy was concerned, the four official languages—Malay, Mandarin, Tamil, and English—were to be accorded equal status. In 1970, in the Dillingham Lecture at the East West Center in Honolulu, Lee advocated a change to societal multilingualism but individual asymmetrical bilingualism (Chan 1984). Thereafter, English was given special emphasis as the common language of communication, the language of international trade, technology, and economics. Every Singaporean was asked to develop linguistic abilities in English and his or her mother tongue. The way had been cleared in 1966 when the Wang Gungwu Report on the Chinese-medium Nanyang University recommended the raising of academic standards and a greater emphasis on English as a medium of instruction. This direction had also been advocated by the Thong Saw Pak Report on the Ngee Ann Polytechnic, another Chinese-medium institution. The protests and agitation by left-wing student militants, joined by the Barisan Sosialis, against the two reports were swiftly suppressed by police action, paving the way for change.

Two consequences flowed from the language switch: first, the rapid emergence of Singapore as a global city and a financial and business center, and second, the reshaping of the values and norms of the politically strategic elites as a consequence of education. In 1980, Nanyang University was merged with the English-medium University of Singapore to form the National University of Singapore, thereby eliminating a base of opposition to the government of Chinese-educated intelligentsia who were disadvantaged in the economic market, where the English language was and would continue to be the effective currency. The initial indignation and resistance to the emphasis on English was evident in the *Nanyang siang pau*'s strident campaign to portray the PAP government as killing the Chinese language, but objections were silenced by the detention of the newspaper's senior executives and editors. Simultaneous actions against two

English-language dailies, the *Singapore Herald* and the *Easter Sun*, for alleged links with foreign interests and the subversion of natural values were acts of delicate political balance to maintain parity between the two major language constituencies. The lesson was effectively delivered, as subsequently no cultural elite or language lobby attempted to make its stand in the same way again.

The official adoption of English as the common working language led to far more profound repercussions than Lee had perhaps bargained for. In fact, the promotion of the English language remolded the culture of the people once an English education became widespread. In the 1980s, for example, it was gradually understood that the language switch to English weaned the well-educated Chinese population from traditional Chinese religion and predisposed them for conversion to Christianity on a rather significant scale, with possible implications for political culture (Hinton 1985: 40–42).

Convinced that the survival of Singapore and the creation of a modern industrialized state is dependent upon a special constellation of behavior, the PAP leadership underscored the need to induce the right behavior in its population primarily through the media and the schools. Social engineering in the late 1960s and early 1970s referred to limiting family sizes, creating a sense of national identity, and promoting socially endorsed values and norms of behavior, but by the 1980s, population policies were perceived by the electorate to smack of elitism and genetic engineering.

To sum up, in the period 1966–70, the pressures of ensuring economic growth and political harmony brought about by the sudden independence from Malaysia reinforced the centralizing tendencies of the earlier consolidation years. Faced with external insecurity, the PAP leadership put a high premium on tighter internal organization and social cohesion. The concentration of power matched by high growth performance vindicated the thesis of developmental authoritarianism, which advocates strong, activist government and a strong center for economic development. A philosophy of survival based on a loose structure of ideas about the management of small states thus congealed.

## The Politics of Rapid Economic Growth: 1971–84

The next fourteen years represented a relatively long period of sustained growth interrupted by a short recession in 1974 and 1975, a consequence of sharp increases in the world's oil prices. On the face of it, the PAP had forged a consensus on the nation-building goals of economic development, territorial defense, social redistribution, political participation, and identity creation. The recessionary years amplified the dissatisfaction and divergent views; nonetheless, these differences were diffusible, disorganized, and suppressible, enabling the PAP to occupy the middle ground of the political spectrum and to build in these years what Lee called "a politics of coalition."

The alliance between the politicians and the bureaucrats that effectively defeated the Communists now spearheaded the economic revolution. Institutionally, a number of new statutory boards were created to handle new functions. In addition to those previously established, the Monetary Authority of Singapore (MAS) was set up in 1971, the Post Office Savings Bank (POSB) in 1972, the Sentosa Development Corporation (SDC) in 1972 for resort development, the Industrial Training Board (ITB) in 1973, the Telecommunication Authority of Singapore (TAS) and the Urban Renewal Authority (URA) in 1974, and the Singapore Broadcasting Corporation (SBC) in 1980, to name but a few. Apart from providing an environment favorable to investment in employment-creating and output-raising industries, the government involved itself in the direct ownership and control of many industrial, financial, and commercial enterprises that were wholly or partly state owned. Moving away from their traditional role of executing policy, bureaucrats turned into entrepreneurs directing economic activity. This was necessary in certain risk-taking ventures, as the private sector was weak. The traditional development of Singapore as a trading port meant that the class of indigenous industrialists and entrepreneurs with the requisite experience to head the drive for industrialization was absent.

This configuration of political and economic institutions and the decision-making structure earned Singapore the description of an "administrative state." The emergence of the "administrative state" transformed the political system in three ways. First, it enforced a changed political style, one that emphasizes orderly allocation and management as a way of handling political demands and the depoliticization of the general political realm. Second, bureaucratic dominance in the political system was expanded and entrenched not only in administrative structures but in economic sectors, too. A group of trusted senior bureaucrats appointed to an interlocking network of directorates of government companies, for the first time wielding both economic power and political power, played a major role in Singapore's development. Their enhanced participation once legitimized by their success and effectiveness made the shrinking of the public sector in subsequent years more problematic, a serious issue in the political transition. Third, the decision-making structure monopolized initiative at the top, within the cabinet, and within the very upper echelons of the bureaucracy. The formulation of policy in the decade of the 1970s did not seem to involve the input even of the back bench of parliament.

In the electoral arena, the ruling party gained invincibility. After 1968, the general elections of 1972, 1976, and 1980 repeated the clean sweep of all the seats in the legislature, clinching between 69 and 76 percent of the total votes cast each time and institutionalizing a hegemonic party system. Opposition parties made their regular debuts, seeking to mobilize the growing pockets of discontent of those untouched or adversely affected by the development process. The number of opposition parties registered in Singapore ranged from sixteen to twenty, but those participating in the elections were half that number. In 1972, J. B. Jeyaratnam, a lawyer, entered electoral politics through the Workers' party, but it was only in 1981 that he was returned to parliament in the by-election at Anson. His reelection in the 1984 general election demonstrated that the Singapore electorate was pushing for some checks and balances in the system. Similarly, Chiam See Tong, another lawyer, launched his crusade to enter parliament in 1976 as an independent candidate and gained his seat after several attempts in the general elections and by-elections in 1984 when he formed the Singapore Democratic party.

This is not to say that no intellectually rigorous opposition existed in the society. The relentless drive for economic growth together with an apparent lack of interest on the part of the political leadership for workers' rights and welfare ushered in a general sense of disillusionment and discontent among the population. In the 1970s, the escalating costs of living were not assuaged by the tight wage policies, regarded as necessary for economic competitiveness. Singapore leaders saw the republic as a "global city" tied into the international economic system and a base for the foreign multinational companies (Rajaratnam 1987: 223–30). During the economic trough of the worldwide oil recession in 1974, when twenty thousand workers, or 2 percent of the total work force, were retrenched and the government's response was to call for belt-tightening, self-reliance, and social discipline, radical student politics made its appearance on the University of Singapore campus.

Student activism in the English-language institutions of higher education was without a strong tradition, unlike campus politics at Nanyang University, the Chinese-language university, which had a history of alienation from political authority. However, neo-Marxist thinking and the antiwar and counterculture movement ascendant in North America now found adherents among the students at the University of Singapore. There were also the contagious influence and networking of student groups, which started from the Thai student revolution of October 1973. When the radical student union leadership identified with the workers' strike action and the campaign for squatters' rights across the causeway in Johore Bahru, the PAP government cracked down on student political activity. To prevent the politicization of the student body in the future, parliament passed the University of Singapore Amendment Bill in July 1976. The act divided the University of Singapore Students' Union into eight faculty clubs and three non-faculty bodies, including a Political Association in which only students who were Singapore citizens were permitted to participate. It also ruled that no constituent student body other than the Political Association was allowed to engage in politics or make pronouncements of a political nature (Republic of Singapore Parliament 1976). Left-wing opposition to the political system did not abate but was externally directed to embarrass the PAP internationally through securing its expulsion from the Socialist International. This move was orchestrated by some domestic left-wing critics, a radical wing of the Dutch Labor party, and a faction of the British Labour party. The PAP withdrew from the organization before the resolution was voted upon by the International.

Ideologically, the PAP had traveled some distance from its original doctrinal orientation (Tan 1983). Even in its early partnership with the Communists, PAP socialism was of a pragmatic variety rejecting nationalization pledges of the orthodox socialists. Rapid economic growth within a free-enterprise framework placed precepts of profit making, accumulation of savings, meritocracy, and efficiency ahead of social equality, redistribution, and welfare action. Definitely, by the late 1970s, the intellectual credo of the regime explicitly rested upon a philosophy of self-reliance and self-help, a throwback to the rugged individualism of the American brand of capitalism. Nonetheless, it still regarded itself to be a socialist party and in its own defense pointed to its record of social policies, activist intervention in the economy, and the regulation of the private sector as touchstones of a socialist order.

At the end of the 1970s, changes in the world situation made their impact upon Singapore. Global recession, protectionism in the industrialized countries, and increasing competition from other newly industrializing countries convinced Lee that Singapore's growth momentum could only be sustained by scaling the technological ladder. This entailed restructuring the economy away from labor-intensive manufacturing and services toward industries with high value-added content and incorporating more capital, higher skill, and technology. This restructuring exercise, known as the second industrial revolution, was formally launched in 1979 with upward wage adjustments, the promotion of mechanization, automation, computerization, and an accelerated program of manpower training and skills development.

Vast economic changes dramatically remodeled the social base by expanding the middle sector. The creation of a large middle class is the triumph of PAP's rule. In 1960, some 350,000 students were enrolled in schools, mostly in primary education (figures rounded from Republic of Singapore Department of Statistics 1983: table 9.1). Only 60,000 students had a place in secondary schools. The university and college population was 8,000 students. By 1980, there were about half a million students in primary and secondary schools, and the tertiary institutions had an enrollment of 22,000. Technical and vocational education, which was nonexistent in 1960, now had strong support. In 1986, of the 550,000 students in schools, over 270,000 were enrolled in primary schools; as many as 201,000 were in secondary schools. Tertiary education was pursued by 42,000 students, and another 20,000 were in vocational institutions (Republic of Singapore Information Division 1987). The professional, managerial, and executive class doubled between 1960 and 1980, and an upgrading generally of occupations had taken place (table 9.1). Even the same category of description of workers does not adequately describe the level of sophistication at which the same service or job was conducted.

More families moved from lower-income status to middle-income security with increased household incomes (table 9.2). In 1987, in a National Day Rally speech, Lee asserted that by the homeownership criterion, in fact 80 percent of Singaporeans could be considered to be middle class.

Table 9.1

**Employed Persons Aged 15 Years and Over by Occupational Group, 1960–86 (thousands of persons)**

| Occupational group | 1960 | 1980 | 1986 |
|---|---|---|---|
| Professional, technical, administrative, managerial, and executive workers | 7.0 | 13.6 | 16.9 |
| Clerical and related workers | 11.4 | 15.6 | 15.7 |
| Sales workers | 18.3 | 12.3 | 13.5 |
| Service workers | 15.0 | 10.4 | 11.9 |
| Agricultural workers and fishermen | 7.9 | 1.9 | 1.1 |
| Production transport and other manual workers | 38.0 | 40.4 | 35.8 |
| Workers not classified by occupation | 1.9 | 5.8 | 5.0 |
| Total | 471.9 | 1,077.1 | 1,149.0 |

*Sources:* Republic of Singapore Department of Statistics 1983: 38; Republic of Singapore Information Division 1987: 287.

Growing affluence, better education, and job security did not solder the political allegiance of the electorate to the ruling party. The erosion of political support for the government occurred on several fronts. For one, the Malay community did not progress at the same pace as the other ethnic communities in the growth process. The 1980 population census provided irrefutable evidence of uneven development. Although far more Singapore Malays were better educated, were better housed, and held jobs at a professional level than twenty years before, their achievements did not keep pace with the Chinese and Indians, even though the Indian community was almost half the size of the Malay. Within the civil service, Malay recruits were concentrated primarily in Divisions III and IV. Only 203 Malays made it to Division I and Superscale grades or, the administrative class of the bureaucracy, compared with 7,089 Chinese and 736 Indians (table 9.3).

Furthermore, in 1980, 88 percent of the Malay work force earned incomes of less than U.S. $6,000 annually, whereas the national figure for the percentage of the work force earning less than that sum was 62.4 percent (Mattar 1984: 121). The inability of the Malays to maintain the pace of competition in an environment of strict meritocracy strengthened their minority complex and caused them to turn inward as a defense mechanism and to opt for a strategy of self-strengthening.

The government also began to lose support from private domestic entrepreneurs, small- and medium- business people, and some independent professionals, who were deeply resentful that over the years, in the push to establish an advanced

Table 9.2

**Household Income in Singapore, 1977–78 and 1982–83**

| Amount (U.S. $ per year) | 1977–78 (%) | 1982–83 (%) |
|---|---|---|
| Below $2,999 | 21.5 | 4.8 |
| $3,000–$5,999 | 40.4 | 26.3 |
| $6,000–$8,399 | 19.0 | 21.6 |
| $8,400–$11,999 | 9.0 | 14.8 |
| $12,000–$17,999 | 6.3 | 15.7 |
| $18,000–$23,999 | 2.2 | 7.0 |
| $24,000–$29,999 | 0.8 | 3.8 |
| Above $30,000 | 0.8 | 6.0 |
| Average annual household income | 6,396 | 12,174 |

*Source:* Singapore government survey of household expenses. Sample: 6,000 families. The *Sunday Times*, June 30, 1985.

global city, the PAP government had unrestrainedly expanded public-sector control over the economy on the one hand and freely opened the economy to foreign participation on the other. By the mid-1980s, squeezed between government and foreign competition, a whole class of indigenous entrepreneurs and professionals were patently alienated from the government.

A third center of growing disaffection can be found among the increasing numbers of well-educated, articulate, and materially secure professionals, civil servants, academics, and schoolteachers. The push for modernization and industrialization placed a concomitant emphasis on tertiary education and overseas education. The government took the lead in supporting large numbers of students on scholarships in prestigious universities in the West. This privileged, strategic elite returned to Singapore seeking, among other things, the practice of the promise of democratic government after the Anglo-American model.

The election of the opposition Workers' party candidate, J. B. Jeyaratnam, to the Anson seat in the 1982 by-election was an historic moment, creating the opening wedge to roll back the protracted total dominance of the PAP in parliament. The attitudes of the new and younger electorate in the 1984 general election (40 percent of the voters were below the age of forty) were unpredictable. In fact, the electorate was increasingly vocal about the need for an opposition in parliament. In 1984, in two interviews conducted by the *Straits Times* and the *Singapore Monitor*, a majority of respondents expressed the desire to see opposition representation in the legislature (*Straits Times*, December 4, 1984; Singapore Monitor, December 23, 1984). In the end, after a year of exceptionally controversial policies, the PAP found a heavy vote swing of 12.6 percent against it, and two opposition members were elected in the general election.

Table 9.3

## Government Employees by Ethnic Groups and Salary Grades in Singapore, December 1982

| Ethnic group | % of total population | % of total government employees | % in salary grades* | | | | | |
| --- | --- | --- | --- | --- | --- | --- | --- | --- |
| | | | Superscale | Division I | Division II | Division III | Division IV |
| Chinese | 76.90 | 67.52 | 77.98 | 84.04 | 80.07 | 67.77 | 37.73 |
| Malay | 14.60 | 18.47 | 1.83 | 2.43 | 9.46 | 20.61 | 38.81 |
| Indian | 6.40 | 10.74 | 11.93 | 8.49 | 8.02 | 9.40 | 18.33 |
| Other | 2.10 | 3.27 | 8.26 | 5.02 | 2.45 | 2.20 | 5.13 |
| Total | 100.00 | 100.00 | 100.00 | 99.98 | 100.00 | 99.99 | 100.00 |

*Source*: Percentages derived from data in Mattar 1984: 120.

*Salary grades in 1982 (in U.S. $ per annum according to the Budget for the Fiscal Year 1983–84):
  Superscale: U.S. $2,500–10,850
    Division I: U.S. $400–2,800
    Division II: U.S. $300–1,200
    Division III: U.S. $200–685
    Division IV: U.S. $190–445

## The Politics of Political Transition: 1985–

The coincidence of three transitions—political, social, and economic—left a major mark upon the fast-changing politics of the mid-1980s. At the level of leadership, a political transition was effected in the clear ascendance of the second-generation PAP leaders to cabinet positions of first and second deputy prime minister. The "self-renewal" exercise that began in the late 1970s culminated in 1984, when one-third of the PAP slate of election candidates comprised new recruits. Subsequently, a number were appointed to office, among them the prime minister's son, Brigadier-General Lee Hsien Loong. So extensive was the political renewal with the 1984 general elections that thirty-seven of the seventy-seven PAP members of parliament were newcomers who had entered politics only since 1980. The relentless drive to renew political ranks was propelled by the recognition that an aging leadership (several cabinet ministers until 1980 were first-generation politicians who had been in office since 1959) would be out of sync with the social transition taking place in Singapore, epitomized in the phenomenon of a rejuvenating electorate. The statistics indicated that by 1988, 68.5 percent of the electorate would be less than forty-three years old.

The poor performance of the ruling party in the election forced a reassessment of its political style. The upsurge of antigovernment sentiment in the electorate signaled to the political leadership that authoritarian methods would not be so readily accepted as in the past even if the end results were laudable. In any case, lacking the authority of the first generation, the second-generation leaders embarked upon a consensus-seeking and consultative style to cope with the pressures for participation. In Singapore terms, this represented the first stage of the opening up of a tight system. There was a second good reason for a thoroughgoing review of the existing mode of governmental operation. In 1985, Singapore slid into a severe economic recession, one not experienced since 1964, when the Indonesian confrontation, disrupted the economy. The urgency of the economic crisis called for innovative action, and a restive and increasingly critical population confirmed that an economic recession could provoke negative political attitudes and behavior if prolonged.

Dialogue sessions between the second-generation leaders and key social and economic groups, such as trade unions, grass-roots leaders, businessmen, students, and professional bodies, were organized with vigor. A special Feedback Unit with direct access to First Deputy Prime Minister Goh Chok Tong provided an institutionalized channel for citizen complaints on administrative action and for citizen reactions to government policy to be heard. An Economic Committee composed of industrial, financial, business, and professional leaders under the chairmanship of Brigadier-General Lee prepared a document analyzing Singapore's economic problems and the economic transition, and offering a strategy for recovery. Its work was subsequently applauded for the thoroughness and thoughtfulness of the proposals, and the rapid turnaround of the recession went a long way toward legitimizing the new leadership. Certainly, there was no shortage of opportunities or avenues for participation even for the average constituent. The new PAP leaders took the National Agenda for Action, the party's manifesto for the 1988 election, to the people in open constituency discussions in 1986 and 1987. Taken together, all these efforts could be read as a reformist liberalization of the political process.

There are, however, two important caveats to the opening up. First, the PAP government has not surrendered the initiative for organization and mobilization, and participation was accommodated within state-sponsored channels. Second, in the exchanges, the dialogues appeared to be occasions used by the government more frequently to explain its policies to the people than to listen to and understand the aspirations of the people. The approach is best illustrated in Brigadier-General Lee's statement at the opening of a National Agenda seminar in 1987 that there was such a thing as "fundamentally correct policies" that the government should campaign for. "If the first time we try to persuade people, we fail, the correct answer is not to say no good, start again. The correct answer is to go back, try, try and try again. And if after 10 tries, we still fail, then [we] go back and look at a new approach, but not before that" (*Straits Times*, April 13, 1987). In spite of these compromises, participation is still reasonably high, carrying with it the strong expectations as well as the possibility of a backlash should liberalization be curtailed.

While the PAP leaders are experimenting with liberalization, that is, with the creation of "space" and the tolerance of dissent, if not on a collective basis, at least on an individual level, they do not have democratization in mind in the meaning of accepting competing bases of power. Paralleling the measures of liberalization in the decision-making structure were several indications that Singapore would continue to be run as a tight ship. The geopolitical constraints upon Singapore are, after all, constant, and Singapore's new leaders seem unprepared to jettison a formula that has worked so well in the past. Instead, they have reiterated and acknowledged the fundamental realities of the conditions of a small city-state nation. A small state comes with inherent vulnerabilities that demand the presence of a centralized system and a cohesive population to survive in a competitive world. Consequently, moves aimed at restricting the political arena were introduced even as liberalization in the consultative process was enhanced.

The first of these was the Newspapers and Printing Presses (Amendment) Act, which restricted the circulation of foreign publications deemed to be interfering in the internal politics of Singapore. As the state of press freedom in any country is invariably viewed as a barometer of the political climate, the measure to circumscribe foreign publications willy-nilly affected the perception of domestic political space. The injunction that interest groups and professional bodies should confine their activities and public comments to strictly professional matters and keep off politics was a significant step in laying down the line of political participation. In 1987, this extended to a warning to all religious organizations not to mix religion and politics (*Straits Times*, August 17, 1987). Twenty-two young men and women including four Roman Catholic church workers were detained under the Internal Security Act for involvement in a Marxist conspiracy using the church and social action as a front and means for advancing Marxist political objectives. The threshold of tolerance for the legal opposition, the two elected members of parliament, is equally low. In 1987, J. B. Jeyaratnam, the Workers' party leader, as a result of a series of reckless attacks on the independence of the Singapore judiciary, faced disciplinary action for his abuse of parliamentary privilege. He was eventually disqualified from his parliamentary seat for the criminal offense of making a false declaration of his party's accounts.

It is an interesting statement about the nature of Singapore politics that the middle-class desire to see an opposition in parliament is not matched by organized expression or concerted effort to realize this presence. A general reluctance on the part of the intelligentsia and the average citizenry to enter into the hurly-burly of politics when authorities are patently intolerant of opposition leaves dissenting views underrepresented or unrepresented, opposition diffused, and alienation strengthened. Had the Singapore system deteriorated into a different sort of government—corrupt, ineffective, and clearly delegitimized—the intellegentsia may have acted differently.

In 1988, several turns of events starting with statements by some of the recently released Marxist detainees that they had been tortured, their subsequent rearrests, the further arrests of two lawyers who acted for the detainees and seemingly with them, and the official outcry against external interference to change Singapore's political path left no doubt that economic development and growth need not lead to the same political outcome as that institutionalized in Europe or that which is being structured in East Asia. The revelation that an American diplomat in Singapore had transgressed what to Singapore and by normal diplomatic standards would be considered acceptable diplomatic behavior, by encouraging regime opponents to participate in politics against the government, led to an unexpected confrontation between close strategic friends. In their offensive against external attempts, in this case by the United States, to democratize the Singapore political system, forcing it to keep pace with the democratizing trends in certain other countries in the Asia-Pacific region, Prime Minister Lee and the second-generation leaders are fighting to assert the validity of different models of democracy and of Singapore as one of them. They insist that political systems should be evaluated and accepted for their appropriateness and authenticity arising from the special political, historical, and cultural contexts. Presumably, as there is appropriate technology in development strategies, so is there appropriate democracy. In a philosophical and passionate exposition of the Singapore way of life in a benchmark speech in parliament on June 2, 1988, Prime Minister Lee emphatically stated, "We are different [from South

Korea and Taiwan]. No one race, no one language, no one culture, which these countries have. But of course they have other problems" (*Straits Times*, June 3, 1988). His indignation at the imposition of external judgment was expressed vividly in his question, "And who is to tell Singapore that if they vote for the PAP, that's not democracy? Would we have got here if we had been swapping horses for four years?"

The contours of the Singapore political mode prescribed by the PAP, democracy "Singapore style," had been explicitly outlined and defended several weeks earlier in a public discourse on democratization following the charges of external interference in domestic politics and anger at perceived attempts "to make us more like a Western society." Singapore democracy is above all, said First Deputy Prime Minister Goh Chok Tong to the grass-roots leaders, "based on consensus-building, not dissent. It is a politics of cooperation not confrontation and the supremacy of collective freedom not individual interest" (*Straits Times*, May 15, 1988). Moreover, it is a system that places greater faith in moral men as leaders than in institutional checks and balances to regulate power and the political system. As Goh argued, "I get the impression that Americans generally believe that no one should be entrusted with wide powers because sooner or later he is bound to abuse them," whereas, "on this constitutional framework [the British system of cabinet government] Singaporeans have superimposed a Confucian gentleman, a *junzi*, someone who is upright, morally beyond reproach, someone people can trust" (*Straits Times*, June 1, 1986). Clearly, this model draws its inspiration from the dominant Confucian culture of the Chinese population.

The assumption that these political values will always strike a responsive chord in Singapore rests on the belief that the dominant culture will not undergo transformation. This may be a questionable premise in the long run. Admittedly, one of the aspects of cultural change in Singapore is the persistence and resilient strength of the Chinese language and culture in spite of extensive use of English in the schools and workplace. The language of the family and home is still primarily the mother tongue. This is borne out by the fact that the top ten television programs of the Singapore Broadcasting Corporation are in Mandarin, and Mandarin serial dramas have an avid following in Singapore. Statistics indicate, too, that television news and the highly political "Today in Parliament" have a larger viewership in the Chinese telecast than in English. On one level, this may suggest that Chinese cultural values may be transmitted, absorbed, and reinforced. But on another level, it is unlikely that the Westernization of the Singapore population and the increasing Christianization of the educated Chinese will not go hand in hand with a greater emphasis on individual worth and individual rights. In the upper-middle-class families, English is the first tongue. It is inconceivable that this change will not ultimately erode the culture and rituals over time. How then, is the Singapore leadership to accommodate the dissenting interests that will arise?

## An Authentic Political Model?

The central questions animating this chapter are whether the process of economic development and the forces of modernization, such as education, urbanization, industrialization, and high-technology communications, carry with them the imperatives of homogenization or universalizing political trends that shape political systems in the same way so that, in the end, all societies and states will possess congruent models fashioned after the Anglo-American political model, or do culture, historical experience, and specific political context leave a more significant and permanent imprint of their own, producing variants on the models that the forces of economic development and modernization alone might not lead one to expect?

The path of political development in Singapore, and ultimately the model that will take root, will have to take into account the multiplication of plural interests and the increasing aspirations for participation, both by-products of the modernization process and economic development; but the solution seized upon by the PAP government, for the near future, is a mixture of strategies: to liberalize without democratization, that is, to open up new channels of participation while at the same time applying coercive political measures on a selective basis against the opposition, which in the end forestalls any growth of a power base for significant political challenges. Over the four years after the 1984 general election in the wake of the new political mood in the country and the pressures for political change, the PAP leadership has clarified for itself and the electorate the political limits of what it will not tolerate and the possibilities of what it is prepared to offer.

The political model advocated is one that presumes the necessity of a hegemonic party system and a limited but tame opposition as a requisite for stable government in an island city-state situation. It restrictively defines what constitutes legitimate political issues and the legitimate political arena. It may be asked, will political participation on these terms be acceptable in the long run to Singapore society, or will this represent a transitory and stunted model that will be thrust aside by the increasing momentum and demands by a population, which, more than any other rapidly changing society in the Asia-Pacific region, possesses linguistic access to a world culture? That world culture places a premium on openness and the extension of liberal democracy. Can the Singapore political model be maintained *sui generis*, albeit with constant revision and modification, yet authentic to its needs and situations? And will it in the end be so totally different from the Western model that it replicates the former in form but not in substance? Will such a model work and last so that it comes to be evaluated objectively in a positive way rather than as a failed version of the Anglo-American variety?

The reasons why the Singapore population may be receptive to this model for some time to come are many. Its size lends itself to effective control. It is, after all, diminutive enough to coopt most political aspirants and the activist intelligentsia, leaving aside only a handful of dissidents who may prefer to be in opposition. Singaporeans to a greater or lesser extent accept the vulnerability proposition and the case for compromise arising from the fundamental realities of being a predominantly Chinese state in a Malay region with a plural mix in its population. Furthermore, the disorderly and tense politics in neighboring states are often viewed as negative examples. The belief that prosperity and economic development are obtained at a price is still widely held. But the most persuasive reason for the adherence to the model is the strong legitimacy that the PAP still retains. Not only has it demonstrated its ability to create prosperity and stability against heavy odds in an island-state, recently reconfirming this in the speedy correction of economic recession, but also it has kept itself relatively scandal free. Where scandals are exposed, the initiative is from the government itself, and unlike South Korea, there is no Kwangju equivalent in the nation's recent history to act as a rallying point for populist change.

Against this, the republic is not devoid of emerging forces that seek to transform the political model. A new and younger generation of voters is less inclined to accept the political leadership at face value. The strategic strata of the middle class—comprising professionals, corporate executives, businessmen, journalists, bureaucrats, students, and academics—are definitely expanding, and while they come with diverse aspirations, all are searching for a more open and democratic political system. A tighter economic situation easily politicizes the voter and encourages a more critical and oppositionist stance, as was apparent in the 1985 recession. Finally, Singapore is an unusually open economy and society because of its international trading and business links, and its communication links are among the most modern in the region. It is difficult to see how it can shut out democratic developments elsewhere from having a contagious influence upon segments of the population. Conflicting pulls will be exerted upon the model. There is no doubt that flexibility and responsiveness are the requirements of the political transition if the course is to be a smooth and stable one.

# Part IV
# An Industrial Economy

# 10

---

# Japan:
# There May Be a Choice

## Ikuo Kabashima

JAPAN'S postwar rapid economic growth is often referred to as an "Economic Miracle." Nowadays the level of economic development is so high that few remember Japan was in fact classified as a developing country in the 1950s and 1960s. Not only has Japan's economic growth been rapid, but its developmental path has been at variance with the dominant theories of political development.

Samuel Huntington (1987) suggests five goals of political development: economic growth, economic equality, democracy in terms of broad-based political participation, political order, and national autonomy. The problems for developing countries, he says, is that these five goals are not readily compatible, that a cruel choice must be made among them.

Japan's political history over the postwar period demonstrates, however, that the cruel choices can be avoided, and that there is an alternative model of political and economic development, the success of which has hinged on certain conditions that characterized Japanese society during this period.

### Huntington's Cruel Choices and the Case of Japan

The first cruel choice poses the incompatibility of growth with the equitable distribution of income. Simon Kuznets (1963) suggested this conflict in his U-shaped hypothesis. Countries in a very early stage of economic development, according to Kuznets, would have less income inequality. In a middle, growing stage, the intersectoral inequality between the urban (modern) sector and the rural (traditional) sector deepens; consequently, overall income inequality widens. As countries grow further, however, overall income inequality narrows as income inequality within the urban sector narrows and that between the urban

---

I am grateful to Jeffrey Broadbent for his comments and encouragement. His comments were so extensive that he is almost responsible for the content of this chapter.

and agricultural sectors is reduced. The case of Brazil has been frequently cited as an example of the incompatibility of rapid economic growth and income equality. After a decade of growth in that country, Fishlow (1972: 391) pointed out that "the upper 3.2 percent of the labor force commands 33.1 percent of income in 1970, compared to about 27 percent in 1960."

The second cruel choice alleges the incompatibility of economic growth and the equitable distribution of political power. While economic growth has not necessarily produced equitable distribution of income in developing countries, neither has it necessarily produced political democracy or stability there. Rather, by the mid-1960s, charismatic leaders and militarists had seized power in many of these countries. Huntington focused on the obvious breakdown of governments in many newly independent countries during the 1960s. Socioeconomic modernization increases the demands, hopes, and political participation of citizens, he contends, but it does not ensure that their demands can be met. Thus, a crucial gap appears between demands and possibilities. In Huntington's gap hypothesis, developing countries face an incompatibility between rapid economic development and democracy in terms of both political stability and participation by the poor.

Under these circumstances, political development for Huntington differs from modernization, mobilization, or participation. Political development, he argues, is an increase in the ability of governments to deal with the onslaught of problems that change brings. He sees political danger in the process, especially when elites lack much practice in the "art of assorting together" and lack institutions that can channel the chaos modernization brings. So modernization in the form of high economic development, urbanization, literacy, and so forth bears no necessary relation to political development. In fact, the political system may decay because of socioeconomic progress: political turmoil may grow along with GNP, literacy, education, communication, and participation.

Democratic government and economic development are also thought to be incompatible by Jack Donnelly (1984). He states that a development-oriented authoritarian government rather than a democratic-leaning one is required if higher rates of economic growth are to be achieved. To promote long-term economic development an authoritarian government can concentrate its efforts and centralize scarce resources in capital investment, and not worry in the short term about distributive demands.

Huntington's (1968) proposed inverse relationship between political stability and the social mobilization caused by economic development sums up these viewpoints. This hypothesis states that economic development is followed by urbanization, higher education attainment, spread of mass media, and participation. When the increasing expectations and new demands coming from this social mobilization are not met, social discontent and resistance to the state will result. Where opportunities to "exit" are absent, the participatory "voice" of discontent increases (Hirschman 1970). When there are no responsive political institutions to meet this rising demand for participation, political instability will result. In this view, political "decay," meaning the move to authoritarian government, is one of the normal, not aberrant, paths of political development. New states can have rapid economic growth, or they can have democratic and egalitarian development, Huntington argues, but they usually cannot have both. There is "no easy choice" between these values (Huntington 1968; Huntington and Nelson 1976).

Given this scholarly view, the example of Japan is all the more surprising. In the post–World War II period, Japan managed to achieve high economic growth and at the same time both a narrowing of income inequality and a growing political stability—all under democratic institutions. Over the postwar period, Japan has maintained a democratic electoral system with secret ballot, free-choice voting, and a wide and unrestricted variety of competing political parties. And although money politics remains a problem, Japan has some of the strictest election campaign laws in the world, intended to reduce the differences in financing between the candidates.

This is not to say that Japan has been an ideal democracy. A single party, the Liberal Democratic party (LDP), has managed to maintain power for the entire postwar period through a wide variety of means, both fair and questionable. Nonetheless, the democratic system works. The choice of candidates is open to the voter. Many voters do indeed vote for opposition parties, and, given a declining LDP majority, the LDP must stay somewhat nervous about and responsive to public opinion, enacting publicly favored policies in order to win votes that might otherwise go to the opposition parties. It is this balance between single-party rule on the one hand and democratic accountability on the other that has defined the postwar Japanese political system.

Thus, the Japanese developmental path offers the possibility that there may be another choice: a set of policies that does not require a country to choose between economic growth, income equality, and democratic political development but instead secures all three. What were these policies, and what made this unexpected outcome possible?

To explore this theme to the fullest the analysis should begin in the mid-nineteenth century; but, confining myself to the scope of this volume, I shall concentrate on Japan's postwar years, particularly during the country's rapid-growth stage (1945–70). In the first section, I ask why and how democratization was possible and what forms the process took. Next, what were the conflicts between economic reconstruction and democratization? Finally, what measures did the government take to resolve these conflicts?

The San Francisco Treaty of 1951 brought Japan not only independence but also increased tension between tendencies toward greater state power and the postwar occupation-inspired democratic reforms. The resolution of these tensions occurred as a learning process for the ruling elites. They came to realize that social order could be better maintained by increasing social prosperity through economic growth policies, rather than by increasing police power and national military security. But subsequent growth policies required the concentration of resources. How were they compatible with the other policies supporting the equitable distribution of income? If economic growth policies required centralization of decision making in order to carry out consistent and stable policies, how could broad-based political participation expand in postwar Japan? These are questions central to explaining how the cruel choices were averted in postwar Japan.

To answer these questions, I shall argue that Japan's unusual combination of stability, authoritative policy, and broad participation stemmed first from the occupation in the immediate postwar period and then from the LDP's dominance of the government since that time. "Supportive rural participation"—the overwhelming backing of the LDP by the farmers of Japan—gave the LDP a crucial popular base that enabled it to acquire and maintain power. In return, the farmers have benefited from various kinds of patronage, and in any case they are thoroughly imbued with a deferential political culture (Kabashima 1984). Hence, while participating actively in politics to the extent of voting, they passively accepted the authoritative decision making by the elite in matters of national policy. This broad-based, supportive rural participation admittedly does not fit the citizen-based "town meeting" ideal of democracy. But it helped preserve the democratic system in the period shortly after World War II. It softened the divisiveness and tension among social groups and moderated demands for radical change that accompanied rapid economic development.

By implication, by setting up a system of "supportive political participation" by peasant and farming strata, a developing country may open up a path of development that navigates among the "cruel choices"—unless, of course, the conditions that made this solution possible in Japan were unique to that country. What were these conditions?

## The Occupation as Authoritarian Liberalism

One condition that helped Japan was the authoritative imposition of democratizing and equalizing changes by the occupation. The purposes accomplished by this authoritative power contrast sharply with the self-enhancing use of power by most authoritarian states. General Douglas MacArthur, Supreme Commander for the Allied Powers (SCAP), arrived in Japan on August 30, 1945, with the occupation army shortly after the Japanese government accepted the Potsdam Declaration. Under his direction the General Headquarters of the Allied Forces (GHQ) enforced a number of economic and social reforms designed to facilitate political democracy, including land reform, dissolution of the zaibatsu, legalization of labor movements, extension of the right of women to participate in politics, and educational reforms.

These reforms radically changed the Japanese political system. Before the war, political parties had made some headway, and it is fair to say that a quasi-democracy was functioning in the Taisho period (1912–26). But it had definite limits: the electorate did not include women, unions had a very fragile existence, their political parties were suppressed, and the imperial bureaucracy, topped by a sacred emperor, lent powerful legitimacy to elite decisions. Tenants, under the watchful eye of a landlord class, had little politically independent voice. Workers, many within highly concentrated industrial zaibatsu structures controlled by a few families, also had little independent voice. This concentration of power intensified during World War II, as all quasi-independent organizations like unions were combined into the Imperial Rule Assistance Association to support the war effort without question.

Among the democratization programs pushed by GHQ, the most important one was land reform. The initiative for land reform was taken first by the Japanese government in anticipation of the will of GHQ, but GHQ immediately became involved. For example, the Japanese government proposed limiting the ownership of cultivated land to five hectares. The proposal was later revised by GHQ, limiting ownership to three hectares of self-cultivated land and one hectare for absentee ownership. Before the reforms in 1945, 46 percent of cultivated land was tenant land, and only 56.5 percent of all farmers were landowners. After the reforms in 1950 the former decreased to 10 percent and the number of landowning farmers increased to 87.6 percent. Through the issuance of bonds, the government bought paddy at the rate of 978 yen for 0.1 hectare and sold it back to new tenants at 756 yen. This price was equivalent to only 7 percent of the value of the yearly harvest (Kōsai 1981). In the long run the effects of high inflation made the initial government investment negligible.

The large number of prewar landowners (approximately 3.7 million) and their political clout would have made it difficult for the Japanese government alone to persuade them to give up land. It could do so only because the absolute authority of the occupying forces stood behind it. The effects of land reforms included a more equitable distribution of total agricultural income and the vanishing of tenancy disputes, which had risen to a peak of 6,824 cases in 1935 involving 113,000 people (Kōsai 1981).

GHQ saw the zaibatsu, or family-held conglomerates as possessing inordinate financial power; thus, their dissolution was a major occupation-period concern. In fact, the concentration of power in these financial combines before the war had been extensive. For example, in Mitsui Company, ten related families owned 64 percent of all Mitsui stocks. Other zaibatsu showed similar financial concentration. The government ordered the freezing of the assets of the fifteen largest zaibatsu on November 2, 1945. The Anti-Monopoly Law, enacted under the direction of GHQ in April 1947, and the Law for the Elimination of Excessive Economic Concentration, which passed the Diet in December 1947, further attacked the zaibatsu, eventually putting 325 companies up for dissolution (Uchino 1978). There was also a purging of the prewar and wartime business leaders who were thought to have cooperated with the militarists. The result was an increase in competitiveness among relatively smaller and newer firms and an opening for young and innovative managers who gave a dynamic force to the economy (Kōsai 1981).

Japanese labor unions were modeled on U.S. labor practices, which included freedom to organize unions and the right of assembly, methods for dispute settlement, guarantees of workers' rights, and compensation settlements (Uchino 1978). GHQ in fact encouraged a surge in labor activity, and union membership increased from 38,000 in 1945, or only 4.1 percent of the total labor force, to 4,849,000 in 1946, or 52.1 percent of the labor force. Under predominantly radical leadership, these unions formed the political constituency of various socialist groups opposed to the conservative parties, which later evolved into the LDP.

Ironically, one unintended effect of the occupation, bent on liberalizing the society, was to strengthen the position of the state ministries, especially those doing economic planning (Johnson 1982). To administer the many reforms it wanted to impose on Japan, the occupation needed an extensive, Japanese-speaking bureaucracy. Rather than set up its own, it decided to use the one already in place, the Japanese state. Weakening the other traditional concentrations of power in the society—the zaibatsu and the landlord class—but leaving the state intact meant placing the state in a functionally stronger position than it had been in before the war. This so strengthened the state that Johnson describes the 1940s, both wartime and postwar, as "the high tide of state control" (1982: 195).

As table 10.1 indicates, the destruction from the war was extensive. This strongly affected productive capacity in the immediate postwar years, and the output of mining and manufacturing dropped to 20 percent of prewar peak production. Textiles were in particularly short supply. Agricultural production also declined. Real GNP per capita fell to half. As the prewar production base was relatively small, these drops in production led to a decline in consumer goods, seriously affecting living standards of the population at large. In these circumstances it is not surprising that Engels's coefficient for urban residents, indicating the share of the average family's budget spent on food, increased from 32.5 percent in 1931 to 67.8 percent in 1946, and that, postwar, approximately 10 percent of immediate families were without homes. In addition, the inflation rate was extremely high, showing a fiftyfold increase in 1946 and continuing high throughout the occupation period. Postwar land reform and dissolution of the zaibatsu, combined with this extremely high inflation, contributed to the collapse of the landholding and noble classes, further leveling out economic differences in the society.

Although still lower than prewar levels, the Japanese economy achieved a 20 percent increase of real GNP from 1946 to 1949. How was it possible for Japan to grow when rates of savings and capital formation were so low? One answer seems to be that the destruction resulting from the war fell more heavily on the

Table 10.1

## Economic Indicators of the Reconstruction Period in Japan, 1946–49

| | Prewar and wartime | | 1946 | 1947 | 1948 | 1949 |
|---|---|---|---|---|---|---|
| Real GNP per capita (1970 prices 1,000 yen) | (1934–36) | 188 | 104 | 106 | 121 | 127 |
| Mining & manufacturing output (1955 = 100) | (1944) | 98.20 | 19.20 | 23.90 | 31.10 | 40.00 |
| Rice production (10,000 tons) | (1933) | 1,062 | 921† | 880 | 997 | 938 |
| Textile supply per capita (pounds) | (1937) | 12.67 | 2.11 | 2.07 | 2.33 | 1.91 |
| Dwellings per household | (1942) | 1.06 | 0.91 | 0.86 | 0.87 | 0.88 |
| Engel coefficient for urban workers (percent)* | (1931) | 32.5 | 67.8 | 63.0 | 60.4 | 60.1 |
| Electrical power generating capacity (billion kw) | (1943) | 37.7 | 30.3 | 32.8 | 37.8 | 41.5 |
| Passengers carried by National Railways (JNR) (billion people) | (1944) | 3.1 | 3.2 | 3.3 | 3.3 | 3.0 |
| Consumer price index (1934–36 = 1) | | — | 50.6 | 109.1 | 189.0 | 236.9 |

Source: Kōsai 1981: 37, 53.
*Share of average family expenditures devoted to food.

production base for consumer goods and less on those for heavy industries such as electricity and steel (table 10.1). This meant that Japan could begin to produce relatively quickly, provided labor and raw materials were available. Fortunately, the demobilized armed forces provided a labor force that was skilled both in technical matters and in social organization. With foreign trade restricted, the main economic problem was securing raw materials. In response, the state focused its industrial policy on improving the domestic supply of raw materials, especially coal and steel. Three economic policies were adopted: priority production, channeling of funds into priority industries through the Reconstruction Finance Bank, and subsidizing the difference when the cost of production exceeded the selling price.

Priority production was designed to concentrate resources such as raw materials, capital, and labor on the production of coal and steel. The Reconstruction Bank channeled 30 percent of its funds to the coal industry. Furthermore, to reduce the risks involved in coal and steel production, the government made up the difference when the production cost exceeded the selling price. The government subsidy amounted to 8.7 percent, 11.1 percent, 13.2 percent, and 24.2 percent of government expenditures in 1946, 1947, 1948, and 1949, respectively. The steel industry was the largest recipient of this subsidy (Kōsai 1981). In this way the government was able to concentrate resources to increase coal and steel production. Thus, as the previous discussion indicates, increasing GNP did not necessarily contribute to the immediate needs of people, such as the provision of food, housing, and clothing but focused rather on rebuilding the infrastructure.

As the occupation was extended, there was increasing pressure on the U.S. government to help stabilize the Japanese economy. U.S. taxpayers' mounting criticism of the occupation's cost and their concern with growing cold war tensions compelled the United States to shift the focus of its Japan policy from political reform to lowering inflation and balancing the budget. Joseph Dodge, who was experienced in the financial restructuring of occupied Germany and was then chief executive officer of the Bank of Detroit, was called upon to remedy Japan's ailing financial condition. The so-called Dodge Line placed ceilings on spending, strictly enforced tax collection, reduced subsidies and bank credits, and stabilized wages. Public employee labor unions, which had gained many liberties during the initial occupation period, were prohibited from striking, and radical movement leaders, many of whom had been freed and encouraged by GHQ in the early occupation years, were purged. Although initially unpopular, the Dodge Line policies effectively lowered inflation and rationalized industry. At the same time the fixing of the exchange rate at 360 yen to the dollar, another Dodge Line measure, proved very favorable to an increasingly export-oriented economy and lasted until 1971.

In effect, from 1945 to 1952, the occupation provided what may be termed a functional equivalent to the authoritarian state hypothesized by Huntington and others as characteristic of periods of rapid economic growth. Uncharacteristically, however, being external, transient, and relatively free of domestic constraints, this authority used its power not to consolidate its own strength but to establish a democratic political system and a pluralistic social and economic base that it hoped would support that system. It weakened the ownership basis of the concentrated power of landlords and oligopolists and dispersed political power more widely by granting freedom to unions, opposition political parties, and the press and instituting other democratic freedoms. At times, in the interest of promoting rapid economic growth, the authority restricted and weakened the newly formed unions, but it did not destroy them. Hence, on the whole, this should be termed an authoritatively imposed democracy and economic redistribution. This democratic transformation came eventually to be supported, but it cannot be denied that its initiation, timing, and character were determined uniquely by the intervention of an authoritative external force—the occupation—which was unconstrained by links to a domestic social class or set of classes and which thus could act with a minimum of domestic constraints. The question was: Could the democratic transformation be sustained under conditions of high growth once the occupation's authoritarian props were removed?

## Formation of the Dominant-Party System

The San Francisco Treaty, which came into effect on April 28, 1952, brought the occupation of Japan to an end. It is important to note that the treaty was signed in a cold war atmosphere. The negotiation process excluded the Soviet Union and China, and neither signed, causing a strong reaction by the left-wing political forces, vigorously supported by organized labor and many intellectuals. Contrary to the view of the Yoshida government, these opposition elements preferred to delay the signing of a treaty until the signature of all countries could be secured. The U.S.-Japan Mutual Security Treaty, also signed at this time, brought similar criticism. Along with concerns for the possibility of losing Japan's national autonomy, strong alignment with the United States was seen as likely to involve Japan in a war contrary to the provisions of the constitution and the wishes of the people.

A deep polarization of Japanese politics set in, partly over foreign and security policy and partly over domestic issues. Independence saw the end of GHQ and the start of autonomous Japanese politics. Leaders purged during the occupation now had an opportunity to revive their political activities. A main objective of the more conservative of these postoccupation leaders was to revise what they saw as a mandated constitution. They were concerned also to revise the U.S.-Japan Mutual Security Treaty and build up Japan's own national defense capabilities. In addition, many of the reforms of the occupation period were seen by these leaders as inhibiting the state's power, creating a vacuum that, they felt, with the occupation forces gone, needed to be filled. With the Left opposing such a restoration, Japanese politics seemed headed into an era of high instability. Some doubted whether democracy could survive.

Consolidation of the Socialist party in 1955 placed pressure on the two conservative parties—the Liberal party and the Democratic party—to merge and form the LDP almost immediately thereafter. This merging of conservative parties, which together had the support of the majority of the voting public then and for many years thereafter, ensured the conservatives of long-term control of the government and indirectly served particularly the business and farm interests, which were their major constituencies. Strong resistance continued to be voiced, however, by the opposition parties, which were able to marshal the support of the trade union movement and appeal to popular apprehension about the fragility of peace and the new democratic reforms.

In 1957 these fears were inflamed by the election of Nobusuke Kishi as LDP president, a post that brought him the prime ministership as well. Prime Minister Kishi, a prewar elite bureaucrat and wartime cabinet minister jailed by GHQ and later released, was regarded as a staunch nationalist and anti-Communist. As was often the case with leaders from the prewar period, he believed in elite control of the government rather than popular participation in governmental affairs. One of his most urgent policy objectives was the revision of the U.S.-Japan Mutual Security Treaty, which was considered to be unequal. In September 1958 he anticipated extraparliamentary moves against revision of the treaty by proposing a bill that would have given the police force wider powers. He said, "It is unfortunate that the government has no control of the police force. Before the war the government had control over the police and therefore had political maneuverability. It is troubling that at present there is a weak control of police through the Public Safety Commission" (Masumi 1985: 50). Both the content of these bills and the way the LDP pursued them increased public fear of a return to an authoritarian state. Pressure against this bill by opposition parties, the mass media, and intellectual groups finally forced the Kishi government to drop it. Treaty revision remained on the agenda, however, and in January 1959 negotiations began once more.

In October a treaty revision bill was introduced in the Diet. On May 19, faced with strong minority opposition that frustrated the Japanese preferences for consensual decision making, the Kishi cabinet used its majority to pass the revision, overcoming the opposition's physical resistance by calling in five hundred members of the police force. Outside the Diet an estimated thirty thousand demonstrators and thirty-five hundred police officers confronted each other in a standoff.

The mass media quickly attacked the LDP move as being undemocratic and mobilized public opinion against the bill. After the bill passed the Diet on May 19, the antigovernment movement intensified. Demonstrators numbered an estimated 100,000 on May 20 and 175,000 on May 27. On June 4, 6,000,000 union members participated in a national strike and 20,000 shops closed. On June 10, Presidential Secretary Hagarty arrived to discuss President Eisenhower's proposed visit to Japan, but demonstrations at the airport were so intense he needed police assistance to get to safety. Consequently, the president's visit was canceled. June 15 saw 5,600,000 demonstrating throughout Japan.

These demonstrations were the result of popular fear of a revival of militarism and authoritarianism. The memory of the war was still fresh. The media played a great role in reporting news events and mobilizing sentiment against what it perceived as an antidemocratic movement by the government. One incident illustrates the intensity of the protest demonstration: the chief of police came into the prime minister's study to warn him that the police force could no longer ensure his safety. The prime minister responded, "If this is not a safe place, no other place is safe. If I am to die as prime minister, this is the place to die" (Masumi 1985: 75).

The threat of serious violence eventually turned the press and public against the demonstrations. The crisis in the streets subsided, and in the next election the public sustained the LDP in power. The upheaval did, however, represent a turning point in the thinking of the LDP leadership, a turn away from preoccupation with strengthening the state to a primary concern for economic growth. Hayato Ikeda, who became prime minister in 1960, focused on more positive means of strengthening LDP rule: economic policies designed to "double personal income." Subsequently, Japan achieved this doubling and went beyond it.

## Economic Growth and Social Mobilization

In the years following the occupation, Japanese economic growth proceeded rapidly (table 10.2). The 1955–60 GNP increased at a surprising average of 8.7 percent per year. Of this, growth of the labor force composed 2.2 percent, and growth in labor productivity, 6.5 percent. As the key to economic growth, the rapid increase in labor productivity seen here is very significant: it was due to both capital formation and technological improvement, with the former about double the weight of the latter. The trend of high growth continued up to 1970 and was sustained at a more moderate rate thereafter. This raises several questions. Where did this capital come from? Was it mainly state-led or private capital investment?

Certainly, high capital formation is not possible without a high savings rate. As table 10.3 illustrates, the savings rate in Japan was quite high across all income groups. According to economic theory, because higher-income groups have high savings propensities, unequal distribution of income may be needed for economic growth. But in Japan, rapid redistribution of income occurred along with economic growth, as will be discussed later. This relatively equitable distribution of income in Japan, however, did not bring on a deficiency of capital; both rich and poor, farmers and workers showed high savings propensities. Capital formation was thus possible during a process of equitable growth and did not depend on one particular sector's taking a very high share of income and saving part of it.

Table 10.2

**Rates and Factors of Growth in Japan, 1955–79 (percent)**

|  | 1955–60 | 1960–65 | 1965–70 | 1970–75 | 1975–79 |
|---|---|---|---|---|---|
| Real growth rate | 8.7 | 9.7 | 12.2 | 5.1 | 5.6 |
| Factors of growth rate in terms of labor: |  |  |  |  |  |
| Increase of employment | 2.2 | 1.7 | 1.8 | 0.4 | 1.2 |
| Increase in productivity in terms of labor, capital, and technology: | 6.5 | 8.0 | 10.4 | 4.7 | 4.4 |
| Labor force | 2.4 | 0.8 | 1.3 | 0.3 | 1.5 |
| Capital | 4.0 | 5.3 | 5.4 | 3.7 | 1.9 |
| Technological improvement | 2.3 | 2.4 | 5.5 | 1.7 | 2.5 |
| Consumer price index | 1.5 | 6.1 | 5.4 | 11.5 | 5.3 |
| Unemployment rate | 2.0 | 1.3 | 1.2 | 1.4 | 2.1 |

*Source:* Kōsai 1981: 2, 5, 7.

Another important aspect of economic growth in Japan with significant political consequences was the sustained low unemployment rate. According to Huntington's gap hypothesis, lack of jobs for an increasingly mobile population increases social unrest. This in turn brings on a participation explosion and subsequent political instability. To the contrary, as will be shown, combined high economic growth and low unemployment in Japan provided a stable political environment.

High economic growth had a powerful effect on Japan's social structure, including large-scale urban migration, shifts in the occupational structure, and education expansion. In Huntington's gap hypothesis, this kind of social mobilization stimulates popular and competing demands for political participation to the point of immobilizing politics, thus calling forth an authoritarian state as the only efficient policy-making possibility. In Japan, as has been seen, political confrontation did occur in this high-growth period, but not to the extent of seriously destabilizing the system—either its democratic structure or its one-party dominance. What is there in Japan's social mobilization experience that may help to explain this?

Table 10.4 indicates the migration to the cities from 1945 to 1985. In 1945 only one-fourth of the population lived in urban areas. A rapid urban migration occurred, however, especially during the 1950s and 1960s and continuing at a slower pace in the 1970s. This migration was especially pronounced in the larger cities such as Tokyo and Osaka. For example, from 1950 to 1970 population growth in these areas averaged 1.2 million per year. Villagers previously tied to traditional social and cultural networks suddenly became weakly affiliated urbanites. Such a decline in social integration is often seen as one cause of social unrest.

Table 10.3

## Savings Rate in Japan, 1952–85 (percent)

| Year | All | Households Worker | Farm | I | Annual income quintile goups II | III | IV | V |
|------|-----|-------|------|------|------|------|------|------|
| 1952 | 10.3 | 4.4 | 8.1 | | | | | |
| 1953 | 7.8 | 5.8 | 6.0 | | | | | |
| 1954 | 9.6 | 7.4 | 3.4 | | | | | |
| 1955 | 13.4 | 9.2 | 10.0 | | | | | |
| 1956 | 13.7 | 11.8 | 3.6 | | | | | |
| 1957 | 15.6 | 12.5 | 6.2 | | | | | |
| 1958 | 15.0 | 12.6 | 7.5 | | | | | |
| 1959 | 16.7 | 13.9 | 9.2 | | | | | |
| 1960 | 17.4 | 14.9 | 12.1 | | | | | |
| 1961 | 19.2 | 16.5 | 8.6 | | | | | |
| 1962 | 18.6 | 16.2 | 13.6 | | | | | |
| 1963 | 18.0 | 15.7 | 13.6 | 9.4 | 14.9 | 16.4 | 17.2 | 18.7 |
| 1964 | 16.7 | 16.8 | 14.4 | 12.3 | 14.3 | 16.8 | 18.3 | 20.6 |
| 1965 | 17.8 | 16.8 | 15.6 | 12.1 | 15.6 | 16.9 | 17.6 | 21.4 |
| 1966 | 17.9 | 17.5 | 17.1 | 14.4 | 16.0 | 16.7 | 18.5 | 20.7 |
| 1967 | 19.4 | 17.9 | 18.9 | 13.1 | 17.4 | 17.8 | 20.1 | 22.6 |
| 1968 | 19.7 | 18.4 | 13.1 | 13.1 | 17.4 | 18.6 | 19.7 | 23.8 |
| 1969 | 19.2 | 19.1 | 15.8 | 13.5 | 17.2 | 18.9 | 19.6 | 23.9 |
| 1970 | 17.9 | 19.9 | 15.4 | 14.2 | 17.8 | 20.5 | 22.3 | 24.2 |
| 1971 | 17.8 | 19.6 | 14.7 | 13.0 | 16.6 | 19.8 | 21.5 | 23.9 |
| 1972 | 18.2 | 21.3 | 18.8 | 14.1 | 17.3 | 20.4 | 22.7 | 25.7 |
| 1973 | 20.4 | 22.2 | 22.0 | 15.2 | 18.8 | 21.9 | 24.4 | 27.0 |
| 1974 | 23.2 | 23.8 | 24.6 | 25.6 | 26.0 | 27.1 | 27.7 | 18.6 |
| 1975 | 22.8 | 22.6 | 25.8 | 28.5 | 24.8 | 25.6 | 26.1 | 16.0 |
| 1976 | 23.2 | 22.2 | 24.1 | 17.1 | 20.0 | 21.9 | 24.6 | 25.1 |
| 1977 | 21.8 | 22.0 | 22.5 | 13.6 | 18.1 | 22.1 | 24.6 | 28.0 |
| 1978 | 20.8 | 22.4 | 22.6 | 12.6 | 19.1 | 21.1 | 25.3 | 28.5 |
| 1979 | 18.2 | 22.2 | 20.6 | 14.7 | 18.6 | 22.1 | 24.8 | 26.2 |
| 1980 | 17.9 | 21.3 | 18.1 | 13.2 | 18.8 | 22.2 | 23.9 | 26.0 |
| 1981 | 18.3 | 20.6 | 18.7 | 11.4 | 17.4 | 20.6 | 22.6 | 25.6 |
| 1982 | 16.5 | 20.8 | 19.3 | 12.5 | 18.0 | 21.4 | 21.6 | 24.3 |
| 1983 | 16.3 | 20.6 | 19.4 | 11.6 | 18.6 | 20.1 | 23.5 | 24.4 |
| 1984 | 16.0 | 21.1 | 19.4 | 11.5 | 18.0 | 21.5 | 23.5 | 25.2 |
| 1985 | 16.0 | 22.2 | 18.3 | 12.8 | 18.5 | 23.6 | 23.7 | 26.9 |

*Source*: Kokumin Seikatsu Sentā 1970, 1976, and 1987.

Table 10.4

**Migration in Japan, 1945–85**

| Year | Population in cities (1,000s) | (%) | Population in rural areas (1,000s) | (%) |
|------|------|------|------|------|
| 1945* | 20,022 | 27.8 | 51,976 | 72.2 |
| 1950 | 31,366 | 37.3 | 52,749 | 62.7 |
| 1955 | 50,532 | 56.1 | 39,544 | 43.9 |
| 1960 | 59,678 | 63.3 | 34,622 | 36.7 |
| 1965 | 67,356 | 67.9 | 31,853 | 32.1 |
| 1970 | 75,429 | 72.1 | 29,237 | 27.9 |
| 1975 | 84,967 | 75.9 | 26,972 | 24.1 |
| 1980 | 89,187 | 76.2 | 27,873 | 23.8 |
| 1985 | 92,889 | 76.7 | 28,160 | 23.3 |

*Source*: Asahi Shinbunsha 1987: 63.
*Okinawa is not included.

Table 10.5 illustrates changes in occupational structure. In 1947 those employed in agriculture, forestry, and fisheries industries accounted for just over half of the total labor force. The remainder was spread almost evenly between secondary and tertiary industries. After that time, the primary agricultural labor force declined rapidly. This led to a decrease in support for the LDP. The tertiary sector, on the other hand, registered gradual increase, especially in services. Small businesses dominated wholesale and retail trade, creating a stable and increasing portion of the labor force supporting the LDP.

Despite the rapid growth in manufacturing output, the secondary-sector labor force increased only moderately: 22 percent to 33 percent over forty years. Within this sector, the high economic growth period of 1955–70 contributed to an increase of manufacturing-sector labor to a peak in 1970, but it declined thereafter. While this sector has many unionized workers, it also contains a small but steadily increasing percentage of construction industry workers. The construction companies in Japan consist of smaller enterprises whose owners are usually core backers of local support groups (*kōenkai*) of LDP politicians. They are able usually to exercise influence over these small employee groups during election time. The gradual decline of the small yet vocal mining labor force implied a loss of radical support for the opposition parties.

On balance, structural changes in the labor force lowered support for the LDP, but not to the point where it would lose control of the Diet. The LDP slowed its decline in the Diet by delaying a readjustment of Diet seats according to population shifts to the cities. Hence, although weakening the democratic representativeness of the Diet, the LDP preserved the democratic system and its own hegemony at the same time.

Higher education is also said to increase the demand for political participation. At the same time education provides "human capital" indispensable for

Table 10.5

**Employed Persons by Industry in Japan, 1947–85 (percent)**

| Year | Primary[a] | Secondary | | | | Tertiary | | | | | | |
|------|---------|---------|--------------|---------------|-------|--------------------------|-------------------------------------|-----------------------------------------------------|---------|-----------------|-------|-------|
| | | Mining | Construction | Manufacturing | Total | Wholesale and retail trade | Finance, insurance, and real estate | Transportation, communication, and public utilities | Service | Govern-ment | Other | Total |
| 1947 | 53.4 | 2.0 | 4.0 | 16.3 | 22.3 | 6.3 | 0.8 | 5.1 | 8.0 | 2.7 | 1.3 | 22.9 |
| 1950 | 48.3 | 1.7 | 4.3 | 16.0 | 21.9 | 11.1 | 1.0 | 5.1 | 9.2 | 3.3 | 0.1 | 29.7 |
| 1955 | 41.0 | 1.4 | 4.5 | 17.6 | 23.5 | 13.9 | 1.6 | 5.2 | 11.3 | 3.5 | 0.0 | 35.5 |
| 1960 | 32.7 | 1.2 | 6.1 | 21.7 | 29.1 | 15.8 | 1.8 | 5.5 | 12.0 | 3.0 | 0.0 | 38.2 |
| 1965 | 24.7 | 0.7 | 6.4 | 24.4 | 31.5 | 17.8 | 2.4 | 6.6 | 13.8 | 3.1 | 0.0 | 43.7 |
| 1970 | 19.3 | 0.4 | 7.5 | 26.1 | 34.0 | 19.3 | 2.6 | 6.8 | 14.6 | 3.3 | 0.1 | 46.6 |
| 1975 | 13.8 | 0.2 | 8.9 | 24.9 | 34.1 | 21.4 | 3.3 | 6.9 | 16.4 | 3.7 | 0.3 | 51.8 |
| 1980 | 10.9 | 0.2 | 9.6 | 23.7 | 33.6 | 22.8 | 3.6 | 6.9 | 18.4 | 3.6 | 0.1 | 55.4 |
| 1985 | 9.3 | 0.2 | 9.1 | 23.7 | 33.0 | 23.1 | 3.8 | 6.6 | 20.5 | 3.5[b] | — | 57.5 |

*Source:* Japan MCA, various years.

[a]Primary includes agriculture forestry and fisheries.

[b]Includes both government and other.

economic growth. Figure 10.1 shows changes in the levels of educational attainment. The ratio of junior high school graduates who advanced to high school increased significantly from 1945 to 1975. After 1975 approximately 90 percent of these graduates went to high school. Of those who graduated from high school, significant numbers went on to college (including junior colleges, especially for female students).

In Japan, research on voting behavior shows that higher education is correlated with more votes for the opposition parties (Watanuki 1967). So the prediction that education will cause more demand for an issue-conscious critical form of participation is borne out. Up to this point, however, this demand has not grown to the extent of seriously destabilizing the continuing LDP hold on the government. Control of over 50 percent of Diet seats is essential to the LDP because that permits control of Diet committees and decision making. According to recent research, a critical swing vote group with higher than average education lodges a protest vote against the LDP when that party controls a large margin of seats in the Diet (Kabashima and Broadbent n.d.). But the same group returns to vote for the LDP when it has only a small margin in the Diet. In other words, because it has a stake in the status quo, this group of swing voters is pursuing a conscious strategy of keeping the LDP in power. But, afraid of LDP tendencies toward corruption and authoritarian regression, it wants to keep the LDP in power by only a slim margin of Diet seats. This, it hopes, will keep the LDP nervous and responsive to voters. Thus, with the security treaty issue largely resolved and the shift in LDP priorities to economic growth, the social mobilization effect of education has not produced the kind of political confrontation that some development theorists predicted. Rather, it produces a second kind of "supportive participation." The level of education enjoyed by Japan's work force in 1950 also was unique among developing countries. So was the close coordination between its education and employment systems. For all the criticisms of the rigidity of these systems, little talent was allowed to go to waste or to drift. It was carefully graded and channeled into a similarly ranked hierarchy of companies and government offices, thus avoiding unemployment of intellectuals and giving most people a stake in the status quo.

Another significant development was the diffusion of mass media. Recent research shows that Japanese leaders from a wide variety of institutions believe the mass media exert a powerful impact on Japanese society (Kabashima and Broadbent 1986). This also implies a strong effect on politics. Radio broadcasting recipients increased from 39 percent of total households in 1945 to about 95 percent in 1962, at which time most households possessed radios. As seen in table 10.6, television broadcasting expanded from an insignificant level in 1952 to a saturation point in the late 1960s. The reader will note significant increases in 1958 and 1959 and once again in 1964, respectively timed with the wedding of the crown prince and princess and the Tokyo Olympics (Uchikawa 1978). Newspaper circulation was already at high levels at the end of the war, with

**Figure 10.1. Ratio of Lower, Secondary, and Upper-Secondary School Graduates Who Advanced to Schools of Higher Grade**

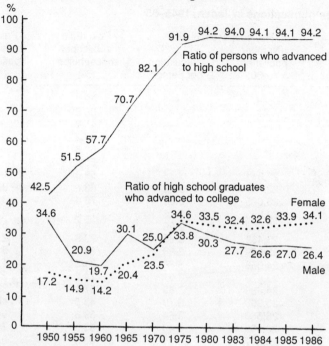

*Source:* Japan MCA 1987b: 644.

about one newspaper circulated per 3.73 individuals, or about one newspaper per household. A slight increase is observed in 1985.

Since the media in Japan are more commercially than politically oriented, they present images from all sectors of society and serve usually to liberalize and moderate politics (Kabashima and Broadbent 1986). Rather than the increase in circulation rates after the war, the most politically important change affecting the media was the acquisition of press freedom. The press played a significant role in political mobilization during several postwar crisis periods, such as the 1960 Japan-U.S. security treaty and the 1970s' pollution crisis. It was not enough, however, to unseat the LDP regime. Rather, given the broad support for many aspects of the status quo, it served as a reformist influence, moderating the more reactionary aspects of the LDP and opposing violence by the opposition.

## Economic Growth and Income Equality

Previous studies have shown that if economic development proceeds far enough, income inequality declines in the long run. But in the short run, in early stages of development, rapidly growing economies tend to exacerbate income inequality. Growing, overall inequality, Kuznets argues, stems from two different sources:

Table 10.6

**Mass Communications in Japan, 1945–85**

| Year | Newspaper circulation* (Number published, 1,000) | Circulation per person) | Paid radio subscriber households (%) | Paid TV subscriber households (%) |
|------|------|------|------|------|
| 1945 | — | — | 39.2 | — |
| 1946 | — | — | 38.6 | — |
| 1947 | — | — | 40.6 | — |
| 1948 | — | — | 47.2 | — |
| 1949 | — | — | 53.8 | — |
| 1950 | — | — | 55.4 | — |
| 1951 | 22,311 | 3.73 | 58.6 | — |
| 1952 | 22,737 | 3.72 | 63.6 | 0.01 |
| 1953 | 23,625 | 3.66 | 70.4 | 0.10 |
| 1954 | 22,853 | 3.88 | 75.3 | 0.30 |
| 1955 | 22,688 | 3.96 | 73.8 | 0.90 |
| 1956 | 23,489 | 3.87 | 77.8 | 2.30 |
| 1957 | 23,689 | 3.88 | 81.2 | 5.10 |
| 1958 | 24,058 | 3.86 | 81.3 | 11.0 |
| 1959 | 23,473 | 3.96 | 74.7 | 23.1 |
| 1960 | 24,438 | 3.89 | 57.2 | 33.2 |
| 1961 | 25,903 | 3.70 | 45.8 | 49.5 |
| 1962 | 26,550 | 3.64 | 89.6 | 64.8 |
| 1963 | 28,103 | 3.46 | 93.8 | 75.9 |
| 1964 | 29,677 | 3.31 | 96.3 | 83.0 |
| 1965 | 29,776 | 3.34 | 85.4 | 75.6 |
| 1966 | 30,935 | 3.25 | 89.8 | 79.8 |
| 1967 | 32,447 | 3.12 | 93.4 | 84.2 |
| 1968 | 33,792 | 3.02 | — | 88.1 |
| 1969 | 35,073 | 2.93 | — | 91.7 |
| 1970 | 36,304 | 2.85 | — | 94.8 |
| 1971 | 36,562 | 2.86 | — | 84.4 |
| 1972 | 38,162 | 2.80 | — | 87.0 |
| 1973 | 39,847 | 2.72 | — | 88.7 |
| 1974 | 40,006 | 2.74 | — | 91.7 |
| 1975 | 40,513 | 2.74 | — | 82.6 |
| 1976 | 42,120 | — | — | — |
| 1977 | 43,114 | — | — | — |
| 1978 | 44,277 | — | — | — |
| 1979 | 45,852 | — | — | — |
| 1980 | 46,391 | — | — | — |
| 1981 | 47,256 | — | — | — |
| 1982 | 47,993 | — | — | — |
| 1983 | 47,041 | — | — | — |
| 1984 | 47,515 | — | — | — |
| 1985 | 48,232 | — | — | — |

*Source:* Nihon Hōsō Kyōkai 1977.
*Morning and evening editions.

intrasectoral income inequality within the urban and rural sectors and intersectoral inequality and differential population growth across these two sectors. Japan, however, traveled a somewhat uncommon development path: the income inequality narrowed rather than widened as the economy grew. How then can one explain such an unusual evolution of income distribution?

The third column of table 10.7 shows that the nonagricultural sector in Japan experienced a decline in income inequality from a Gini coefficient of 0.33 in 1959 to one of 0.27 in 1969. (The Gini coefficient attempts to represent the degree of inequity of income distribution, the closer to zero the less the inequity.) Rapid economic growth resulted in reduced profit differentials between big plants and small plants; a shortage of young workers in the labor force, increasing the incomes of young, less experienced people; and diminishing earning inequality across cities (Mizoguchi 1974). As described before, the land reform significantly equalized the income of farmers. The degree of variation and the direction of change of income inequality within the agricultural sector after this initial effect are not significant, as the fourth column shows.

Overall income trends do not show quite the same even pattern. From 1955 to 1963 they register a slight increase in inequality, while the trend is reversed from 1963 to 1975. The explanation would seem to be found in the differences of income levels between sectors. Table 10.8 illustrates the differences in the growth of household income between workers' households and farmers' households. With the beginning of postwar economic development following the recovery of prewar levels by 1955, the income of workers increased rapidly, overtaking that of farmers; as a result, the intersectoral inequality between workers' and farmers' households increased sharply. This progression of the intersectoral inequality between 1955 and 1963 corresponds with the progression of the overall inequality in that period. After 1963, however, intersectoral inequality declined rapidly, corresponding to the diminishing of overall inequality. The expansion of farmers' income proceeded more rapidly than that of workers' income, with the former eventually outstripping the latter.

This expansion of rural income directly contradicts the expectation of mainstream development theory that resources must be squeezed from the peasantry for the capital accumulation necessary for industrial takeoff, as well as the corollary expectation that this process will result in protest and resistance. In the Japanese case, the farmers saved their extra income (which was then used for more growth-producing investment) without generating much political protest.

A possible explanation for the increase in farmers' income is the increase in the number of part-time farmers. Economic growth drew youth to the cities, causing a shortage of agricultural labor. This led to the mechanization of agriculture, which went so far as to give farmers the time to work in local industry while farming on weekends. These part-time farmers, of course, benefited from the growth of wage income. At the same time, they received a good income from their farming activities. The question then becomes, what makes the income from

Table 10.7

## Distribution of Income Measured by Gini Coefficient and the Rate of Economic Growth in Japan, 1952–85

| Year | Gini coefficient[a] for | | | | Real GNP growth rate[f] |
|---|---|---|---|---|---|
| | Whole population | | Nonagricultural sector[d] | Agricultural sector[e] | |
| | Data 1[b] | Data 2[c] | | | |
| 1952 | — | — | — | — | 11.7 |
| 1953 | — | — | — | — | 7.7 |
| 1854 | — | — | — | — | 2.8 |
| 1955 | — | — | — | 0.25 | 10.8 |
| 1956 | 0.35 | — | — | 0.25 | 6.1 |
| 1957 | — | — | — | 0.27 | 7.8 |
| 1958 | — | — | — | — | 6.0 |
| 1959 | 0.37 | — | 0.33 | 0.25 | 11.2 |
| 1960 | — | — | 0.33 | 0.25 | 12.5 |
| 1961 | — | — | 0.32 | 0.25 | 13.5 |
| 1962 | 0.40 | 0.36 | 0.30 | 0.27 | 6.4 |
| 1963 | — | 0.35 | 0.30 | 0.26 | 12.5 |
| 1964 | — | 0.34 | 0.29 | 0.26 | 10.6 |
| 1965 | 0.35 | 0.32 | 0.30 | 0.25 | 6.0 |
| 1966 | — | — | 0.20 | 0.24 | 11.4 |
| 1967 | — | 0.33 | 0.29 | 0.24 | 11.1 |
| 1968 | 0.31 | 0.32 | 0.27 | 0.24 | 13.0 |
| 1969 | — | 0.31 | 0.27 | 0.25 | 12.1 |
| 1970 | — | 0.30 | 0.27 | 0.25 | 8.3 |
| 1971 | 0.30 | — | 0.28 | 0.26 | 5.3 |
| 1972 | — | 0.31 | 0.27 | 0.26 | 9.7 |
| 1973 | — | 0.30 | 0.27 | 0.24 | 5.3 |
| 1974 | — | 0.30 | — | — | 0.2 |
| 1975 | — | 0.31 | — | — | 3.6 |
| 1976 | — | 0.33 | — | — | 5.1 |
| 1977 | — | 0.32 | — | — | 5.3 |
| 1978 | — | 0.32 | — | — | 5.1 |
| 1979 | — | 0.31 | — | — | 5.3 |
| 1980 | — | 0.32 | — | — | 4.5 |
| 1981 | — | 0.32 | — | — | 3.3 |
| 1982 | — | 0.33 | — | — | 3.3 |
| 1983 | — | 0.32 | — | — | — |
| 1984 | — | 0.34 | — | — | — |
| 1985 | — | 0.35 | — | — | — |

[a]The Gini coefficient attempts to measure the degree of inequality of income distribution; the closer to 0, the less the inequality.
[b]Mizoguchi 1974.
[c]Kojima 1988.
[d]Japan EPA 1975b: 198.
[e]Ibid.: 203 and 210.
[f]Japan EPA, various years.

Table 10.8

**Intersectoral Differences in the Growth of Mean Household Income in Japan, 1955–75**

| Year | Workers' households | Farmers' households | Intersectoral differences |
|------|---------------------|---------------------|---------------------------|
| 1955 | $   973 | $   995 | $–22 |
| 1957 | 1,089 | 946 | 143 |
| 1959 | 1,229 | 1,035 | 194 |
| 1961 | 1,504 | 1,276 | 228 |
| 1963 | 1,776 | 1,374 | 402 |
| 1965 | 2,171 | 1,832 | 339 |
| 1967 | 2,624 | 2,951 | 33 |
| 1969 | 3,255 | 3,127 | 120 |
| 1971 | 4,152 | 4,056 | 96 |
| 1973 | 5,228 | 5,985 | –757 |
| 1975 | 7,871 | 8,844 | –973 |

*Source:* Japan OPM 1977: 7.
*Note:* Unit is U.S. dollar based on the exchange rate in 1965 ($1.00 = Y360).

farming—with farmers spending so little time on their small farms—so high?

The answer is that the income of farmers has been affected by politics. To raise the income of farmers, the government has maintained high price supports and protection for agricultural products and has substantially subsidized the improvements that have made the mechanization of agriculture possible. To improve the economic situation of farmers in the long run, it was necessary to introduce new technologies. Since small farmers in Japan had neither the capacity to finance large investments in agricultural machinery nor a way to make the land suitable for modern machinery, the government of Japan subsidized them heavily.

Table 10.9 reports the share of government spending that has supported the farming population in Japan (above any general services offered by other government ministries), as well as governmental expenditures on agricultural price support programs. In 1955, 11 percent of the national expenditure was allocated to the agricultural sector. That this ratio remained at the same high level throughout the 1950s and 1960s is particularly significant in view of the fact that the number of farm households declined drastically over the same period. A significant portion of the government's total expenditure on agriculture is allocated to the price support program for rice and other agricultural commodities. Governmental spending on the agricultural sector in Japan has been disproportionately high in comparison with that in the United States, England, Germany, or France. In the latter countries, agricultural support as a share of total spending amounts to between 2 and 4 percent of the national budget, whereas in Japan it has been 8–12 percent (Kabashima 1984). The evidence suggests that in Japan, a redistribution of income occurs from the nonagricultural to the agricultural sector through the political system.

Farmers' political participation explains this high level of rice price support. Figure 10.2 shows that voters in rural areas have participated consistently more than their urban counterparts in Lower House elections since 1955. The participation study of the Cross-National Program in Political Change conducted in 1966 also showed that the rate of participation by farmers in voting, campaigning, and communal activities was approximately 0.1–0.2 standard deviations higher than the average (Kabashima 1984: 330). Moreover, as shown in table 10.10, farmers in Japan have also shown higher than average support for the LDP. It is plausible that, because of this higher level of supportive participation, farmers have been able to apply strong pressure on the government, thereby reversing the natural tendency toward widening inequality between the rural and urban sectors during the period of rapid growth.

The impact of rural participation is further amplified by the fact that the electoral district system favors rural districts. Reischauer writes:

> In the 1976 election ten candidates failed to gain seats although each received more than 100,000 votes, while nine others were elected with less than half as many votes. The result of this situation has been a gross under-representation of big cities, where almost all the post war population increase has occurred, and an over-representation for rural areas which have seen a steady erosion of population. (Reischauer 1977: 270)

Supportive rural participation during the country's period of rapid growth was based to a significant degree on traditional village solidarity that was institutionalized through various intermediate groups. Although in the prewar and immediate postwar years local influentials played a dominant role in relating these local social networks of the village to political processes at higher levels, administrative amalgamations of local governmental units in the 1950s and early 1960s created the need for intermediate organizations on a broader scale.

Agricultural cooperatives filled this role on one level; on another, conservative politicians organized constituency-wide individual support groups (kōenkai). These organizations have become the principal means for mobilizing rural voters and distributing governmental benefits. The intense concern of rural voters with improvement of local conditions has made them particularly receptive to politicians from the party in power, who can respond with governmental largess. Moreover, those who are elected from rural districts, since they have a stable support base, are able to advance in the power hierarchy in politics more rapidly. Thus, rural voters have a more powerful representative voice than their urban counterparts. As a result, the farmers receive preferential treatment through rice price supports and public works. This substantially equalized the intersectoral economic inequality that might otherwise have resulted from rapid growth.

Table 10.9

## The Structure of Governmental Expenditures in Japan, 1955–75 (unit = 100 million yen)

| | A<br>Total expenditure | B<br>Agriculture | | B1<br>Agricultural price supports | | C<br>Defense | | D<br>Social welfare | |
|---|---|---|---|---|---|---|---|---|---|
| | Amount | Amount | (B/A) | Amount | (B1/A) | Amount | (C/A) | Amount | (D/A) |
| 1955 | 10,133 | 1,113 | (.11) | — | — | 1,347 | (.13) | 1,038 | (.10) |
| 1957 | 11,846 | 1,183 | (.10) | 150 | (.01) | 1,430 | (.12) | 1,161 | (.10) |
| 1959 | 15,121 | 1,512 | (.10) | 0 | (.00) | 1,556 | (.10) | 1,480 | (.10) |
| 1961 | 20,074 | 2,296 | (.11) | 660 | (.03) | 1,835 | (.09) | 2,454 | (.12) |
| 1963 | 30,568 | 2,984 | (.10) | 740 | (.02) | 2,476 | (.08) | 3,891 | (.13) |
| 1965 | 37,447 | 3,981 | (.11) | 1,205 | (.03) | 3,054 | (.08) | 5,458 | (.15) |
| 1967 | 52,034 | 6,158 | (.12) | 2,415 | (.05) | 3,870 | (.07) | 7,396 | (.14) |
| 1969 | 69,309 | 8,244 | (.12) | 3,530 | (.05) | 4,949 | (.07) | 9,743 | (.14) |
| 1971 | 96,590 | 11,452 | (.12) | 2,601 | (.03) | 6,935 | (.07) | 13,418 | (.14) |
| 1973 | 152,726 | 18,709 | (.12) | 5,380 | (.04) | 9,790 | (.06) | 22,196 | (.15) |
| 1975 | 212,888 | 21,768 | (.10) | 7,520 | (.04) | 13,273 | (.06) | 39,269 | (.18) |

*Source:* Japan MOF 1960, 1965, 1970, 1975.

**Figure 10.2. Urban-Rural Difference in Voter Turnout in the House of Representatives Elections**

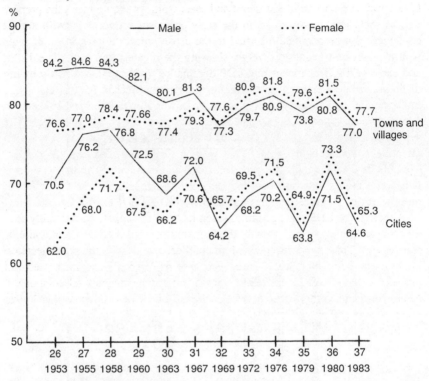

*Source:* Japan MHA 1987

## Mobilization and Stability

Postwar political stability may be attributed in part to the dominance of the LDP since 1955. Economic growth itself, however, by accelerating social mobilization, has worked against LDP dominance. These changes occurred in occupational structure, educational levels, and urbanization. Economic growth decreased the number of primary-sector workers and lesser educated and rural citizens, while increasing the number of salaried secondary- and tertiary-sector workers and highly educated, urban citizens. As the former always show higher support for the LDP, overall LDP support declined proportionally with economic development through the 1950s (Ishida 1963).

The LDP reacted to these structural changes by delaying redistricting in response to population shifts. Figure 10.3 shows the seats won and the proportion of votes cast for the LDP in the House of Representatives elections, 1955–86. The white section of the bar graph shows the proportion of the votes cast for the LDP, and the total bar graph height represents the proportion of LDP seats gained in the House of Representatives. The shaded area indicates the difference between the proportion of votes cast and seats won. As shown there, the proportion of seats won to votes cast in the early period of economic growth almost coincided. But as population shifted to the urban areas, the proportion of seats won to votes cast began to diverge, showing the greatest gap in the late 1960s and early 1970s. This means that LDP dominance was maintained partly by the disproportionate weight given to rural areas. Another reason for this gap is the multimember constituency system used for Lower House elections. In this system each electoral district is assigned a specific number of seats in the Diet. The system favors the larger LDP because it can minimize the "waste" vote more effectively than smaller parties. That is, in a given three-member district, for example, two LDP candidates can each receive 30 percent of the total votes and win, while their single opponent may receive 40 percent and win, the opponent thus "wasting" 10 percent of the opposition votes.

Although the LDP managed to broaden its base of support considerably during the years of economic growth, the farmers provided the consistent and crucial margin. Their support remained crucial because, despite the rapid decrease in the farm population, rural areas were overrepresented, and most electoral districts in the Lower House retain a small but critical agricultural component. Moreover, rural voters participated an average of 10 percent more than urban voters in Lower House elections, which slowed the decrease in LDP support.

Huntington's gap hypothesis suggests that rapid urbanization may cause political destabilization. The social and political effects of urbanization in Japan were moderated, however, by a number of factors: social policy, plentiful jobs, and strong social institutions. Social policy such as the occupation land reform and LDP rural patronage and rice price support made life on the farm more attractive, reducing the number of migrants somewhat. Strong, inclusive institutions and indigenous social networks transferred migrants from country to city through relatives and friends and held them within a constant social framework when they arrived, thus lessening their disorientation.

Moreover, for those who did migrate, the employment situation was favorable. The rapidly growing Japanese economy produced a high demand for labor, especially among young workers such as the rural migrants. The possibilities for sales outstripped the ability to produce (given the relatively labor-intensive techniques of the time), bringing about a labor shortage. This produced relatively high wages, even for those without a high school education. This provided well-paying jobs for the migrants and helped equalize the distribution of income.

Rapid growth also caused a shift in the national occupational structure, from the manual labor–oriented industries such as mining to "clean job" industries. This reduced the harshness of work conditions, a frequent spur to radical opposition politics. Miners, for instance, have a long history of vocal and radical support for opposition parties. As such occupations gave way to clerical and

Table 10.10

## Party Support by Occupation, Education, and Place of Residence (percents)

| | November 1955 | | | | | May 1960 | | | | | August 1965 | | | | | June 1970 | | | | | June 1975 | | | | |
|---|---|---|---|---|---|---|---|---|---|---|---|---|---|---|---|---|---|---|---|---|---|---|---|---|---|
| | LDP | OP | ID | NA | Com. | LDP | OP | ID | NA | Com. | LDP | OP | ID | NA | Com. | LDP | OP | ID | NA | Com. | LDP | OP | ID | NA | Com. |
| **Occupation** | | | | | | | | | | | | | | | | | | | | | | | | | |
| White collar (manager) | 37 | 50 | 5 | 8 | 16 | 28 | 58 | 7 | 7 | 18 | 37 | 57 | 2 | 4 | 20 | 39 | 53 | 4 | 4 | 23 | 38 | 51 | 7 | 4 | 24 |
| Blue collar (salesperson) | 36 | 53 | 2 | 9 | 20 | 26 | 57 | 6 | 11 | 25 | 50 | 43 | 6 | 1 | 3 | 55 | 39 | 5 | 1 | 5 | 52 | 40 | 6 | 2 | 6 |
| Small business | 62 | 22 | 5 | 11 | 19 | 49 | 30 | 9 | 12 | 18 | 59 | 36 | 3 | 3 | 10 | 64 | 29 | 3 | 5 | 10 | 53 | 33 | 10 | 5 | 15 |
| Farmers and fishers | 52 | 20 | 4 | 24 | 41 | 50 | 25 | 7 | 18 | 37 | 59 | 24 | 3 | 14 | 25 | 64 | 26 | 1 | 9 | 17 | 62 | 24 | 2 | 12 | 18 |
| Other | 49 | 25 | 6 | 20 | 4 | 37 | 32 | 11 | 20 | 2 | 52 | 26 | 5 | 17 | 3 | 55 | 21 | 4 | 20 | 3 | 45 | 33 | 7 | 15 | 4 |
| **Education level** | | | | | | | | | | | | | | | | | | | | | | | | | |
| 0–6 years | 44 | 19 | 5 | 32 | 34 | 40 | 22 | 9 | 29 | 26 | 40 | 34 | 6 | 20 | 21 | 50 | 26 | 3 | 21 | 14 | 48 | 27 | 8 | 17 | 13 |
| 7–9 | 53 | 35 | 3 | 9 | 40 | 41 | 42 | 7 | 10 | 43 | 48 | 43 | 3 | 6 | 43 | 50 | 42 | 3 | 5 | 39 | 47 | 42 | 4 | 7 | 33 |
| 10–12 | 47 | 45 | 4 | 4 | 20 | 40 | 48 | 7 | 5 | 25 | 45 | 49 | 3 | 3 | 27 | 49 | 44 | 3 | 4 | 36 | 45 | 43 | 6 | 6 | 40 |
| More than 13 | 40 | 54 | 4 | 2 | 6 | 28 | 63 | 8 | 1 | 6 | 44 | 52 | 2 | 2 | 9 | 45 | 48 | 6 | 1 | 11 | 38 | 50 | 9 | 3 | 14 |
| **Place of residence** | | | | | | | | | | | | | | | | | | | | | | | | | |
| 7 largest cities | | | | | | | | | | | 37 | 58 | 2 | 3 | 20 | 44 | 47 | 5 | 4 | 19 | 44 | 43 | 7 | 6 | 21 |
| Cities > 100,000 | | | | | | | | | | | 44 | 44 | 4 | 8 | 18 | 49 | 42 | 3 | 6 | 27 | 39 | 46 | 8 | 7 | 26 |
| Cities < 100,000 | | | | | | | | | | | 48 | 41 | 3 | 8 | 29 | 47 | 42 | 5 | 6 | 25 | 45 | 42 | 5 | 8 | 28 |
| Towns and villages | | | | | | | | | | | 48 | 37 | 4 | 11 | 33 | 54 | 36 | 2 | 8 | 29 | 53 | 35 | 3 | 9 | 25 |

*Notes:*

LDP = Liberal Democratic Party; OP = Opposition Parties; ID = Independent; NA = No answer; Com. = Composition: Share of each category in the sample

*Source:* Asahi Shimbunsha 1976.

service-sector manual jobs, the workers had less incentive to protest violently against the immediate harshness of their work conditions. This led to waning support for opposition parties, which in turn reduced the tendency of the ruling conservatives to react with coercive suppression. Thus, in Japan at least, rapid economic growth was a positive factor in establishing a foundation for political stability.

## Supportive Participation with Economic Growth

The key to Japan's having been able to avoid the "cruel choice" and to maintain a degree of democracy and broad political participation along with rapid economic growth lies in the relationship of "supportive participation" between the ruling party and the rural population. The term "supportive" is meant to indicate that the mass of the rural population favored, or at least did not oppose, the policies of the elite. The term "participation" means that their support was not entirely passive, acquiescent, or without choice; they had, in fact, effective means of expressing political choice, usually by vote, and also by petition or demonstration. This power injected some representative quality into the decisions of the political elite. In the Japanese case, such representativeness focused on meeting the material demands of the rural supporters, leaving the elite a free hand to design and pursue other broad national policies.

The policy-making style developed in Japan since the 1970s further reinforced this pattern of combining supportive participation with substantial redistribution. So long as broad policy lines are set and issues remain essentially incremental in character, elite bureaucrats have dominated decision making, leaving the parties to act as agents of outsiders pressing claims against the bureaucracy. In contrast to the bureaucrats' efforts to concentrate resources, party politicians have had a strong redistributive orientation.

The success of rural voters and politicians in disseminating government funds to their rural districts is of course partly dependent on the availability of these funds. Economic growth and the subsequent increase in government revenues have made massive resources available for redistribution to the rural sector. In 1955, total governmental expenditure amounted to barely one trillion yen; by 1975, it had increased to approximately twenty-one trillion yen (table 10.9). Since the ratio of agricultural expenditures to total governmental spending remained constant during this period while the number of farm households declined drastically, the absolute amount allocated to individual farmers increased substantially. This increase in agricultural spending through rapid economic development reinforced supportive participation.

Certainly, a system of supportive participation is only a limited form of democracy. It supports a political elite, authoritative if not authoritarian, that is only partially responsive to public demand and criticism. But in the Japanese case, it enabled the country to stabilize its democratic system in a period when

Figure 10.3. Seats Won and Proportions of Votes Cast for the LDP in the House of Representatives (1955–86)

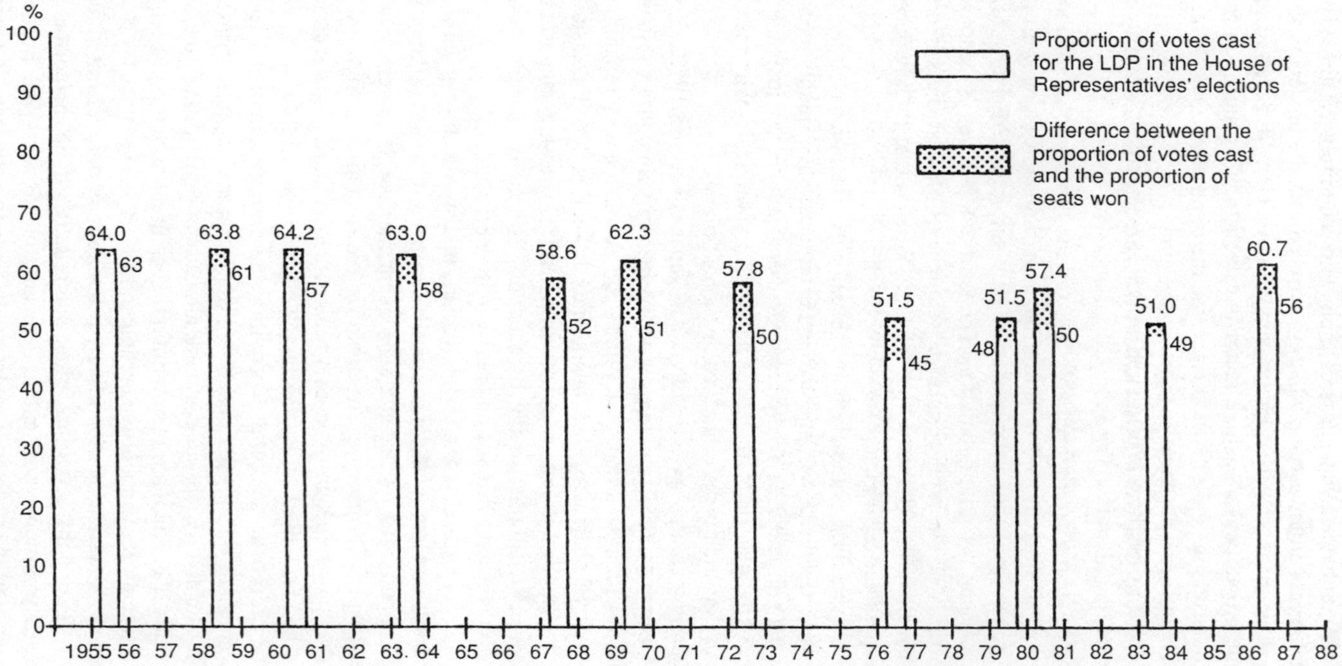

rapid economic growth might have been expected to lead to a different outcome. In summary, among the special conditions that made this system and outcome possible were the following:

—Land reform.

—Authoritarian liberalism.

—High economic growth, which reversed the trend of the gap hypothesis.

—High propensity to save for capital formation.

—Social infrastructure in education and mass media that created an egalitarian liberal culture supporting democracy and equality.

—Efficient and uncorrupt bureaucracy.

—Economic infrastructure.

—Strong social network extending from the villages to the cities.

No doubt the total combination of these conditions is unique to Japan. That is not to say, however, that a system of supportive participation will not develop or cannot be constructed elsewhere. Not all the conditions may be necessary in the exact form they appeared in Japan. Given the paucity of cases of this type, it is difficult to distinguish scientifically which are necessary, sufficient, or unnecessary and whether functional equivalents can substitute for those that are key.

# Part V
# Conclusion

# 11

# The Dynamics of
# Political Change

## Harold Crouch and James W. Morley

THERE is no question that over the past twenty to forty years economic growth has had a major impact on political change in the Asia-Pacific region, but the relationship has not been transparent. Higher rates of growth have been associated with a stabilization of democracy in Japan, a democratic transformation in South Korea, the beginning of a democratizing trend in Taiwan, the emergence of a quasi-democratic system in Thailand, and an erosion of the Leninist regime in China. On the other hand, the era of rapid economic growth has also seen the strengthening of authoritarian governments in Indonesia and Singapore and an uncertain trend toward strengthening authoritarian impulses in the quasi-democratic system in Malaysia.

Is there a pattern in this diversity? We believe there is but that it has been obscured for two reasons. First, it can be misleading to focus too much on the *rate* of economic growth—the speed of change from year to year—rather than on the *level* of growth attained. And second, no study of political change can afford to focus on economic growth alone without taking into account the many other factors that can either reinforce or counter, at least temporarily, political pressures arising from the growth process.

It is a common misconception that high rates of growth necessarily favor the regime in power. Certainly there is some evidence to support this proposition, and most leaders in power probably assume it to be true. Who can doubt that in Japan, for example, the democratization of its system in the occupation period has been legitimized at least in part by the high economic growth it has sustained throughout the postwar period; or that in China it was the growth in the early 1950s that gave the Communist regime one of its first claims to legitimacy; or that the varying degrees of support enjoyed by authoritarian regimes, such as those of Park in South Korea in the 1960s, Marcos in the Philippines in the early 1970s, and over the years Chiang K'ai-shek and particularly Chiang Ching-kuo in Taiwan, Suharto in Indonesia, and Lee Kuan Yew in Singapore, were derived in part from their ability to initiate or sustain economic growth?

But high growth can also undermine existing regimes. The extraordinary successes of the economic policies of the Kuomintang not only provided the regime with legitimacy but also stimulated the liberalizing pressures to which it felt forced to begin to concede by 1985. Similarly, in South Korea, the vigorous growth initiated under President Park, and the resumption of high growth under President Chun after the 1979–80 recession, provided the context for the democratic transformation of 1987. Similar pressures have been felt elsewhere.

On the other hand, failure to grow can also have political consequences. Economic failure has often been a stimulant to opposition and demands for political reforms that sometimes lead to regime change, such as the collapse of the Sukarno regime in Indonesia in 1965–66 and of the Marcos regime in the Philippines in 1986. But failure to sustain economic growth has certainly not always led to transforming political change. Most of the Asia-Pacific regimes have withstood brief economic setbacks, and the Chinese Communist regime managed to do so for more than twenty years.

To rise above these apparent contradictions one needs, first, to focus less on the rate of economic growth and more on the level of development achieved. If we take the GNP per capita as a rough indicator of the level of development and relate it to each of the Asia-Pacific countries in our sample, we find that in general, despite exceptions, there is today more of a broad pattern than might have been supposed (table 11.1).

If Singapore and the Philippines are removed from the table, the remaining Asia-Pacific states seem to be arrayed in a generally orderly pattern, something like flying geese. The simile was first used by the Japanese economist Akamatsu Kaname to describe the relationship of the Asia-Pacific economies to each other (Akamatsu 1962). It seems to us adaptable to the relationship of the region's polities: Japan as the economic leader and most established democracy flying in the lead, the NIE-democratic or democratizing echelon coming next, the quasi-democratic systems still feeling the tug of authoritarianism coming after, the less developed, more authoritarian regimes bringing up the end of the line, and with each regime experiencing pressures that tend to push it up to the echelon ahead.

It may be objected, of course, that such a pattern would not have emerged if we had made this analysis some years earlier. In 1975, for example, the only democratic states were Japan and Thailand, the one with the highest GNP per capita and the other with a relatively low one; and if it had been made in 1965, the only democratic state besides Japan was the Philippines, another low per capita income society. Is the correlation we now see any more significant than its apparent lack in these earlier years? We believe it is, and that much of the earlier lack of correlation can be explained as evidence of the instability commonly associated with the lower levels of development that obtained, or with the power of noneconomic factors that in those times may have temporarily overshadowed the pressures generated by economic growth—and that in fact go a long way as well to explain the deviations of Singapore and the Philippines from the pattern.

Table 11.1

**Growth Level and Regime Type**

| Country | GNP per capita (1987) U.S. dollars | Regime type |
|---|---|---|
| Industrial | | |
| Japan | $15,760 | Democratic |
| NIEs | | |
| Singapore | 7,940 | Authoritarian |
| Taiwan | 4,630 | Quasi-democratic |
| S. Korea | 2,690 | Democratic |
| Developing | | |
| Malaysia | 1,810 | Quasi-democratic |
| Thailand | 840 | Quasi-democratic |
| Philippines | 590 | Democratic |
| Indonesia | 450 | Authoritarian |
| Giant | | |
| China | 290 | Eroding Leninist |

*Sources:* Except for Taiwan all data are from *World Bank, 1989:* 14–17. Data for Taiwan are from Republic of China DGB 1989: 93.

## The Underlying Rationale

This correlation of the current level of growth and regime type—rough and not without exceptions though it is—does not seem to be accidental. We cannot demonstrate that mathematically—the necessary data are not available even if we knew how to weight and relate them, which we do not—but by standing on the shoulders particularly of the modernization theorists and the statist theorists, we believe we can see a dynamic that makes sense and that is consistent with the historical material assembled in the preceding chapters. All other things being equal, it is a dynamic comprising three distinct but interrelated processes:

> Economic growth drives social mobilization.
> Social mobilization drives political mobilization.
> Political mobilization drives regime change.

In the initial process—a process that continues as long as growth continues—economic growth drives social mobilization. To improve the factors of production, a dynamic process must be set in motion by which the quality of labor is steadily upgraded, more and more capital is accumulated and invested, and higher and higher technology is introduced. Concomitantly, as the quality and quantity of these factors change, the factors themselves must be redirected to meet ever more rationally evolving economic needs.

In the late and late-late developing countries in our sample it has been the state that usually initiates the process. Infrastructures are needed that only the state can provide: roads, education systems, legal structures, and the like, to be sure. But equally needed, if development is to go forward, are technological and managerial expertise, as well as mechanisms of capital accumulation and investment. In ex-colonies these are mainly in foreign hands during the colonial period and continue to be largely foreign controlled after independence. In the absence of strong indigenous business classes, the state sooner or later feels a need to enhance its direct role in the economy either in place of foreign capital or at least alongside it. Typically, therefore, the state plays a major direct role in economic development. While this does not necessarily lead to anthoritarianism, it tends to strengthen the state vis-à-vis society.

Such a development process cannot go forward without churning up the previously existing social order. Characteristically, redundant rural populations have moved into cities and thence into factory production and eventually into higher levels of the service sector while education levels have been raised and communications systems improved. In the course of these events, old ideas and old associations are melted down. New social forces tend to congeal around new ideas, and new social classes and strata are formed, particularly important being the industrial working class, the urban, educated middle class; and the business class, each with its own skills, interests, and ambitions. Karl Deutsch (Deutsch 1961: 493ff.) observed similar changes taking place in other parts of the developing world a generation ago and identified them as part of a single process he termed social mobilization.

These changes appear to set in motion a second process in which social mobilization drives political mobilization; that is, it stimulates a growing awareness of group identity and interests, and it encourages the organization of the new groups and strata into politically active bodies—farmers into cooperatives; industrial workers into labor unions; students into student unions; lawyers, doctors, and teachers into professional associations; and businessmen into industrial clubs, chambers of commerce, and the like, while new organizations representing ethnic and communal interests are also formed. Most important, political parties develop and establish deeper roots in society partly through links with organizations representing the newly mobilized social groups and classes.

In this process, the members of civil society and the agencies of the state are natural rivals, for each seeks to bring these organizations under its own control. The state's primary interest is to prevent the emerging groups from being organized in hostility to the state's purposes. It also seeks to secure the cooperation of those groups that can provide information and skills the state may require to formulate and execute its own plans. The civil leaders of particular groups, on the other hand, are not characteristically moved to serve the state's interests. On the contrary, political mobilization seems necessary as a means of securing influence over the state and bringing it to act in their group's interests. At the very least, they are anxious to constrain the state from acting adversely to those interests.

It is of critical importance whether it is the society or the state that is most successful in the political mobilization process, for success in this endeavor is one of the principal determinants of the regime's internal balance of power, and it is that balance of power that determines in large part the structure of the regime. To the extent that the state is able to direct the flow of information, control the structure of the new organizations, and utilize them to effect its purposes, it enhances its own autonomous influence, moving the regime in a more authoritarian direction. Conversely, to the extent that it is civil society that controls and enhances its relative power most in the process, the regime is driven in a liberalizing direction. For a considerable period of time, in fact throughout the lower and middle level-of-growth periods, the political mobilization struggle continues. It is in fact this tug-of-war that goes a long way to explain the political instability that characteristically occurs at this time—a phenomenon first pointed out a generation ago by James Coleman (1960: 544) and confirmed again more recently in a study of 120 countries by Zehra Arat (1988: 30), but not related by them to the growth process.

The struggle between old and newly mobilized groups does not always lead to the establishment of authoritarian regimes. Sometimes a more or less stable balance between groups permits the emergence of quasi-democratic systems. But the most common outcome of this struggle is the rise sooner or later of a state strong enough to impose its rule on the various competing groups. The ways such states come into existence vary enormously—whether through revolutions, military coups, or the gradual elimination and cooptation of opposition groups. Some states prove more capable than others of maintaining political stability, but those that are able to create a stable political order are usually also fairly successful in promoting economic development. In the early and intermediate states of growth, the fruits of development are normally very unevenly distributed, with the result that many sections of society feel disadvantaged and frustrated. These groups often constitute threats to the government, which continues to rely on repressive means to maintain itself in power.

Eventually, however, the economy becomes too large and too complex to be controlled or managed from a single point or by a single bureaucracy. The decisions required are too numerous, the talents needed are too diffused in the population, and the capital and technology that must be rationally coordinated are held too widely. The state feels forced, whether it wishes to or not, to move beyond cooptation and to experiment with various reforms involving a decentralization of the economic decision-making process and an acceptance, at least in part, of the determination of the market. Its desire, of course, is to maintain itself in authority by reforming the economy without reforming the polity.

It is a vain hope. Before long it becomes clear that such reforms are not enough. At this level of economic growth, the society has evolved too far for economic reforms alone to work. The modern classes—the working, middle, business, and, sometimes, farming (as opposed to peasant) classes—have become too large, too highly educated, too politically conscious, and too well mobilized under their own leadership to accept any longer the authority of a state that excludes them from real political participation, and when the balance of power between state and society has shifted decisively, the new social forces demand and secure, whether by negotiation or violence, movement toward the democratic transformation of the political system.

It is, therefore, not accidental that medium levels of economic growth are commonly associated with authoritarianism and instability while the higher levels are generally correlated with democracy. All other factors being equal, these correlations would appear to be in large part the effects of the growth process itself, mediated through the social and political processes it generates.

How well do the Asia-Pacific countries reflect this pattern?

## The Asia-Pacific "Fit"

When the experiments with political democracy that were undertaken to some degree throughout the region in the immediate postindependence period (excluding only China and Taiwan) collapsed almost everywhere, the need for stable political systems to provide favorable conditions for growth contributed to the state's increasing its domination over society. China adopted a Communist structure and most of the others became authoritarian: in Korea, the Rhee-Park-Chun versions; in Taiwan, the Kuomintang rule; in Indonesia, first the regime of Sukarno, then of Suharto; in Singapore, the PAP regime under Lee Kuan Yew; and in Thailand, the resumption of essentially military leadership, interrupted by coups and brief episodes of liberalization. Japan, of course, had undergone the same move to modern authoritarianism in the early Meiji period, when society there too was not yet ready to lead the growth process, and the leadership of the state seemed to be required. In Malaysia and the Philippines relatively democratic systems lasted longer, but in the 1970s authoritarian rule was established in the Philippines, and Malaysia moved in a more authoritarian direction.

In the early stages of growth, relatively large results were achieved by most of these authoritarian states. By improving education, holding down wages, forcing returns into investment, establishing state enterprises, encouraging the substitution of domestic manufactures for foreign imports, and the like—and preventing the emerging new social forces from interfering in the political process—they were able to bring into production relatively large amounts of hitherto underutilized resources. But as time went on, a clear differentiation set in. Some economies moved ahead faster than others. Japan, building on nearly a century of growth and turning to its well-established strategy of export-led industrialization, soon resumed the trend line that the war and its destruction had interrupted. The other economies had had far less previous growth and generally speaking preferred to pursue a different growth strategy, that of import substitution.

Eventually, however, the import-substitution industrialization strategy ran out its string. If growth was to be sustained, structural changes were required, which meant the adoption of new economic strategies. Japan, of course, was already keyed to exports—its structural adjustment problem was rather to move out of labor- and into more capital- and technology-intensive production—but for the other resource-poor countries, the challenge was to expand exports. Korea made the shift when Park Chung Hee seized power, Taiwan between 1958 and 1961, and Singapore in 1968 after the props had been pulled out from its economy by its expulsion from Malaysia and the announcement of the British withdrawal of its forces east of Suez. As one would expect, similar pressures were felt in the resource-rich developing countries a bit later, in the 1970s and 1980s, but there import-substitution policies were more supplemented than replaced. In China it was not until 1978 that a different type of crisis resulted in a shift to the "four modernizations" policy, which was made possible by a leadership change.

Thus, while economic growth has generally been sustained throughout the region, each economy has proceeded from its own starting level and with its own resource mix. Each has experimented with its own economic strategies and experienced its own varying rates of growth. The result is that the levels of per capita income achieved generally differentiate them into three categories of economies: developing, newly industrializing, and advanced.

As our model would lead us to expect, the pressures of growth have generated a mobilization of society throughout the Asia-Pacific region, but one that varies from country to country in general accord with the level of growth attained (table 1.12). Japan, for example, the country with the most advanced economy in the region, has also the highest level of education, the most advanced communications, and the highest share of its work force in the service sector. Its urbanization is topped only by Singapore, a city-state without a hinterland. At the next level of economic development, the social mobilization indicators for the NIEs (Singapore, South Korea, and Taiwan) are also high. Although generally not so high as those for Japan, nevertheless, the degree of social mobilization in these countries clearly sets them apart from the third category, the developing countries. Thus, about two-thirds of the population of both Taiwan and South Korea (and almost 100 percent of Singapore) are urbanized while the urbanization rates in the developing countries range between one-fifth and two-fifths. Similarly, statistics for literacy, secondary and tertiary education, and newspaper reading confirm lower levels of social mobilization there (although there are some surprising exceptions in the case of particular indicators).

Modern social classes also have become differentiated. Generally speaking, in each society they have expanded in rough correspondence with the level of per capita income attained. In most cases, the tug-of-war between the state and society for control of their political mobilization also has intensified with the level of growth and has resulted in the political instability our model suggests.

The history of the industrial working class shows this clearly. In the early stages of economic growth this class is naturally small, difficult to organize, and lacking in bargaining power because of widespread unemployment and under-employment. In the developing countries in our study, the working class is still relatively small, the proportion of the work force employed in manufacturing and construction being only 13 percent in Indonesia and the Philippines, and 15 percent in Thailand (FEER 1989: 6–7), and a substantial number in fact work in small, "traditional" industries. The potentially organizable workers in the "modern" sector constitute a small minority, and in any case the influence of trade unions remains limited in the context of large-scale unemployment and underemployment. In Malaysia, whereas 14.5 percent of the work force is employed in manufacturing, the potential political influence of trade unions is dissipated by communalism. It is only in the NIEs and in Japan that the working class constitutes a more significant proportion of the population.

It is not surprising, then, that the struggle to mobilize labor politically has the longest history in Japan. It began there in the first half of the century, when private, party, and state elements fought to dominate the burgeoning labor organizations. With the coming of the Pacific war, the state seemed to have won, subsuming all private bodies under so-called patriotic associations. But, in the postwar period, the dissolution of the old control bodies and the enforcement of freedom of association and other human rights freed not only former interest groups, including industrial labor, to re-form, but a host of new ones to arise and take ever more political action. The result is that in Japan it is society rather than the state that has finally won the struggle for political leadership of the unions, and indeed of other new social forces.

In China, too, the competition had been intense in the prewar period. But with the consolidation of Communist power in 1949, it took a diametrically opposite course from that of Japan. The Stalinist model of transmission belt mobilization was introduced, vast efforts being made to win the commitment and cooperation of the various emerging social sectors—peasants, workers, professionals, and ethnic groups—for executing the will of the party-state.

Autonomous labor union movements in Korea, Taiwan, and Singapore pre-dated the formation of the independent state as we know it today and were looked on by the new authorities of each as threats to their power. (The discussion of unions in these three countries, which follows, is drawn largely from Deyo 1982.) The first measures taken, therefore, were to destroy union autonomy. Martial law, repressive legislation, secret police infiltration, and leadership purges were among the instruments used, and they were largely successful. Having emasculated the unions of civil control, these states then moved to restructure them for the state's purposes, although the states lacked the coercive power of the Chinese model. Instead, the state-union relationship was based on various forms of corporatism in which the state was the dominant force.

In Taiwan, having broken the labor movement's autonomy and effectively excluded it from the political process shortly after its arrival on the island, the KMT moved to make it a cooperative element in its own power structure. It took the lead in organizing unions, principally at the enterprise level, and placed them under a KMT-controlled Chinese Federation of Labor. It then brought them partially into its administration by making them members of local labor-management councils, where dispute settlements and worker benefits were largely decided and where local KMT cadres and their allies in management could exercise the desired degree of control without suppression.

Singapore and Korea have had roughly similar experiences, although the Singapore state—or perhaps it is more accurate to say its ruling party, the People's Action party (PAP)—has been more successful in repressing union autonomy. In both societies, the first round went to society, the labor unions under colonial rule having been led by anticolonial militants. The second and third rounds, following independence, went largely to the state. By 1965 the PAP in Singapore had broken the leftist unions and brought the rest into its National Trades Union Congress (NTUC). There they were used in the 1970s to administer productivity campaigns, training programs, and the like, and a cabinet minister was appointed as secretary general of the NTUC. In what appears to be a third round in the 1980s, controls were decentralized, company unions were encouraged, and enterprises were given more scope in dispute settlement and welfare administration, although the state remained dominant.

In Korea, the struggle has been more prolonged. In the Rhee, Park, and Chun administrations, the government managed to purge and silence the unions and bring them under its own Federation of Korean Trade Unions. In the 1970s and 1980s it also experimented with some of the same corporatist methods Taiwan and Singapore were using, such as devolving worker assistance programs to union offices and increasing company welfare programs. But it was never able to secure the degree of domination achieved by its fellow NIEs, possibly in part because its militant union movement has a longer history and in part because the larger size of its manufacturing enterprises makes unionization more appealing.

In the non-Communist developing economies, where social mobilization stimulated by economic development has been more limited, the industrial working class has been smaller and less confident of its political potential. As a consequence, its political mobilization is less advanced. It has therefore been easier for the state to establish its domination over the labor movement. In colonial Malaya the British encouraged the formation of the Malayan Trade Union Congress (MTUC) as an alternative to the Communist unions, and the MTUC today continues to be a moderate organization, hemmed in by many restrictive laws. In Indonesia a government-sponsored labor federation replaced independent unionism, which collapsed with the crushing of the Communist party in 1965. In Thailand the union movement is small and fragmented, some sections being under the influence of groups in the military and the government. Only in the Philippines does the leftist union movement represent some sort of challenge to the government, but it is still a relatively weak force.

The urban, educated middle class, consisting of professionals, white-collar employees, small-business people, intellectuals, and students, also has been growing throughout the region. It could be expected that members of this class would have a strong interest in expanding democratic representation because they would be among the major beneficiaries. They are usually sensitive to both the abuse of power and corruption, which often accompany authoritarianism, and they have a greater capacity than the members of the lower classes to organize themselves in pursuit of what they conceive to be their rights and interests. They now include the overwhelming bulk of the Japanese population and form a powerful base for the democratic regime there. In Korea, it was the student uprising in the spring of 1987, backed by a less radical but not less determined urban middle class, that finally forced an end to the military rule. In Taiwan, it was intellectuals and professionals, often Western educated, who finally devised a strategy that persuaded the KMT that the time had come to begin some sort of transition to democracy.

In most developing countries, however, the middle class is still very weak. Especially in Indonesia and Thailand it is numerically small, and most of its members are employed by the government and therefore inhibited, although not absolutely precluded, from becoming involved in movements demanding an autonomous voice in the government. In Malaysia, where the middle class is larger, a substantial proportion of the middle class is Chinese—as it is in Indonesia—so that its political influence tends to be dissipated by communalism.

The two exceptions to these generalizations are Singapore and the Philippines. In Singapore, where the middle class is large, only partly employed in government service, and predominantly Chinese in a predominantly Chinese society, it could be expected that it would take the lead in demanding further democratization. In fact, it has been fairly quiescent politically. In the Philippines, where the low level of economic development would incline one to expect a rather undeveloped middle class, this class is in fact disproportionately large and politically energetic, contributing the leadership and most of the bodies that monitored the crucial 1986 election and blocked the path of Marcos's troops on the EDSA Boulevard.

The key to the middle class's ethos and effectiveness would seem to be found partly in its economic status, which becomes increasingly independent of the state as growth continues, but even more in its education. In general, we should expect the development of education to be dependent on the level of economic growth, since growth depends on education to improve human resources, and an expanding educational system requires the allocation of more and more of the state's resources. In general, the statistics bear out this expectation. The significance of higher education becomes clear when one realizes that, regardless of the economic level, those countries where the middle class—including the students, who seek generally to enter it—has been the most active in the drive for democratization and its strongest supporter once achieved (Japan, the Philippines, Korea, and Taiwan) are exactly those countries with the highest percentage of the population receiving higher education. At the other extreme, China, where the state looked with suspicion on higher education for so long and, during the Cultural Revolution, nearly destroyed its institutions, has not only the lowest percentage of its population highly educated but also the lowest level of growth and the most autocratic political system.

The big-business class might be expected to have pursued its interests in the political arenamore vigorously and independently than the other modern classes. In most Asia-Pacific countries, however, businessmen have generally been reluctant to take a political lead until the economy is relatively well advanced. In the developing economies, the big-business class, while contributing financial support to various political parties and other ruling groups, has been relatively successfully coopted, being deterred from antigovernmental action by intermarriage or financial ties between officials and businessmen and by the establishment of advisory organs under bureaucratic leadership. In Korea, too, even the largest conglomerates have depended on the government's support. In Taiwan, where enterprises were less dependent, they were the objects of such solicitude by the government that they have had little to complain of. In Japan, too, during the first twenty years or so of the postwar period, when government institutions continued to control much of the country's capital as well as the licensing of imports and foreign exchange, which the war-devastated economy was so short of, big business took a relatively low posture. But as the economic situation improved, this class has emerged as a growing force for change in Korea and Taiwan and as a central pillar of the democratic regime in Japan. .

A significant independent, commercially oriented, small farmer class has not yet come into being in the developing countries, where agriculture is still carried out largely by peasants or on plantations. It is only in Japan, Korea, and Taiwan, following capitalistic land reform, that this class has become large and politically conscious. There, support by its members has been carefully solicited by the governments in power, and during the authoritarian periods in Korea and Taiwan, their interests were so well looked after that they raised few questions about the nature of the regimes. Only when, at a higher level of income, political stability seemed to become unmanageable did they in both cases begin gradually to shift their support to the forces for democratization. In Japan that shift had occurred much earlier, in the late 1940s, when defeat and occupation broke not only the authoritarian system, but its mystique as well.

One might suppose that increased social and political mobilization and the changes in the class structure associated with economic growth would have a natural tendency to drive the state toward a quasi-democratic transformation. After all, might not Malaysia and Thailand be examples, each having a quasi-democratic structure and occupying a political and economic position between Indonesia and China with their lower levels of per capita income and authoritarian or Communist polities, and Japan and Korea with their higher levels of per capita income and democratic structures? We are not inclined to believe that this is necessarily true. This model appears more or less to fit Thailand. Although the Thai polity has not moved in a straight line but has wavered back and forth between quasi-democratic and authoritarian forms, the secular trend appears to be away from authoritarianism and toward quasi-democracy as economic development has taken place. But in the Malaysian case, the quasi-democratic system was established when the state was founded, before the era of rapid growth, while that growth was accompanied in fact by a trend toward increased reliance on authoritarian means of control. Moreover, the NIEs went through no such quasi-democratic phase at the same level of growth.

Relatively weak though these new classes may be at the intermediate level of growth, their members, particularly the middle-class technocrats and businessmen, have usually been cultivated assiduously by the various states, and increasingly so as the economy becomes more complex. Increased consultation, however, should not be confused with democratization. The state has usually acted very selectively, bringing elements of the new classes in to offer advice or execute its decisions, but it has not given up its decision-making power unless forced to. There have, of course, been occasions when society has challenged the state. The student uprising in South Korea in 1960, the struggle for political control in Singapore in 1959–65, the alternating quasi-democratic and authoritarian eras in Thailand, and the demonstrations by students and intellectuals in China in 1986 and 1989, among other events, all testify to the pressure of rising social forces. But in no instance have these forces been able more than temporarily to wrest control, except perhaps in the Philippines. At this level of growth they have been too weak to transform the system.

We are inclined, therefore, to believe with Zehra Arat that in the Asia-Pacific region as elsewhere, the correlation between economic growth and political change is generally curvilinear, that characteristically economic growth does not drive the state to give up its arbitrary power gradually as social forces gain in strength (Arat 1988). Rather, in these circumstances, the state is more apt to hold out as long as it can, giving in to democratization only at a higher level of growth when the balance of power between it and society has finally tipped—not partially, but as a whole.

But what about the experience at higher levels of growth? If our model holds, we should expect the economy then to have become too complex for the state to manage alone. We should also expect that at least some of the new social classes would have become too large and politically conscious to be willing any longer to defer to the judgments of the bureaucracy or to be excluded from the political process. An important threshold should be crossed, the internal balance of power should tip, and authoritarian rule should give way to a democratic transformation. And that, we submit, is exactly what happened or is happening in several Asia-Pacific countries that have entered or are about to enter the status of advanced economies.

The democratization of Japan occurred, of course, in the early postwar years at the direction of foreign occupying forces. It might not have been so thorough if it had not been for those forces, and it might not have been accomplished at precisely that time. Nevertheless, the wide welcome given that transformation, together with the rapid growth that followed it, suggests that the pressures of the economy, the society, and the polity were already driving toward exactly such a change. During the early part of the century Japanese society had been transformed with the growth of industry, which necessitated urbanization, the spread of education, and the growth of both the working and middle classes as well as a business elite. The war and its aftermath provided the occasion for the democratization of Japan, but democracy was imposed on a society that was already prepared to receive it.

The cases of South Korea and Taiwan are less ambiguous. Throughout the 1950s, 1960s, and 1970s, the pressure for political change had been intensifying as the economies had been growing from developing to newly industrializing levels, but it was not until they approached the threshold of advanced status that the political crisis came to a head. By that time, around the mid-1980s, the economy in each had clearly become too complex for a small bureaucratic center to handle; greater decentralization and privatization seemed imperative if the growth was to continue. A better economic plan was needed; and better techniques had to be devised for mobilizing the emerging social forces to support the plan. And in each, the modern classes had become too large and too politically conscious for them to accept any longer the low levels of pseudoparticipation that have been offered hitherto. To be sure, Taiwan is proceeding at a slower pace than South Korea, but both would seem to be engaged in the same kind of historic political transformation that our model suggests.

Thus, the political impact of economic growth on the political systems of Asia-Pacific countries would seem generally to correspond to the pattern we have derived. Nevertheless, there remain nagging questions that cannot be ignored. If a high level of income is such an important element in this transformation, how, for example, can one explain the restoration of democracy in the Philippines at a time when most of its citizens had hardly begun to experience economic improvement, and how can one explain the recent liberalizing pressures in China at an even lower income level? How does one explain the quasi-democratic systems of Malaysia and Thailand if growth at the early and intermediate stages is so conducive to unstable authoritarianism? And if high income levels have driven Japan, South Korea, and Taiwan to democratize—or, in Japan's case, to accept democracy or, in Taiwan's case, to begin the process—why did not Singapore, with a per capita income level roughly twice as high as those of South Korea and Taiwan, not follow suit? In fact, why did it not set the pace?

## Influence of Other Factors

Our model has been derived from a composite of the experiences of nine different countries on the artificial premise that all other factors are equal, that, for example, all the geographic, social, political, cultural, and external forces that make up the tangled web of a particular society have no independent effect on the shape or evolution of its political regime. Reality, of course, is far different. To be sure, most of these other forces are affected by the processes unleashed by economic growth, but they also contribute independently to the development of the political system. The political outcomes of the processes unleashed by economic growth are sometimes augmented, sometimes mitigated, and indeed on occasion overwhelmed by these same forces. What we have is a theory not of prediction, but of probability. In a specific case, therefore, it is a critical matter whether these other forces are in large part supportive of or obstructive to the normal pattern of growth's influence. In the early and intermediate stages of growth in the Asia-Pacific region, to what degree do they advance, retard, or otherwise modify the tendency toward instability and authoritarianism? At the more advanced stage of growth, what is their impact on the tendency toward reform and democratization?

## Geographic Factors

The importance of differences in resource endowments among the countries of the Asia-Pacific region has already been noted. Here we should like to point out several other geographic factors, particularly size and regionalism, that have been significant in the evolution of the political systems of certain of these countries.

*Size*

Singapore, after all, is no larger than a medium-sized city. It lacks the space to produce its own food, supply its own water, dig its own minerals, or retreat into in time of military emergency. Moreover, its small population means that its armed forces must be tiny in comparison to those of its neighbors. One should hardly be surprised that a deep sense of insecurity pervades the society and inclines the citizens to turn more to authority for protection than its economic level might lead one otherwise to expect. At the same time, Singapore's small size means that its population forms a relatively intimate community, one in which information is widely shared, conformity is likely to be encouraged, and dissidence can be almost instantly detected and effectively suppressed.

China's geographic situation is almost the opposite. It is in fact so large that conditions in one part of the country can be significantly different from those in another. We have referred to statistics on a national basis, statistics that clearly place China at a low level of economic development—and consequently a low level also of social mobilization. How, then, can one explain, for example, the upwelling of intellectual protest in the period of the Hundred Flowers movement in the late 1950s and again in 1986 and 1989? At least one explanation must surely be that in some ways a massive country like China must be thought of not as a single entity, but as a collection of regions and subregions, each as large as many of the separate medium-sized countries of the world, and each at a somewhat different stage of economic development. With that in mind, it is not difficult to understand that in the more highly developed regions, such as those around the coastal cities in Fujian and Guangdong with their extensive ties to Hong Kong and overseas Chinese generally, growth has been faster and social mobilization has proceeded further than in the country at large. The modern classes compose a larger share of the population in those regions than in the nation at large, and the political consequences in these areas, so long as they are not constrained, are quite similar in character and scale to those in countries at the intermediate level of growth—as became evident in the intellectuals' protest in Beijing and Shanghai in May and June 1989 and the apparent weakness in the repression that followed in the South.

*Regionalism*

Regionalism is another important factor in almost all pregrowth societies, but, to the extent that its divisions are not reinforced by communal differences, its role tends to decline as systems of communication and transportation are improved and national education systems, national markets, and other national institutions are formed. Nevertheless, it remains a particularly marked feature of Korean politics as well as of the politics of the four developing countries—and of China, as we have already noted. To varying degrees in each, power at the center is checked either by regional blocs of voters and by regional factions of officials or by both, thereby constraining authoritarianism and strengthening the pressures for liberalization, and in Korea for democratization.

## Social Factors

Economic growth does not, of course, take place in a social vacuum. Different societies already have different class structures and communal patterns, which in one way or another continue to influence the nature of the political regime regardless of the speed of economic growth. The presence of relatively autonomous social classes and communal groups can make democratization easier or at least make it harder to maintain an authoritarian regime, while their absence often provides a favorable environment for authoritarianism.

*Inherited Class Structure*

In the first section of this chapter the evolution of the class structure as a result of economic growth was seen as a major factor causing, first, political instability in authoritarian systems and, finally, political change in the direction of liberalization and democratization. But not all characteristics of the class structure of a particular country are the result of recent economic change. Countries also inherit part of their class structure from the past. Pressures emanating from this inherited class structure may outweigh the demands of the new social classes produced by economic change. It is also possible that some features of the old class structure may favor democratization while others may retard it. In countries where there are no strong inherited social classes outside the government bureaucracy, we can expect the state to be able to rule for a considerable period without having to take much account of extrabureaucratic interests, but in countries where there are strong inherited classes independent of the state, we would expect the state to be compelled to respond to their pressures. In such circumstances the inherited class structure would tend to act as a check on authoritarianism and make democratization easier.

Among such inherited classes, experiences elsewhere suggest that the big-landlord and the peasant classes may be the most significant. In the Asia-Pacific region, such a big-landlord class exists only in the Philippines—a factor that helps to explain the longevity of the postindependence democratic system as well as the eventual collapse of the Marcos dictatorship in spite of the low level of per capita income. In the Philippines a regionally dispersed big-landlord class had been allowed to develop under Spanish colonialism in the nineteenth century. It consolidated its position under American rule in the first half of the twentieth century. After independence, land reform programs sponsored by several presidents were far too modest to weaken it fundamentally. Under the democratic system the power of the central government was checked partly by the real political power wielded by the landlords in their own regions. At the same time, rivalries between landlord interests helped to ensure that the two-party democratic system continued until the crisis of the early 1970s, when President Marcos established his authoritarian martial-law regime. The landlord class formed much of the so-called oligarchy that Marcos tried but failed to break, and its reassertion contributed to the fall of Marcos and the restoration of a democratic system after 1986.

In no other Asia-Pacific country has such an independent, large landlord class survived. In Japan most landlords lost their properties at the end of the war. In Korea and Taiwan, Japanese landlordism did not outlast the colonial era, and domestic landlords were swept away by land reform. Large landlords were also swept away in China, in the course of the land reform in the early 1950s. In the resource-rich areas in Southeast Asia, where the plantation sector in colonial days had been almost completely owned by foreigners, the large holdings passed with independence largely into government or government-related hands. In Indonesia, Dutch plantations were nationalized in the 1950s. In Malaysia, the main British plantations passed into the hands of government-connected companies in the 1970s and early 1980s. Singapore, of course, is an urban island without a rural hinterland.

As for the inherited peasantry in the developing countries of Southeast Asia, it has remained, generally speaking, mired in poverty and politically inert except when mobilized by the left as in Indonesia in the 1950s and early 1960s and in the Philippines in the 1970s and 1980s. In Thailand and Malaysia as well as Indonesia since 1966 and many parts of the Philippines today, peasant acceptance of the status quo, whether authoritarian or quasi-democratic, has been achieved in large part through the peasantry's integration into ubiquitous networks of patron-client ties. The peasantry has therefore usually been a force for stability and the maintenance of the existing order.

Differences in the inherited business class have also been significant, in both size and ethnic composition. In some of the Asia-Pacific societies—Japan and the NIEs, as well as China—this group had no ethnic burden, but in most of the developing countries of Southeast Asia, it had an overwhelming preponderance of Chinese, so that it was ethnically distinct from the indigenous population. In Indonesia and Thailand, where the Chinese minority is small, this has made it particularly reluctant to assert itself publicly lest it increase the discrimination it suffered. Instead, it has sought close ties to the government through patronage arrangements, although there have been signs since the late 1970s of increasing independence in Thailand, partly because assimilation has been much easier than in Indonesia. In Malaysia, the Chinese business group, although on the defensive, has been more able to protect its interests. The Chinese community there makes up about 30 percent of the population, giving its business leaders a base of political support that is not present elsewhere. Among the developing countries, it is only in the Philippines that the indigenous component of the inherited business class was relatively high, a fact, together with its larger size, that helps to explain why that class has dared to take more significant political initiatives at lower levels of growth than did its neighbors—as, for example, in pursuit of democratization during the latter part of the Marcos regime.

*Communalism*

The degree to which each society has been divided by ethnic, religious, and cultural differences among its indigenous inhabitants or between its indigenous inhabitants and later immigrants, has been a powerful force in the politics of a number of Asia-Pacific countries apart from its consequences for the emergence of an independent business class.

Generally speaking, where these divisions have been deep, they have been seen as threats to national unity and have provided additional justification for authoritarianism regardless of the dynamics of economic growth. In Indonesia, for example, where the Javanese are the largest single community (although constituting only 45 percent of the population), the alienation of various non-Javanese communities was a principal cause of the regional rebellions that broke out in the 1950s, and the felt need to suppress them was an important rationale for the authoritarian regime that followed. In Taiwan, all during the period of early and intermediate growth, politics was embittered by the conflict between the "mainlanders," a minority that came to the island with the Kuomintang in the immediate postwar period and seized control, and the majority "Taiwanese," also Han Chinese, but whose ancestors came to Taiwan a century or more ago and who differed in dialect, devotion to the island, and historic experience, having been ruled by the Japanese for fifty years. For an entire generation, during the period of early and intermediate growth, martial law was justified in part as essential for the maintenance of "mainlander" Kuomintang power in the face of the hostility of the activists in the "Taiwanese" majority.

On the other hand, in the countries where democratization has taken place—Japan and Korea—internal ethnic conflict has not been a problem, and in Taiwan it is not without significance that the Kuomintang has thought it safe to begin democratization only after communal hostilities had begun to subside as a result in large part of the relatively equitable distribution of the benefits of growth and the introduction into the party and the government of a large number of the "Taiwanese" majority.

But do communal divisions necessarily lead to or strengthen authoritarianism? Authoritarianism is the normal response when intercommunal antagonisms express themselves in rioting, rebellion, and civil war. On the other hand, intercommunal rivalries and tensions do not always threaten national survival. In such cases it could be argued that the presence of distinct groups with strong senses of ethnic self-identity can contribute to the balance of political forces that provides a social foundation for democracy or quasi-democracy. The presence of strong ethnic minorities often means that dominant groups have to take such minorities' interests into account and make sure that they are represented in the government. Thus, in Indonesia the country's communal composition made it difficult for any single ethnic group to dominate completely in the years immediately after independence, with the result that it was easier to practice a quasi-democratic system. It was only when ethnic rivalries led to open rebellion and the prospect of separatism that this system proved to be inadequate and was replaced by a more authoritarian regime. Similarly, the communal structure of the Philippines probably represents a barrier to authoritarianism. As no linguistic-cultural community is even remotely near to constituting a majority—the largest group, the Cebuano, making up only 22 percent of the population—the government must consist of representatives from the various communities, all of which are minorities. As a consequence, governments can never be "captured" by a single ethnic or regional group.

In Malaysia, where the society is divided into Malay and other indigenous (60 percent), Chinese (31 percent), and Indian and other (9 percent) communities, the relatively open democracy practiced in the 1960s was greatly restricted following the emergency declared to deal with the racial rioting in 1969. Racial tension again provided the rationale for tightening the screws throughout the 1970s and 1980s. But on balance, it is this same high level of communal consciousness that appears to offer one of the most persuasive explanations of the existence there of a quasi-democracy at a level of economic growth that would seem to have favored authoritarianism. The minorities in Malaysia are both numerically and economically so important that suppression cannot be the only answer. The interests of these minorities must be taken into account and their representatives provided a place in the government—for the sake of political stability as well as for the sake of economic growth. Although the Malaysian government has moved in an authoritarian direction since the beginning of the 1970s, the multicommunal nature of the political elite, despite Malay predominance, provides an important check on the government's powers as interests represented by non-Malay components of the government have to be given at least part of their due, and each party in the ruling coalition has an interest in preserving at the very least a sufficient degree of democratic space to enable it to keep its own supporters mobilized.

## Political Factors

Political change is not caused by economic and social change alone but also has its own dynamic. Even when economic and social factors seem to favor liberalization and democratization, essentially political factors can obstruct and even prevent political change, at least in the short run. Similarly, such factors can push a system in the direction of democratization even when economic and social factors are not especially favorable.

Among the essentially political factors that have affected the types of regime that have evolved in the Asia-Pacific region are the nature of existing political institutions, the degree of elite cohesion, and the influence of personalities and fortuitous events.

### Political Institutions

The impact of rapid economic growth on a political system takes place through existing political institutions, which are gradually modified as a result of that growth. The types of political institutions that had been established in the Asia-Pacific region before modern growth began differed greatly from each other. In some countries political parties were strong, in others weak. In some the military was strong and highly politicized, but in others weak or relatively professional in outlook. The strength of the bureaucracy must also be taken into account. These differences have had significant effects on the evolution of the political systems involved.

In Japan, following the occupation, a democratic system was firmly established independently of the process of economic development, although it is undeniable that economic success contributed greatly to the legitimacy of the new system. Strong political parties were encouraged, the discipline of the bureaucracy was reinforced, and the military was placed firmly under civilian control. But, as was suggested earlier, party and bureaucratic institutions had a long history in Japan on which to build, and the trauma of defeat and occupation effectively weakened and depoliticized the military.

In most of the other countries of the Asia-Pacific region, political parties and democratic institutions had failed to develop strong roots by the time that rapid economic growth began. In China, the Communist party was completely dominant and permitted no challenge to its monopoly of power. Similarly, in Taiwan, the KMT was identified with the state and did not perform the normal representative functions of political parties in democracies. In Korea, the old political parties were easily pushed aside when the military took power in 1962, and in Thailand political parties had no real roots in society and were periodically banned by military-dominated governments.

In the ex-colonies of Southeast Asia, however, political parties had developed either with the encouragement of the colonial power, as in the Philippines, or as part of nationalist movements demanding the end of colonialism. This did not, however, ensure that a democratic political system would become entrenched. In Indonesia the political parties were soon discredited because of their failure to establish strong and effective governments during the period of liberal democracy immediately after independence. There had been, after all, no single party leading the nationalist struggle. Instead, each party had its roots in particular sections of society, representing particular regions, religions, or social classes, and it was the inability of these parties to work out enduring coalition arrangements that contributed to the collapse of the democratic system. On the other hand, in Malaysia the main moderate parties involved in the struggle for independence were able, almost fortuitously, to come to terms with each other. Thus, an initially uneasy coalition among parties representing the Malay, Chinese, and Indian communities was eventually transformed into the alliance that has dominated Malaysian politics ever since. It is partly the ability of the ruling alliance (now expanded and known as the National Front) to guarantee its own electoral victories that explains why opposition parties have been given relatively wide, although limited, scope to mobilize support, with the result that a quasi-democratic system has become firmly entrenched in Malaysia. In Singapore, too, a strong political party emerged from the nationalist struggle for independence, but, in contrast to Malaysia, the opposition was severely crushed, leaving opposition parties with little more than token forces in Singapore.

In the Philippines, on the other hand, the emergence of nonideological parties on the American model was encouraged by the United States as the colonial power, and for more than a quarter of a century after independence, regular elections were held in which power was transferred back and forth between the two major parties. Nevertheless, the parties were not sufficiently institutionalized to prevent the introduction of martial law under Marcos, and although constitutional democracy was restored after the fall of Marcos, the old party system did not reappear immediately or in the same form.

For most of the Asia-Pacific countries in the early and intermediate stages of growth, the main alternatives to party rule have been rule by the civil bureaucracy and the armed forces or both—that is, by the instruments of the state in which society has usually had only a small influence. In some cases the bureaucracy and military have ruled together or in association with a dominant party or individual. The character of these instruments, therefore, has been important in determining the degree and duration of authoritarianism as well as the timing and the ease or difficulty in making the transition to democracy at higher levels of growth.

States with strong and able civil bureaucracies have been able to meet the needs of the citizenry more effectively, thereby deterring the mobilization of social opposition. They have also been advantaged in exercising authoritarian control. States with weak, corrupt, and factionalized bureaucracies, on the other hand, have had greater difficulty meeting citizen needs and have had to rely more heavily on coercion by a party or army for regime maintenance.

Imperial China, of course, had the longest bureaucratic tradition, but by the twentieth century its selection and decision-making processes had broken down, and in any event, the long tradition had been destroyed by the politicization that had occurred first under the Kuomintang and then under the Communist party. The state was, therefore, seriously handicapped in advancing growth, on which its legitimacy has partly depended, and was forced to rely more heavily than it might otherwise have done on the party, the armed forces, and other instruments of coercion.

Indonesia also found little to build on, the Dutch colonial administration having been relatively small and having recruited relatively few colonial people into its service. The Philippines was slightly better off, modern concepts of administration having been introduced by the United States; however, the American emphasis on political and civil, rather than bureaucratic, action did not result in a highly trained Filipino officialdom. Unfortunately, postindependence developments did not protect it against either politicization or corruption, which reached a peak in the Marcos period. Thailand, on the other hand, had not been colonized and had not been so seriously penetrated by modern, external practices. It also had a centuries-old tradition of government administration that had served the premodern monarchy efficiently. Nevertheless, by the time economic growth began to mobilize the society, the bureaucracy had become factionalized, inefficient, and often corrupt.

But in the other states in the region, the quality of the bureaucracies was relatively high when growth began. This was the product in Japan of an unbroken tradition of meritocratic selection and disciplined and honest decision-making procedures going back centuries. Imperial Japan introduced the same principles in Korea and Taiwan, where they also inherited the prestige of the unbroken older tradition of Chinese-style practice. The British played a similar role in their colonies, which were to become Malaysia and Singapore. Each of these bureaucracies had to be reoriented to cope with the problems of growth, but this has been easier to do than to create an efficient bureaucracy de novo, and there can be no question of the advantage this has conferred on their respective states, despite various weaknesses, in maintaining growth and thereby securing a higher degree of public support than might otherwise have been the case.

As we have pointed out, at the higher stages of economic growth even an efficient and technically skilled bureaucracy cannot alone handle the complexities involved and must call on the help of society and finally defer in large part to it (Singapore's size making it somewhat of an exception). While most bureaucracies, skilled as well as unskilled, face that issue unwillingly and may therefore obstruct for a time the reforms and ultimate transformation that seem to be required, the most disciplined bureaucracies with the longest unbroken experience, including those in Japan, Korea, and Taiwan, seem to make the adjustment best.

The character and strength of the military and other coercive establishments also have had a major impact on regime formation and change in this region in the early and intermediate stages of growth, often either as the ruling elite themselves or as the main source of support for a civilian-led authoritarianism. In China the military has been highly politicized, playing a major role in the administration of the economy in significant parts of the country as well as sharing intimately in the political decision making of the state. At the same time the military has been ultimately subordinate to the Communist party. Similarly, in Taiwan, the military was initially politicized but was eventually brought under control through highly efficient infiltration and supervision by the KMT.

In other countries, the military has been an independent political force in its own right. In Korea the military has had a powerful role model in the U.S. armed forces, with which it has been intimately involved since the Korean war. The professional backbone is therefore stronger than one might imagine in a country emerging from colonialism under Japan, whose prewar and wartime military had been highly politicized. Nevertheless, particularly under the strain of the northern confrontation, various of its middle-level officers became increasingly distrustful of the ability of civilian politicians and officials to preserve the nation. From the spring of 1961 to the summer of 1987, such officers moved in to establish first the Park and then the Chun regimes, but they did not so much displace the civilians as constrain or guarantee the execution of their policies, a role that seems to have made it easier for them to pull back in the summer of 1987—by which time civilian opposition forces had become formidable—and permit the transformation toward democracy to take place.

In Indonesia, the military has always been involved in politics, having been founded in 1945 in order to participate in the armed struggle for independence, and it makes no pretense of being an apolitical, professional force. The Indonesian armed forces' doctrine recognizes its "dual function" as an organization concerned with the broad welfare of the nation as well as defense and security in a narrow sense. Thus, after the collapse of the democratic system in the 1950s the military moved in first as a partner in Sukarno's "Guided Democracy" and then as the dominant element in the government under Suharto's "New Order." In Thailand also, the military has always participated in politics, and for much of the postwar period it has played a dominant role while at other times it has stood in the wings ready to intervene if circumstances warranted it.

In the other three countries the military inherited professional, apolitical traditions from the colonial power. These traditions have remained strong in Malaysia and Singapore, where civilian rule has in any case been effective, but were greatly eroded during the period of martial law in the Philippines when President Marcos needed military support to suppress the political parties and other opponents. The military in the Philippines became increasingly politicized, but also fragmented, and in the post-Marcos period several factions launched coup attempts although the leadership always remained loyal to the constituted civilian authority.

## Elite Cohesion

The nature of the political elite and the degree of elite cohesion constitute another important factor that has its own dynamic independent of broader economic and social factors. The presence of a long-established and cohesive elite can often obstruct political change even when other factors are pushing in the direction of change. Authoritarian rulers are usually able to maintain themselves in power as long as they can retain the loyalty of other members of the ruling elite; however, once that elite becomes divided, whether along personal, political, communal, or other lines, it is less capable of meeting challenges from outside itself. When the elite is divided, it is often difficult for it to determine its strategy in facing opposition, and there is always the possibility that some of its components might even ally themselves with that opposition. The less cohesive an elite, the less it is able to resist pressures toward liberalization and democratization.

In Korea and Taiwan, the dominant elites, headed by the military and the Kuomintang, respectively, were essentially united up to the 1980s, in terms of both support for the particular individuals holding the post of president and agreement on the basic political and economic strategies of the government. Despite growing popular opposition to the government in Korea, authoritarian rule remained firm until sections of the elite began to reassess the long-term viability of the regime. Although open factionalism was not obvious in the regime of Chun Doo Hwan, large blocs among the ruling elements—the military, the bureaucrats, the technocrats, and their political supporters—simply became unwilling, in the face of the national reaction to the bloody suppression of the Kwangju uprising in May 1980 and the massive, nationally supported street demonstrations in the spring of 1987, to maintain their power any longer by force. Something similar seems to be happening in Taiwan, where the liberalization is being advanced by a Kuomintang that is itself undergoing a liberalization—a revitalization by the recruitment of the educated young, including many "Taiwanese" who might otherwise have gone over to the opposition, and a restructuring of the thinking of the leadership that began under Chiang Ching-kuo's chairmanship. The transition in Taiwan is still in progress, but there, as in Korea, the transformation is being made through the challenging of old ideas within the ruling group without, initially at least, that group's losing its dominant position. One possible reason for the less dramatic pace of reform in Taiwan may be the capacity of the ruling elite to maintain its essential unity of approach. In Singapore, however, there have been few signs of liberalization, and the government remains firmly under the grip of the PAP. The PAP leadership has been extraordinarily united since the party's formation in the 1950s, and there have been no signs of factionalism since the breakaway of the Barisan Sosialis in 1963. The lack of factional conflict within the ruling party has given little opportunity for the emergence of a strong opposition.

Of the developing countries, Indonesia, too, has remained under cohesive leadership since the military takeover of power in 1966. In Indonesia the government has been controlled by a single institution, the military, with its own ethos and objectives. Although factionalism has been common, the rivalries are among Suharto loyalists and have not involved challenges to Suharto himself. In the other three developing countries, governments have been far less cohesive, with the result that government repression of opposition has been less firm, and opposition groups have been able to exert some influence on government policy.

In Thailand, the military-dominated government of Thanom and Praphat collapsed in 1973 in the face of mass demonstrations, partly because of internal divisions within the military that culminated in the unwillingness of the army commander to suppress the demonstrations. During the next three years of civilian party rule, internal rivalries prevented the military from reasserting itself, different military factions forming links with different civilian parties. Although the military intervened in coups in 1976 and 1977 and once again established itself as the main political force in the country, it was still unable to overcome factional rivalries, with the result that it could not reestablish its pre-1973 dominance. Instead, rival military factions sought to bolster themselves against each other by, among other things, trying to win over civilian support. Although the first two prime ministers after 1977 were former supreme commanders of the armed forces, they increasingly relied as much on civilian allies as the military to remain in power; the third prime minister, also a former general, clearly relies primarily on his own party machine and the alliances he has struck in parliament. As long as the military remains internally divided, it is unable to take complete power, while the longer it remains divided, the more scope there is for the civilian parties to extend their organizations and consolidate their popular support. Although the quasi-democracy in Thailand rests on shaky foundations and is probably still vulnerable to a military challenge if some future military leader were to establish unchallenged dominance over the armed forces, the longer the present system lasts, the deeper its roots will become.

In the Philippines, too, the downfall of the Marcos dictatorship was caused in part by factional rivalries. Open competition among sections of the political elite had been an established part of the pre–martial law democratic system and had been only partially suppressed after the declaration of martial law in 1972. In contrast to Thailand, where the pre-1973 regime had been dominated by a single institution—the army—which, no matter how factionalized, still had a common ethos and institutional interest, in the Philippines the Marcos regime itself consisted of coteries of politicians, bureaucrats, businessmen, and military officers who seemed tied to the regime more by personal than by institutional interests. The lack of institutional domination of the state in the Philippines, in contrast to military domination in Thailand and Indonesia or party domination in Malaysia and Singapore, made the restoration of democracy much easier.

In Malaysia, however, competition within the political elite has been institutionalized in the multiparty National Front government. Because the rival components of the Malaysian government have strong communal roots, as discussed earlier, the check on authoritarianism is all the more effective. Although the Malaysian political system has steadily become more authoritarian since the 1969 racial riots, the government continues to be fairly responsive to demands from society expressed through its constituent parties, the opposition parties, and various interest groups. In the past few years, however, there has been a marked increase in internal factionalism within the government parties, which for several years virtually immobilized the main Chinese party, the MCA, and has now, more significantly, culminated in a split in the dominant Malay party, UMNO. While factionalism within UMNO might be expected to further check authoritarian tendencies in the government leadership, there is also the danger in the Malaysian communal context that rival UMNO groups will try to outbid each other in demonstrating their commitment to the "Malay cause" and bring about a further increase in racial tensions, which could threaten the whole political order and thus create conditions in which authoritarian intervention is more possible.

Like Malaysia, Japan also has institutionalized competition within the ruling elite. Although the LDP has remained in power since 1955, it has never been a tightly knit party under cohesive, PAP-style leadership. Factions within the party are formally organized and in sharp competition with each other. Two results of factional competition have been a steady turnover of prime ministers and regular cabinet reshuffles. Governments are never monopolized by any single faction but always consist of coalitions of major LDP groups (in the Nakasone administration, joined also by one of the smaller opposition parties). The inability of any one faction to maintain domination of the government for long periods makes it difficult to establish the sort of governmental cohesion needed for authoritarian repression. Thus, opposition parties have flourished, and a wide range of independent social organizations are able to carry out activities in defense of their interests.

While rivalries within the elite act as a break on any trend toward authoritarianism, democratization will, however, be endangered if conflict reaches a level at which effective government is undermined. Democracy was abandoned in Indonesia in 1957, for example, partly because the numerous political parties seemed unable to work out enduring coalition arrangements among themselves at a time when regional movements were threatening the unity of the state. Korea's earlier democratic experiment under Chang Myon in 1960–61 ended in a military coup when discipline could not be imposed on the disparate elements seeking power. Similarly, the brief period of political party rule in Thailand after 1973 ended in 1976 when parliament was unable to produce an effective coalition government.

*Fortuitous Events and Personalities*

In seeking to explain political change we should not overlook the sometimes crucial importance of "special factors"—the unexpected and fortuitous events that take place for reasons largely unconnected with politics. Nor should we ignore the significance of particular personalities in the national leadership at particularly crucial times.

Thus, for example, we can ask whether the transition to democracy in Korea would have been as rapid as it was in 1987 if it had not been for the coincidence that Seoul was to host the Olympic Games in 1988. Would the Thai military have remained as politically fragmented as it was in the 1970s if General Kris Sivara, the man who had refused to fire on students during the 1973 uprising, had not died shortly afterward? How would Thai politics have developed without the restraining influence of the particular man who happens to be king? Would UMNO have split in Malaysia if the leadership of the party had passed to a less abrasive personality than Dr. Mahatir? Does the personality of Lee Kuan Yew provide the real explanation for the thorough suppression of virtually all opposition in Singapore? What influence has Javanese mysticism had on the political decisions of both Sukarno and Suharto? Would Philippine politics have taken the course it did if Benigno Aquino had not decided to return to Manila and the fateful decision to murder him had not been taken? And can anything be said about China without taking account of the personalities of Mao Zedong or Deng Xiaoping? The precise impact of factors such as these is difficult, if not impossible, to measure, but their significance should not be ignored.

## Political Culture

To what extent can deviations from the expected pattern be explained in terms of political culture, thought of as embracing both basic cultural attitudes and political ideology? Autocratic rule was no stranger to the region and in fact had been the customary form of government in most of the Asia-Pacific countries. Japan had been under authoritarian rule until its defeat in World War II, and autocratic tradition remained strong. China had experienced a succession of autocratic rule at the hands of the imperial dynasts, the warlords, the KMT, and the Communist party. Like Thailand, where absolute monarchy was succeeded by indigenous authoritarian rule in 1932, most of the other countries had long traditions of centralized autocratic rule before falling under what was usually no less autocratic colonial rule: Korea and Taiwan under Japan, and the other countries of Southeast Asia under various Western powers. But despite the bad memories of some of these experiences, there were also other memories of rule by "good kings" of the past as well as habits of deference and obedience that continued to shape common perceptions of how modern governments should behave. It was therefore not surprising that most of these societies turned to the state when the requirements of growth first began to emerge, and, indeed, for much of the population in many countries, authoritarian rule is still seen as natural or at least acceptable.

These historical experiences were not, however, identical. To some extent the Western colonial powers successfully implanted a liberal tradition alongside more traditional ideas. Liberalism took deepest root in the Philippines, where there was no tradition of great indigenous kingdoms or sultanates (except in Mindanao in the south) before the Spanish established their centralized autocracy. Then the Philippines came under the colonial rule of the United States, which preached democracy for more than forty years, established democratic institutions by stages, and gradually transferred power into Filipino hands. When independence came and the problem of growth was presented, society had already penetrated the state, and a democratic political regime was in place. At first, society was not prepared to accept very much control or even guidance by the state to hasten the course of economic growth. While the strength of the inherited liberal tradition was not sufficient to prevent the imposition of martial law by President Marcos in 1972, it did later contribute to his overthrow in 1986.

In Malaysia and Singapore, the British accepted the idea of preparing their colonies for independence only toward the end of the colonial era. They had, however, propagated the rule of law and the habits of judicial procedure, and they introduced at least partially elected assemblies, so that when independence did come, democratic political forms seemed natural, although they were qualified by security provisions designed to face Communist insurgency. The idea of democracy and related ideas such as the rule of law remain as important parts of the political tradition of both Malaysia and Singapore, and to some extent represented obstacles to the authoritarian trends of the 1970s and 1980s. Democratic ideas were far less developed by the Dutch in Indonesia and were rigorously excluded by the Japanese from Korea and Taiwan. Democratic ideology (at least in the Western sense) was also weak in China.

Religion, in the form of either institutions or beliefs, also contributes to political culture. Traditional religion—or modernized versions of it—can give powerful support to the state, as did state Shintoism in prewar and wartime Japan. In contemporary Thailand, Buddhism tends to be identified with the state, while in the Philippines the Catholic church has helped to legitimize both the Marcos regime and its successor. Indonesian governments under both Sukarno and Suharto have derived part of their legitimacy, at least in the most populous island of Java, by adhering to the practices of ancient Javanese mysticism, while in Malaysia, Islam is the official religion.

But the legitimizing role of religion is ambivalent. The church in the Philippines also played a major role in the downfall of Marcos, while Islam provides a challenge to the governments of both Malaysia and Indonesia. Indeed, in some countries, such as Malaysia and Indonesia, religion tends to reinforce communal differences and to fragment political culture. The contribution of religion to political culture, therefore, depends on the particulars of the case. In some circumstances in the Asia-Pacific region, it has backed authoritarianism, but in other cases it has played a crucial role in undermining the legitimacy of authoritarian regimes.

The ideological content of the political culture may be as important as perceptions inherited from the past. Most Asia-Pacific states in the early stage of state formation found it desirable to try to bolster their authority by disseminating general principles on which the political regime was founded. Only three, however, presented "elaborate and guiding ideologies," to use Juan Linz's phrase (Linz 1973: 185). In prewar and wartime Japan it took the form of an emperor-centered Japanism. In post-1949 China, it was Marxism-Leninism-Maoism. In Taiwan, following the arrival of the Kuomintang, it was the "Three People's Principles" of Sun Yat-sen. These ideologies sought to justify a concentration of power in the state in a period when growth was in its early and intermediate stages and continued to favor state domination later. In Japan the dominant ideology was replaced only following the collapse of the state itself at the end of the war, while in China it continues to justify the limitation of democratic expression.

But in the case of Taiwan, the Kuomintang from the beginning championed an ideology of tutelage. The party's role was not to rule forever, but to prepare the way for democracy. The transition seemed a long way off in the Chiang Kai-shek and Chiang Ching-kuo years, when the ideology strongly backed the authoritarian structure. But once the economy reached a point where democratization pressures had become acute in the 1980s, the democratic construct in the party's ideology provided a serviceable rationale for party members and oppositionists alike to begin the democratizing transformation that had long been promised.

The other Asia-Pacific countries in our sample, including contemporary Japan, do not have "elaborate and guiding ideologies." Those that have already adopted democratic systems—Japan, the Philippines, and South Korea—have rather a broad commitment to democracy itself together with varying emphases on nationalism, capitalism, growth, and welfare. Others have gone farther to adopt specific principles that are more aptly described, again following Linz, as "mentalities" rather than "ideologies." Here the principles are looser and broader and are less capable of serving as guides to policy. Indonesia's Pancasila (Five Principles), Thailand's reverence for "Nation, King, and Religion," Malaysia's *Rukunegara* (National Principles), and Singapore's neo-Confucianism provide examples. In these cases governments also try to appropriate the concept of democracy and claim to be working toward some form of "democracy Asian-style" in which the national leadership is held in high esteem and opposition muted.

In all the countries of the region, however, democratic aspirations are present. In some, governments themselves have adopted democratic procedures, while in others, significant sections of the population have raised the banner of democracy in their challenge to existing governments and political systems. The strength of such popular commitment to democracy, however, varies enormously among the countries of the region.

## External Environment

One of the most complex influences on the evolution of the political systems of the Asia-Pacific region has been the external environment. Its influence is felt in all aspects of these regimes and in varying degrees, from threatening to competitive to supportive. In the military sphere, it is a common observation that the more threatening the environment—or the more it is perceived to be threatening—the greater the power of the state grows. Thus, in the early and intermediate stage of growth, the sense of military threat in this region would seem to have augmented the normal pressures for authoritarianism that growth engenders. Certainly, the danger perceived from the North gave the Korean government extensive popular support for strengthening the instruments of authority in the Rhee, Park, and Chun regimes. The same may be said for China, facing the United States and then later the USSR; Taiwan, facing China across the Straits; Thailand, facing Vietnam; and Singapore, a small country with large neighbors. The counterpart of these threats in the other developing states consisted of the armed, Communist-led insurrections in the 1940s, 1950s, and 1960s, all of which had domestic roots but international connections.

To what extent has the perception of external military threat blocked the process of political change? Military defeat and the subsequent security treaty with the United States eliminated that block for Japan. Korea and Taiwan gained similar protection from a close defense relationship with the United States, but in the end it was only when the immediate military threat from their neighbors began to ease that either felt it safe to begin the transition to democracy. On the other hand, the continuing intensity of the sense of vulnerability that Singapore feels as a small Chinese island in a vast Malay sea may go a long way to explain its reluctance to take the same road.

Of course, Singapore is not worried only or perhaps even primarily about external military threats. Its leaders seem to feel extremely vulnerable to what are perceived as ethnic threats from their neighbors, and to cultural and economic threats from the world at large, on which the Singapore economy is so dependent. No doubt the small size of Singapore heightens these feelings, but to varying degrees they are pervasive throughout most of the region, where the impact of the Western media, Western and Japanese multinationals, and international financial institutions seems often to crowd out local interests and local values.

Enough has already been said to underline the influence of the external environment in the economic sphere—the roles that the openness of its markets, the size of its demand, and the availability of its capital and technology play in the character and strength of a country's economic growth. But there is an additional influence that calls for special emphasis—the role that foreign knowledge, attitudes, and values play in changing the capabilities, desires, and expectations of a local population. The correlation among states in this region between the degree of political liberalization and the extent of their cultural and intellectual openness is too high to be accidental. Clearly, cultural openness drives in the same ultimately liberalizing direction as economic growth.

## The Deviant Cases

It would certainly be desirable if these various noneconomic forces could be measured with precision, and if some coherent theory were available to explain their interaction,; but there is no such theory available, and it is beyond the scope of this work to attempt to build one, our own more modest aim having been to try to throw some additional light only on the political impact of economic growth. Nevertheless, it does remain for us to try at least to show how the deviation of certain countries in our sample, namely, Singapore, the Philippines, and to an extent China, from the flying geese pattern, which we believe economic growth helps to propel, can be persuasively explained by the impact of some of these other noneconomic factors.

The PAP government of Singapore presents a unique case in the region where, in spite of the high level of economic growth attained, the countervailing forces that growth would be expected to have nurtured have not in fact pressed as hard for democratization as might have been expected. It is not that social mobilization failed to take place. Growth did produce a complex, differentiated class structure, including a strong middle class and a large working class. Why, then, has neither pressed harder for liberalization? One explanation would appear to be the country's small size, which makes the population more ready to accept discipline in an effort to overcome its perceived vulnerability. Another would

seem to lie in the extraordinary economic achievements of the present government and also in its success in ensuring that the key potential social bases of
political opposition have benefited materially. The Singapore middle class has
clearly prospered, but so has the large working class, despite the absence of a
militant trade union movement. The early low-wage policy was accompanied by
a huge expansion in public housing, schools, and health services, while during
1979–81 the government implemented a series of sharp wage increases. Immigrant laborers, the worst-off section of the Singapore work force, have not
counted politically.

On the side of the state, one may ask as well, why have its leaders been so
much less willing to risk political liberalization than the leaders of Korea and
Taiwan? Here again the small size of the country and its perceived fragilities
would seem to be crucial. Let us list some of them. First, Singapore's lack of a
substantial domestic market makes it extremely dependent on maintaining its
competitive position in world trade, so that it feels it cannot take the risk of an
outbreak of uncontrolled labor demands pushing up costs. Second, Singapore's
overwhelming reliance on foreign capital and its aspiration to consolidate its
position as the regional center for financial and commercial services make it
imperative that its reputation for political stability be maintained. Third, unlike
most Third World governments, the Singapore government has no rural base of
support on which it can fall back in the event of urban political upheaval, so it
has to be doubly sure of its urban base. Fourth, the government is acutely aware
of Singapore's position as a small Chinese community in a vast Malay world.
While the government has no reason to feel threatened by the present governments in neighboring states, it tries to maintain a high level of national discipline
in order to be prepared to meet any emergency in the future. It is particularly
concerned to avoid communal strife at the expense of its Malay minority because
of the likely political implications for its relations with its neighbors. In these
circumstances, democratization seems unlikely until a greater sense of security is
achieved.

The Philippines is unique in the opposite way. It is the only case in the region
where a developing economy is supporting a political democracy, although admittedly one that is resting on foundations that are by no means firm. The Philippine
state, one should recall, came to independence with a fairly long preparatory democratic experience and an ideological devotion to democracy. The state is, in fact, weak,
having arrayed against it an indigenous large-landlord class; a powerful, independent
Catholic church; a middle class with a level of higher education that is unique in the
region; and a growing working class. After a quarter of a century of democracy,
however, the general public's frustration with apparently ineffective government and
a growing fear, especially on the part of the upper and middle classes, of the rising of
the poor under NPA leadership enabled Marcos briefly in the 1970s to try to construct
an authoritarian regime, but the presence of the relatively powerful and independent
interests outside the government and the lack of cohesion and common purpose within

it, including its military component, made it difficult to establish a strong authoritarian regime. The democratic transformation in 1986 was facilitated by the fact that it did not involve the overthrow of the dominant social classes, but rather their restoration to the direct control of the political process, which they had lost under Marcos's rule.

All of this is not to indicate that a strong democratic regime is inevitable in the Philippines. Quite the opposite. The level of economic growth is still too low for the society to be sufficiently mobilized to support such a regime. In years past, the balance between elite interests represented in the government and those in the Congress had prevented strong action to ameliorate the conditions of the increasingly assertive lower classes, represented in part by the recently formed New People's Army (NPA). While it became increasingly clear that Marcos used his authoritarian powers to benefit a small elite of which he was part, he was also able to begin the implementation of limited reforms, especially land reform at the expense of the landlord class and in favor of the peasantry. The post-Marcos restoration of democracy has to a considerable extent returned the Philippines to the pre-1972 situation and the challenges with which the democratic system seemed unable to cope then. The NPA has grown weaker and the government has attracted a number of new and concerned leaders, but democracy without social reform may prove as ineffective after 1986 as it was before 1972.

China, too, has pursued an exceptional path. At least, during the Maoist period, economic growth and many of the mobilizing and reforming pressures that such growth normally generates were forcibly contained. The economic reforms adopted since the 1970s have begun to release these pressures at last. If China were now to follow the pattern of the other Asia-Pacific states, one would expect its communism to soften into a more restrained authoritarian system, in which forces for ultimate political transformation might be expected to grow.

This is not, of course, what the Chinese leadership appears to have in mind. Nor is an ultimate democratic transformation what most of the ruling elites of the authoritarian and quasi-democratic states in the region have in mind. They do not share our view of the dynamics of change. Most of the leaders of these regimes seem to feel that they have now found or are about to find a way to continue economic growth without destabilizing the political systems over which they preside. The formula is sometimes referred to as Chinese, Indonesian, Thai, or Singaporean democracy, or simply democracy Asian-style. Elections have been conducted in each country throughout the authoritarian and, in the case of China, Communist period. These elections vary considerably as to the extent of opposition that is allowed, but in no case can the decision-making elite be said to be selected exclusively by popular vote, freely expressed, and the champions of "Asian democracy" do not believe it should be.

The hallmark of true democracy, they argue, is governmental responsiveness, not to private interests nor to those that emerge successfully from a competitive struggle among such interests as in "the West," but to the common good of the entire community, and in Asia, it is claimed, that result is best guaranteed by having a strong state that is above the control of society's conflicting private interests. Such a state needs instrumentalities for knowing what the people want, for drawing on their experience, and for trying to reach with them a consensus on public policy, but it should reserve ultimate decision making for itself, since only it can rise above private interests to understand and effect the common good.

It is too early to say whether in these instances responsiveness can be secured without responsibility, but history does not make one sanguine. Pregrowth states in the Confucian tradition, from which these constructs would seem partly to be drawn, tended ultimately to be self-serving. In the West, too, the modern corporatist regimes, which have drawn on organic-statist approaches that bear a strong resemblance to those of "Asian democracy," have characteristically tended toward authoritarianism (Stepan 1978: 49–50), and in the end these have not proved sufficiently flexible to cope effectively with the requirements and consequences of sustained growth—without a democratic breakthrough.

The experiences of three of the four most economically advanced Asia-Pacific states—Japan, Korea, and Taiwan (all of which incidentally also have a strong Confucian tradition)—strengthen this skepticism. The pattern in these states seems to be that as growth continues to ever higher levels, it becomes more and more apparent that the structural changes required at one level of growth prove to be inappropriate for the next.

It is of course possible that some more inclusionary form of corporatism, to use Stepan's phrase (1978: 73–113), may be found that would allow greater participation in the political process without completely upsetting the rule of the elites in power. The Malay leadership in Malaysia after all has been experimenting for a number of years with a quasi-democratic system in which the government accepts its responsibility to the electorate, but in which much of the leadership of the Malay, Chinese, and Indian ethnic communities has been coopted into the Barisan Nasional, a national political front in which the most serious intercommunal bargaining takes place.

But what has happened or is happening in the most advanced of the Asia-Pacific economies appears not to be a transition to an inclusionary corporatism. Instead, it is a transformation into a democracy—and a democracy that is not consensual but contestational in form, not "Asian" but "Western." Japan, Korea, and, increasingly, Taiwan provide examples. We disagree, therefore, with these conservative elites. We believe there is a dynamic at work that, so long as growth continues, will drive toward political change and ultimately toward a democratic transformation.

But there is no guarantee that full democracy will be achieved. Many other factors—geographic, social, political, cultural, and external—can slow or even reverse the process.st Our analysis is therefore best seen not as a formula for precise prediction, but as an instrument for sensitizing one to some of the more potent forces with which we shall all have to grapple.

# Bibliography

Abeuva, J. V. 1979. "Ideology and Practice Under the New Society." In *Marcos and Martial Law in the Philippines*, ed. D. A. Rosenberg. Ithaca: Cornell University Press.

Adelman, Irma. 1979. "Growth, Income Distribution and Equity-Oriented Development." In *The Political Economy of Development and Underdevelopment*, ed. Charles K. Wiber. 2d ed. New York: Random House.

Adrian, C., and C. Press. 1964. "Decision Costs in Coalition Formation," *American Political Science Review* 62 (June): 556–63.

Agence France Press, Hong Kong, July 17, 1987, in FBIS no. 137, July 17, 1987, pp. 0–1.

———. June 30, 1988, in FBIS no. 217, July 1, 1988, p. 17.

Akamatsu, Kaname. 1962. "A Historical Pattern of Economic Growth in Developing Countries," *The Developing Economies* (Tokyo). Preliminary Issue, no. 1 (March-August): 3–25.

Almond, G. B., and J. S. Coleman, eds. 1960. *The Politics of the Developing Area*. Princeton: Princeton University Press.

Anderson, Benedict. 1972. *Java in a Time of Revolution*. Ithaca: Cornell University Press.

———. 1978. "Last Days of Indonesia's Suharto?" *Southeast Asia Chronicle*, no. 63: 2–17.

———. 1983. "Old State, New Society: Indonesia's New Order in Comparative Perspective," *Journal of Asian Studies* 42, 3: 477–96.

———. 1988. "Current Data on the Indonesian Military Elite," *Indonesia*, no. 45: 137–60.

Anderson, Benedict, and Ruth McVey. 1971. *A Preliminary Analysis of the October 1, 1965 Coup in Indonesia*. Ithaca: Cornell Modern Indonesian Project.

Apter, David. 1961. "Some Reflections on the Role of Political Opposition in New Nations," *Comparative Studies in Society and History* 4: 154–68.

Arat, Zehra F. 1988. "Democracy and Economic Development: Modernization Revisited," *Contemporary Politics* 21, 1 (October): 21–35.

Asahi Shimbunsha. 1987. *1987 Asahi nenkan* (Asahi yearbook 1987). Tokyo: Asahi Shimbunsha.

———. 1976. *Nihonjin no seiji ishiki* (Political attitudes of Japanese voters). Tokyo: Asahi Shimbunsha.

Asian Development Bank. Various years. *Key Indicators of Developing Member Countries of ADB*. Makati, Philippines: Economic Office, Asian Development Bank.

———. 1971. *Southeast Asia's Economy in the 1970s* [the Hla Myint Report]. London: Longman.

Ayoob, M., and Ng Chee Yuen, eds. 1988. *Southeast Asian Affairs, 1988*. Singapore: Institute of Southeast Asian Studies.

Baldwin, Frank, ed. 1973. *Without Parallel: American-Korean Relationship since 1945*. New York: Pantheon Books.

*Bangkok Post*. Various issues.

Banister, Judith. 1984. "Population Policy and Trends in China, 1978–83," *China Quarterly* 100 (December): 717–41.

Bates, Robert H. 1981. *Markets and States in Tropical Africa*. Berkeley: University of California Press.

Baum, Richard. 1986. "Modernization and Legal Reform in Post-Mao China: The Rebirth of Socialist Legality," *Studies in Comparative Communism* 19 (Summer): 69–103.

Bellows, Thomas. 1970. *The People's Action Party of Singapore: Emergence of a Dominant Party System*. Monograph Series no. 14, Yale University, Southeast Asia Studies. New Haven: Yale University Press.

"Be Prepared for Two or Three Hard Years." 1988. *Renmin ribao*, December 26, in FBIS no. 248, December 27, 1988, pp. 36–37.

Bernstein, Thomas P. 1977. *Up to the Mountains and Down to the Villages: The Transfer of Youth from Urban to Rural China*. New Haven: Yale University Press.

———. 1984. "Stalinism, Famine, and Chinese Peasants: Grain Procurement during the Great Leap Forward," *Theory and Society* 13, 3 (May): 339–77.

Bernstein, Thomas P., and Anonymous. 1983. "Starving to Death in China," *New York Review of Books* 30, 10 (June 16).

Bix, Herbert P. 1973. "Regional Integration: Japan and South Korea in America's Asian Policy." In *Without Parallel: American Korean Relationship since 1945*, ed. Frank Baldwin. New York: Pantheon Books.

Blum, Albert, ed. 1981. *International Handbook of Industrial Relations*. Westport: Greenwood Press.

Bonner, R. 1987. *Waltzing with a Dictator. The Marcoses and the Making of American Policy*. New York: Time Books.

Booth, Anne. 1986. "Survey of Recent Developments," *Bulletin of Indonesian Economic Studies* 20, 1: 83–97.

Booth, Anne, and P. McCawley. 1981. *The Indonesian Economy During the Suharto Era*. Singapore: Oxford University Press.

Bourchier D. 1984. *Dynamics of Dissent in Indonesia: Savito and the Phantom Coup*. Ithaca: Cornell Modern Indonesian Project, Interim Reports Series, no. 63.

Breidenstein, Gerhard. 1973. "Capitalism in South Korea." In *Without Parallel: American-Korean Relationship since 1945*, ed. Frank Baldwin. New York: Pantheon Books.

Bresnan, John F., ed. 1986. *Crises in the Philippines: The Marcos Era and Beyond*. Princeton: Princeton University Press.

Brillantes, A. B. 1987. *Dictatorship and Martial Law: Philippine Authoritarianism in 1972*. Quezon City: Great Books Publisher.

Buchanan, Ian. 1972. *Singapore in Southeast Asia: An Economic and Political Appraisal*. Indon: G. Bell and Sons.

Cardoso, Fernando. 1988. "Entrepreneurs and the Transition Process: The Brazilian Case." In *Transition from Authoritarian Rule*, ed. Guillermo O'Donnell. Baltimore: Johns Hopkins University Press.

Carroll, J. 1965. *The Philippine Manufacturing Entrepreneur*. Ithaca: Cornell University Press.

Chai-Anan Samudavanija. 1971. "The Politics and Administration of the Thai Budgetary Process," Ph.D. dissertation, University of Wisconsin.

———. 1982. *The Thai Young Turks*. Singapore: Institute of Southeast Asian Studies.

————. 1988. "Macro-economic Decision-Making and Management of Economic Policies," paper presented at the conference on Who Determines Thai Economic Policies, Thammasat University, Bangkok, February.

————. 1989. "Thailand: A Stable Semi-Democracy." In *Democracy in Developing Countries: Asia*, ed. Larry Diamond et al. Boulder: Lynne Rienner.

Chai-Anan Samudavanija and Suchit Bunbongkarn. 1985. "Thailand." In *Military-Civilian Relations in Southeast Asia*, ed. Haji Amad Zakaria and Harold Crouch. Singapore: Oxford University Press.

Chai-Anan Samudavanija and Sukhumbhand Paribatra. 1987. "In Search of Balance: Prospects for Stability in Thailand during the Post CPT Era." In *Durable Stability in Southeast Asia*, ed. Kusuma Snitwongse and Sukhumbhand Paribatra. Singapore: Institute of Southeast Asian Studies.

————. 1988. Interviews with ten people who sat on the Joint Public and Private Consultative Committee at the national and provincial levels, in Bangkok, Songkla, and Chiangmai, March–May.

Chan, Anita, Richard Madsen, and Jonathan Unger. 1984. *Chen Village*. Berkeley: University of California Press.

Chan Heng Chee. 1971. *Singapore: The Politics of Survival 1965–1967*. Kuala Lumpur: Oxford University Press.

————. 1975. "Politics in an Administrative State: Where Has Politics Gone?" In *Trends in Singapore*, ed. Seah Chee Meow. Singapore: Singapore University Press.

————. 1984. "Language and Culture in Singapore," *Ilmu Masyarakat*, January–June.

————. 1985. "Singapore." In *Military-Civilian Relations in Southeast Asia*, ed. Haji Ahmad Zakaria and Harold Crouch. Singapore: Oxford University Press.

Chan Heng Chee and Obaid ul Haq, eds. 1987. *S. Rajaratnam: The Prophetic and the Political*. Singapore: Graham Brash.

Chang Won-jong. 1971. "Son'go Kyongje ron" (Electoral economics), *Shin Dong-a*, June: 98–111.

Chattip Nart-supha. 1970. *The Economic Development of Thailand 1956–1965*. Bangkok: Prae Pittaya.

Chen Chieh-hsien. 1977. "The Eighth National Congress of the Kuomintang," *China Forum* 4, 1 (January): 199.

Chen Sheng-shih. 1977. "The Seventh National Congress of the Kuomintang," *China Forum* 4, 1 (January): 199.

Chen Yang-teh. 1978. *T'ai-wan min hsuan ti fang ling tao jen wu pien tung chih fen hsi* (The analysis of leadership change in Taiwan's local elective offices), Ph.D. dissertation, National Chengchi University.

Chen Yun. 1979. "Tiaozheng guomin jingji, jianchi an bili fazhan" (Adjust the national economy; persist in developing according to proportions). In *San Zhong chuan hue yilai: Zhongyao wenjian xuanpian*, ed. Zhonggong Zhongyang Wenjian Yanjiu Shi. Beijing: Renmin Chubanshe, p. 74.

Cheng Tun-jen. 1987a. "Politics of Industrial Transformation: The Case of the East Asian NICs," Ph.D. dissertation, University of California, Berkeley.

————. 1987b. "The Rise and Limits of the East Asian NICs," *Pacific Focus* 2, 2 (Fall): 54–55.

————. 1989a. "Democratizing the Quasi-Leninist KMT Regime in Taiwan," *World Politics* (July).

————. 1989b. "Development Strategies and Regime Dynamics: South Korea and Taiwan." In *Manufactured Miracles: Patterns of Development in Latin America and East Asia*, ed. Gary Gereffi and Donald Wyman. Princeton: Princeton University Press.

Cheng Ying. 1988. "Mass Riots on the Mainland Rise One After the Other," *Chiushi nientai* 222 (July 1), in FBIS 128 (July 5, 1988): 39.

Chin Kin Wah, ed. 1987. *Defense Spending in Southeast Asia*. Singapore: Institute of Southeast Asian Studies.

*China Daily*. Various dates.

*Chinese Law and Government*. 1976–77. "Mao Tse-tung: Speeches at the Chengchow Conference" (February and March 1959) 9, 4 (Winter).

*Chung yang jih pao* (Central daily news), August 4, 1987, p. 2.

Coleman, James S. 1960. "Conclusion: The Political Systems of the Developing Area." In *The Politics of the Developing Area*, ed. G. B. Almond and J. S. Coleman. Princeton: Princeton University Press.

"Confidential Document: A Speech of Deng Xiaoping for Restricted Use Only." 1986. *Pai Hsing* (Hong Kong) 122 (June 16), in FBIS 117 (June 18, 1986): W1–2.

Crouch, Harold. 1974. "The 15th January Affair in Indonesia," *Dyason House Papers*, no. 1.

———. 1978. *The Army and Politics in Indonesia*. Ithaca: Cornell University Press.

———. 1979. "Patrimonialism and Military Rule in Indonesia," *World Politics* 31, 4.

———. 1980. "From Alliance to Barisan Nasional." In *Malaysian Politics and the 1978 Election*, ed. H. Crouch et al. Kuala Lumpur: Oxford University Press.

———. 1984. *Domestic Political Structures and Regional Economic Cooperation*. Singapore: Institute of Southeast Asian Studies.

———. 1989. "Malaysian Politics in the 1990s: The Limits to State Power," paper presented at the Conference on New Directions in Asian Studies, Singapore.

Crouch, Harold, Lee Kam Hing, and M. Ong, eds. 1980. *Malaysian Politics and the 1978 Election*. Kuala Lumpur: Oxford University Press.

Dahl, Robert. 1971. *Polyarchy: Participation and Opposition*. New Haven: Yale University Press.

———, ed. 1973. *Regimes and Oppositions*. New Haven: Yale University Press.

Das, K. 1987. *Malay Dominance?* Kuala Lumpur: K. Das Ink.

*Deemar Media Index*, 1986.

de Guzman, R., and M. Reforma. 1988. *Foundation and Dynamics of Philippines Government and Politics*. Singapore: Oxford University Press.

Dernberger, Robert F. 1987. "The Chinese Economy in the New Era: Continuity and Change," paper presented at the Conference on China in a New Era: Continuity and Change, Manila, August 24–29.

Deutsch, Karl. 1961. "Social Mobilization and Political Development," *American Political Science Review* 60, 3 (September): 493–514.

Deyo, Frederick C. 1987. "State and Labor: Modes of Political Exclusion in East Asian Development." In *The Political Economy of the New Asian Industrialism*, ed. Frederick C. Deyo. Ithaca: Cornell University Press.

Deyo, Frederick C., ed. 1987. *The Political Economy of the New Asian Industrialism*. Ithaca: Cornell University Press.

Diamond, Larry, Juan J. Linz, and Seymour Martin Lipset, eds. 1989. *Democracy in Developing Countries: Asia*, vol. 3. Boulder: Lynne Rienner.

Diamond, Larry, Seymour Martin Lipset, and Juan Linz. 1987. "Building and Sustaining Democratic Government in Developing Countries: Some Tentative Findings," *World Affairs* 150, 1 (Summer): 5–20.

Diokno, Jose W. 1985. *The Political Economy of the New Asian Industrialism*. Ithaca: Cornell University Press.

Dittmer, Lowell. 1987. "China in 1986: Domestic Politics." In *China Briefing, 1987*, ed. John S. Major and Anthony J. Kane. Boulder, CO: Westview Press.

———. 1990. "China in 1989: The Crisis of Incomplete Reform," *Asian Survey* 30, 1 (January): 26–31.

Domes, Jurgen. 1981. "Political Differentiation in Taiwan: Group Formation Within the Ruling Party and the Opposition Circles, 1979–1980," *Asian Survey* 21 (October): 1023–42.

Donnelly, Jack. 1984. "Human Rights and Development: Contemporary or Competing Concerns?" *World Politics* 36, 2: 255.

Doronila, A. 1985. "The Transformation of Patron-Client Relations and Its Political Consequences in the Postwar Philippines," *Journal of Southeast Asian Studies*, 16, 2: 99–116.

Drummond, S. H. 1987. "The Malaysian Elections: Mahathir's Successful Gamble." In *The Round Table* (London) 301 (January): 93–109.

Drysdale, John. 1984. *Singapore: Struggle for Success.* Singapore: Times Books International.

Emmerson, D. K. 1983. "Understanding the New Order: Bureaucratic Pluralism in Indonesia," *Asian Survey* 23, 11: 1120–41.

Esman, M. 1972. *Administration and Development in Malaysia.* Ithaca: Cornell University Press.

Esposito, John L., ed. 1987. *Islam in Asia: Religion, Politics and Society.* New York: Oxford University Press.

*Far Eastern Economic Review.* Various issues.

Far Eastern Economic Review. 1989. *Far Eastern Economic Review, Asia Yearbook 1989.* Hong Kong: Far Eastern Economic Review.

Fegan, B. 1985. "Rural Philippines: Central Luzon." In *The Philippines after Marcos*, ed. R. J. May and F. Nemenzo. London: Croom Helm.

Feith, Herbert. 1962. *The Decline of Constitutional Democracy in Indonesia.* Ithaca: Cornell University Press.

———. 1968. "Suharto's Search for a Political Format," *Indonesia*, no. 6 (October).

Fincher, John. 1989. "Zhou's Fall, China's Loss," *Foreign Policy* 76 (Fall): 3–25.

Fischer, Ernst. 1970. *Marx in His Own Words.* Harmondsworth, Middlesex, England: Penguin Books.

Fishlow, Albert. 1972. "Brazilian Size Distribution of Income," *American Economic Association Papers and Proceedings* 62: 391–402.

Fletcher, Nancy. 1969. *The Separation of Singapore from Malaysia.* Cornell University, Department of Far Eastern Studies, Southeast Asia Program, Occasional Paper. Ithaca: Cornell University.

Foreign Broadcast Information Service. *Daily Report—China.* Washington. Various issues.

"Foreign Investments in Thai Firms." 1987. *Bangkok Post*, February 13.

Forster, Keith. 1990. "Impressions of the Popular Protest in Hangzhou, April/June 1989," *Australian Journal of Chinese Affairs* 23 (January 1990): 98–99.

Fourth Plenary Session of the CPC's 13th Central Committee. 1989. Amended by New Star Publishers. Beijing: New Star Publishers.

Francis, Corinna-Barbara. 1989. "Reform in the Role of the Communist Party of China." Ph.D. dissertation, Columbia University.

Gale, Bruce. 1981. *Politics and Public Enterprise in Malaysia.* Singapore: Eastern Universities Press.

Gates, Hill. 1979. "Dependency and the Part-Time Proletariat in Taiwan," *Modern China* 5 (July): 381–408.

Geertz, Clifford. 1963. *Agricultural Involution: The Process of Ecological Change in Indonesia.* Berkeley: University of California Press.

George, T. J. S. 1973. *Lee Kuan Yew's Singapore*. London: Andre Deutsch.

Gereffi, Gary, and Donald Wyman, eds. 1989. *Manufactured Miracles: Patterns of Development in Latin America and East Asia*. Princeton: Princeton University Press.

Ghazali Shafie, Tan Sri. 1985a. Interview. September.

———. 1985b. "Nation Building and the Crisis of Values." In *Rukunegara: A Statement of Hope*.

Glassburner, Bruce, ed. 1971. *The Economy of Indonesia: Selected Readings*. Ithaca: Cornell University Press.

Goh Keng Swee. 1973. "Investment for Development: Lessons and Experience of Singapore, 1959 to 1971," paper presented at the Third Economic Development Seminar on Investment for Development in Saigon, January 17.

Golay, Frank. 1961. *The Philippines: Public Policy and National Economic Development*. Ithaca: Cornell University Press.

Gold, Thomas B. 1986. *State and Society in the Taiwan Miracle*. Armonk, NY: M. E. Sharpe.

Grossholtz, Jean. 1964. *Politics in the Philippines*. Boston: Little, Brown.

*Guangming Ribao (GMRB)* (Brightness daily), December 17, 1987; March 29, 1988, in FBIS 70 (April 12, 1988); December 4, 1988, in FBIS 247 (December 23, 1988): 22–23; July 22, 1989, in FBIS 151 (August 4, 1989): 30–33.

Hackenberg, R. A., and B. H. Hackenberg. 1987. "The Urban Working Class in the Philippines: A Casualty of the New Society, 1972–1985." In *Leaders, Factions, and Parties: The Structure of Philippine Politics*, ed. Carl Lande. Monograph no. 6. New Haven: Yale Southeast Asia Studies.

Hadi Soesastro. 1989. "The Political Economy of Deregulation in Indonesia." *Asian Survey* 29, 9: 853–69.

Haggard, S. C., and Cheng Tung-jen. 1987. "State and Foreign Capital in the East Asian NICs." In *The Political Economy of the New Asian Industrialism*, ed. F. C. Deyo. Ithaca: Cornell University Press.

Hahm Pyong-choon. 1974. "Toward a New Theory of Korean Politics: A Reexamination of Traditional Factors." In *Korean Politics in Transition*, ed. E. R. Wright. Berkeley: University of California Press.

Han Sung-joo. 1974. *The Failure of Democracy in South Korea*. Berkeley: University of California Press.

———. 1975. "South Korea: The Political Economy of Dependency," *Asian Survey* 15 (January).

———. 1988. "South Korea 1987: The Politics of Democratization," *Asian Survey* 28 (January).

Harding. Harry. 1988. *China's Second Revolution*. Washington, DC: Brookings Institution.

Harvey, Barbara. 1977. *Permesta: Half a Rebellion*. Ithaca: Cornell Modern Indonesia Project Monograph Series.

Hawes. G. 1987. *The Philippine State and the Marcos Regime: The Politics of Export*. Ithaca: Cornell University Press.

Henderson, Gregory. 1968. *Korea: The Politics of the Vortex*. Cambridge: Harvard University Press.

Heng Pek Koon. 1988. *Chinese Politics in Malaysia*. Singapore: Oxford University Press.

Hernandez, Carolina G. 1985. "The Philippines." In *Military-Civilian Relations in Southeast Asia*. London: Oxford University Press.

Hicks, G. L., and G. McNicol. 1971. *Trade and Growth in the Philippines: An Open Dual Economy*. Ithaca: Cornell University Press.

Hill, Hal. 1982. "The Philippine Economy Under Marcos: A Balance Sheet," *Australia Outlook* 36, 3: 32–39.

————. 1988. *Foreign Investment and Industrialization in Indonesia.* Singapore: Oxford University Press.

Hill, Hal, and J. A. C. Mackie, eds. 1989. *Indonesia Assessment 1988.* Political and Social Change Monograph no. 8. Canberra: Australian National University.

Hill, Hal, and Sisira Jayasuriya. 1985. *The Philippines: Growth, Debt and Crisis: Economic Performance During the Marcos Era.* Canberra: Development Studies Center, ANU.

Hinton, Keith. 1985. *Growing Churches, Singapore Style: Ministry in an Urban Context.* Singapore: Singapore Overseas Missionary Fellowship.

Hirschman, Albert O. 1970. *Exist, Voice and Loyalty.* Cambridge: Harvard University Press.

*Hong Kong Standard,* April 9 and 11, 1988, in FBIS 70 (April 12, 1988): 45–46.

Hsian Chang-chuan. 1971. *T'ai-wan ti fan hsuan ju* (Local elections in Taiwan). Taipei: Shang Wu.

Hsieh, Milton. 1970. Speech in *The Kuomintang.*

Hu Chiaomu. 1978. "Observe Economic Laws, Speed up the Four Modernizations," *Peking Review* 47 (November 24): 13–21.

Hu Fu. 1988. Interview, Columbia University, June.

Huang, Mab. 1976. *Intellectual Ferment for Political Reforms in Taiwan, 1971–73.* Ann Arbor: Center for Chinese Studies, University of Michigan.

Huntington, Samuel. 1970. "Social and Institutional Dynamics of One Party Systems." In *Authoritarian Politics in Modern Society,* ed. Samuel P. Huntington and Clement H. Moore. New York: Basic Books.

Huntington, Samuel P. 1984. *Political Order in Changing Societies.* New Haven: Yale University Press.

————. 1984. "Will More Countries Become Democratic?" *Political Science Quarterly* 9 (Summer): 201.

————. 1987. "The Goals of Development." In *Understanding Political Development,* ed. Myron Weiner and Samuel P. Huntington. Boston: Little, Brown.

Huntington, Samuel P., and Clement H. Moore, eds. 1970. *Authoritarian Politics in Modern Society.* New York: Basic Books.

Huntington and Moore 1970., Huntington, Samuel and Moore, Clement H., eds, *Authoritarian Politics in Modern Society* New York: Basic Books.

Huntington, Samuel P. and Joan M. Nelson. 1976. *No Easy Choice: Political Participation in Developing Countries.* Cambridge: Harvard University Press.

Ichimura Shinichi, ed. 1987. *Indonesian Economic Development.* Tokyo: Japan International Cooperation Agency.

————. 1988a. "The Pattern and Prospects of Asian Economic Development." In *Challenge of Asian Developing Countries: Issues and Analyses,* ed. Ichimura Shinichi. Tokyo: Asian Productivity Organization.

————, ed. 1988b. *Challenge of Asian Developing Countries: Issues and Analyses.* Tokyo: Asian Productivity Organization.

Ikemoto Yukio. 1986. "Technical Progress and Level of Technology: 1970–1980," *Developing Economies* 24, 4 (December): 368–90.

Ileto, R. 1985. "The Past in the Present Crisis." In *The Philippines after Marcos,* ed. R. J. May and F. Nemenzo. London: Croom Helm.

Im Hyug Baeg. 1987. "The Rise of Bureaucratic Authoritarianism in South Korea," *World Politics* 15, 4 (January).

Ingram, James C. 1954. *Economic Change in Thailand since 1850.* Stanford: Stanford University Press.

International Bank for Reconstruction and Development. 1959. *A Public Development Program for Thailand.* Baltimore: Johns Hopkins University Press.

Ishida, Hirohide. 1963. "Hoshutō no vision," *Chūō kōron,* January.

Jackson, Karl. 1977. "Bureaucratic Polity: A Theoretical Framework for the Analysis of Power and Communication in Indonesia." In *Political Power and Communications in Indonesia*, ed. Lucien W. Pye and Karl D. Jackson. Berkeley: University of California Press.

Jackson, Karl D., Sukhumbhand Paribatra, and J. Soedjati Djiwarndono, eds. 1985. *ASEAN in Regional and Global Context*. Berkeley: Institute of East Asian Studies, University of California.

Japan. Economic Planning Agency. Various years. *Kokumin shotoku tōkei* (National income statistics).

———. Management and Coordination Agency, Statistics Bureau. Various years. *Kokusei chōsa* (National census).

———. Ministry of Home Affairs, Election Department. 1987. "Tōhyōritsu nado ni kansuru shiryō" (Materials relating to election turnout, etc.), January.

———. Ministry of Finance. 1960, 1965, 1970, 1975. *Kuni no yosan* (The national budget).

———. 1987. *Nihon tōkei nenkan 1987* Japan Statistical Yearbook 1987.

———. 1975. *Shotoku shisan bunpai no jittai to mondaiten* (Status and problems of income and wealth distribution). Tokyo: Ōkurashō Insatsukyoku.

———. Office of the Prime Minister, Bureau of Statistics. 1977. *Kakei chōsa* (Family income and expenditure survey).

———. *Japan Statistical Yearbook*.

Jenkins, David. 1984. *Suharto and His Generals: Indonesian Military Politics 1975–1983*. Ithaca: Cornell Modern Indonesia Project.

Jiang Ping-lung and Wu Wen-cheng. 1989. "The Changing Role of the KMT in the Political System in Taiwan." Paper presented at the Conference on Democratization in the Republic of China, Taipei, January 9–11.

Johns, A. H. 1987. "Indonesia. Islam and Cultural Pluralism." In *Islam in Asia: Religion, Politics and Society*, ed. John L. Esposito.New York: Oxford University Press.

Johnson, Chalmers. 1982. *MITI and the Japanese Miracle*. Stanford: Stanford University Press.

———. 1988. "Political Institutions and Economic Performance: The Government-Business Relationship in Japan, South Korea and Taiwan," In *Asian Economic Development: Present and Future*, ed. R. Scalapino et al. Berkeley: Institute of East Asian Studies, University of California.

———, ed. 1970. *Change in Communist Systems*. Stanford: Stanford University Press.

Joint Publications Research Service.

Josey, Alex. 1968. *The Critical Years Ahead: Republic of Singapore General Election, 1968*. Singapore: Donald Moore Press.

Kabashima, Ikuo. 1984. "Supportive Participation with Economic Growth: The Case of Japan," *World Politics* 36, 3: 309–38.

Kabashima, Ikuo, and Jeffrey Broadbent. 1986. "Referent Pluralism: Mass Media and Politics in Japan," *Journal of Japanese Studies* 12, 92: 329–61.

———. N.d. "Keeping the LDP on a Tight Reign: Voter Rationality Under a Dominant Party Regime," ms.

Kahin, Audrey. 1985. *Regional Dynamics of the Indonesian Revolution: Unity from Diversity*. Honolulu: University of Hawaii Press.

Kahin, George McT. 1952. *Nationalism and Revolution in Indonesia*. Ithaca: Cornell University Press.

Karl, Terry Lynn. N.d. "Dilemmas of Democratization in Latin America," paper presented at the Conference on Latin America at the Threshold of the 1990s, Institute of Latin America of the Chinese Academy of Social Sciences, Beijing.

Kerkvliet, Benedict. 1977. *The Huk Rebellion: A Study of Peasant Revolt in the Philippines*. Berkeley: University of California Press.

Khong Kim Hoong. 1986. "Results of the 1986 Malaysian General Elections," *Review of Indonesian and Malaysian Affairs* 20, 1 (Summer): 186–215.

————. 1987. "The Role of Public Interest Groups in a Democratic Society," paper presented at the anniversary conference on Issues and Challenges for National Development, Faculty of Economics, University of Malaya, December 15–16.

Kim Se-jin. 1971. *The Politics of Military Revolution in Korea*. Chapel Hill: University of North Carolina Press.

Kokumin Seikatsu Sentā. 1970, 1976, 1987. *Kokumin seikatsu tōkei nenpō* (Annual report of Japanese consumer information). Tokyo: Shiseidō.

Kōsai, Yutaka. 1981. *Kōdo seichō no jidai: Gendai Nihon keizai-shi nōto*. Tokyo: Nihon hyōronsha. English translation by Jacqueline Kaminsky, *The Era of High-Speed Growth: Notes on the Post-War Japanese Economy*. Tokyo: Tokyo University Press.

Krirkiat Phipatseritham. 1983. "The World of Finance: The Push and Pull of Politics," paper presented at the Seminar on National Development of Thailand: Economic Rationality and Political Feasibility, Thammasat University, Bangkok, September 6–7.

Kuomintang. 1970. *The Kuomintang: Selected Historical Documents, 1894–1969*. New York: St. John's University Press.

Kusuma Snitwongse and Sukhumbhand Paribatra, eds. 1987. *Durable Stability in Southeast Asia*. Singapore: Institute of Southeast Asian Studies.

Kuznets, Simon. 1963. "Quantitative Aspects of Economic Growth of Nations: Part VII, The Distribution of Income by Size," *Economic Development and Cultural Change* 11: 1–80.

————. 1966. *Modern Economic Growth*. New Haven: Yale University Press.

Lande, Carl. 1965. *Leaders, Factions, and Parties: The Structure of Philippine Politics*. Monograph no. 6. New Haven: Yale Southeast Asia Studies.

————, ed. 1987. *Rebuilding a Nation: Philippine Challenge and American Policy*. Washington: Washington Institute Press.

Lee Chae-jin. 1973. "South Korea: The Politics of Domestic-Foreign Linkage," *Asian Survey*, January.

Lee Chong-sik. 1981. "South Korea in 1980: The Emergence of a New Authoritarian Order," *Asian Survey* 21 (January): 125–43.

Lee Hong Yung. 1988. "The Transition from Revolutionary Cadres to Bureaucratic Technocrats in China," ms.

Lee Kuan Yew. 1959. Speech at the official opening of the Civil Study Center, August 15.

————. 1984. Speech at the National Residents' Committee Presentation at the World Trade Center Auditorium, October 27.

Lerman, Arthur J. 1978. *Taiwan's Politics: The Provincial Assemblyman's World*. Washington, DC: University Press of America.

Lev, Daniel S. 1979. "Judicial Authority and the Struggle for an Indonesia Rechsstaat," *Law and Society Review* 31, 1.

Lewis, John W., and Xue Litai. 1988. *China Builds the Bomb*. Stanford: Stanford University Press.

Li, K. T. 1988. *The Evolution of Policy Behind Taiwan's Development Success*. New Haven: Yale University Press.

Liddle, R. W. 1983. "The Politics of Shared Growth: Some Indonesian Cases," *Comparative Politics* 19, 2.

————. 1985. "Suharto's Indonesia: Personal Rule and Political Institutions," *Pacific Affairs* 58, 1.

Lijphart, Arend. 1975. *The Politics of Accommodation*. 2d ed. Berkeley: University of California Press.
————. 1984. *Democracies*. New York: Yale University Press.
Lim Chong Yah et al. 1988. *Policy Options for the Singapore Economy*. Singapore: McGraw-Hill.
Lim, David. 1975a. "The Economic, Political and Social Background to Development Planning in Malaysia." In *Readings on Malaysian Economic Development*, ed. D. Lim. Kuala Lumpur: Oxford University Press.
Lin Bin. 1988. "Food Subsidies Float with Price Index," *Beijing Review* 31, 14 (April 4–10): 7.
Lin Cheng-chieh et al. 1983–84. Articles in various issues of *Ch'ien chin* (Progress).
Lin Chia-lung. 1988. "Kuo-min-tang yu Min-chin-tang ti chun chung chi ch'u: Tai-wan hsuan min cheng tang chih shih ti pi chiao fen hsi" (The mass bases of the KMT and DPP: A comparative analysis of electoral supports to political parties), Ph.D. dissertation, National Taiwan University.
Lindblom, Charles. 1977. *Politics and Markets*. New York: Basic Books.
Linz, Juan J. 1973. "Opposition to and Under an Authoritarian Regime: The Case of Spain." In *Regimes and Oppositions*, ed. Robert Dahl. New Haven: Yale University Press.
Lipset, Seymour Martin. 1963. *Political Man*. London: Mercury Books.
————. 1981. "Economic Development and Democracy." In *Political Man*, expanded ed. Baltimore: Johns Hopkins University Press.
Lipset, Seymour Martin, and Frederick C. Turner. 1987. "Economic Growth and Democratization: The Continuing Search for Verification," ms.
Lipset, Seymour Martin, and Stein Rokkan. 1967. *Party Systems and Voter Alignments: Cross-National Perspectives*. New York: Free Press.
*Los Angeles Times*. Various issues.
Lowenthal, Richard. 1970. "Development vs. Utopia in Communist Policy," In *Change in Communist Systems*, ed. Chalmers Johnson. Stanford: Stanford University Press.
Luo Bing. 1990. "Zhongong pi ge de juemi wenjian," *Cheng ming* 2: 6–8. This is the top secret document in which Gorbachev was criticized.
Luo Rongxing, Zhu Huaxin, and Cao Huanrong. 1987. "Different Interest Groups under Socialism," *Beijing Review* 30, 48 (November 30–December 6): 18–19.
McCawley, Peter. 1978. "Rural Electrification in Indonesia—Is It Time?" *Bulletin of Indonesian Economic Studies* 14: 34–69.
McDonald, Hamish. 1980. *Suharto's Indonesia*. Blackburn, Victoria, Australia: Fontana Books.
MacFarquhar, Roderick. 1989. "The End of the Chinese Revolution," *New York Review of Books*, June 22, pp. 8–10.
Machado, K. 1978. "The Philippines: A Return to Normalcy?" *Asian Survey* 18, 2: 202–11.
————. 1979. "The Philippines: Authoritarian Consolidation Continues," *Asian Survey* 19, 2: 131–40.
MacIntyre, Andrew. 1988. "Politics, Policy, and Participation: Business-Government Relations in Indonesia," Ph.D. dissertation, Australia National University.
Mackenzie, Ann. 1987. "People Power or Palace Coup: the Fall of Marcos." In *Regime Change in the Philippines: The Legitimation of the Aquino Government*, ed. M. Turner. Political and Social Change Monograph. Canberra: Australia National University.
Mackie, J. A. C. 1967. *The Problem of Inflation in Indonesia*. Ithaca: Cornell Modern Indonesia Project.

———. 1989a. "Indonesia Political Developments, 1987–88." In *Indonesia Assessment 1988*, ed. Hal Hill and J. A. C. Mackie. Canberra: Australia National University.

———. 1989b. "Property and Power in New Order Indonesia," ms.

McVey, Ruth. 1970. "Nationalism, Islam and Marxism: The Management of Ideological Conflict in Indonesia." Introduction to Sukarno, *Nationalism, Islam and Marxism*. Ithaca: Cornell University Indonesia Project.

———. 1971, 1972. "The Post-Revolutionary Transformation of the Indonesian Army," *Indonesia*, 11: 131–76; 13: 147–82.

Mahathir Mohamad. 1970. *Malay Dilemma*. Singapore: Donald Moore.

———. 1985. "A Prescription for a Socially Responsible Press." Speech delivered at a meeting of ASEAN journalists in Kuala Lumpur and printed in *Far Eastern Economic Review*, October 10, 1985, pp. 26–28.

———. 1986. *The Challenge*. Petaling Jaya: Pelanduk Publications.

Major, John S., and Anthony J. Kane, eds. 1987. *China Briefing, 1987*. Boulder: Westview Press.

"Malaysia—In Shape." 1989. *The Economist*, September 16–22, pp. 23–24.

Malaysia. 1969. *The May 13 Tragedy: A Report*. Kuala Lumpur: National Operations Council.

———. 1985. *Mid-Term Review of the Fourth Malaysia Plan (1981–1985)*. Kuala Lumpur: Government Printer.

———. 1989. *Mid-Term Review of the Fifth Malaysia Plan (1986–1990)*. Kuala Lumpur: Government Printer.

Malaysian Bar Council. 1987. "Possible Restoration of Malaysia's Mismanaged Economy—The Appointment of a Commission of Enquiry." In *INSAF* Kuala Lumpur, 20.

Mao Zedong. 1956. "On the Ten Great Relationships." In *Chairman Mao Talks to the People*, ed. Stuart Schram. New York: Random House, 1974.

———. 1959. "Speech at the Lushan Conference." In *Chairman Mao Talks to the People*, ed. Stuart Schram. New York: Random House, 1974.

Marlay, R. 1987. "The Political Legacy of Marcos: The Political Inheritance of Aquino." In *Leaders, Factions, and Parties: The Structure of Philippine Politics*. Monograph no. 6. New Haven: Yale Southeast Asia Studies.

Masumi, Junnosuke. 1983. *Sengo seiji 1945–55*. Tokyo: Tokyo University Press. English trans. by Lonny E. Carlile, *Postwar Politics in Japan, 1945–1955*. Berkeley: Center for Japanese Studies, Institute for East Asian Studies, University of California, 1985.

———. 1985. *Gendai seiji: 1955-nen igo* (Contemporary politics in Japan: Since 1955). Tokyo: Tokyo University Press.

Mattar, Ahmad. 1984. "Changes in the Social Economic Status of the Malays," *Petir 30th Anniversary Issue*. Singapore: People's Action Party.

Mauzy, Diane K. 1983. *Barisan Nasional: Coalition Government in Malaysia*. Kuala Lumpur: Marican and Sons.

———. 1987. "Malaysia in 1986: The Ups and Downs of Stock Market Politics," *Asian Survey* 37, 2 (February).

May, R. J., and F. Nemenzo, eds. 1985. *The Philippines after Marcos*. London: Croom Helm.

Medhi Krongkaew. 1987. "The Current State of Poverty and Income Distribution in Thailand," paper presented at the International Conference on Thai Studies, Australian National University, Canberra, July.

Mehmet, Ozay. 1986. *Development in Malaysia*. London: Croom Helm.

Meyer, Alfred G. 1960. *Communism*. New York: Random House.

Milne, R. S., and Diane K. Mauzy. 1986. *Politics and Government in Malaysia*. Singapore: Federal Publications.

*Ming pao*, Hong Kong, October 21, 1986, in FBIS 38 (October 23, 1986): K7.

*Ming pao yue-k'an (MPYK)*, Hong Kong, 247 (July 1986): 27–28, in JPRS-CPS–87–020, April 8, 1987, pp. 60–63.

Mizoguchi, Toshiyuki. 1974. "Sengo Nihon no shotoku bunpu to shisan bunpu" (The distribution of income and wealth in postwar Japan), *Keizai kenkyū* (Economic research) 25, 4 (October): 345–66.

Moore, Barrington, Jr. 1966. *Social Origins of Dictatorship and Democracy*. Boston: Beacon Press.

Morell, David, and Chai-Anan Samudavanija. 1981. *Political Conflict in Thailand: Reform, Reaction, Revolution*. Cambridge: Oelgeschlager, Gunn & Hain.

Morfitt, M. 1982. "Pancasila: The Indonesian State Ideology According to the New Order Government," *Asian Survey* 21, 8: 838–51.

Mortimer, R. 1972. *The Indonesian Communist Party and Land Reform 1959–1965*. Monash Papers on Southeast Asia. Clayton: Monash University, Centre for Southeast Asian Studies.

Muzaffar, Chandra. 1984. "A Call for Clean Politics in UMNO," *Far Eastern Economic Review*, July 19, p. 24.

Myrdal, Gunnar. 1968. *Asian Drama: An Inquiry into the Poverty of Nations*, vol. 1. London: Allen Lane (Penguin Press).

Nathan, Andrew J. 1985. *Chinese Democracy*. New York: Alfred A. Knopf.

———. 1988. Review of Harding's *China's Second Revolution*, in *New Republic*, April 18, pp. 43–46.

———. 1990. "Chinese Democracy in 1989: Continuity and Change," *Problems of Communism* 38, 5 (September–October): 17–29.

Nemenzo, F. 1985. "The Left and the Traditional Opposition." In *The Philippines after Marcos*, ed. F. Nemenzo. London: Croom Helm.

———. 1986. "Military Intervention in Philippines Politics," *The Dilman Review*, nos. 5–6: 16–25.

Ness, Gayl D. 1967. *Bureaucracy and Rural Development in Malaysia*. Berkeley: University of California Press.

*New Straits Times*, July 26, 1986.

*New York Times*. Various issues.

Nihon Hōsō Kyōkai, ed. 1977. *Hōsō gojūnen-shi* (Fifty-year history of broadcasting). Tokyo: Nihon hōsō shuppan kyōkai.

*1987 Year-End Economic Review*. Bangkok: Bangkok Post.

Noble, Lela G. 1986. "Politics in the Marcos Era." In *Crisis in the Philippines: The Marcos Era and Beyond*, ed. John F. Bresnan. Princeton: Princeton University Press.

———. 1987. "Muslim Grievances and the Muslim Rebellion." In *Rebuilding a Nation: Philippine Challenge and American Policy*, ed. Carl Lande. Washington, DC: Washington Institute Press.

Nordlinger, Eric A. 1987. "Taking the State Seriously." In *Understanding Political Development*, ed. M. Weiner and S. Huntington. Boston: Little, Brown.

Nugroho Notosusanto and Ismail Saleh. 1968. *The Coup Attempt of the September 30th Movement in Indonesia*. Jakarta: Pembimbing Masa.

O'Brien, Kevin. 1988. "China's National People's Congress: Reform and Its Limits," *Legislative Studies Quarterly* 8, 3 (August): 343–74.

O'Donnell, Guillermo. 1973. *Modernization and Bureaucratic-Authoritarianism*. Berkeley: Institute of International Studies, University of California.

———. 1978. "Reflections on Patterns of Change in Bureaucratic Authoritarian States," *Latin American Research Revue* 13, 1.

O'Donnell, Guillermo, and P. C. Schmitter. 1986. *Transitions from Authoritarian Rule: Prospects for Democracy*. Baltimore: Johns Hopkins University Press.

O'Donnell, Guillermo, Philippe C. Schmitter, and Laurence Whitehead, eds. 1986. *Transitions from Authoritarian Rule: Comparative Perspective*. Baltimore: Johns Hopkins University Press.

Oey, Hong Kee. 1974. *Indonesia After the 1971 Elections*. London: Oxford University Press.

Oksenberg, Michel. 1987. "China's 13th Party Congress," *Problems of Communism* 36, 6 (November–December): 1–17.

"On Questions of Party History." 1981. In *Beijing Review* 24, 27 (July 6): 10–39.

"On the Reform of the System of Party and State, August 18, 1980." 1984. In *Selected Works of Deng Xiaoping, 1975–1982*. Beijing: Foreign Languages Press, pp. 302–25.

Overholt, W. H. 1986. "The Rise and Fall of Marcos," *Asian Survey* 26, 11: 1137–63.

Ozbudun, Ergun. 1987. "Turkey." In *Comparative Elections in Developing Countries*, ed. M. Weiner and E. Ozbudun. Durham: Duke University Press.

Paisal Sricharatchanya. 1988. "Not Just Chicken Feed," *Far Eastern Economic Review*, March 3.

Pang Cheng Lian. 1971. *Singapore's People Action Party: Its History, Organization and Leadership*. Kuala Lumpur: Oxford University Press.

Pang Eng Fong. 1981. "Singapore," In *International Handbook of Industrial Relations*, ed. Albert Blum. Westport: Greenwood Press.

Pempel, T. J. N.d. "One Party Dominant Regimes," ms.

People's Republic of China. 1988. *China Statistical Yearbook*. English edition. Hong Kong: International Centre for the Advancement of Science and Technology.

"The Petrochemical Industry in ASEAN." 1988. *The Nation*, May 10.

*Phu Jad Karn*. Various issues.

Porter, G. 1987. "Communism in the Philippines," *Problems of Communism* 36: 14–35.

"The Price China Has Paid: An Interview with Liu Binyan." 1989. *New York Review of Books* 35, 21–22 (January 19): 31–35.

Puthucheary, M. 1978. *The Politics of Administration, the Malaysian Experience*. Kuala Lumpur: Oxford University Press.

Pye, Lucian. 1985. *Asian Power and Politics*. Cambridge: Belknap Press, Harvard University Press.

Pye, Lucian W., and Karl D. Jackson, eds. 1977. *Political Power and Communications in Indonesia*. Berkeley: University of California Press.

Quah, Jon S. T. 1981. "Statutory Boards." In *Government and Politics of Singapore*, ed. Jon S. T. Quah, Chan Heng Chee, and Seah Chee Meow. Singapore: Oxford University Press.

Race, J. 1985. "Whither the Philippines?" *Prisma*, no. 5: 30–42.

Rajaratnam, S. 1987. "Singapore: Global City." In *S. Rajaratnam: The Prophetic and the Political*, ed. Chan Heng Chee and Obaid ul Haq. Singapore: Graham Brash.

Rao, V. V. Bhanoji. 1980. *Malaysia, Development Pattern and Policy, 1947–1971*. Singapore: Singapore University Press.

Reeve, David. 1985. *Golkar of Indonesia: An Alternative to the Party System*. Singapore: Oxford University Press.

Reid, A. J. S. 1974. *The Indonesian National Revolution*. Melbourne: Longmans Studies in Contemporary Southeast Asia.

Reischauer, Edwin. 1977. *The Japanese*. Cambridge: Harvard University Press.

*Renmin ribao (RMRB)* (People's daily), January 15, 1988, in FBIS 21 (February 2, 1988): 22; June 29, 1988, in FBIS 140 (July 21, 1988): 55.

———, overseas ed., September 10, 1988, in FBIS 178 (September 14, 1988): 26–27; July 25, 1989, in FBIS 143 (July 27, 1989): 21–22; October 17, 1989, in FBIS 199 (October 17, 1989): 8–12.

Republic of China. Directorate-General of Budget, Accounting and Statistics, Executive Yuan. 1989. *Statistical Yearbook of the Republic of China*. Various years. Taipei.

————. Economic Research Center for U.S. Aid, Executive Yuan. Various years. *Taiwan Statistical Data Book.* Taipei.

————. Legislative Yuan. 1985. *Lao tung chi jung fa* (The basic labor law). The Secretariat, special collection of the legislative debates, no. 73. Two volumes.

Republic of Singapore. Department of Statistics. 1983. *Economic and Social Statistics, 1962–1980.* Singapore: Department of Statistics. 1970.

————. Housing and Development Board. 1970. *First Decade in Public Housing.* Singapore: HDB.

————. Information Division, Ministry of Communications and Information. 1987. *Singapore 1987.* Singapore: IDMCI.

————. Information Division, Ministry of Culture. 1984. *Singapore: An Illustrated History, 1941–1984.* Singapore: IDMC.

————. Parliament. 1976. "University of Singapore Amendment Act," *Asia Research Bulletin* 6, 1.

Riedel, R. 1988. "Economic Development In East Asia: Doing What Comes Naturally?" In Hughes 1988.

Riggs, Fred. W. 1966. *Thailand: The Modernization of a Bureaucratic Polity.* Honolulu: East-West Center Press.

Riskin, Carl. 1987. *China's Political Economy—The Quest for Development Since 1949.* New York: Oxford University Press.

Robison, Kevin Hewison, and Richard Higgot, eds. 1987. *Southeast Asia in 1980s: The Politics of Economic Crisis.* Sydney: Allen & Unwin.

Robison, Richard. 1986. *Indonesia: The Rise of Capital.* Sydney: Allen & Unwin.

————. 1987. "After the Gold Rush: The Politics of Economic Restructuring in Indonesia in the 1980s." In *Southeast Asia in the 1980s: The Politics of Economic Crisis,* ed. Kevin Hewison Robison and Richard Higgot. Sydney: Allen & Unwin.

————. 1988. "Authoritarian States, Capital-Owning Classes and the Politics of the Newly Industrializing Countries: The Case of Indonesia." In *World Politics* 41, 1: 52–74.

Robson, A. 1987. "The 1987 Congressional Election in the Philippines: Context, Conduct and Outcome." In *Regime Change in the Philippines: The Legitimation of the Aquino Government,* ed. M. Turner. Political and Social Change Monograph. Canberra: Australia National University.

Rosca, Ninotchka. 1987. *Endgame: The Fall of Marcos.* New York: Franklin Watts.

Rosen, Stanley. 1988. "The Impact of Reform Policies on Chinese Youth." Paper presented at the Conference on Social Consequences of the Chinese Economic Reforms, Harvard University, May 13–15.

Rosenberg, D. A., ed. 1979. *Marcos and Martial Law in the Philippines.* Ithaca: Cornell University Press.

————. 1984. "Communism in the Philippines," *Problems of Communism* 33, 5: 24–46.

Salleh Abbas, Tun, with K. Das. 1989. *May Day for Justice.* Kuala Lumpur: Percetakam A-Z.

Saravanamuttu, Johan. 1989. "Kelas Menengah Dalam Politik Malaysia: Tonjolan Perkauman Atau Kepentingan Kelas?" (The middle class in Malaysian politics: The salience of ethnicity or class interests?), paper presented at the Political Science Seminar, "Whither Malaysian Politics," Penang, February 3–4.

Scalapino, Robert. 1988. "Political Trends in Asia and Their Implications for the Region." In *Asia and the Major Powers: Domestic Politics and Foreign Policy,* ed. R. Scalapino et al. Berkeley: Institute of East Asian Studies, University of California.

Scalapino, Robert, Seizaburo Satō, and Jusuf Wanandi. 1988. *Asian Economic Development: Present and Future.* Berkeley: Institute of East Asian Studies, University of California; reprint of 1985 volume.

Schoenhals, Michael. 1987. "Original Contradictions: On the Unrevised Text of Mao Zedong's 'On the Correct Handling of Contradictions among the People,' " ms.

Schram, Stuart, ed. 1974. *Chairman Mao Talks to the People*. New York: Random House.

Schumpeter, Joseph A. *Capitalism, Socialism, and Democracy*. New York: Harper & Row. 1975.

Schurmann, Franz. 1966. *Ideology and Organization in Communist China*. Berkeley: University of California Press.

Scott, James C. 1972. "The Erosion of Patron-Client Bonds and Social Change in Southeast Asia," *Journal of Southeast Asian Studies*, no. 1: 5–37.

Seah Chee Meow, ed. 1975. *Trends in Singapore*. Singapore: Singapore University Press.

———. 1981. "The Civil Service." In *Government and Politics of Singapore*, ed. Jon S. T. Quah et al. Singapore: Oxford University Press.

Shamsul, A. B. 1988. "The Battle Royal: The UMNO Elections of 1987." In *Southeast Asian Affairs, 1988*, ed. M. Ayoob and Ng Chee Yuen. Singapore: Institute of Southeast Asian Studies.

Share, Donald. 1987. "Transitions to Democracy and Transition Through Transaction." In *Comparative Political Studies* 19, 4 (January): 525–48.

Sheu Jia-you. 1987. "The Class Structure in Taiwan and Its Change," paper presented at the International Conference on Taiwan, R.O.C.: A Newly Industrializing Society, National Taiwan University, September 3–5.

Shirk, Susan. 1982. *Competitive Comrades*. Berkeley: University of California Press.

*Siam Rath*.

Sicat, Gerardo. 1984. "A Historical and Current Perspective on the Philippines Economic Prospects," ms.

Simbulan, Dante. 1966. "A Study of the Socio-Economic Elite in Philippines Politics and Government." Ph.D. dissertation, Australia National University.

*Singapore Monitor*, December 23, 1984.

Smail, John R. W. 1964. *Bandung in the Early Revolution, 1945–1946*. Ithaca: Cornell Modern Indonesia Project.

Smith, Kwanchai. 1980. "Concept of Poverty and Problems of Poverty Identifications," paper presented at workshop on Socioeconomic Aspects of Poverty in Thailand, Thai University Research Association, January 4–6.

Snodgrass, D. R. 1980. *Inequality and Economic Development in Malaysia*. Kuala Lumpur: Oxford University Press.

Snoh Unakul. N.d. Interview with Dr. Snoh, who was formerly governor of the Bank of Thailand and is at present Secretary-general of the NESDB.

Soedjatmoko. 1956. "The Pole of Political Parties in Indonesia." In *Nationalism and Progress in Free Asia*, ed. Philip W. Thayer. Baltimore: Johns Hopkins University Press.

Solinger, Dorothy J., ed. 1984. *Three Visions of Chinese Socialism*. Boulder: Westview Press.

———. 1987. "Urban Reform in Wuhan, 1984–1987: The Mix of Market and Plan." Paper presented at the Conference on China in a New Era: Continuity and Change, Manila, August 24–29.

———. 1989. "Democracy with Chinese Characteristics," *World Policy Journal* 6, 4 (Fall): 621–32.

Solomon, Richard. 1971. *Mao's Revolution and the Chinese Political Culture*. Berkeley: University of California Press.

Sompop Manarungsan. 1987. "Macro-national and Regional Economic Development of Thailand After W. W. II." Paper presented at workshop on Development of Modern Entrepreneurs in Various Regions of Thailand, Bangkok, December 4–5.

————. 1988. *Economic Development in Thailand, 1850–1950: Response to the Challenge of the World Economy*. Groningen: Faculty of Economics, University of Groningen.

Somsakdi, Xuto, et al. 1983. *Strategies and Measures for the Development of Thailand in the 1980s*. Bangkok: Research Institute of the Thai University Association.

Sopiee, Mohamed Noordin. 1974. *From Malayan Union to Singapore Separation: Political Unification in the Malaysian Region 1945–1965*. Kuala Lumpur: Penerbit Universiti Malaya.

Starner, Frances. 1961. *Magsaysay and the Philippine Peasantry: The Agrarian Impact on the Philippines' Politics, 1953–1956*. Berkeley: University of California Press.

Steinberg, D. 1987. *Regime Change in the Philippines: The Legitimation of the Aquino Government*. Political and Social Change Monograph. Canberra: Australia National University.

Stepan, Alfred. 1978. *The State and Society: Peru in Comparative Perspective*. Princeton: Princeton University Press.

————. 1986. "Paths Toward Redemocratization: Theoretical and Comparative Consideration." In *Transitions from Authoritarian Rule: Comparative Perspective*, ed. G. O'Donnell et al. Baltimore: Johns Hopkins University Press.

*Straits Times*, Various dates.

Suchit Bunbongkarn. 1987. *The Military in Thai Politics 1981–86*. Singapore: Institute of Southeast Asian Studies.

"Su Shaozhi Discusses Political Structural Reform." 1986. *Dushu* 9 (September 10), in JPRS-CPS–87–020, April 8, 1987, pp. 25–30.

Suchit Bunbongkarn and Sukhumbhand Paribatra. 1986. "Thai Politics and Foreign Policy in the 1980s: Plus Ça Change, Plus C'est la Même Chose?" In *ASEAN in Regional and Global Context*, ed. Karl D. Jackson et al. Berkeley: Institute of East Asian Studies, University of California.

Sukarno. 1970. *Nationalism, Islam and Marxism*. Ithaca: Cornell Modern Indonesia Project.

Sukhumbhand Paribatra. 1987a. *From Enmity to Alignment: Thailand's Evolving Relations with China*, ISIS Paper no. 1. Bangkok: Institute of Security and International Studies, Chulalongkorn University.

————. 1987b. "Thailand: Defense Spending and Threat Perception." In *Defense Spending in Southeast Asia*, ed. Chin Kah Wah. Singapore: Institute of Southeast Asian Studies.

Summers, Robert, and Alan Heston. 1988. "A New Set of International Comparisons of Real Product and Price Levels Estimates for 130 Countries, 1950–1985," *Review of Income and Wealth* 34, 1 (March): 1–25 and supplemental diskette.

Sundhassen, Ulf. 1977. "The Military in Indonesia." In *Political Power and Communications in Indonesia*, ed. Lucian W. Pye and Karl D. Jackson. Berkeley: University of California Press.

Sundrum, R. M. 1986. "Indonesia's Rapid Economic Growth," *Bulletin of Indonesian Economic Studies* 23, 3.

————. 1988. "Indonesia's Slow Economic Growth 1981–86," *Bulletin of Indonesian Economic Studies* 24, 1.

*Ta hsueh tsa chih* (The intellectuals). Various issues.

Tadem, C., ed. 1988. "Status and Prospects of Agrarian Reform in the Philippines," *Katipunan* (May): 11–14.

Tai Hung-chao. 1970. "The Kuomintang and Modernization in Taiwan." In *Authoritarian Politics in Modern Society*, ed. Samuel P. Huntington and Clement H. Moore. New York: Basic Books.

Tan, Augustine H. H. 1986. "Singapore's Economy: Growth and Structural Change," In *Southeast Asian Affairs 1986*. Singapore: Institute of Southeast Asian Studies.

Tan, Augustine H. H., and Kapur Bauar, eds. 1983. *Pacific Growth and Financial Interdependence*. Sydney: Allen & Unwin.

Tan Teng Lang. 1983. "The Evolving PAP Ideology: Beyond Democratic Socialism." B.A. Hons. thesis, Department of Political Science, National University of Singapore.

Tandrup, Anders. 1984. "Privatisation under Bureaucrat Capitalism: Some Comments on Malaysia's New Economic Policy," paper presented at the seminar on Statens rolle i den sydostasiatiske udviklingsproces, Copenhagen, August 25–26.

Tanner, Harold M. 1988. "Democracy and the Intelligentsia: An Analysis of the Views of Fang Lizhi and Liu Binyan," seminar paper, Columbia University, May.

*TDRI Newsletter*. Bangkok: Thai Development Research Institute.

Teh Cheang Wan. 1979. "Public Housing in Singapore," *Petir 25th Anniversary Issue*. Singapore: People's Action Party.

Thailand. Statistical data supplied by the following offices: Board of Investment; Board of Trade; Bank of Thailand; Department of Business Economics, Ministry of Commerce; Labour Research Branch, Labour Studies and Planning Division, Department of Labour, Ministry of Interior; National Economic and Social Development Board; National Statistical Office.

Thailand, National Economic and Social Development Board. 1982. *Fifth National Economic and Social Development Plan, B.E. 2525–2529*. Bangkok: Office of the Prime Minister.

Thayer, Philip W., ed. 1956. *Nationalism and Progress in Free Asia*. Baltimore: Johns Hopkins University Press.

Thee Kian Wee and Yoshihara Kunio. 1987. "Foreign and Domestic Capital in Indonesian Industrialization," *Southeast Asian Studies* (Kyoto), March.

*The Mirror* 2, 30 (July 25, 1966): 1.

*The Nation*. Various issues.

Tien, Hung-mao. 1989. *The Great Transition: Political and Social Change in the Republic of China*. Stanford: Hoover Institution Press.

Tiewes, Frederick. 1984. *Leadership, Legitimacy, and Conflict in China*. Armonk, NY: M. E. Sharpe.

Toh Kin Woon. 1982. *The State, Transnational Corporations and Poverty in Malaysia*. Research Monograph no. 16. Sydney: Sydney University.

Turner, M. 1987. "The Quest for Political Legitimacy in the Philippines: The Constitutional Plebescite of 1987." In *Regime Change in the Philippines: The Legitimation of the Aquino Government*, ed. M. Turner. Political and Social Change Monograph. Canberra: Australia National University.

Twatchai Yongkittikul and Chaiyawat Wibulswasdi. 1983. "Strategies and Measures for Thailand's Economic Development in the 1980s." In *Strategies and Measures for the Development of Thailand in the 1980s*, ed. Yuto Somsakdi et al. Bangkok: Research Institute of the Thai University Association.

Uchikawa Yoshimi. 1978. "Political Process under the Development of Mass Communications in Post-war Japan," *The Annals of the Japanese Political Science Association*: 303–21.

Uchino Tatsurō. 1978. *Japan's Postwar Economy: An Insider's View of Its History and Its Future*. Tokyo: Kodansha International.

United Nations. 1961. *A Proposed Industrialization Program for the State of Singapore: Report of the United Nations Industrial Survey Mission*.

United Nations. Various years. *UN Statistical Yearbook*.

United States Agency for International Development. 1989. *Development and the National Interest: U.S. Economic Assistance into the 21st Century: A Report by the Administrator.* Washington, DC: Agency for International Development.

U.S. House of Representatives. 1974. *Human Rights in South Korea: Implications for U.S. Policy,* Hearings before the Subcommittee on Asian and Pacific Affairs of the Committee of Foreign Affairs, 93d Congress, 2d Session. Washington, DC: Government Printing Office.

Vasil, R. K. 1971. *Politics in a Plural Society.* Kuala Lumpur: Oxford University Press.

Vasil, Raj. 1988. *Governing Singapore.* Singapore: Times Books International.

Villegas, B. 1986. "The Economic Crisis." In *Crises in the Philippines: The Marcos Era and Beyond,* ed. John F. Bresnan. Princeton: Princeton University Press.

Vogel, Ezra. 1969. *Canton under Communism.* Cambridge: Harvard University Press.

————. 1989. *One Step Ahead: Guangdong under Reform.* Cambridge: Harvard University Press.

von Vorys, Karl. 1975. *Democracy Without Consensus: Communalism and Political Stability in Malaysia.* Princeton: Princeton University Press.

Wagner, Rudolf C. 1989. "Das Wahre Gesicht der Unruhen" (The true face of the turmoil), *Die Zeit,* September 1, 1989.

Walder, Andrew. 1986. *Communist Neo-Traditionalism: Work and Authority in Chinese Industry.* Berkeley: University of California Press.

————. 1989. "The Political Sociology of the Beijing Upheaval of 1989," *Problems of Communism* 38, 5 (September–October): 330–40.

Wang, N. T. 1988. Personal communication.

Ward, K. 1974. *The 1971 Election in Indonesia: An East Java Case Study.* Monash Papers on Southeast Asia. Clayton: Monash University, Centre for Southeast Asian Studies.

Watanabe Toshio. 1978. "Heavy and Chemical Industrialization and Economic Development in the Republic of Korea," *The Developing Economies* 15, 4 (December): 389.

Watanabe Toshio and Kajiwara Hirokazu. 1983. "Pacific Manufactured Trade and Japan's Options," *The Developing Economies* 21, 4 (December): 313–39.

Watanuki, Jōji. 1967. "Patterns of Politics in Present Day Japan." In *Party Systems and Voter Alignments: Cross-National Perspectives,* ed. Seymour Martin Lipset and Stein Rokkan. New York: Free Press.

Weiner, Myron, and Ergun Ozbudun. 1987. *Comparative Elections in Developing Countries.* Durham: Duke University Press.

Weiner, Myron, and Samuel P. Huntington. 1987. *Understanding Political Development.* Boston: Little, Brown.

*Wen hui bao,* Shanghai, December 2, 1989, in FBIS 237 (December 12, 1989): 18–23.

Wiber, Charles K., ed. 1979. *The Political Economy of Development and Underdevelopment.* 2d ed. New York: Random House.

Wilson, David. 1962. *Politics in Thailand.* Ithaca: Cornell University Press.

Winckler, Edwin A. 1984. "Institutionalization and Participation on Taiwan: From Hard to Soft Authoritarianism?" *China Quarterly* 99 (September): 481–99.

Wolgan Chosun. 1987. December: 189–225.

Wong, Christine P. W. 1988. "Interpreting Rural Industrial Growth in the Post-Mao Period," *Modern China* 14, 1: 3–30.

Woradej Chantasorn. 1979. "The Expansion of Agencies in Thai Bureaucracy," paper presented at the seminar on Thailand in the 1980s, Pattaya, Thailand, December 13–16.

World Bank. Various years. *World Development Report.* New York: Oxford University Press.

———— Various years. *World Tables*. Baltimore: Johns Hopkins University Press.

Wright, Edward Reynolds, ed. 1974. *Korean Politics in Transition*. Berkeley: University of California Press.

Wu Na-teh. 1980. "Emergence of the Opposition Within an Authoritarian Regime: The Case of Taiwan," ms.

Wurfel, D. 1979. "Elites of Wealth and Elites of Power in the Philippines." In *Southeast Asian Affairs 1979*. Singapore: Institute of Southeast Asian Studies.

————. 1989. *The Philippines*. Ithaca: Cornell University Press.

Xinhua (New China News Service), Beijing, December 29, 1986, in FBIS 6 (January 9, 1987): K6–9; August 18, 1987, in FBIS 159 (August 8, 1987): K3; January 12, 1988, in FBIS 13 (January 21, 1988): 25; April 4, 1988, in FBIS 65 (April 5, 1988): 16–17; April 13, 1988, in FBIS 72 (April 14, 1988): 32; June 30, 1988, in FBIS 217 (July 1, 1988): 17–18; September 5, 1988, in FBIS 174 (September 8, 1988): 50; December 9, 1988, in FBIS 242 (December 16, 1988): 53; August 22, 1989, in FBIS 162 (August 23, 1989): 15–18.

Xinhua Commentator. 1985. *Xinhua*, Beijing, December 18, in FBIS 245 (December 20, 1985): K21–22.

"Yi hao wenjian yao guan 'erh hao wenjian' " (No. 1 document must govern the no. 2 document). 1984. In *Renmin ribao*, June 12.

Young, Hugo. 1988. "Judge Not, That Ye Be Not Removed," *The Guardian* (London), November 8.

Yue Daiyun and Carolyn Wakeman. 1985. *To the Storm—The Odyssey of a Revolutionary Chinese Woman*. Berkeley: University of California Press.

Yung Wei. 1982. "Hsian tuan chi ho hsieh min chu ti tau lu mai chin" (Make headway on the road to unity, harmony, and democracy), *Chung yang jih pao* (Central daily news), October 7.

Z. 1990. "To the Stalin Mausoleum," *Daedalus* (Winter): 295–344.

Zakaria Haji Ahmad. 1977. "The Police and Political Development in Malaysia: Institution Building of a 'Coercive' Apparatus in a Developing, Ethnically Divided Society." Ph.D. dissertation, Massachusetts Institute of Technology.

————. 1987. "Stability, Security, and National Develoment in Malaysia: An Appraisal." In *Durable Stability in Southeast Asia*, ed. Kusuma Snitwongse and Sukhumbhand Paribatra. Singapore: Institute of Southeast Asian Studies.

————. 1988. "Malaysian Foreign Policy and Domestic Politics: Looking Outward but Moving Inward." In *Asia and the Major Powers, Domestic and Foreign Policy*, ed. R. Scalapino et al. Berkeley: Institute of East Asian Studies, University of California.

————. 1989. "Malaysia: Quasi-Democracy in a Divided Society." In *Democracy in Developing Countries: Asia*, ed. Larry Diamond et al. Boulder: Lynne Rienner.

Zakaria Haji Ahmad, and Harold Crouch, eds. 1985. *Military-Civilian Relations in Southeast Asia*. Singapore: Oxford University Press.

Zhao Lukuan et al. 1987. "A New Idea on Solving the Problem of Unfair Distribution of Personal Income," *Jingji yanjiu* 7 (July 20), in JPRS-CAR-88-057, September 20, 1988, pp. 20–26.

Zhao Ziyang. 1987. "Advance Along the Road of Socialism with Chinese Characteristics," *Beijing Review* 30, 45 (November 9–15): 1–27.

————. 1988. "Report to the Third Plenum of the 13th Central Committee," *Renmin ribao*, overseas ed., October 28, in FBIS 209 (October 28, 1988).

*Zhong bao* (New York), January 21, 1987.

Zhonggong Zhongyang Wenjian Yanjiu Shi, ed. 1982. *San Zhong chuan hui yilai: Zhongyao wenjian xuanpian* (Since the Third Plenum: Selected important documents). Beijing: Renmin Chubanshe.

*Zhongguo qingnian bao*, February 17, 1989.

*Zhongguo Tongji Nianjian* (Chinese statistical yearbook). 1987. Beijing: Zhongguo Tongji Chubanshe.

Ziegler, Harmon. 1988. *Pluralism, Corporatism, and Confucianism: Political Association and Conflict Regulation in the United States, Europe, and Taiwan*. Philadelphia: Temple University Press.

Zweig, David. 1985. "Strategies of Policy Implementation: Policy 'Winds' and Brigade Accounting in Rural China," *World Politics* 37, 2 (January): 267–93.

# Index

## STUDIES OF THE EAST ASIAN INSTITUTE

*The Ladder of Success in Imperial China*, by Ping-ti Ho. New York: Columbia University Press, 1962.

*The Chinese Inflation, 1937–1949*, by Shun-hsin Chou. New York: Columbia University Press, 1963.

*Reformer in Modern China: Chang Chien, 1853–1926*, by Samuel Chu. New York: Columbia University Press, 1965.

*Research in Japanese Sources: A Guide*, by Herschel Webb with the assistance of Marleigh Ryan. New York: Columbia University Press, 1965.

*Society and Education in Japan*, by Herbert Passin. New York: Teachers College Press, 1965.

*Agricultural Production and Economic Development in Japan, 1873–1922*, by James I. Nakamura. Princeton: Princeton University Press, 1967.

*Japan's First Modern Novel: Ukigumo of Futabatei Shimei*, by Marleigh Ryan. New York: Columbia University Press, 1967.

*The Korean Communist Movement, 1918–1948*, by Dae-Sook Suh. Princeton: Princeton University Press, 1967.

*The First Vietnam Crisis*, by Melvin Gurtov. New York: Columbia University Press, 1967.

*Cadres, Bureaucracy, and Political Power in Communist China*, by A. Doak Barnett. New York: Columbia University Press, 1968.

*The Japanese Imperial Institution in the Tokugawa Period*, by Herschel Webb. New York: Columbia University Press, 1968.

*Higher Education and Business Recruitment in Japan*, by Koya Azumi. New York: Teachers College Press, 1969.

*The Communists and Peasant Rebellions: A Study in the Rewriting of Chinese History*, by James P. Harrison, Jr. New York: Atheneum, 1969.

*How the Conservatives Rule Japan*, by Nathaniel B. Thayer. Princeton: Princeton University Press, 1969.

*Aspects of Chinese Education*, edited by C.T. Hu. New York: Teachers College Press, 1970.

*Documents of Korean Communism, 1918–1948*, by Dae-Sook Suh. Princeton: Princeton University Press, 1970.

*Japanese Education: A Bibliography of Materials in the English Language*, by Herbert Passin. New York: Teachers College Press, 1970.

*Economic Development and the Labor Market in Japan*, by Koji Taira. New York: Columbia University Press, 1970.

*The Japanese Oligarchy and the Russo-Japanese War*, by Shumpei Okamoto. New York: Columbia University Press, 1970.

*Imperial Restoration in Medieval Japan*, by H. Paul Varley. New York: Columbia University Press, 1971.

*Japan's Postwar Defense Policy, 1947–1968*, by Martin E. Weinstein. New York: Columbia University Press, 1971.

*Election Campaigning Japanese Style*, by Gerald L. Curtis. New York: Columbia University Press, 1971.

*China and Russia: The "Great Game,"* by O. Edmund Clubb. New York: Columbia University Press, 1971.

*Money and Monetary Policy in Communist China*, by Katharine Huang Hsiao. New York: Columbia University Press, 1971.

*The District Magistrate in Late Imperial China*, by John R. Watt. New York: Columbia University Press, 1972.

*Law and Policy in China's Foreign Relations: A Study of Attitude and Practice*, by James C. Hsiung. New York: Columbia University Press, 1972.

*Pearl Harbor as History: Japanese-American Relations, 1931–1941*, edited by Dorothy Borg and Shumpei Okamoto, with the assistance of Dale K. A. Finlayson. New York: Columbia University Press, 1973.

*Japanese Culture: A Short History*, by H. Paul Varley. New York: Praeger, 1973.

*Doctors in Politics: The Political Life of the Japan Medical Association*, by William E. Steslicke. New York: Praeger, 1973.

*The Japan Teachers Union: A Radical Interest Group in Japanese Politics*, by Donald Ray Thurston. Princeton: Princeton University Press, 1973.

*Japan's Foreign Policy, 1868-1941: A Research Guide*, edited by James William Morley. New York: Columbia University Press, 1974.

*Palace and Politics in Prewar Japan*, by David Anson Titus. New York: Columbia University Press, 1974.

*The Idea of China: Essays in Geographic Myth and Theory*, by Andrew March. Devon, England: David and Charles, 1974.

*Origins of the Cultural Revolution: I, Contradictions Among the People, 1956-1957*, by Roderick MacFarquhar. New York: Columbia University Press, 1974.

*Shiba Khan: Artist, Innovator, and Pioneer in the Westernization of Japan*, by Calvin L. French. Tokyo: Weatherhill, 1974.

*Insei: Abdicated Sovereigns in the Politics of Late Heian Japan*, by G. Cameron Hurst. New York: Columbia University Press, 1975.

*Embassy at War*, by Harold Joyce Noble. Edited with an introduction by Frank Baldwin, Jr. Seattle: University of Washington Press, 1975.

*Rebels and Bureaucrats: China's December 9ers*, by John Israel and Donald W. Klein. Berkeley: University of California Press, 1975.

*Deterrent Diplomacy*, edited by James William Morley. New York: Columbia University Press, 1976.

*House United, House Divided: The Chinese Family in Taiwan*, by Myron L. Cohen. New York: Columbia University Press, 1976.

*Escape from Predicament: Neo-Confucianism and China's Evolving Political Culture*, by Thomas A. Metzger. New York: Columbia University Press, 1976.

*Cadres, Commanders, and Commissars: The Training of the Chinese Communist Leadership, 1920-45*, by Jane L. Price. Boulder, CO: Westview Press, 1976.

*Sun Yat-sen: Frustrated Patriot*, by C. Martin Wilbur. New York: Columbia University Press, 1977.

*Japanese International Negotiating Style*, by Michael Blaker. New

York: Columbia University Press, 1977.

*Contemporary Japanese Budget Politics*, by John Creighton Campbell. Berkeley: University of California Press, 1977.

*The Medieval Chinese Oligarchy*, by David Johnson. Boulder, CO: Westview Press, 1977.

*The Arms of Kiangnan: Modernization in the Chinese Ordnance Industry, 1860–1895*, by Thomas L. Kennedy. Boulder, CO: Westview Press, 1978.

*Patterns of Japanese Policymaking: Experiences from Higher Education*, by T. J. Pempel. Boulder, CO: Westview Press, 1978.

*The Chinese Connection: Roger S. Greene, Thomas W. Lamont, George E. Sokolsky, and American-East Asian Relations*, by Warren I. Cohen. New York: Columbia University Press, 1978.

*Militarism in Modern China: The Career of Wu P'ei-fu, 1916–1939*, by Odoric Y. K. Wou. Folkestone, England: Dawson, 1978.

*A Chinese Pioneer Family: The Lins of Wu-Feng*, by Johanna Meskill. Princeton University Press, 1979.

*Perspectives on a Changing China*, edited by Joshua A. Fogel and William T. Rowe. Boulder, CO: Westview Press, 1979.

*The Memoirs of Li Tsung-jen*, by T.K. Tong and Li Tsung-jen. Boulder, CO: Westview Press, 1979.

*Unwelcome Muse: Chinese Literature in Shanghai and Peking, 1937–1945*, by Edward Gunn. New York: Columbia University Press, 1979.

*Yenan and the Great Powers: The Origins of Chinese Communist Foreign Policy*, by James Reardon-Anderson. New York: Columbia University Press, 1980.

*Uncertain Years: Chinese-American Relations, 1947–1950*, edited by Dorothy Borg and Waldo Heinrichs. New York: Columbia University Press, 1980.

*The Fateful Choice: Japan's Advance into Southeast Asia*, edited by James William Morley. New York: Columbia University Press, 1980.

*Tanaka Giichi and Japan's China Policy*, by William F. Morton. Folkestone, England: Dawson, 1980; New York: St. Martin's

Press, 1980.

*The Origins of the Korean War: Liberation and the Emergence of Separate Regimes, 1945-1947*, by Bruce Cumings. Princeton: Princeton University Press, 1981.

*Class Conflict in Chinese Socialism*, by Richard Curt Kraus. New York: Columbia University Press, 1981.

*Education Under Mao: Class and Competition in Canton Schools*, by Jonathan Unger. New York: Columbia University Press, 1982.

*Private Academies of Tokugawa Japan*, by Richard Rubinger. Princeton: Princeton University Press, 1982.

*Japan and the San Francisco Peace Settlement*, by Michael M. Yoshitsu. New York: Columbia University Press, 1982.

*New Frontiers in American-East Asian Relations: Essays Presented to Dorothy Borg*, edited by Warren I. Cohen. New York: Columbia University Press, 1983.

*The Origins of the Cultural Revolution: II, The Great Leap Forward, 1958-1960*, by Roderick MacFarquhar. New York: Columbia University Press, 1983.

*The China Quagmire: Japan's Expansion of the Asian Continent, 1933-1941*, edited by James William Morley. New York: Columbia University Press, 1983.

*Fragments of Rainbows: The Life and Poetry of Saito Mokichi, 1882-1953*, by Amy Vladeck Heinrich. New York: Columbia University Press, 1983.

*The U.S.-South Korean Alliance: Evolving Patterns of Security Relations*, edited by Gerald L. Curtis and Sung-joo Han. Lexington, MA: Lexington Books, 1983.

*Discovering History in China; American Historical Writing on the Recent Chinese Past*, by Paul A. Cohen. New York: Columbia University Press, 1984.

*The Foreign Policy of the Republic of Korea*, edited by Youngnok Koo and Sungjoo Han. New York: Columbia University Press, 1984.

*State and Diplomacy in Early Modern Japan*, by Ronald Toby. Princeton: Princeton University Press, 1983 (hc); Stanford:

Stanford University Press, 1991 (pb).

*Japan and the Asian Development Bank*, by Dennis Yasutomo. New York: Praeger Publishers, 1983.

*Japan Erupts: The London Naval Conference and the Manchurian Incident*, edited by James W. Morley. New York: Columbia University Press, 1984.

*Japanese Culture*, third edition, revised, by Paul Varley. Honolulu: University of Hawaii Press, 1984.

*The Foreign Policy of the Republic of Korea*, edited by Youngnok Koo and Sung-joo Han. New York: Columbia University Press, 1985.

*Japan's Modern Myths: Ideology in the Late Meiji Period*, by Carol Gluck. Princeton: Princeton University Press, 1985.

*Shamans, Housewives, and other Restless Spirits: Women in Korean Ritual Life*, by Laurel Kendell. Honolulu: University of Hawaii Press, 1985.

*Human Rights in Contemporary China*, by R. Randle Edwards, Louis Henkin, and Andrew J. Nathan. New York: Columbia University Press, 1986.

*The Pacific Basin: New Challenges for the United States*, edited by James W. Morley. New York: Academy of Political Science, 1986.

*The Manner of Giving: Strategic Aid and Japanese Foreign Policy*, by Dennis T. Yasutomo. Lexington, MA: Lexington Books, 1986.

*Security Interdependence in the Asia Pacific Region*, James W. Morley, Ed., Lexington, MA: D.C. Heath and Co., 1986.

*China's Political Economy: The Quest for Development since 1949*, by Carl Riskin. Oxford: Oxford University Press, 1987.

*Anvil of Victory: The Communist Revolution in Manchuria*, by Steven I. Levine. New York: Columbia University Press, 1987.

*Urban Japanese Housewives: At Home and in the Community*, by Anne E. Imamura. Honolulu: University of Hawaii Press, 1987.

*China's Satellite Parties*, by James D. Seymour. Armonk, NY: M.E. Sharpe, 1987.

*The Japanese Way of Politics*, by Gerald L. Curtis. New York: Columbia University Press, 1988.

*Border Crossings: Studies in International History*, by Christopher Thorne. Oxford & New York: Basil Blackwell, 1988.

*The Indochina Tangle: China's Vietnam Policy, 1975-1979*, by Robert S. Ross. New York: Columbia University Press, 1988.

*Remaking Japan: The American Occupation as New Deal*, by Theodore Cohen, edited by Herbert Passin. New York: The Free Press, 1987.

*Kim Il Sung: The North Korean Leader*, by Dae-Sook Suh. New York: Columbia University Press, 1988.

*Japan and the World, 1853-1952: A Bibliographic Guide to Recent Scholarship in Japanese Foreign Relations*, by Sadao Asada. New York: Columbia University Press, 1988.

*Contending Approaches to the Political Economy of Taiwan*, edited by Edwin A. Winckler and Susan Greenhalgh. Armonk, NY: M.E. Sharpe, 1988.

*Aftermath of War: Americans and the Remaking of Japan, 1945-1952*, by Howard B. Schonberger. Kent, OH: Kent State University Press, 1989.

*Single Sparks: China's Rural Revolutions*, edited by Kathleen Hartford and Steven M. Goldstein. Armonk, NY: M.E. Sharpe, 1989.

*Neighborhood Tokyo*, by Theodore C. Bestor. Stanford: Stanford University Press, 1989.

*Missionaries of the Revolution: Soviet Advisers and Chinese Nationalism*, by C. Martin Wilbur Julie Lien-ying How. Cambridge, MA: Harvard University Press, 1989.

*Education in Japan*, by Richard Rubinger and Edward Beauchamp. New York: Garland Publishing, Inc., 1989.

*Financial Politics in Contemporary Japan*, by Frances Rosenbluth. Ithaca: Cornell University Press, 1989.

*Suicidal Narrative in Modern Japan: The Case of Dazai Osomu*, by Alan Wolfe. Princeton: Princeton University Press, 1990.

*Thailand and the United States: Development, Security and Foreign*

*Aid*, by Robert Muscat. New York: Columbia University Press, 1990.

*Race to the Swift: State and Finance in Korean Industrialization*, by Jung-En Woo. New York: Columbia University Press, 1990.

*Anarchism and Chinese Political Culture*, by Peter Zarrow. New York: Columbia University Press, 1990.

*Competitive Ties: Subcontracting in the Japanese Automotive Industry*, by Michael Smitka. New York: Columbia University Press, 1990.

*China's Crisis: Dilemmas of Reform and Prospects for Democracy*, by Andrew J. Nathan. Columbia University Press, 1990.

*The Study of Change: Chemistry in China, 1840–1949*, by James Reardon-Anderson. New York: Cambridge University Press, 1991.

*Explaining Economic Policy Failure: Japan and the 1969–1971 International Monetary Crisis*, by Robert Angel. New York: Columbia University Press, 1991.

*Pacific Basin Industries in Distress: Structural Adjustment and Trade Policy in the Nine Industrialized Economies*, edited by Hugh T. Patrick with Larry Meissner. New York: Columbia University Press, 1991.

*Business Associations and the New Political Economy of Thailand: From Bureaucratic Polity to Liberal Corporatism*, by Anek Laothamatas. Boulder, CO: Westview Press, 1991.

*Constitutional Reform and the Future of the Republic of China*, edited by Harvey J. Feldman. Armonk, NY: M.E. Sharpe, 1991.

*Sowing Seeds of Change: Chinese Students, Japanese Teachers, 1895-1905*, by Paula S. Harrell. Stanford: Stanford University Press, forthcoming.

*Driven by Growth: Political Change in the Asia-Pacific Region*, edited by James W. Morley. Armonk, NY: M. E. Sharpe, forthcoming.

*Locality and State: Schoolhouse Politics During the Chinese Republic*, by Helen Chauncey. Honolulu: University of Hawaii Press, forthcoming.

*Social Mobility in Contemporary Japan*, by Hiroshi Ishida. Stanford: Stanford University Press, forthcoming.

*Pollution, Politics and Foreign Investment in Taiwan: The Lukang Rebellion*, by James Reardon-Anderson. Armonk, NY: M. E. Sharpe, forthcoming.

*Managing Indonesia: The Political Economy from 1965 to 1990*, by John Bresnan. New York: Columbia University Press, forthcoming.

*Tokyo's Marketplace*, by Theodore C. Bestor. Stanford: Stanford University Press, forthcoming.